THE POLITICS
OF SHARED POWER

Number One:
Joseph V. Hughes, Jr., and Holly O. Hughes
Series in the Presidency and Leadership Studies
James P. Pfiffner, General Editor

The Politics of Shared Power

Congress and the Executive

FOURTH EDITION

Louis Fisher

Texas A&M University Press
College Station

The paper used in this book meets the minimum requirements
of the American National Standard for Permanence
of Paper for Printed Library Materials, Z39.48-1984.
Binding materials have been chosen for durability.

Library of Congress Cataloging-in-Publication Data

Fisher, Louis.
    The politics of shared power : Congress and the executive /
Louis Fisher. — 4th ed.
        p. cm.—(Joseph V. Hughes, Jr., and Holly O. Hughes
    series in the presidency and leadership studies; no.1)
    Includes bibliographical references and index.
    ISBN 0-890996-806-3 ✓
    1. United States. Congress—Power and duties. 2. Sepa-
    ration of powers—United States. 3. Executive power—
    United States. I. Title.
    JK305.F54 1998
    320.473'04—dc20   00000
                                                        CIP

Texas A&M University Press expresses its appreciation for support in publishing works on the presidency and leadership to

The Center for Presidential Studies
George Bush School of Government and Public Service
Texas A&M University

To my parents,
for giving room to a child's curiosities

CONTENTS

PREFACE

◆

To study one branch of government in isolation from the others is usually an exercise in make-believe. Very few operations of Congress and the presidency are genuinely independent and autonomous. For the most part, an initiative by one branch sets in motion a series of compensatory actions by the other branch—sometimes of a cooperative nature, sometimes antagonistic. Like tuning forks when struck, the branches trigger complementary vibrations and reverberations.

Even a study on executive-legislative relations, if narrowly construed, is a contrivance. Congress and the presidency function within a political environment that consists of the judiciary, the bureaucracy, independent regulatory commissions, political parties, state and local governments, interest groups, and foreign nations. This book concentrates on the intersection where congressional and presidential interests converge. Despite the heavy traffic, head-on collisions are rare. Instead, individual drivers merge safely at high speeds. After passing through an elaborate cloverleaf, they exit to prepare for future exchanges. Standing in the midst of this intersection gives one the impression of anarchy and chaos, but distance and perspective bring a sense of order and purpose.

Although major personalities and pivotal events make their impacts, institutional patterns persist. The 1976 election of Jimmy Carter to the presidency, accompanied by Democratic majorities in each house of Congress, did not by itself ensure a constructive and effective partnership between the executive and legislative branches. Party leadership and affiliation could not bridge the deep divisions existing then or the more enduring disagreements on policy goals and constitutional duties.

Ronald Reagan's 1980 election victory for the Republicans presented a different set of power relationships. Although his party gained control of the Senate, he faced a Democratic House of Representatives. In 1981 he was able to build a bipartisan-conservative majority in the House and enjoyed partisan loyalty from the Republican Senate. Within a year, however, he faced stiff opposition from both houses. His reelection in 1984, along with a Democratic House and a Republican Senate, did not translate into political control of Congress.

The overwhelming victory by George Bush in 1988 maintained Republican control of the White House, but Bush often operated through the negative instrument of a veto to deny a Democratic Congress the programs it wanted. Regardless of who occupies the White House, members of Congress have their own constitutional obligations to discharge and their unique constituencies to represent.

Bill Clinton's victory in 1992, combined with Democratic majorities in each House, appeared to give the presidency a decided advantage in pressing legislative goals. However, the Clinton health plan floundered from the start, picked apart by Democrats and Republicans in Congress. One of Clinton's major legislative victories—passage of the NAFTA trade agreement with Mexico—required bipartisan support in both houses.

When the Republicans gained control of Congress in the 1994 elections, they thought they had the legislative majorities to dictate public policy. They soon learned that they had the power to pass legislation but not the power to override Clinton's vetoes. The bellicose partisan tone of 1995 gradually evolved into a search for bipartisan solutions in 1996. Clinton's reelection in 1996 and continued Republican control of Congress put pressure on both branches to discover middle-ground policies that had a chance of enactment.

A substantial part of the politics of executive-legislative relations is conducted through the courts. It is shortsighted to push this material to the side by calling it "judicial" or "legal." This activity is as political as anything else in the nation's capital. The courts review cases brought to them by members of Congress, the president, and agency heads. Judges referee disputes between the two political branches. When political activists decide that their interests will not be satisfied by Congress or the executive branch, they turn to the courts. Adjudication is politics by another name. Decisions by the judiciary determine individual rights, allocation of federal funds, and the prerogatives of the legislative and executive branches.

This book is shaped by a central question: How does the separation of power doctrine work in practice? This question gives rise to a number of issues. To what degree does the president participate as legislator? How much does Congress intervene in administrative matters? What are the political and constitutional problems for this sharing of power? Separate chapters on the bureaucracy and the independent regulatory commissions probe these questions more deeply and from different angles. A chapter on war powers and foreign affairs studies executive-legislative disputes that affect global relations, including the Iran-Contra affair, the Persian Gulf War in 1991, and Clinton's military initiatives in Haiti and Bosnia. The final chapter examines the sharing of budgetary powers through the Budget Act of 1974, the Gramm-Rudman statutes of 1985 and 1987, the Budget Enforcement Acts of 1990 and 1993, and the Line Item Veto Act of 1996. An epilogue reviews the concepts and words in our vocabulary that interfere with an accurate understanding of executive-legislative relations.

I appreciate the interest and support of the Texas A&M University Press in publishing a new edition of this book. James P. Pfiffner and the editorial board of the Joseph V. Hughes, Jr., and Holly O. Hughes Series in the Presidency and Leadership Studies, as well as one anonymous reviewer, offered many good suggestions. As always, I am blessed with talented and knowledgeable colleagues at CRS, including Stan Bach, Rogelio Garcia, Fred Kaiser, Ron Moe, Walter Oleszek, Harold Relyea, and Mort Rosenberg.

THE POLITICS
OF SHARED POWER

CHAPTER I

◆

Constitutional Underpinnings

Even sophisticated students of government make the mistake of describing Congress and the presidency as detached and disconnected institutions. Writing in 1885, Woodrow Wilson claimed that it was impossible that the framers of the Constitution "could believe that executive and legislature could be brought into close relations of cooperation and mutual confidence without being tempted, nay, even bidden, to collude." How could either branch, he asked, maintain its independence "unless each were to have the guaranty of the Constitution that its own domain should be absolutely safe from invasion, its own prerogatives absolutely free from challenge?"[1]

Scholars today are more likely to emphasize sharing than separation. As noted by Richard Neustadt: "The constitutional convention of 1787 is supposed to have created a government of 'separated powers.' It did nothing of the sort. Rather, it created a government of separated institutions sharing powers."[2]

Close examination of executive-legislative disputes shows how difficult it is to capture in a few words the essence of separated powers. Every concise formulation seems unsatisfactory in light of specific cases and circumstances. The Constitution, for both theoretical and practical reasons, anticipates a government of powers that are largely shared but sometimes exclusive.

Separation Doctrine: Theory and Practice

The record of the Continental Congress convinced the framers of the Constitution that they needed a separate branch of government to promote administrative efficiency. From 1774 to 1781, Congress had to perform all the functions of government: legislative, administrative, and adjudicative. There was no executive or judicial branch.

In an effort to allow more time for legislative duties, members of Congress experimented with various makeshift arrangements to handle administrative matters. First they relied on committees, then on boards staffed by men recruited from outside the legislature, and finally, in 1781, decided on single executives to administer four areas: foreign affairs, finance, war, and marine affairs. Although these executives were agents of Congress and totally dependent on the legislative body for their existence, a measure of independence and autonomy evolved.[3]

Between 1781 and 1787, the framers concluded that it was essential to vest administrative responsibilities and permanency in a separate executive branch. At the Philadelphia Convention, however, no one knew how much separation should exist between the legislative and executive branches. James Madison had decided neither the manner in which the executive should be constituted nor "the authorities with which it ought to be clothed."[4] The Virginia Plan, presented to the convention on May 29, 1787, authorized the legislature to select the executive. Many "prerogatives" we now associate with the president were initially assigned to Congress. For example, the Virginia Plan called on the legislature to choose members of a national judiciary. Two months later the delegates voted to have judges appointed solely by the Senate.[5] In a later draft of the Constitution, the Senate retained sole power to make treaties and appoint ambassadors.[6]

As the convention progressed, these features of congressional government were replaced by the constitutional provisions familiar to us today. The Senate and the president share the appointment and treaty powers. The president is chosen by electors rather than by the legislature (unless a tie vote or three-candidate race throws the election into the House of Representatives). The president possesses a qualified veto, in part to protect against legislative encroachments.

Other devices were considered to limit the legislative branch. Madison reminded the delegates that experience had proved "a tendency in our governments to throw all power into the Legislative vortex. The Executives of the States are in general little more than Cyphers; the legislatures omnipotent." James Wilson feared that the "natural operation of the Legislature will be to swallow up the Executive." Gouverneur Morris and John Mercer also warned of legislative aggrandizement and usurpation.[7] Serious consideration was given to the creation of a revisionary council (joining the executive with the judiciary) to check legislative ambitions. Madison urged that the judiciary be introduced in "the business of Legislation—they will protect their Department, and uniting [with] the Executive render their Check or negative more respectable."[8] This proposal was rejected. Compared to the executive departments under the Articles of Confederation, the president possessed far greater independence and autonomy. Yet for government to function, all three branches must cooperate as part of a common endeavor. The ironies and subtleties of our constitutional system were captured by Justice Robert H. Jackson: "While the Constitution diffuses power the better to secure liberty, it also contemplates that practice will integrate the dispersed powers into a workable government. It enjoins upon its branches separateness but interdependence, autonomy but reciprocity."[9]

By the late 1780s, the doctrine of a strict separation of powers had lost ground to the idea of checks and balances. Each branch shares in the powers of another branch: the Senate confirms presidential appointments and ratifies treaties, the House may impeach the president, and the president may veto bills but these vetoes can be overridden. A contemporary of the framers, publishing his views in 1788, ridiculed the separation doctrine as a "hackneyed principle" and a "trite maxim."[10] Madison, in *Federalist* 37, 47, and 48, took great pains to explain and justify the sharing between branches. Alexander Hamilton, in *Federalist* 66, said that the true meaning of the separation maxim was "entirely compatible with a partial intermixture" and that overlapping was not only "proper, but necessary to the mutual defense of the several members of the government, against each other."

Alexander White, a member of the First Congress, dismissed as fantasy the call for a separation of powers: "We are told, that we ought to keep the Legislative and Executive departments distinct; if we were forming a constitution, the observation would be worthy of due consideration, and we would agree to the principles; but the Constitution is formed, and the powers blended; the wished-for separation is therefore impracticable."[11] When the First Congress debated the list of constitutional amendments that became the Bill of Rights, it rejected a proposal that would have strictly allocated the powers of government among three separate branches.[12]

No one has successfully defined the boundaries between the legislative, executive, and judicial branches. In *Federalist* 37, Madison compared the problem to naturalists who had difficulty drawing an exact line between vegetable life and the animal world. Such difficulties, however, do not deny the existence of vegetables and animals. Nor is the distinction between earth, air, and water rendered meaningless by the existence of dust, mud, and clouds.[13]

Two principles, seemingly irreconcilable, operate side by side: (1) the separation of powers and (2) the system of checks and balances. Far from being contradictory, they complement and support one another. An institution cannot check unless it has some measure of independence; it cannot retain independence without the power to check.

Exclusive Powers

The Supreme Court cautions against an indiscriminate embrace of the "sharing of power" thesis. As the Court noted in 1974, the judicial power vested in the federal courts by Article III of the Constitution "can no more be shared with the Executive Branch than the Chief Executive, for example, can share with the Judiciary the veto power, or the Congress share with the Judiciary the power to override a Presidential veto."[14]

The system of separated powers is safeguarded by several provisions in the Constitution. For example, Article I, Section 6 prohibits members of Congress from holding appointive office. The delegates at the Philadelphia Convention wanted to avoid the corruption of the British system, which allowed members of Parliament to create offices for their own profit.[15] Under the U.S. system, no person holding a federal office can be a member of Congress, and legislators cannot be appointed to a federal office if that office has been created, or its salary increased, during the legislator's term of office.

Other provisions in the Constitution protect the independence of each branch. Congress is expressly proscribed from passing a bill of attainder, which would encroach upon the judiciary by inflicting punishment without a trial.[16] The Speech or Debate Clause (Article I, Section 6) gives legislators a general immunity from lawsuits, protecting them from executive or judicial harassment. For any speech or debate in either house, senators and representatives "shall not be questioned in any other place."[17] To protect the independence of the president and the courts, Congress may not reduce the compensation of the president or federal judges.

The budget process includes a number of discrete powers. The appropriations power belongs to Congress alone: "No Money shall be drawn from the Treasury, but in Consequence of Appropriations made by Law." The exclusive power to originate tax bills is reserved for the House of Representatives, although by custom the House originates appropriation bills as well. The House of Representatives has the sole power of impeachment; the Senate has the sole power to try all impeachments. Each house is the judge of the "Elections, Returns and Qualifications" of its own members, but Congress may not add to the qualifications specified in the Constitution.[18] Each house determines the rules of its proceedings and may punish and expel its members.

The president's "exclusive" powers fall principally under three headings: (1) the power to nominate, (2) the power to negotiate with foreign countries, and (3) the power to pardon. Exclusivity does not mean that these executive prerogatives operate without legislative participation. Congressional interest and the intervention of outside groups can limit all three powers.

Power to Nominate

Chief Justice John Marshall once called the nomination process the "sole act of the president" and "completely voluntary."[19] Congress may not establish a nominating procedure that puts before the president a single name. To design a method of selection that takes from the president the exercise of judgment and will, and limits the chief executive to one name and no other, is no different in constitutional principle from insisting that "he shall appoint John Doe to that office."[20] To preserve this constitutional discretion, generally the president is furnished at least three names for each vacancy.[21] There are situations, such as a senator's recommendation of someone for U.S. attorney, in which the president's *political* options are limited to one name.

Congress has discovered a number of ways to circumscribe the president's authority to nominate. It may stipulate the qualifications of appointees, itemizing in great detail the qualities the president must consider before sending forth a name. For federal district judges, U.S. attorneys, and marshals, it has been the custom for senators to "nominate" the individuals, allowing the president to give "advice and consent." For appellate courts and some district courts, panels were formed under President Carter to recommend nominees for federal judges. The element of presidential choice was preserved by having each panel recommend five candidates for each vacancy.[22]

President Ronald Reagan abolished the judicial nominating commissions established to select appellate judges. His administration also announced that the attorney general would invite Republican senators, with the assistance of advisory groups, to identify prospective candidates for federal district judges. For states with no Republican senators, the attorney general would solicit suggestions and recommendations from the Republican House members of that state.[23] During the Bush and Clinton administrations, the nominating process for selecting federal judges followed a variety of practices: screening committees or panels to help senators choose a nominee, recommendations from the state bar or lawyers associations, and an informal structure for interviewing and recommending candidates for judgeships.

The president can decide whom to appoint but cannot decide whether an agency should exist and function.[24] Once an office has been authorized by Congress, it must be filled. Otherwise the statutory purpose would be nullified by the president's failure to appoint officials to carry out the law. When an agency consists of several members at the top and can operate without a full staff on board, there are precedents for not filling each office. The Interstate Commerce Commission (ICC) was authorized eleven commissioners, but President Carter deliberately kept its size to seven by not filling all the vacancies. In 1982 Congress passed legislation to reduce the number of ICC commissioners to seven by January 1, 1983, and to five by January 1, 1986.[25] Legislation in 1995 terminated the ICC and shifted some of its functions to a newly created board within the Department of Transportation.[26]

Nominees are frequently caught in a political cross-fire. In 1986, Senator William S. Cohen, Republican of Maine, blocked the nomination of Peter C. Myers as deputy secretary of agriculture to protest the administration's treatment of potato farmers in his state. After the Agriculture Department agreed to purchase 2.2 million pounds of surplus Maine potatoes, Cohen removed his objection to the nomination. To get the department's attention on another dispute, Senator George J. Mitchell, Democrat of Maine, blocked the nomination of a member of the White House staff to be general counsel of agriculture.[27] Also in 1986, Senator Slade Gorton, Republican of Washington, made headlines by switching his vote to support the nomination of Daniel A. Manion to be a federal judge on the Seventh Circuit. Gorton changed his position after the White House promised to nominate his choice for a federal judgeship in his state.[28] The White House kept its promise, but Senate Democrats retaliated by preventing action on Gorton's nominee.[29] Gorton was defeated in the November 1986 elections after his opponent made an issue of the vote switch. Gorton was re-elected to the Senate in 1988.

Power to Negotiate

In terms of express constitutional powers, executive prerogatives in foreign affairs are quite limited. From the constitutional duty to receive "Ambassadors and other public Ministers," the president serves as our primary channel of communication with other nations.[30] The Logan Act of 1799 attempted to protect this responsibility. It was directed against private citizens who "usurp the Executive authority of this Government, by commencing or carrying on any correspondence with the Governments of any foreign Prince or State."[31]

Routinely violated, this statute has resulted in the indictment of only one individual, and he was found not guilty. In fact, the Logan Act is of doubtful constitutionality because it is vague in meaning and restrictive of First Amendment freedoms.[32] Its enforceability is reflected in this comment in 1979 by President Carter (the nation's chief law enforcement officer), after Americans had traveled to the Mideast to talk to Arab and Israeli leaders: "I don't have any authority, nor do I want to have any authority, to interrupt or to interfere with the right of American citizens to travel where they choose and to meet with whom they choose. I would not want that authority; I think it would be a violation of the basic constitutional rights that are precious to our Nation."[33]

A trip to Cuba in 1975 by two Democratic senators, John Sparkman of Alabama and George McGovern of South Dakota, raised the question of whether they had violated the Logan Act. The State Department concluded that nothing in the act "would appear to restrict members of the Congress from engaging in discussions with foreign officials in pursuance of their legislative duties under the Constitution." Both senators told the Cuban officials that they had no authority to negotiate on behalf of the United States.[34] When Richard Nixon's trip to China was challenged in 1976 as a possible violation of the Logan Act, the State Department explained that his visit had been undertaken entirely as a private citizen and that the department was "unaware of any basis for believing that Mr. Nixon acted with the intent prohibited by the Logan Act."[35] The trip, taken at the time of the New Hampshire presidential primary, provoked Senator Barry Goldwater, Republican of Arizona, to say that Nixon would do the United States a favor by remaining in China.[36]

When more than fifty Americans were held hostage in Iran, beginning in November 1979, an assortment of American legislators, professors, members of the clergy, and parents of the hostages traveled to that country to try their hands at negotiation. Carter's tolerance came to an end the following summer when a former attorney general, Ramsey Clark, attended a conference in Iran despite a presidential ban. Carter announced his inclination to prosecute Clark and several others who had violated his directive.[37] This amounted to presidential pique, however, and the threat was soon forgotten.

During the Reagan years, the Reverend Jesse Jackson traveled to a number of foreign countries, talking to government leaders in Syria, Cuba, Central America, and other regions, often negotiating for the release of U.S. citizens. His visits to Cuba in 1984 and his talks with Fidel Castro prompted President Reagan to remind reporters that "there is a law, the Logan Act, with regard to unauthorized personnel, civilians, simply going to—or citizens—to other countries and, in effect, negotiating with foreign governments. Now, that is the law of the land." However, he said he had no plans to take legal action.[38] A trip by Louis Farrakhan in 1996 to African and Middle Eastern countries, including Libya, Nigeria, Iraq, and Iran, prompted some legislators to charge that he had violated the Logan Act.[39] Nothing came of this dispute, either.

From the constitutional power to receive "Ambassadors and other public Ministers," the president derives the power to recognize foreign governments. Although this is largely an exclusive power for the president, there have been occasions where the president decided that the act of recognizing a country might lead to war and has therefore deferred to Congress.[40] Courts consider themselves bound by the president's determination of which political group to recognize as the government of a foreign country.[41] President George Bush exercised this authority in 1991 in recognizing a number of nations that had declared their independence from the Soviet Union.

Power to Pardon

Article II of the Constitution gives the president the power to grant "Reprieves and Pardons for Offenses against the United States, except in Cases of Impeachment." This power may take a variety of forms: full pardon, conditional pardon, clemency for a class of people (amnesty), commutation (reduction of the sentence), and remission of fines and forfeitures.[42]

The power of pardon is one of the few "exclusive" powers available to the president. In 1981 the responsibility fell to President Reagan to pardon former FBI officials Edward Miller and Mark Felt, who had been convicted of authorizing illegal break-ins. As with other powers exercised by the government, however, a number of limitations and checks operate. The power of pardon is limited to offenses against the United States (not against the individual states and localities). Presidents cannot use the power to compensate individuals for what has been done or suffered, nor can they draw money from the treasury, except as expressly authorized by an act of Congress.[43]

Through its appropriations and taxing powers, Congress may remit fines, penalties, and forfeitures, thereby participating in "pardons." Congress, with the support of the Supreme Court and the Justice Department, has vested that discretion in the secretary of the treasury and in other executive officials.[44] Congress may also legislate a general pardon or amnesty by repealing a law that had imposed criminal liability. The Congress derives this power not by "sharing" the president's pardon power but through its power to legislate and to repeal legislation.[45] Certain statutory restrictions have been struck down by the Supreme Court as invalid interferences with the pardon power.[46] When a proviso in an appropriations act attempts to control the president's power to pardon, as well as to prescribe for the judiciary the effect of a pardon, the statutory provision cannot stand.[47]

Many of these principles apply to recent controversies over the pardon power: President Gerald Ford's pardon of Nixon, President Carter's granting of amnesty to those who had violated the draft laws during the Vietnam War, and President Bush's pardons of six individuals involved in the Iran-Contra affair.

On September 8, 1974, President Ford granted a full pardon "for all offenses against the United States which Richard Nixon has committed or may have committed or taken part in during the period from January 20, 1969, through August 9, 1974." Some members of Congress suspected that Nixon made a deal with Ford when nominating him to be vice president. If Nixon had conditioned the nomination on the promise of a pardon, or conditioned his own resignation on a pardon, the House might have charged Ford with accepting a bribe, which is itself an impeachable offense. To allay such concerns, Ford took the extraordinary step of appearing before the House Judiciary Committee to explain the basis for his action.[48]

To some legislators it seemed improper for Ford to grant a pardon before formal charges had been lodged and without a formal admission of guilt from Nixon. It is established, however, that a pardon may be granted prior to a conviction and even before indictment.[49] Still, it is generally regarded as unwise and inexpedient to invoke the power prior to trial and condemnation. The president, without the benefit of all the facts that can be produced through the normal trial procedure, may inadvertently grant a pardon for offenses that have not yet come to light.[50]

A pardon carries an "imputation of guilt." Upon acceptance of a pardon, an individual in effect confesses guilt.[51] On both points—guilt and confession—Nixon equivocated. Philip W. Buchan, counsel to President Ford, interpreted Nixon's statement as one of "contrition," which is an expression of sorrow, not necessarily of guilt. Buchan believed that Nixon's words came "very close to saying that he did wrong, that he did not act forthrightly."[52]

In 1977, President Carter clashed with Congress over two appropriation acts that prohibited him from using funds to carry out his amnesty order. With certain exceptions, the order granted an unconditional pardon for Vietnam-era violators of the selective service laws. Some of the appropriation restrictions had no practical effect by the time Carter signed the bills. His cancellation of indictments for certain violations of the selective service laws, and termination of investigations regarding those violations, did not depend on appropriations. But he objected, in particular, to a statutory prohibition concerning the exclusion of aliens because of possible violations of selective service laws. Carter considered this feature an unconstitutional interference with his power to pardon, a bill of attainder, and a denial of due process.[53]

The Iran-Contra affair, which occurred during the Reagan administration, involved the sending of arms to Iran and the supply of military assistance to the Contra rebels in Nicaragua. A number of mid-level and low-level officials in the Reagan administration were convicted for their participation, as were several individuals in the private sector. On December 24, 1992, in one of his last actions in office, President Bush pardoned six individuals for their conduct in the Iran-Contra affair: former Secretary of Defense Caspar Weinberger, former Assistant Secretary of State Elliot Abrams, former National Security Adviser Robert McFarlane, and three individuals from the Central Intelligence Agency (Duane Clarridge, Alan Fiers, and Clair George). The pardon of Weinberger, in particular, was criticized by some because Bush had a direct and apparent conflict of interest. The defense in the Weinberger prosecution had indicated that it might call Bush and subject him to cross-examination for his role in the Iran-Contra affair.[54]

Concurrent Powers

The American political system operates primarily on the basis of concurrent powers. One branch can do very little without the support and countenance of the others. Justice Oliver Wendell Holmes, Jr., once noted: "[H]owever we may disguise it by veiling words we do not and cannot carry out the distinction between legislative and executive action with mathematical precision and divide the branches into watertight compartments, were it ever so desirable to do so, which I am far from believing that it is, or that the Constitution requires."[55]

The framers tried to produce a document that would allow government to operate more effectively and with greater powers than were possible under the Articles of Confederation. They spent an entire decade prior to the Philadelphia Convention in an anxious and persistent search for a more workable form of government.[56] Although the framers adopted a separation of powers, they "endeavored to prove that a rigid adherence to it in all cases would be subversive of the efficiency of the government, and result in the destruction of the public liberties."[57]

Justice Louis Brandeis argued that the doctrine of separated powers was adopted "not to promote efficiency but to preclude the exercise of arbitrary power."[58] That is a half-truth. The framers believed that a separation of powers would act in the interest of efficiency. To achieve that objective, public officials must act with moderation and common sense, ever respectful of the rights and privileges of other branches, constitutional limitations, and the larger purposes of government. The antithesis of that attitude took shape in the extremism and doctrinal wrangling of the Lyndon Johnson and the Richard Nixon administrations.

Clash of Prerogatives

The exercise of prerogatives by Congress and the president often puts the two branches on a collision course, requiring an accommodation that is satisfactory to both. Two examples where this often occurs are (1) access to information and (2) the presidential veto.

EXECUTIVE PRIVILEGE DISPUTES. In no area of federal activity is the need for compromise so essential as access to information. Although the courts have recognized that Congress has an implied power to investigate and that the president has an implied power to withhold information (executive privilege), neither power is absolute. When legislators seek documents that an executive wants to withhold, something has to give.[59]

In 1976, Representative John Moss, Democrat of California, operating through his subcommittee, requested from the American Telephone and Telegraph Company (AT&T) information on "national security" wiretaps by the administration. The Justice Department sued to prohibit the company from complying with the subcommittee subpoena, arguing that compliance might lead to public disclosure of vital information and could adversely affect national security. A district court decided that if a final determination had to be made about the need for secrecy and the risk of disclosure, "it should be made by the constituent branch of government to which the primary role in these areas is entrusted. In the areas of national security and foreign policy, that role is given to the Executive."[60]

This attempt by the judiciary to assign discrete tasks to the executive was soon overturned. Five months later an appellate court remanded the decision to the district court, in part because the election of Jimmy Carter gave the two branches an opportunity to resolve their dispute without judicial compulsion. The appellate court, acting as referee, urged executive and legislative officials to settle their differences out of court. The appellate court believed that a compromise worked out between the branches was "most likely to meet their essential needs and the country's constitutional balance."[61]

The Justice Department and the subcommittee continued to disagree, however, forcing the appellate court to intervene and give additional guidance. Judge Harold Leventhal of the D.C. Circuit rejected the idea that the dispute between the two branches represented a "political question." When a dispute consists of a clash of authority between the executive and legislative branches, "judicial abstention does not lead to orderly resolution of the dispute." Neither branch, he said, had "final authority in the area of concern." When the process of negotiation founders and stalemate beckons, the court may intervene to promote the "smooth functioning of government."[62]

Leventhal emphasized the need to resolve conflicting viewpoints and seek intermediate positions. He noted that the framers, in adopting a Constitution with general and overlapping provisions, anticipated that "a spirit of dynamic compromise would promote resolution of the dispute in the manner most likely to result in efficient and effective functioning of our governmental system." An adversarial relationship, with neither party willing to be flexible, is alien to a system of coordinate branches. Leventhal advised the contestants to avoid polarization: "each branch should take cognizance of an implicit constitutional mandate to seek optimal accommodation through a realistic evaluation of the needs of the conflicting branches in the particular fact situation."[63] By putting pressure on both parties to clarify their major concerns, Leventhal continued to push in the direction of an acceptable compromise. The case was dismissed on December 21, 1978, after the Justice Department and the subcommittee amicably resolved their differences.[64]

A similar pattern developed during the Reagan administration. The oversight subcommittee of the House Public Works Committee sought documents from the Environmental Protection Agency (EPA) as part of the subcommittee's investigation of the Superfund program, a $1.6 billion program established by Congress to clean up hazardous waste sites and to prosecute companies responsible for illegal dumping. There was reason to suspect that the major chemical companies were not paying their full share of the costs, leaving the balance to be picked up by taxpayers.

The Reagan administration told the subcommittee that it could not see documents in active litigation files. The administration expressed concern that sensitive documents would become public, especially after other committees had requested access to the same information. Acting under instructions from President Reagan, Anne Gorsuch, EPA administrator, refused to turn over "sensitive documents found in open law enforcement files." If Congress accepted this policy, oversight efforts would have to wait years until the government completed its enforcement actions.

The Public Works Committee held Gorsuch in contempt and the House of Representatives voted 259-105 to support the contempt citation. To underscore the institutional interests of the legislative branch, 55 Republicans joined 204 Democrats to build the majority.[65] The administration immediately went to court to declare the House action an unconstitutional intrusion into the president's authority to withhold information from Congress. In 1983 the court dismissed the government's suit on the grounds that judicial intervention in executive legislative disputes "should be delayed until all possibilities for settlement have been exhausted." The court urged both parties to devote their energies to compromise and cooperation, not confrontation.[66] Shortly thereafter, the Reagan administration agreed to release the documents to Congress.

There were no significant executive privilege disputes during the Bush administration, but the election of Bill Clinton in 1992 and of a Republican Congress in 1994 set the stage for numerous collisions over legislative requests for information from the White House. After the 1994 elections, the House Committee on Government Reform and Oversight began a detailed probe of the firing of seven Travel Office employees from the Clinton White House. Frustrated by the slow release of documents, in 1996 the House passed a resolution conferring special authorities on the committee. The resolution authorized the committee chairman, after consulting with the ranking Democrat on the committee, to direct a member or staff of the committee to take affidavits and depositions pursuant to notice or subpoena and under oath. This procedure allowed the staff to depose over fifty potential witnesses and thus expedite the inquiry.[67] After the White House invoked executive privilege to shield thousands of documents in the "Travelgate" affair, the House Committee on Government Reform and Oversight voted 27 to 19 to hold White House Counsel Jack Quinn in contempt. Before the matter could be taken to the floor, the disputed documents were released to the committee.[68]

In 1995, the Clinton administration refused to release records subpoenaed by the Senate Whitewater Committee, which had requested notes taken by someone in the White House Counsel's office. The White House argued that the notes were protected under the attorney-client privilege, a claim rarely asserted by the president. Clinton said that he believed the president "ought to have a right to have a confidential conversation with his minister, his doctor, his lawyer," adding that he should not "be the first president in history" to give up his right to attorney-client privilege.[69] However, the meeting was not between Clinton and his personal attorney to discuss private legal matters. Government attorneys, supposedly paid to conduct government business, attended the meeting. After the Senate voted to go to court to enforce the subpoena, the White House surrendered the notes.[70] On June 23, 1997, the Supreme Court let stand a decision by an appellate court forcing the White House to release notes that it had claimed were protected by the attorney-client privilege. The notes were handed over to Independent Counsel Kenneth Starr.

On three occasions in 1996, Clinton asserted executive privilege to deny Congress access to documents. He refused to give Congress a secret internal report on his decision to overlook weapons shipments from Iran to Bosnian Muslims, withheld forty-seven documents subpoenaed by House investigators probing the murder of political opponents in Haiti, and denied a House panel a memorandum from FBI Director Louis Freeh, who was reportedly critical of the administration's drug policy.[71]

POCKET VETO DISPUTES. The pocket veto controversy represents another clash of prerogatives: the president's power to veto versus Congress's power to override. The Constitution provides that any bill not returned by the president within ten days (Sundays excluded) shall become law "unless the Congress by their Adjournment prevent its Return, in which Case it shall not be a Law." The latter technique of negating a bill is known as the "pocket veto."

Toward the end of 1970, President Nixon returned a bill to Congress as a pocket veto. The Senate was absent for four days during the winter holidays; the House was gone for five. Many Democratic members of Congress felt that Nixon had blatantly misused his pocket veto authority.

In 1973 a district court held that the holiday adjournment had not prevented Nixon from returning the bill to Congress as a regular bill, giving both houses a chance to override him. The following year an appellate court upheld that decision. The bill was eventually printed as a public law (P.L. 91-696) and backdated to December 25, 1970, which marked the end of the ten-day period provided in the Constitution for executive review of bills.

In deciding the case, the district court emphasized the twofold purpose of the veto power: (1) to give the president suitable opportunity to consider bills presented by Congress, and (2) to give Congress suitable opportunity to consider the objections in a veto message and to override them.[72] The courts interpreted the pocket veto clause in a manner that would protect both legislative and executive interests.[73]

As a result of this litigation, the Justice Department announced an accommodation on April 13, 1976. It stated that President Ford would use the return veto rather than the pocket veto during congressional recesses and adjournments, whether in the middle of a session or between the first and second sessions. The pocket veto would be exercised only after the period following a final (*sine die*) adjournment at the end of the second session of a Congress. The two houses of Congress had to specifically authorize an officer or other agent to receive return vetoes during recess periods.[74]

The accommodation announced by the Ford administration was honored by President Carter. President Reagan also agreed not to exercise the pocket veto during the middle of a session. The agreement collapsed, however, regarding pocket vetoes between the first and second sessions. After Congress had adjourned on December 16, 1981, at the end of the first session of the 97th Congress, to return in about six weeks, Reagan used the pocket veto for a special relief bill for a bankrupt Florida firm.[75] At the end of the first session of the 98th Congress, he used the pocket veto for a bill that required certification of human rights practices in El Salvador as a precondition for sending military aid. The House had adjourned on November 18, 1983, and did not return until January 23, 1984—nine weeks later.

A bipartisan group of thirty-three members of the House of Representatives filed suit to require that the bill be published as a public law. In 1984 a federal district judge upheld the pocket veto, but he was later overturned by the D.C. Circuit.[76] When the Supreme Court accepted the case it appeared that the confusion about the pocket veto was about to be cleared up. However, the Court held that the controversy was moot because the bill vetoed by Reagan had expired by its own terms.[77]

The Court seemed to invite the two political branches to work out an accommodation. In 1990, after hearings, the House Rules Committee reported legislation that restricted the pocket veto to the end of a Congress; the House Judiciary Committee held hearings and also reported the bill favorably.[78] No further legislative action has been taken.

President Bush exercised the pocket veto a few times, but in peculiar fashion. In claiming that he exercised a pocket veto, Bush would also *return* the bill to Congress as though it were a regular veto subject to override. He used a pocket veto on December 3, 1989, against a Chinese immigration relief act but returned the bill to Congress, where an override vote failed. Congress counted his veto as a regular veto rather than a pocket veto. When he vetoed a bill in the middle of a session or at the end of the first session, Congress regarded those "pocket vetoes" as invalid and claimed that the bills became law at the end of the ten-day waiting period. For example, on December 20, 1991, Bush said that he used a pocket veto on a bill creating a Morris K. Udall Foundation. Congress passed legislation the next year reauthorizing the foundation but also included a section that repealed the previous bill, which Congress now treated as a public law. By signing the new bill, Congress hoped that Bush would concede that the previous bill had indeed become law and that no pocket veto had been applied. Bush did sign the new bill, but stated: "S. 2184 purports to 'repeal' S. 1176, passed in the last session of the Congress and presented to me in December. Because the bill came to me during an adjournment of the Congress and I withheld my signature, S. 1176 never became law. Therefore, the section of S. 2184 purporting to repeal S. 1176 can have no effect."[79] There were no pocket veto disputes during the Clinton years.

Reconciling Theory and Practice

The purpose of this book is to help the reader understand how the federal government operates within the context of the separation of powers theory. Action and theory have a symbiotic quality. Executive-legislative actions shape theory; theory constrains action. The constant interaction between the branches supplies definition and substance to their powers and relationships.

Chapters 2 and 3 examine the executive and legislative branches from two contrary and contrasting positions: president as legislator and Congress as administrator. These titles indulge in some hyperbole, but allow us to examine the day-to-day functioning of the two political branches: the president engaged in the legislative process and members of Congress participating in the administration of programs. It took more than a century for us to accept—formally at least—the president's role in legislation. The right of Congress to intervene in administration is still being resisted.

After these two chapters, it is possible to probe more deeply into the structure of government, focusing first, in Chapter 4, on the bureaucracy in the executive departments and then, in Chapter 5, on the independent regulatory commissions. The executive departments are pulled in two directions. They respond to Congress, which creates them and provides authorizations and appropriations, and to the president, who appoints the principal officers to manage agency activities. Both Congress and the president, through longstanding practices, attempt to direct the operations of the executive departments. Indeed, it is inconceivable to think of the departments as wholly subservient to one branch.

The independent regulatory agencies, such as the Federal Trade Commission and the Interstate Commerce Commission, have been described variously as "arms of Congress," administrative bodies, and quasi-judicial agencies. No one is sure, at any given time, where these agencies fit into the scheme of things. Some agencies had their beginning within an executive department, only to gain independence at a later date. They are an anomaly and defy orderly placement within the three branches of government. However mystifying they are in organizational terms, these agencies respond concretely to the supervision of Congress and the president. Chapter 5 explains the techniques of control, as well as recent recommendations to strengthen the president's hand.

Chapter 6 focuses on foreign affairs, the war power, and covert operations. The two branches generally coordinate their roles in these areas smoothly, but the exceptions to that general rule are important ones: the Korean War, the Vietnam War, the Iran-Contra affair, the Persian Gulf War under President Bush, and the military initiatives by President Clinton in Haiti and Bosnia. The virtues and vices of the War Powers Resolution of 1973 are also examined. Chapter 6 supplies a constitutional and historical framework to study these disputes and profit from them.

Budgetary controls are covered in Chapter 7. The attempt to control spending, deficits, and priorities takes the reader through such landmark statutes as the Budget and Accounting Act of 1921, the Congressional Budget and Impoundment Control Act of 1974, and the Gramm-Rudman-Hollings Act of 1985. A key feature of the latter statute was declared unconstitutional in 1986 by the Supreme

Court, forcing Congress and the executive to search for alternative controls. The poor results with this statute led to Gramm-Rudman II in 1987 and the Budget Enforcement Act of 1990 and its extension in 1993. Chapter 7 concludes by analyzing the Line Item Veto Act of 1996. An epilogue identifies loaded words and concepts that prevent us from properly understanding executive-legislative relations.

CHAPTER 2

President as Legislator

To a literalist, the Constitution limits the president to two forms of legislative activity: (1) the right to recommend to Congress such measures "as he shall judge necessary and expedient" and (2) the power to veto a bill. To this list can be added the president's power (shared with the Senate) to make treaties, which the Constitution defines as part of "the supreme Law of the Land." A fourth source of influence, which has been exercised on rare occasions in the past, permits him to convene both houses or either of them. In case they disagree on the time of adjournment, the president can adjourn them "to such Time as he shall think proper."[1]

The Supreme Court has held that in the "framework of our Constitution the President's power to see that the laws are faithfully executed refutes the idea that he is to be a lawmaker." According to this view the Constitution limits the president's functions in the lawmaking process to "the recommending of laws he thinks wise and the vetoing of laws he thinks bad."[2] And yet superimposed upon the president's express constitutional authorities are other legislative powers either implied in the Constitution or developed by custom (often with the blessing of the courts). Some of these legislative powers are expressly delegated by Congress to the president and the executive agencies. Others result from agency regulations, presidential proclamations, and executive orders.

Express Powers

Article II of the Constitution is remarkable for its laconic treatment of presidential power. Over 60 percent of the language is devoted to the term of office, election, qualifications, removal, compensation, and oath of office. The remainder of the article describes the president's power only in general terms; the veto power is set forth in Article I.

Recommending Legislation

The Constitution requires the president "from time to time" to give Congress "Information of the State of the Union, and recommend to their Consideration such Measures as he shall judge necessary and expedient." The first presidents, George Washington and John Adams, appeared before Congress to deliver their annual messages, but in 1801 President Thomas Jefferson discontinued that practice, preferring to submit his message in writing. More than one hundred years elapsed before President Woodrow Wilson, in 1913, revived the custom of addressing Congress in person.[3]

The annual State of the Union message was typically a lackluster product, consisting mainly of departmental and agency reports on their activities. These messages were seldom used to recommend specific legislation. President William Henry Harrison, in his inaugural address of March 4, 1841, enunciated the classic Whig interpretation of the president's legislative role. He could not conceive that by a fair interpretation of the Constitution "any or either of its provisions would be found to constitute the President a part of the legislative power." The power to recommend, Harrison said, was "a privilege which he holds in common with every other citizen; and although there may be something more of confidence in the propriety of the measures recommended in the one case than in the other, in the obligations of ultimate decision there can be no difference."[4]

President Grover Cleveland broke ranks with this attitude by devoting his entire 1887 State of the Union message to the subject of tariff reform. The message had a profound impact on Congress and the press, created a split in Cleveland's Democratic party, and contributed to his defeat the following year.[5] From time to time other presidents advocated legislation to satisfy party commitments. For example, President William Howard Taft believed the president could exercise

> a controlling influence in the securing of legislation by his personal intervention with members of his party who are in control in each House. I think he ought to have very great influence, because he is made responsible to the people for what the party does, and if the party is wise, it will bend to his leadership as long as it is tolerable, and especially where it is in performance of promises that the party has made in its platform. . . . [6]

Since Taft's time, presidents regularly use the State of the Union message to pursue legislative goals. The message, delivered in person to Congress, typically reviews the government's failures and successes (giving disproportionate attention to the latter), restates the administration's priorities, and appeals to Congress and the public at large for support.

In addition to the constitutional requirement for the State of the Union message, statutes direct the president to submit legislative recommendations. The two major documents transmitted to Congress each year are the budget message, prescribed by the Budget and Accounting Act of 1921, and the economic report, submitted in compliance with the Employment Act of 1946. Hundreds of other presidential reports, messages, communications, and suggestions for legislation flow to Capitol Hill in response to statutory directives. Although members of Congress periodically criticize the president for invading their legislative domain, major policy departures often await the president's initiative.

In modern times, members of Congress expect the administration to present a bill as a starting point. One committee chair reportedly advised an administration witness: "Don't expect us to start from scratch on what you people want. That's not the way we do things here—*you* draft the bills and *we* work them over."[7]

President Clinton's bill for health-care reform is a good example of how presidential leadership can go awry. During the 1992 campaign, he advocated a revamping of the nation's health-care system and pressed hard for legislation in 1993 and 1994. With Democrats in control of both houses of Congress, the prospects for passage looked good. A combination of forces, however, derailed his bill.

Part of the problem was the sheer scope and complexity of Clinton's proposal. Probably no other legislative initiative contained such technical detail and so many political landmines. Clinton could have chosen a more incremental approach—making marginal but realizable improvements—but he decided to submit a comprehensive package that eventually fell of its own weight. In January 1993, Clinton promised to send Congress a proposal within ninety days and hoped Congress would complete its work by the end of the year. Clinton did not address Congress until September 22 and several more months were needed to convert the proposal to bill form.

Resistance appeared from many quarters. One objection was Clinton's decision to place his wife, Hillary Rodham Clinton, as head of the health-care task force. The apparent purpose was to signal that health reform had the highest priority within the administration. But presidents need task force leaders they can blame, sack, or replace, and that cannot be done with a spouse. Second, Hillary Clinton had no particular expertise or credentials to qualify for the position. Third, her presence inhibited internal debate and rigorous analysis. If task force members thought that she had settled on a position, or was leaning in a particular direction, they were not likely to advocate another policy and challenge the First Lady.

The task force was widely criticized for conducting its business in secret. The Association of American Physicians and Surgeons filed suit on the ground that the closed-door nature of the task force's meetings violated the Federal Advisory Committee Act. The litigation, at the district and appellate court levels, continued throughout 1993.

The September 1993 plan released by President Clinton depended upon the creation of health-care "alliances" to permit consumers to compete more evenly with insurance companies. But the alliances, a new quasi-governmental entity, were criticized as massive bureaucratic creatures that might threaten an individual's freedom to select a personal doctor. The legislation, in the form of a bill that ran 1,342 pages, proved to be too difficult for members of Congress and their constituents to understand. Passage of the bill seemed too big a gamble, possibly doing irreparable harm to a health system that was generally regarded as the best in the world. After numerous efforts in 1994 to move the bill through Congress, Senate Majority Leader George Mitchell announced on September 26 that a compromise bill had failed to attract sufficient votes. Without a floor vote in either the House or the Senate, Clinton's proposal was shelved.[8]

Clinton's health initiative failed in part because he received no support from the Republicans. The opposite was true with one of Clinton's major legislative victories in 1993: passage of the North Atlantic Free Trade Agreement (NAFTA) to expand trade with Mexico. A number of leading Democrats, including House Majority Leader Richard Gephardt, actively opposed the legislation. Republican support was crucial. The bill passed the Senate 61 to 38, including 34 of 44 Republican Senators voting in favor. The margin in the House was close: 234 to 200. Republicans backed the measure 132 to 43, whereas Democrats opposed it, 156 to 102. Another vote against the legislation came from an Independent.

Congress may initiate major pieces of legislation. In 1996, the Republican Congress passed fundamental and far-reaching reforms in the nation's welfare system. President Clinton, under heavy pressure to veto the message, eventually decided to sign it after vetoing two earlier versions.

The president's ability to recommend legislation has been simplified in recent years by a process called fast-track procedures. Under usual procedures, a presidential proposal can be ignored, buried in committee, or altered by Congress almost beyond recognition. The fast-track procedure, incorporated in the Trade Act of 1974, provides that Congress must vote on a president's proposal, either by passing it or defeating it, and it may not be amended by Congress, either in committee or on the floor. Committees must act within a specified number of days, and Congress must complete floor action within a deadline established by Congress.

The prohibition on congressional amendments, while technically correct, is lifted through informal means. Typically, the president's proposal is put in draft form and circulated within Congress and the committees of jurisdiction. If the administration is interested in having the legislation passed, it will accommodate many of the changes requested during this review process.

The Veto Power

The framers, after decisively rejecting a proposal for an absolute veto, gave the president a qualified veto, subject to an override by a two-thirds majority of each house of Congress. The Supreme Court later decided that two-thirds of a quorum present in each house, rather than of the total membership, would suffice.[9] This is still a demanding standard, generally requiring the support of more than 60 senators and 260 to 270 House members.

Some of the Antifederalists in 1788 were deeply offended by the veto power, claiming that it was an error to allow the executive power a negative "or in fact any kind of control over the proceedings of the legislature."[10] But Alexander Hamilton in *Federalist* 73 argued that the power was an essential instrument for protecting the president against legislative encroachments. In addition to protecting the presidency, Hamilton singled out other justifications for the veto power. It would permit the president to prevent the enactment of "improper laws" that result from haste, inadvertence, or design. James Madison also described the veto as multipurpose, available not merely to restrain Congress from encroaching on other branches but also to prevent Congress "from passing laws unwise in their principle, or incorrect in their form" and from violating the rights of the people.[11]

The *threat* of a veto can be an effective weapon for exacting changes in a pending bill. In 1817, when President James Monroe announced that Congress lacked constitutional authority to appropriate money for internal improvements, a House committee reacted with indignation. It expressed shock that a president would try to interfere with the ability of Congress to express its will.[12] Such "interference," while common today, is not always effective. In 1980 President Carter told Congress that he would veto any bill that disapproved his gasoline conservation fee. Undaunted, Congress proceeded with the bill and then quickly and decisively overrode the veto. Members of Congress who manage a bill can use the threat of a veto to eliminate unwanted amendments, claiming that such provisions invite a veto. Even entire bills are shelved in the face of presidential opposition.

The veto power today is fundamentally different from the original design. Both branches have forced changes in the system. Congress developed the practice of presenting to the president bills that had many elements, often unrelated, instead of allowing the president to consider a discrete measure. This practice became more coercive by attaching irrelevant amendments ("riders") to appropriation bills, assuming the president could not afford to veto a money bill in the closing days of a fiscal year. President Rutherford B. Hayes fought Congress on this issue and prevailed with a number of vetoes,[13] but presidents continue to receive complex bills filled with miscellaneous items. Congress, despite House and Senate rules to the contrary, continues to add "legislation" to appropriation bills.[14] The Hyde amendment (restricting the use of federal funds for abortion) is a prominent example of a rider to an appropriation bill.

The Constitution expressly recognizes a "pocket veto." Any bill not returned by the president within ten days (Sundays excluded) shall become law "unless the Congress by their Adjournment prevent its Return, in which Case it shall not be a Law." The pocket veto required several decisions by the Supreme Court to determine what conduct by Congress would "prevent" the return of a bill for legislative consideration. Although the scope of the pocket veto has been gradually restricted by these rulings, litigation has not fully resolved the constitutional dispute. Much has been left to accommodations reached by the political branches (pp. 18–20).

The veto is one of the more effective weapons in the president's arsenal. Of the 1,466 regular vetoes from Washington through Clinton, Congress has managed to override only 105. More than half of those vetoes came during the administrations of Grover Cleveland and Franklin D. Roosevelt, with the vast majority aimed at private relief bills (see Table 2-1). There have also been 1,067 pocket vetoes, with Cleveland and Roosevelt again accounting for more than half.

The threat of a presidential veto can be answered by the threat of a legislative override, producing complex results that defy statistical analysis. President Bush vetoed several bills in a row, each time escaping a congressional override. However, when he vetoed the Civil Rights Bill of 1990, Congress mounted an extensive fight to save the bill. The override vote in the Senate fell short by only one vote. Over the next year, Bush had increasing difficulty in supporting his claim that the legislation constituted a "quota" system for minorities.

TABLE 2-1

Presidential Vetoes, 1789–1997

YEARS	PRESIDENT	REGULAR VETOES	VETOES OVERRIDDEN	POCKET VETOES	TOTAL VETOES
1789–1797	George Washington	2	0	0	2
1797–1801	John Adams	0	0	0	0
1801–1809	Thomas Jefferson	0	0	0	0
1809–1817	James Madison	5	0	2	7
1817–1825	James Monroe	1	0	0	1
1825–1829	John Q. Adams	0	0	0	0
1829–1837	Andrew Jackson	5	0	7	12
1837–1841	Martin Van Buren	0	0	1	1
1841–1841	W. H. Harrison	0	0	0	0
1841–1845	John Tyler	6	1	4	10
1845–1849	James K. Polk	2	0	1	3
1849–1850	Zachary Taylor	0	0	0	0
1850–1853	Millard Fillmore	0	0	0	0
1853–1857	Franklin Pierce	9	5	0	9
1857–1861	James Buchanan	4	0	3	7
1861–1865	Abraham Lincoln	2	0	5	7
1865–1869	Andrew Johnson	21	15	8	29
1869–1877	Ulysses S. Grant	45	4	48	93
1877–1881	Rutherford B. Hayes	12	1	1	13
1881–1881	James A. Garfield	0	0	0	0
1881–1885	Chester A. Arthur	4	1	8	12
1885–1889	Grover Cleveland	304	2	110	414
1889–1893	Benjamin Harrison	19	1	25	44
1893–1897	Grover Cleveland	42	5	128	170
1897–1901	William McKinley	6	0	36	42
1901–1909	Theodore Roosevelt	42	1	40	82
1909–1913	William H. Taft	30	1	9	39
1913–1921	Woodrow Wilson	33	6	11	44
1921–1923	Warren G. Harding	5	0	1	6
1923–1929	Calvin Coolidge	20	4	30	50
1929–1933	Herbert Hoover	21	3	16	37
1933–1945	Franklin D. Roosevelt	372	9	263	635
1945–1953	Harry S. Truman	180	12	70	250
1953–1961	Dwight D. Eisenhower	73	2	108	181
1961–1963	John F. Kennedy	12	0	9	21
1963–1969	Lyndon B. Johnson	16	0	14	30
1969–1974	Richard M. Nixon[a]	26	7	17	43
1974–1977	Gerald R. Ford	48	12	18	66
1977–1981	Jimmy Carter	13	2	18	31

1981–1989	Ronald Reagan	39	9	39	78
1989–1993	George Bush[b]	29	1	17	46
1993–1997	Bill Clinton[c]	18	1	0	18
Total		1,466	105	1,067	2,533

SOURCE: *Presidential Vetoes, 1789–1988*, compiled by the Senate Library (Washington, D.C.: Government Printing Office, 1992), ix; Bush and Clinton figures are taken from *Weekly Compilation of Presidential Documents*.

[a] Two "pocket vetoes," overruled in the courts, are counted here as regular vetoes.

[b] Bush claimed to pocket veto two bills (H.R. 2712 in 1989 and H.R. 2699 in 1991), but actually returned them to Congress, which attempted to override the veto on the first bill; these vetoes are counted here as regular vetoes because they were returned to Congress. Congress argued that two other pocket vetoes by Bush (H.J. Res. 390 in 1989 and S. 1176 in 1991) were invalid and that the bills became law. Because the National Archives did not recognize these bills as enacted into law, they are counted here as pocket vetoes.

[c] As of June 20, 1997.

Congressional support solidified to the point where an override looked likely. Faced with possible defeat, Bush found a way to sign a slightly rewritten civil rights act in 1991.

This conflict underscores an important point. When the veto record is focused on nationally significant legislation (after eliminating private relief bills and minor legislation), Congress is more successful with its override efforts. A persistent Congress can win out, if not under one president, then under the next. In struggles over important bills, Congress is much more of a coequal institution.[15]

President Clinton did not veto a single bill during his first two years in office, when the Democrats controlled Congress. But when the 1994 elections gave Republicans control of Congress, the veto strategy changed. Republicans hoped to use their legislative agenda—called "Contract with America"—to shove through a number of bold initiatives. Legislative success in the House was dramatic and rapid, but progress slowed because of two hurdles: the Senate and President Clinton. The "Contract with America" was the creation of House Republicans; Senate Republicans had less enthusiasm for the reform proposals. And for legislative ideas that happened to emerge from Congress, President Clinton was ready with his veto. Republicans conceded that they lacked a two-thirds majority in each House for an override. Of Clinton's 11 vetoes in 1995, only one was overridden. In 1996, he vetoed six more Republican initiatives without a single override.

Implied and Evolved Powers

Some constitutional scholars believe that an act of the federal government is illegal unless based upon a power enumerated in the Constitution. They take comfort in the statement of Henry Lee at the Virginia ratification convention: "When a question arises with respect to the legality of any power, exercised or assumed," the question will be, "Is it enumerated in the Constitution? . . . It is otherwise arbitrary and unconstitutional."[16] Not only is this doctrine impractical and unrealistic, but these scholars must themselves make room for implied powers: the power of Congress to investigate, the president's power to remove executive officials, and the power of the Supreme Court to review executive and legislative actions.

The president's power as legislator expands as a result of several developments: authority delegated by Congress; the president's implied authority to issue regulations, proclamations, and executive orders; and the personal ability and institutional strength of a president to lobby for legislative proposals.

Delegated Authority

Strict interpretations of the Constitution would prohibit Congress from delegating its power to another branch. This theory finds expression in the ancient maxim *delegata potestas non potest delegari* (delegated power cannot be delegated). According to this doctrine, the power delegated by the people to Congress may not be transferred elsewhere.[17]

Practice has not kept pace with theory, however. From an early date, the Supreme Court allowed Congress to supply general guidelines for national policy, leaving to other branches the responsibility for "filling in the details."[18] Although time after time the Court has paid homage to the nondelegation doctrine, claiming that it would be "a breach of the National fundamental law" were Congress to transfer its legislative power to the president, the Court typically upholds the delegation in question.[19] Delegation by Congress, said the Court in 1940, "has long been recognized as necessary in order that the exertion of legislative power does not become a futility. . . . The burdens of minutiae would be apt to clog the administration of the law and deprive the agency of that flexibility and dispatch which are its salient virtues."[20]

On only two occasions, both occurring in 1935, did the Supreme Court strike down a delegation of legislative authority to the president.[21] The Court objected to vague language and inadequate legislative standards. How little bearing those cases have on delegation today is underscored by the Economic Stabilization Act of 1970, which authorized the president to "issue such orders and regulations as he may deem appropriate to stabilize prices, rents, wages, and salaries at levels not less than those prevailing on May 25, 1970."[22] Nowhere in the statute does one find the procedural safeguards that usually accompany broad delegations of power: giving notice to interested parties before issuing a presidential order, providing a hearing for affected groups, and establishing the machinery for judicial review. A federal court upheld the delegation by noting that some congressional guidelines were imbedded in committee reports and other portions of the legislative history.[23] Allowing Congress to pass laws by placing crucial details outside the bill, however, is not always satisfactory, as Congress periodically discovers. Agencies are bound by law, but not necessarily by nonstatutory controls (see pp. 78–80).

The nondelegation doctrine has not lost its force entirely. Justices of the Supreme Court, usually in dissent, still raise it as a standard for reviewing statutes passed by Congress.[24] A decision in 1980 was significant because four members of the *majority* (in particular Justice William H. Rehnquist) challenged the scope of power granted to an agency by Congress. The other three members, Chief Justice Warren Burger and Justices John Paul Stevens and Potter Stewart, appeared to insist that Congress at least clarify its policy by using less ambiguous language.[25]

Regulations, Proclamations, and Executive Orders

To carry out authority delegated by Congress, executive officials often issue rules and regulations that "must be received as the acts of the executive, and as such, be binding upon all within the sphere of his legal and constitutional authority.[26] In theory, regulations are not a substitute for general policy making. That power is reserved to Congress and may be enacted only in the form of public law.[27] While administrative regulations are entitled to respect, "the authority to prescribe rules and regulations is not the power to make laws, for no such power can be delegated by the Congress."[28] According to the courts, a regulation that is out of harmony with a statute "is a mere nullity."[29]

So much for general theory. Vague grants of delegated power by Congress give administrators substantial discretion to make policy. During the Senate vote in 1981 to confirm James Watt as secretary of the interior, Senator Dale Bumpers, Democrat of Arkansas, recalled that Watt had told his committee: "I believe in complying with the law." Bumpers continued: "Do you know what the law is so far as the management of the public lands is concerned? Most of the time it is whatever the Secretary of the Interior says it is."[30]

Even when statutory language is relatively clear and specific, one provision may conflict with another in the same bill. Faced with inconsistent and perhaps contradictory congressional demands, the president and agency officials try to "harmonize" competing provisions. In 1979 a federal court ruled that the Environmental Protection Agency (EPA) acted properly by adopting a regulatory scheme that bridged conflicting provisions in the Clean Air Act. Instead of Congress resolving the policy conflict, the EPA manufactured an administrative solution.[31]

Presidential proclamations are a second instrument of administrative legislation. Often they are routine in nature, without legislative effect. During 1980 President Carter used proclamations to make statements for Mother's Day, Father's Day, and Salute to Learning Day.[32] Also during that period, however, he issued proclamations that had substantive impact, including import quotas on cotton and on television parts.[33] Several other substantive proclamations issued by Carter in 1980, imposing a fee on imported oil, were declared illegal by a federal court.[34] The judicial decision came against a backdrop of congressional moves to strip Carter of his power to impose import fees.[35]

In a controversial action in 1971, President Nixon issued a proclamation imposing a 10 percent surcharge on articles imported into the United States. After extensive litigation a federal court decided that although the president lacks an independent power to regulate commerce or set tariffs, and any valid proclamation had to be based on authority delegated by Congress, in this case Nixon had acted consistently with statutory authority.[36] When a statute prescribes a particular procedure and the president follows a different course, the proclamation can be declared illegal and void.[37]

A third form of administrative legislation is the executive order. President Franklin D. Roosevelt issued a number of executive orders in 1941 to seize industrial plants, shipbuilding companies, a cable company, a munitions plant, and approximately four thousand coal companies. Two years passed before Congress supplied statutory authority for his actions.[38] During World War II, President Roosevelt created several agencies by executive order, without the slightest shred of statutory support. An opponent of this practice, Senator Richard Russell, Democrat of Georgia, said he "never believed that the President of the United States was vested with one scintilla of authority to create by an Executive order an action agency of Government without the approval of the Congress of the United States." Russell successfully secured the adoption of an amendment, still in effect today, that prohibits the use of any appropriation to pay the expenses of an agency established by executive order "if the Congress has not appropriated any money specifically for such agency or instrumentality or specifically authorized the expenditure of funds by it."[39]

The use of executive orders to eliminate employment discrimination in private industry began with President Franklin D. Roosevelt and continued with Truman, Eisenhower, Kennedy, and Johnson. These initiatives were further carried forward by President Nixon, who issued an executive order that required federal contractors to set specific goals for hiring members of minority groups (the "Philadelphia Plan"). The comptroller general concluded that the plan conflicted with the Civil Rights Act of 1964. Here the federal courts upheld the administration's action.[40] Another executive order by Nixon attempted to rejuvenate the Subversive Activities Control Board. Congress intervened in this case to prohibit the administration from using appropriated funds to carry out the order. Senator Sam Ervin, Democrat of North Carolina, complained that board members had done little "except draw their breath and their salaries."[41] When executive orders exceed presidential authority, the judiciary has struck them down.[42]

The scope and limits of administrative legislation are illustrated by two examples from the Clinton administration. In 1987, the Reagan administration had issued a proposed rule (the "gag rule") prohibiting family-planning clinics from using federal funds to counsel women on abortions or refer them to a doctor for abortion, even if women requested that information. Congress placed language in a conference report stating that changes in existing law must be achieved through the constitutional process rather than through agency regulations.[43] Nevertheless, the Reagan administration made the regulations final in 1988.

In 1991, by a 5 to 4 majority, the Supreme Court upheld the regulations.[44] In that same year, Congress added language to an appropriations bill to prohibit the use of funds to enforce the rule that barred abortion counseling, but President Bush vetoed the bill. Late in 1992, the D.C. Circuit nullified the Gag Rule because when the administration modified it (to permit physicians to counsel patients on abortion), it had failed to submit the regulation for public notice and comment.[45] During the 1992 presidential campaign, Bill Clinton promised to cancel the Gag Rule if elected. On January 22, 1993, in one of his first acts as president, he lifted the restriction on abortion counseling.[46]

Although successful in this instance, Clinton was checked by the courts when he tried to use an executive order in the field of labor law. In 1994, he urged Congress to pass legislation that would ban employers from replacing striking workers. After a Republican filibuster in the Senate blocked the measure, the Republican takeover of Congress in the 1994 elections convinced Clinton that he could expect no legislative support from Congress on this issue. Turning to administrative action, he issued an executive order to declare that it is the policy of the executive branch "in procuring goods and services that, to ensure the economical and efficient administration and completion of Federal Government contracts, contracting agencies shall not contract with employers that permanently replace lawfully striking employees."[47] Federal courts held that the order was an improper attempt to set broad labor policy and violated the National Labor Relations Act by interfering with the right of private employers to hire replacements.[48]

OMB's Review of Agency Regulations
In response to an antiregulation mood in the 1970s, presidents from Ford to Clinton tried to create a system to monitor government regu-

lations that impose heavy costs on businesses and consumers. The Council on Wage and Price Stability (COWPS) in the Ford White House was one effort, followed by the creation under President Carter of the Regulatory Analysis Review Group (RARG). The most ambitious attempt to centralize control over agency regulations is Executive Order 12291, issued by President Reagan in 1981. He designated the Office of Management and Budget (OMB) as the central agency to review regulations and subject them to cost-benefit analysis. The purpose was to "reduce the burdens on existing and future regulations, increase agency accountability for regulatory actions, provide for presidential oversight of the regulatory process, minimize duplication and conflict of regulations, and insure well-reasoned regulations."[49]

By making OMB the central clearinghouse for agency regulations and arming it with a vague cost-benefit weapon, Reagan's order raised serious questions of due process. OMB could use the cost-benefit concept to delay or kill regulations the administration did not want. Moreover, OMB officials could meet privately with industry representatives to discuss pending agency rules. These ex parte contacts were contrary to the standards adopted in the Administrative Procedure Act, which calls for public "notice and comment" of proposed rules.[50]

Although OMB was frequently criticized for its role in reviewing agency regulations, a strong congressional counterattack did not come until 1986. The House Appropriations Committee voted to cut off all funds for the office within OMB that performed regulatory review: the Office of Information and Regulatory Affairs (OIRA). The director of OMB, James C. Miller III, asserted that Congress could not use its power of the purse to prevent the president from carrying out the constitutional duties to oversee the work of the executive branch. If funds were deleted, Miller threatened to do the work in the White House. If Congress cut off funds again, he said, "We will do it in the Justice Department. If you take the office out of the Justice Department, we will do it in Commerce."[51]

The House Appropriations Committee ignored Miller's threat and deleted all funds for OIRA. The committee acted with the support of several committee heads, including Representative John Dingell, Democrat of Michigan, of the House Committee on Energy and Commerce. Dingell urged that funds be eliminated because OMB had violated its charter:

OMB has sought to exercise veto power over agency decisions notwithstanding the absence of any legislative grant of such regulatory review authority;

OMB has subverted public participation procedures enacted by Congress by allowing favored interests to plead their cases in secret meetings with OMB;

Congressional directives, including those designed to protect the public health and the environment, can be easily circumvented in a regulatory review process which is shrouded in secrecy and unbounded by statutory constraints; and

OMB'S activities represent a fundamental threat to the separation of powers embodied in our Constitution.[52]

Several Senate committees were also critical of OIRA. A report issued in May 1986 by the Senate Committee on Environment and Public Works charged that the secrecy and delay imposed by OMB compromised the principles of openness and fairness required for agency rulemaking.[53] On July 31, 1986, the Senate Governmental Affairs Committee reported a bill to reorganize OMB. Included in the bill were provisions to strengthen congressional control over OIRA by making its administrator subject to Senate advice and consent. The report also explained new procedures that would require greater disclosure of OIRA documents and activities.[54] Senator Carl Levin, Democrat from Michigan, insisted that OMB open up its process: "No longer will OMB operate within the shade-drawn, doors-closed, no-fingerprints environment in which it has operated for the past five years. From this point on, OMB's input into the rulemaking process will be a matter of public record, available for all who are so interested to see and judge."[55]

Because of these developments on the Senate side, the Senate Appropriations Committee provided funding for OIRA.[56] The continuing resolution sent to President Reagan at the end of 1986 included $5.4 million for the office. It appeared that concessions wrung from the administration made it unnecessary for Congress to enact statutory limitations on OIRA. Ambiguities in the agreement, however, led to renewed struggles between the branches. In 1989, OMB Director Richard Darman accepted new statutory language, but that fell through when White House Counsel C. Boyden Gray and White House Chief of Staff John Sununu objected that the agreement had not been brought to them.

The uncertainty over the status of OIRA created a vacuum that was soon filled by the Council on Competitiveness, chaired by Vice President Dan Quayle. President Bush created the Council in 1989 to improve U.S. competitiveness in the international market. On June 15, 1990, Bush assigned the Council responsibilities for regulatory review. Critics complained that the Council operated as a conduit for industry and private interests that sided with business against the environment—the original objections leveled against OIRA. Operating within the shelter of the vice president's office, the Council was not subject to the standards of public accountability expected of OIRA. At the end of 1991, legislation (S. 1942) was introduced in Congress to establish statutory procedures for the public disclosure of all agencies that review federal regulations, but no final action was taken.[57] In 1992, the House voted to delete funding for the salaries of staffers on the Quayle Council, using the power of the purse to punish the administration for its secrecy. However, in the face of a threatened Bush veto, the Senate restored the funds.[58]

The Clinton administration continued to conduct centralized review of regulatory agencies but adopted reforms to avoid the insulated and secretive practices of the Reagan and Bush years. On January 21, 1993, in his first full day in office, President Clinton abolished the Council on Competitiveness and asked Vice President Al Gore to recommend new regulatory review procedures. The new procedures were incorporated in Executive Order 12866, released on September 30, 1993. If disagreements between agencies and OIRA cannot be resolved by OIRA, they may be decided by the president or the vice president.[59] In 1996, Congress passed legislation (110 Stat. 868) that allows Congress to review and disapprove federal agency regulations. Major rules are delayed for sixty days to give Congress an opportunity to pass a joint resolution of disapproval. Joint resolutions must be presented to the president and may be vetoed.

Executive Organization and Leadership

The operations of government require constant interaction between executive and legislative leaders. Congress and the president can seldom afford to spin in separate orbits. Among the fundamental duties of the executive branch, since 1789, is the need to structure itself for a continuing dialogue with Congress on legislation, appointments, and other matters that demand close consultation and cooperation.

Early Networks and Linkages

Contacts between Congress and George Washington's administration were smoothed by common bonds of familiarity, friendship, and public service that had been forged in the years of the Continental Congress. Many of the delegates to the Constitutional Convention in Philadelphia were later to serve in the First Congress and in Washington's administration. In the midst of partisan strains between Federalists and Antifederalists, public officials tried to place the new government on secure footing while at the same time protecting the prerogatives of the branch they served.

James Madison, while serving in the First Congress, provided valued counsel to Washington on many legislative matters. Washington sought his advice concerning a possible veto of a bill for compensation to members of Congress.[60] Even though Madison was a member of the House of Representatives, with no constitutional responsibility for reviewing nominations submitted by the president, Washington wanted Madison's opinion on specific nominations. He also turned to him to ask whether executive communications to the Senate should be transmitted by written or oral means. Washington's correspondence contains other efforts to solicit the advice of senators on nominations.[61]

Through various communications to the Senate, Washington suggested that the senators function as an advisory council on appointment and treaty matters. In the handling of treaties, Washington told the Senate, "oral communications seem indispensably necessary." The issues not only required careful consideration, "but some of them may undergo much discussion; to do which by written communications would be tedious without being satisfactory."[62] Although he was severely disappointed by his effort to discuss an Indian treaty with senators, face to face, Washington continued to seek the Senate's advice by written communications.[63]

Presidential bill-drafting is sometimes considered a twentieth-century phenomenon, but the practice existed from the start. Washington wrote down his ideas for a bill on the national militia and sent them to Henry Knox, his secretary of war, for legislative action. In 1790 Washington conferred with two senators in an effort to reverse an action the House had taken on appropriations for the foreign service. Two years later he sent Secretary of State Jefferson to speak privately to members of a House committee investigating the heavy losses by Major General Arthur St. Clair in an Indian raid.[64]

As another way to link the executive branch with Congress, legislators were invited to dine with the president. Washington, sensitive to the precedents being established, entertained members of Congress with great reserve. Senator William Maclay of Pennsylvania, not one of Washington's greatest admirers, remembered these occasions as stiff and formal. After returning from one he wrote: "[I]t was the most solemn dinner I ever sat at." The next year, following another evening with Washington, he recorded in his diary: "The President is a cold, formal man; but I must declare that he treated me with great attention."[65]

Legislative-executive contacts during the Washington administration were tentative and sporadic. Each branch tested the boundaries of the constitutional system, ever on the watch for transgressions and encroachments. This sensitivity is illustrated by the opposition of Congress in 1789 to a proposal that would have authorized the secretary of the treasury to report to Congress on financial recommendations. Some members feared that this might open the door to excessive executive influence, especially in the hands of so formidable a secretary as Alexander Hamilton. The particular language under consideration would have directed the secretary to "digest and report" plans for the improvement and management of the revenue. Representative John Page of Virginia warned that the bill would establish a precedent "which might be extended, until we admitted all the ministers of the Government on the floor, to explain and support the plans they have digested and reported; thus laying a foundation for an aristocracy or a detestable monarchy."[66]

As enacted into law, the language was changed to "digest and prepare." And yet the statute also required the secretary of the treasury to "make report, and give information to either branch of the legislature, in person or in writing (as he may be required), respecting all matters referred to him by the Senate or House of Representatives, or which shall appertain to his office." Some scholars credit Hamilton with drafting the bill that created the Treasury Department.[67] The statutory language suggested that the secretary of the treasury would help bridge the gap between the executive and legislative branches. The secretary, although the head of an executive department, would also serve as an agent of Congress.

Hamilton assumed an activist role in Washington's cabinet. According to the journals of Senator William Maclay, Hamilton believed that his official duties required close contact with legislative leaders. When his plan for a funding system was in jeopardy, Hamilton "was here early to wait on the Speaker, and I believe spent most of his time in running from place to place among the members." When the Senate considered the excise bill, Hamilton "sat close with the committee." Hamilton attended to each detail of the legislative process. After a Senate committee agreed that the power of excise inspectors should extend only to importations and distillations, Maclay discovered that Hamilton "will have even to modify this to his mind. Nothing is done without him." The loyalty of some Federalist legislators prompted Maclay to remark: "It was, however, only for Elsworth, King, or some of Hamilton's people to rise, and the thing was generally done."[68]

Eventually Congress rebelled against Hamilton. In 1792, when he asked to come before Congress to answer questions concerning the public debt, legislators vehemently objected to this mixing of the two branches. Some took the position that departmental heads should never originate legislation or even voice an opinion that might affect congressional decisions. Legislative investigations in 1793 and 1794, although fruitless in unearthing damaging information about Hamilton, so poisoned the relationship between the branches that he resigned from office.[69]

The Jeffersonians

Much of the suspicion and tension between the executive and legislative branches eased during Thomas Jefferson's first term as president. The use of the congressional caucus to nominate presidential candidates provided chief executives a ready circle of supporters (and some political debts) on Capitol Hill. By the time Jefferson was ensconced in office, the party apparatus had so joined the branches that he could draft bills and give them to friendly members of Congress for action. On one occasion he told Albert Gallatin, his secretary of the treasury, of a proposed draft on embargo enforcement: "If you

will prepare something on these or any other ideas you like better
. . . Mr. Newton [of Virginia] . . . will push them through the House."
The periodicals of the day referred to Representative William B. Giles,
Democrat of Virginia, as the leader of the "ministerial phalanx." Giles
served as Jefferson's link to Congress for a few years and was succeeded by John Randolph, another Virginian. When the post of House
majority leader again fell vacant, Jefferson urged Wilson Cary Nicholas, also of Virginia, to make himself available as administration leader
in the House.[70]

Critics of the administration objected to these organizational ties,
complaining that Jefferson's methods were those of an autocrat. Senator Timothy Pickering, a Federalist from Massachusetts, said that
Jefferson was deceptive in his public deference to the legislative
branch: "[H]e secretly dictates every measure which is seriously proposed and supported."[71] But Jefferson could not operate by mere command, even among his close followers. He had to work within the
political limits imposed by the times:

> It was in this calm and seductive manner, careful to avoid all ap-
> pearance of being a master, that he had drawn around him his great
> party, and held it together, year after year, until he had marched
> with it to victory. And it was this spirit which was to give him
> such marked success in directing the work of his administration.
> Such methods only could succeed in handling followers like Giles,
> Randolph, and Macon, men often responding readily to suggestion
> and capable of loyalty but perfectly independent and ready to re-
> sent too free a use of the party lash.[72]

The record shows that Jefferson employed the same liaison techniques that had been pioneered by Hamilton. So long as the executive departments assisted Congress "subtly and with proper
deference," the drafting of a few bills by the executive "for guidance
only" was acceptable to most legislators.[73] Jefferson and Gallatin took
responsibility for initiating the main outlines of party measures. They
followed legislative deliberations carefully, intervening whenever
necessary to preserve the basic goals of the administration. Gallatin,
who had previously served on the House Ways and Means Committee, remained in close touch with his former colleagues, attending

committee meetings in the same manner as Hamilton.[74] By maintaining his residence on Capitol Hill, Gallatin was able to continue his friendships with legislators. As noted by Henry Adams, the principal supporters of the administration in Congress were "always on terms of intimacy in Mr. Gallatin's house, and much of the confidential communication between Mr. Jefferson and his party in the Legislature passed through this channel. . . . But the communication was almost entirely oral, and hardly a trace of it has been preserved either in the writings of Mr. Gallatin or in those of his contemporaries."[75]

Jefferson had cultivated many personal relationships from the time he served in the Continental Congress. From 1797 to 1801 his ties with Congress were deepened by his experience as vice president. Much of his time was devoted to the constitutional duty of president of the Senate. He took time out to write a manual on Senate rules. While in that service he lived at one of the largest boardinghouses on Capitol Hill, sharing company and political insights with members of Congress.[76]

As president, Jefferson laid heavy emphasis on the wining and dining of legislators at the executive mansion. In contrast to the practices established by Washington, he held small dinners "almost nightly when Congress was in session, with legislators predominating among the guests. The dinners were the talk of Washington. In the judgment of observant diplomats from abroad, for whom food and wine were standard accessories of political persuasion, they were the secret of Jefferson's influence."[77]

Jefferson's persuasive innovations did not survive his administration. After the collapse of the rival Federalist party (a rallying point for Jefferson's opponents), his own Democratic party developed signs of division and factionalism. President James Madison and his immediate successors in the White House lacked the personal qualities and political skills that Jefferson had used to maintain party unity and executive-legislative cooperation.

Other structural and organizational changes complicated presidential influence on Capitol Hill. The executive departments, as they grew in number, responsibility, and complexity, drifted beyond the president's immediate control. And in those early decades of the nineteenth century, Congress developed its present system of standing committees, dispersing power away from congressional leaders to "little legislatures." As a result of such changes, presidents succeeding Jefferson had to face decentralized and independent blocs of power, within both the executive branch and Congress.

Reform Efforts, 1864–1921

In the decades following the Civil War, various proposals were put forth to stimulate closer contacts between the executive and legislative branches. In 1864 Democrat George Pendleton of Ohio introduced a bill to provide that departmental heads "may occupy seats on the floor of the House of Representatives." In later years this reform was associated with greater executive influence, but Pendleton thought his proposal would make more information about departmental activities available to Congress. Cabinet officers would have the right to participate in debate and explain the business of their departments. The clerk of the House would keep a "notice book" that contained questions requiring a response from cabinet officials. The objective was to make the executive more accountable, converting a secret operation into one that was "open, declared and authorized."[78]

Opponents of Pendleton's bill predicted that the departmental heads would either be put through the "torture of a cross-examination" or, alternatively, exhibit such awesome mastery of the legislative process that disreputable bills would be enacted into law. In addition, if departmental heads refused to appear, what sanctions (short of impeachment) could Congress use to enforce compliance? Opponents doubted that the Pendleton procedure would put an end to executive "intrigue" in law-making. They warned that passage of the bill would be "a step toward the absorption of the power of Congress by the Executive." After extensive debate, the bill was put aside without further action.[79] Pendleton returned to Congress in 1879, this time as an Ohio senator, and promptly reintroduced his bill to allow cabinet officers to speak on the floor of each house. Two years later a Senate select committee reported the bill favorably, but the bill never came up for a vote. By that time Pendleton was devoting his energy to civil service reform.[80]

During Theodore Roosevelt's administration, Congress explicitly acknowledged the president's role as a legislative leader. In 1906 Congress passed a bill authorizing up to $25,000 a year in traveling expenses for the president.[81] In prior years the railroads had given the president free transportation, a privilege about to be eliminated by the Hepburn Act. Representative Charles Cochran, Democrat of

Missouri, argued that these expenses should now be covered by Congress, because in the

> operation of our constitutional system the President has become the chief leader of public thought and exponent of public opinion— quite as much a source of valuable suggestion for the enactment of laws as a mere executive charged with enforcing the laws, and since the circulation of the President throughout the country aids practically and decisively in promoting salutary legislation, by giving effective direction to public opinion, should not his expenses incurred in rendering such important public service be borne out of the public Treasury?[82]

To Representative J. Swagar Sherley, Democrat of Kentucky, Roosevelt's travels "not only did good by his speeches, but I think his traveling did him a tremendous amount of good." Trips to different sections of the country helped educate the president on the "actual conditions that confront us, and make him a better President for the whole people of the United States."[83]

Pendleton's proposal continued to resurface, but its purpose was changed to give executive officials a dominant voice in the legislative process. One study in 1913, in addition to recommending seats in both houses for cabinet members, advocated two other ways to augment presidential power: (1) by restricting executive messages to "a few definite recommendations embodying the policies in favor of which the party has pronounced in its platform or those for which the President is willing to assume the responsibility," and (2) by allowing the president to initiate bills and giving precedence to administration bills over other measures.[84]

Pendleton's proposal continued to attract interest. Under the "question period" advocated by Senator Estes Kefauver, Democrat of Tennessee from 1943 to 1953, the heads of executive departments and agencies would appear periodically before Congress, for up to two hours, to answer written or oral questions. In 1978 Representative Lee Hamilton, Democrat of Indiana, and his staff assistant recommended that senior executive officials appear frequently before Congress in a "question hour" as part of a cooperative process in foreign affairs and national defense.[85] The idea retains some advocates.

Despite the logic and apparent good sense behind these proposals, they consistently fail to generate the necessary support. Part of the reason is that the advantages, by this time, are largely theoretical. The political process adjusted long ago to permit departmental heads a formal and continuing role in presenting their ideas to Congress.

Institutionalizing Power, 1921–1998

By creating the Budget Bureau in 1921, Congress added an institution that enhanced the president's role as legislative leader. This influence grew because of executive initiatives and statutory interpretation, at times with the support of important power centers in Congress.

The first budget director, Charles G. Dawes, established procedures to control the flow of bills traveling from the executive branch to Congress. The Budget Bureau derived this responsibility from Section 206 of the Budget and Accounting Act of 1921, which prohibited agencies from submitting their financial proposals to Congress unless first requested by either house. The Bureau reasoned that Congress expected it to review all departmental reports to Congress on proposed or pending legislation. Although Section 206 related only to estimates or requests for appropriations, Dawes concluded that "it is necessary for a full compliance with its spirit that all requests or recommendations for legislation, the effect of which would be to create a charge upon the public Treasury or commit the Government to obligations which would later require appropriations to meet them, should be first submitted to the President before being presented to Congress." Several years passed before this policy was systematically enforced.[86]

Dawes's directive appeared to be a power grab by the Budget Bureau, but the initiative came from Congress. The House Appropriations Committee had expressed concern about the lack of supervision over agency requests. Chairman Martin Madden, Republican of Illinois, learned that an agency had asked a legislative committee for authority to divert appropriated funds from the purposes originally specified. Madden told Dawes that "matters of this character should come through the Bureau of the Budget. . . . I have called them to your attention in order that you may take . . . steps . . . to include [such] requests . . . in the control which the Bureau has over direct estimates."[87]

This process of "central clearance" evolved over the years until it embraced three main functions. The Budget Bureau reviewed agency proposals sent to Congress to determine that they were "in accord with the program of the president." It coordinated departmental advice on legislation originating in Congress and advised the president to sign or veto enrolled bills presented to him by Congress. By 1939, when the Budget Bureau was transferred from the Treasury Department to the Executive Office of the President, it had become responsible for clearing proposed executive orders and proclamations and for reviewing the testimony of executive officials who appeared before congressional committees.[88]

Until recent years, central clearance was performed by a staff of Budget Bureau professionals in the legislative reference division. Other participants included the budget examiners assigned to various departments and agencies, with assistance from the general counsel's office in the White House.

The Budget Bureau was expected to supply objective, analytical advice on the merits of bills, leaving political and partisan judgments to the White House. The influence of the legislative reference division declined during the John Kennedy and Lyndon Johnson administrations, due to competition from White House staff. Central clearance was increasingly relegated to handling the "thousands of legislative items not commanding presidential attention, with the White House handling the major items and articulating the president's priorities."[89] In 1970 the Budget Bureau was replaced by the Office of Management and Budget (OMB). Much of the leverage within the OMB shifted from career civil servants to political appointees; objectivity and professionalism lost ground to a more partisan operation.[90]

Initiating Legislation

The search for the source of legislation inevitably takes the traveler on a convoluted and twisted journey, full of surprises. Peel away one "source" and you discover another. The process continues to repeat itself with little hope of reaching the core. As Woodrow Wilson remarked, "Legislation unquestionably generates legislation. Every statute may be said to have a long lineage of statutes behind it."[91]

Senator James E. Murray, Democrat of Montana, is generally credited with supplying the "spark of will" that transformed an idea into the Employment Act of 1946. This legislative achievement, however, owes a major intellectual debt to two British economists, John Maynard Keynes and Sir William Beveridge; to such private organizations as the National Planning Association; and to legislative staff members who worked in concert with executive agencies, interest groups, and private individuals. An annotated bibliography of the major books and articles on full employment written between 1943 and 1945 came to "fifty-six tightly packed pages."[92]

Robert A. Dahl expressed a widely held view of legislative activity in foreign policy: "Perhaps the single most important fact about Congress and its role in foreign policy . . . is that it rarely provides the initiative."[93] Yet other studies credit individual representatives and senators with a significant voice in shaping foreign policy. Francis O. Wilcox, writing from the perspective of chief of staff for the Senate Foreign Relations Committee from 1947 to 1955 and assistant secretary of state for international organization affairs from 1955 to 1961, concluded that "some of the most imaginative and constructive foreign policies since World War II have originated in Congress." As leading examples he cited the exchange-of-persons program, the use of surplus agricultural commodities in the foreign aid program, the International Development Association, the Peace Corps, and the U.S. Arms Control and Disarmament Agency. "Not infrequently," he noted, "an idea is born on Capitol Hill and then, when it is brought to fruition, the President receives political credit for it."[94]

More recently, as a result of the build-up in professional staff within Congress, structural changes within the institution, and greater visibility of foreign policy issues among the public, Congress has been able and willing to assert itself on a continuous basis. Legislative actions—such as terminating the war in Vietnam, restricting presidential policy in Cyprus and Angola, enacting the War Powers Resolution in 1973 over Nixon's veto, restricting the Central Intelligence Agency, and scrutinizing arms sales—have been initiated by Congress with the assistance of outside groups and individuals. During the Reagan years, Congress consistently challenged the president's foreign policy in such areas as the Philippines, arms control, and South Africa.[95] The Bush and Clinton administrations also witnessed strong challenges by Congress to foreign policy initiatives by the president.[96]

Legislation is often rooted in causes that never come to light. A member of a legislator's staff, after playing a pivotal role in initiating and shaping a bill, may decide to conceal that contribution out of deference to a member or because of a self-imposed anonymity. A private organization that conceives the idea embodied in legislation, and perhaps even drafts the bill, might prefer to hide its influence in order to improve the bill's chance for passage. Further complicating the picture, an administration may allow a member of Congress to take the lead in advocating a proposal, not because the legislator conceived the idea but to avoid anticipated criticism that the executive branch is extending its power and promoting expensive programs.[97]

Bills that "originate" in the executive branch are subsequently modified and refined by the suggestions of private groups, committee hearings and markups, and the adoption of floor amendments. Decentralization of Congress in recent years, associated with largely autonomous and well-staffed subcommittees, has produced more floor amendments and challenges to reported bills. As a result, the White House faces the prospect of substantial revisions and often radical alterations in administration bills. In the rare case when an administration bill sails through Congress with little change, this may reflect not so much the president's influence as a decision by the White House to have a draft bill cleared first by the major powers on Capitol Hill.[98]

Scholars devote considerable time and energy in debating which branch of government—legislative or executive—deserves credit for originating most legislation. Writing in 1953, George B. Galloway concluded that very little legislation found its source in Congress. For the most part, he said, legislators are "merely conduits for the executive departments, private organizations, and individual constituents." Samuel P. Huntington, in a 1965 study, suggested that 80 percent of the bills enacted into law originate in the executive branch.[99]

These studies by Galloway and Huntington give far too much credit to the executive branch. Lawrence Chamberlain, after studying ninety major enactments from 1890 to 1940, concluded that no less than seventy-seven developed from bills that had been introduced in earlier years without sponsorship from the administration. A study by Ronald Moe and Steven Teel, published in 1970, agreed with Chamberlain that Congress plays a substantial role in initiating and developing legislation. Chamberlain frames the issue accurately: the *ideas* for legislation seldom originate either in Congress or in the executive branch. "Most legislation is in reality the product of forces external to any government agency."[100]

Executive Lobbying

Prior to World War II, presidents relied on personal assistants within the White House or the executive departments to handle contacts with Congress. The Budget Bureau, created in 1921, marked the starting point for an institutionalized liaison operation with Congress.

The Executive Office of the President (EOP), established in 1939, contained not only the Budget Bureau but other units to improve executive-legislative relations. The EOP White House Office was composed, in part, of secretaries to the president charged with the following mission: "To facilitate and maintain quick and easy communication with the Congress, the individual members of Congress, the heads of executive departments and agencies, the press, the radio, and the general public." The administrative assistants to the president were expected to bridge the gap between the branches.[101]

Agency Initiatives

Although departments have promoted legislation throughout the history of the country, agencies in the 1930s began to realize the value of centralizing control for bill drafting in the counsel's office and assigning to someone in that office a definite responsibility for the task. Most departments had detailed someone in their organization to watch legislation, but usually on a part-time and sporadic basis. In 1934 the Treasury Department created a legislative division with the office of the general counsel. This division was responsible for drafting departmental bills, monitoring their progress after they were introduced in Congress, and working with legislative staff in preparing amendments desired by congressional committees.[102] By 1941, some political scientists were wondering whether executive lobbying had fundamentally altered the governmental process:

> No one would deny that this familiar, slow, democratic process has been materially modified. It is scarcely too strong to say that today the government leads and the people follow; and by government is meant, as all would agree, the executive, or the administrative bu-

reaucracy. This is not to say the executive leadership is new or uncommon in American politics. The strong presidents have all been spirited leaders in legislation. Yet never before in peace-time has there been the degree of legislative direction from administrative quarters that the last few years have brought.[103]

In 1942, two months after the attack on Pearl Harbor, the War Department reorganized its general staff. Under the leadership of Brig. Gen. Wilton B. Persons, the reorganization included the army's first elaborate congressional unit, the legislative liaison division. The Army Organization Act of 1950 established a department legal counselor—a senior civilian reporting directly to the secretary of the army and responsible for monitoring the activities of the office of legislative liaison. In other departments, legislative liaisons also developed out of the departments' general counsels or solicitors.[104]

Organizing the White House, 1941–1969

During the emergency atmosphere of World War II, the task of coordinating the president's program was shared by the White House, the Budget Bureau, and the Office of War Mobilization and Reconversion. After Roosevelt's death, in 1945, Truman tried to pull the entire function back into the Budget Bureau.[105] A small congressional liaison unit was established within the Truman White House. Two assistants were appointed in 1949. Neither had any experience in partisan politics or as congressional staff.[106] Significant liaison responsibilities were carried out by Truman or his associates in the White House, particularly Clark Clifford and Charles S. Murphy. Senior members of the Truman White House characterized the formal liaison unit as "understaffed and relatively ineffectual. The legislative assistants attended the President's staff meetings but rarely spoke up. In the Congress they had little discretion to commit the President or to speak authoritatively for him so as to influence votes, strategy or tactics . . . the legislative assistants were primarily messengers rather than responsible political agents."[107]

By 1953, the first year of the Eisenhower administration, a staff of senior assistants in the White House had been assigned the responsibility of legislative liaison. Starting with three, the unit's staff was increased to eight by 1961.[108] Eisenhower's initial chief liaison officer was General Persons, a close friend and longtime military associate. He had served as a liaison officer for the military under two Democratic administrations. Another member of the liaison team, Bryce Harlow, had known Eisenhower during World War II when Harlow carried out legislative liaison for Gen. George Marshall and Secretary of War Henry Stimson. Later serving as general counsel for the House Armed Services Committee, Harlow remained in contact with Eisenhower.[109] Eventually Harlow replaced Persons as head of the White House liaison unit.

The operation of the liaison staff was limited by Eisenhower's strong belief in the separation of powers doctrine and his respect for congressional prerogatives in legislative matters. But Eisenhower took seriously the promises in his party's platform and the commitments made during the campaign. In 1954 alone he made 232 specific requests for legislation to Congress.[110]

The Kennedy administration, pledged to activist leadership, had an extensive legislative program. Kennedy's razor-thin presidential victory convinced him that a sophisticated, aggressive liaison operation with Congress was indispensable to White House objectives. The chief of the liaison unit was Larry O'Brien. The liaison unit in the Kennedy White House numbered about six full-time professionals. Compared with the Eisenhower staff, they were younger, possessed less experience in dealing with Congress, and had served in highly partisan positions before joining the administration. Several were criticized for displaying "a lack of respect for their elders in the Congress and with using crude tactics more appropriate to the rough-and-tumble of party conventions than to the political process in a coequal branch of the national government."[111]

O'Brien's liaison unit did not try to monopolize congressional relations. Appropriations remained the responsibility of the Budget Bureau. Foreign affairs were left to the president's adviser on foreign affairs, the secretary of state, and the assistant secretary for congressional relations in the State Department (although on some issues, such as foreign aid, the White House liaison team intervened).[112]

When President Johnson, a former Senate majority leader, entered office, he stressed the importance of the congressional liaison operation. He told cabinet members and agency heads: "There's no one more important in your department or agency than the man responsible for congressional relations. You have the responsibility to see to it that you have the best possible man available. You see to it that he's adequately staffed, and you see to it that you maintain your relationship with the Congress every day of the week."[113] In O'Brien's estimate, Johnson's approach to congressional liaison represented a "hard-sell, arm-twisting style of operation which contrasted with Kennedy's more restrained approach."[114]

Nixon to Clinton, 1969–1998

Nixon, like Johnson, came to the presidency with considerable congressional experience: member of the House of Representatives, senator, and vice president. And yet, more than any president before or since, he displayed a contemptuous attitude toward the legislative branch and never seemed comfortable dealing with its members.

To manage his congressional relations staff, President Nixon first turned to Bryce Harlow, veteran White House lobbyist of the Eisenhower years, and to William E. Timmons, who had served as an aide to Republican members of Congress. On December 9, 1970, Harlow resigned his post as counselor to the president. His job had been complicated by attitudes within the Nixon White House. Some senior staffers, including John D. Ehrlichman and H. R. Haldeman, had a limited understanding of Congress or the constitutional system of separated powers and little inclination to learn. Another source of difficulty lay in the heightened expectations of Republican legislators. Many of them remembered Harlow from the Eisenhower days, "when they were so respectful of the General, they asked for little. Part of their trouble is that they expected a great deal of Richard Nixon, who was one of them for so long, who has always been reliably political and completely responsive to their problems."[115]

Harlow was replaced by Clark MacGregor, who had just completed ten years in the House of Representatives. Republican members of Congress praised MacGregor's appointment. On his lapel he wore a button that proclaimed: "I care about Congress." But shortly after MacGregor took office, Nixon issued a sharp attack on the 91st Congress. He said that Congress, because of its record over the previous two years, "will be remembered and remarked upon in history not so much for what it did, but for what it failed to do." The nation, he said, had watched a legislative body "that had seemingly lost the capacity to decide and the will to act."[116]

MacGregor, objecting to this speech, extracted from Nixon a promise that future messages to Capitol Hill would first be routed through him. MacGregor believed that the tense atmosphere of confrontation tactics employed by the Nixon White House should be replaced by a more conciliatory approach. The philosophy he expressed to Nixon, upon accepting the job, was that "bloody defeats in Congress are not helpful to him or the country. My view is that the best politics for Richard Nixon is success for the legislative program."[117] But the Nixon administration was bent on confrontation politics. MacGregor departed to make way for Timmons's hard-hitting style. On July 6, 1972, setting the tone for Nixon's reelection effort, Timmons denounced Congress as "miserable," "irresponsible," "appalling," and "cynical."[118]

The resignations of Ehrlichman and Haldeman, on April 30, 1973, offered another opportunity to mend relations with Congress. Nixon appointed Harlow and Melvin Laird (a former member of Congress and Nixon's first secretary of defense) to the post of White House counselor, where they were supposed to function as Nixon's "ambassadors" to Capitol Hill. Within a year, as pressure mounted for Nixon's resignation, they left the administration.[119]

Max Friedersdorf, Timmons's deputy for House liaison, was appointed to head the liaison unit in the Ford White House. Gerald Ford had spent twenty-five years in the House of Representatives, many of them as minority leader for the Republicans. He was therefore accustomed to the give-and-take of politics. Congressional relations appeared to be off to a good start on August 12, 1974, when President Ford addressed Congress three days after he took office. In contrast to the truculent, pugnacious tone of the Nixon administration, Ford looked forward to a period of trust and harmony: "As president, within the limits of basic principles, my motto toward the Congress is communication, conciliation, compromise, and cooperation." On the whole, executive-legislative relationships improved considerably during the Ford years. Timmons, after leaving his post as White House liaison chief, compared the styles of Nixon and Ford: "If you put in a suggestion for Ford to call up someone, a conferee or a ranking member, he'll do it. Nixon was not comfortable doing that. He did some of it, of course, but it wasn't often, and when he did he really wouldn't like it. It was awkward for him. It was not his nature. Ford is comfortable doing it and he's pretty persuasive in personal negotiations."[120]

Jimmy Carter selected Frank Moore to head his congressional relations team. A native of Georgia, Moore had served as liaison with the Georgia legislature during Carter's term as governor. At no time had Moore ever worked in Washington or on Capitol Hill. Even before Carter took office, congressional Democrats began criticizing Moore's performance. Unreturned phone calls and missed meetings were part of the objections, but the complaints soon broadened to include inadequate consultation on presidential appointments and the energy program.[121]

Some of the problems stemmed from the inexperience of Carter's liaison staff, but other factors contributed to the breakdown in executive-legislative relations. Congressional sensitivity had been heightened by the acerbity of the Nixon years, there was concern that Carter viewed Congress as little more than a national version of the Georgia legislature, and House Speaker Tip O'Neill and Senate Majority Leader Robert Byrd were much more assertive as party leaders than their predecessors, Carl Albert and Mike Mansfield. Moreover, changes in the delegate selection process at the Democratic National Convention allowed someone like Carter to win nomination with less than the usual support from Congress. Carter came in as an "outsider" and would remain one. O'Neill was particularly offended by Carter's top aide Hamilton Jordan, whom O'Neill referred to as Hannibal Jerken. O'Neill expressed his frustration this way: "As far as Jordan was concerned, a House Speaker was something you bought on sale at Radio Shack."[122]

President Reagan's liaison team operated smoothly from the start. Friedersdorf, who had served Nixon and Ford in congressional relations, was selected to head the Reagan liaison unit. His principal assistants, Powell A. Moore (handling the Senate) and Kenneth M. Duberstein (responsible for the House), both had substantial experience on Capitol Hill.

To pass his spending and tax proposals in 1981, President Reagan used all the tools at his disposal. He invited fourteen House Democrats to Camp David for lunch, hoping to build a conservative majority in the House. He carried out his mission partly by dispatching

Air Force planes to bring legislators back to D.C. for a vote. Objecting to this display of presidential largesse and perquisites, a liberal Democrat offered a tongue-in-cheek amendment to an appropriations bill: "No part of any appropriation contained in this title may be used for the purchase or provision of any gift or favor (including, but not limited to, cuff links, helicopter rides, visits to Camp David, and barbecues) to members of Congress for the purpose of influencing their votes on legislation." The amendment was rejected by voice vote.[123]

Reagan's mastery of Congress was short-lived. By 1982 the economy had weakened, his budget policy projected massive deficits, and the Republicans lost twenty-six seats in the House. Republican legislators in both houses began to distance themselves from the president. Initially this display of independence brought threats of sanctions and reprisals from the White House. When White House lobbyists suggested to Charles Grassley, a Republican senator from Iowa, that his criticism of the president's defense program might prevent Reagan from making campaign appearances in his state, the *Des Moines Register* ran a front-page cartoon showing a White House spokesman saying, "And you can forget about the president campaigning for you in '86!" with Grassley responding, "Could I have that in writing?"[124]

At the end of 1986, Reagan's political fortunes sagged further after disclosure of the Iran-Contra affair. In his first year he had put together a remarkable series of legislative victories by carefully orchestrating public opinion and building a working majority in Congress. Operating through constitutional channels had been an outstanding success. Iran-Contra represented the opposite strategy. Officials within the White House and the National Security Council decided to make policy single-handedly. There would be no sharing of power with Congress. Reagan's circumvention of established procedures inflicted lasting damage on his administration (pp. 206–13).

President George Bush assembled a professional team to handle liaison operations with Congress. Frederick D. McClure, his assistant for legislative affairs, received high marks from Capitol Hill. Bush selected for his Cabinet men and women with substantial experience with the Federal Government; many of them had served as members of Congress.

Bipartisan groups of legislators were brought regularly to the White House for discussions. Unlike Reagan, Bush was prepared to discuss substantive issues without having to read from notes, held press conferences more frequently, and seemed to enjoy personal contacts with members of Congress. Bush's previous service in the House and as presiding officer of the Senate gave him a ready circle of congressional friends. After Iraq's invasion of Kuwait in August 1990, he claimed that he could take offensive action against Saddam Hussein without first obtaining authority from Congress. However, Bush decided on January 8, 1991, to seek legislative support and Congress passed the necessary legislation (pp. 202–203). A major irritant in congressional relations was John Sununu, an acerbic White House chief of staff. In early 1992 he was forced out to permit the Republicans to gear up more effectively for the presidential and congressional elections.[125] Removal of an irritant did not translate into electoral success.

President Clinton selected Howard Paster to head the White House legislative affairs office. With substantial experience in the House, the Senate, and the private sector, Paster had a good understanding of the federal legislative process and the tools needed for success. However, a disorganized and largely inexperienced White House staff, coupled with an exceptionally heavy legislative agenda (the health bill, NAFTA, and other proposals), cast a shadow over the first year's effort. Paster left after the first session and was replaced by Patrick Griffin.

In the middle of 1994, Clinton picked OMB Director Leon Panetta to replace Thomas McLarty as White House chief of staff. The move brought order and discipline to all operations, including legislative affairs, but the White House lobbying team had less visibility and impact on Capitol Hill. High turnover within the legislative affairs office was one factor. More significant were the Republican victories in the 1994 elections, shifting the initiative for new legislation from the White House to Congress. In 1996, John Hilley replaced Griffin.[126]

Restrictions on Executive Lobbying

Executive branch lobbying is subject to legal constraints dating back as far as 1913. Congress passed an appropriation bill with this language: "No money appropriated by this or any other Act shall be used for the compensation of any publicity expert unless specifically appropriated for that purpose."[127] Representative Frederick Gillett, Republican of Massachusetts, sponsored this provision after learning that the Civil Service Commission had advertised for a "publicity expert" in the Department of Agriculture. Democrat John Fitzgerald of New York, chairman of the House Appropriations Committee, agreed with Gillett that there was "no place in the Government service for an employee whose sole duty was to extol and to advertise the activities of any particular service of the Government."[128]

In response to this statutory language, agencies concocted new titles for employees. Instead of "publicity expert," agencies created positions for director of information, chief educational officer, supervisor of information research, director of publications, and other imaginative names that circumvented the law.[129] The 1913 legislation remains part of the permanent body of federal law (5 U.S.C. 3107), but it has been diluted by other statutes that specifically authorize and fund publicity efforts. In contrast to the attitude of Representatives Gillett and Fitzgerald, today it is commonplace for Congress to supply funds to agencies and departments for public information officers.

A more significant law passed in 1919. Debate in the House of Representatives reveals that members were offended by bureau chiefs and departmental heads "writing letters throughout the country, sending telegrams throughout the country, for this organization, for this man, for that company to write his Congressman, to wire his Congressman, in behalf of this or that legislation." Statutory language was devised to "absolutely put a stop to that sort of thing."[130] As currently codified (18 U.S.C. 1913), the provision reads:

> No part of the money appropriated by any enactment of Congress shall, in the absence of express authorization by Congress, be used directly or indirectly to pay for any personal service, advertisement, telegram, telephone, letter, printed or written matter, or other device, intended or designed to influence in any manner a Member of Congress, to favor or oppose, by vote or otherwise, any legislation or appropriation by Congress, whether before or after the introduction of any bill or resolution proposing such legislation or appropriation; but this shall not prevent officers or employees of the United States or of its departments or agencies from communicating to Members of Congress on the request of any Member or to

Congress, through the proper official channels, requests for legislation or appropriations which they deem necessary for the efficient conduct of the public business.

In addition to Section 1913 (also known as the "Lobbying with Appropriated Moneys Act"), Congress has enacted other restrictions on departmental lobbying and public relations.[131] Several studies have used the term "legal fiction" to describe these statutory restrictions,[132] but laws have been somewhat effective in limiting the ability of departments to mobilize grass-roots support for or against pending legislation.

Enforcing Statutory Restrictions

Part of the difficulty in controlling executive lobbying by statute is disagreement on what constitutes "publicity," "propaganda," and "liaison." But beyond this issue of definitions is a more fundamental problem. Members of Congress simultaneously oppose and invite executive lobbying. Those who advocate restrictions on departmental lobbying also understand that the legislative process depends on a free flow of information from the executive branch. Even critics of administrative lobbying steer clear of a blanket condemnation. As one legislator remarked: "Certainly, any Administration should be expected to use all legal means at its disposal to encourage acceptance of its programs."[133] Congress has even passed legislation to encourage agency personnel to inform members of Congress about their operations. In a provision that dates back to 1912 (and is reiterated in the Civil Service Reform Act of 1978), Congress declared that the right of federal employees, "individually or collectively, to petition Congress or a Member of Congress, or to furnish information to either House of Congress, or to a committee or Member thereof, may not be interfered with or denied."[134]

Members of Congress do not question the right of presidents to advocate legislative measures, either through the constitutional prerogative to present to Congress information on the state of the union or by other recommendations judged to be necessary or expedient. The president is at liberty to present personal views through press conferences, news broadcasts, and television appearances. Vice President Mondale remarked in 1980: "If you asked me, if I had to give up one—the opportunity to get on the evening news, or the veto power— I think I'd throw the veto power away."[135]

Section 1913 does not prevent executive officials from responding, through appropriate channels, to a legislator's request. Rather, the purpose is to prevent administrators from using their offices to drum up public support or opposition to pending legislation. Members of Congress do not want to be on the receiving end of constituent pressures artificially manufactured by agency telephone calls, telegrams, departmental threats and coercion, and other stimuli originating from within an administration. The General Accounting Office (GAO), as well as the former Budget Bureau, has objected to agency publications that are proselytizing in tone and propagandistic in substance. Agency lobbying is thus subject to legislative as well as executive constraints.[136]

Controversial Actions

In 1948 the House Subcommittee on Publicity and Propaganda reported what it considered a number of illegal and improper agency practices. It expressed particular concern about "an unprecedented flood of news releases from the executive agencies . . . much of it . . . sheer propaganda designed to influence public thinking and to bring pressure upon Congress." The subcommittee found especially objectionable the administration's creation of "health workshops" around the country to promote President Truman's proposal for national health insurance.[137] Although the subcommittee expressed concern about executive lobbying, it hesitated to advocate new statutory controls: "[T]here is a fine line between legitimate information service, and activity on the part of agencies and individuals which is designed to condition the public mind, and [the subcommittee] cautions that it will take legislation drawn with meticulous care to prevent improper action without infringing on legitimate services or the rights of the individual public official."[138]

During the fall of 1961, the Kennedy administration sponsored a series of White House regional conferences around the country. Representative Ancher Nelsen, Republican of Minnesota, criticized the conferences as efforts at the grass roots to foster the objectives of the White House. Postcards were handed out to permit members of the audience to tell the president about their support. Since Section 1913 carries criminal penalties, enforcement depended on the Justice Department, but it participated in the conferences and would have had to pass judgment on its own conduct.[139]

Also during the Kennedy administration, citizens who served on Department of Agriculture committees reported that the meetings were being used primarily to propagandize administration programs. At the urging of the Senate Appropriations Committee, Congress enacted specific language to prohibit the use of appropriated funds to influence the vote of farmers in any referendum and to influence agricultural legislation, except as permitted by Section 1913. The legislation also prohibited funds for salaries or other expenses of members of county and community committees for engaging in any activities other than advisory and supervisory duties and delegated program functions prescribed in administrative regulations.[140]

Several key members of Congress were outraged in 1973 when the Nixon White House prepared a 145-page kit of materials to be used against Congress in the "Battle of the Budget." The kit consisted of guidelines for speeches, "one liners" and "horror stories" about wasteful federal programs—all to be used as part of a coordinated attack on the "spendthrift" Democratic-controlled Congress. Some of the suggested epithets, distributed to top agency officials and public relations aides, included "the buck-passing Congress," "the credit-card Congress," and the "maverick Congress (ignoring the will of the people)." The following are examples of quips that were to be used in lampooning Congress:

> This may look like a Santa Claus Congress—but it's got a bagful of bad news for the taxpayers.

> Just because the Congress passes the buck doesn't mean the President has to spend it.

> When Congress can't add, Senator Scott (the Republican leader) has said the President must subtract. Otherwise the budget will keep on multiplying and the taxpayer's dollars will keep on dividing.[141]

Senators Edmund Muskie of Maine and Hubert Humphrey of Minnesota, both Democrats, asked the GAO to determine whether the White House operation violated Section 1913. Comptroller General Elmer Staats concluded that the kit violated language in an appropriation act, which restricted funds for publicity or propaganda purposes designed to support or defeat pending legislation. Since Section 1913 contains fine and imprisonment provisions, requiring prosecution by the Justice Department, the GAO concluded that it lacked jurisdiction to offer a judgment. After a Ralph Nader litigation unit (Public Citizen, Inc.) went to court claiming that the White House had violated Section 1913, a White House official, in an affidavit, stated that all copies of the kit had been returned for destruction. The suit was subsequently dismissed on the ground that it was moot.[142]

Lobbying by the Ford administration came under fire when several Republican members of Congress complained that White House staffers had threatened to withhold federal favors unless the legislators voted with the administration. Representatives William Cohen and David Emery, both Maine Republicans, said that a White House lobbyist had told them that Ford's appointment of a former Republican governor from Maine to a federal post hinged on their willingness to support Ford's veto of a tax bill. Both legislators voted to override the veto—two of only nineteen Republicans in the House to do so.[143]

A year later, Representative Larry Pressler, Republican of South Dakota, publicly rebuked a White House lobbyist. Pressler said that the lobbyist told him he would be in "political trouble" if he voted against the Ford administration on the natural gas vote. Attacking Pressler in his home district's leading newspaper, the lobbyist called him "paranoid and defensive" and described his reaction to White House pressure as "typical of a freshman Congressman." After the lobbyist apologized, Pressler told President Ford that such tactics were counterproductive and intolerable.[144]

Several complaints were made about the Carter administration's use of public funds to campaign for the SALT II arms control treaty.[145] Also high on the list of agencies criticized for lobbying activities were the Indian Health Services, Commission on Civil Rights, Office of Juvenile Justice, Maritime Administration, and Office of Surface Mining.[146] Especially irritating to some members of Congress was the use of federal funds by the Legal Services Corporation and ACTION (responsible for volunteer programs) to lobby Congress and state and local lawmakers.[147] Three suits were filed in federal court to challenge the attempt by the Carter administration to promote SALT II, trucking deregulation, and civil service reform.[148] The SALT case— brought to court by six senators, four representatives, and the American Conservative Union—was dismissed because they failed to establish specific injury under the standing doctrine.[149]

Legal challenges were brought against the Reagan administration's lobbying of defense funds. GAO accused the Air Force of using a contractor (the Lockheed Corporation) to perform certain types of lobbying activities that would have been illegal for the Air Force. GAO recommended that executive agencies should not ask a contractor to engage in grass-roots lobbying activities that they could not legally perform themselves.[150] This dispute became part of a larger issue: how to control contractors who use federal funds to lobby Congress. Attempts to prevent such actions raise free-speech questions under the First Amendment, but OMB was able to issue guidelines in 1983 to limit abuses.[151] Another dispute during the Reagan administration was the disclosure that the Navy had maintained a rating system for members of Congress, giving them a numerical grade based on their votes on naval-related issues. After legislators and committees denounced the rating system, the Navy discontinued it.[152]

In 1987, GAO concluded that the Reagan administration had engaged in two other activities that violated lobbying rules. In the first, GAO decided that the office for Public Diplomacy for Latin America and the Caribbean had violated a restriction on the use of appropriated funds for publicity or propaganda purposes not authorized by Congress. The office had prepared and disseminated information as part of a campaign to influence the public and Congress to support increased funding for the Contras in Nicaragua.[153] In the second dispute, GAO reported that the Department of Energy violated federal regulations by orchestrating extensive lobbying by a private firm and by nuclear weapons scientists in order to prevent Congress from passing legislation that would ban nuclear tests.[154]

Disputes about executive lobbying continued into the Clinton administration. On April 5, 1995, Edward Perry, Assistant Supervisor of the U.S. Fish & Wildlife Service's field office in State College, Pennsylvania, participated in a press conference sponsored by state and national environmental groups. Because he stated strong opposition to pending revisions to the wetlands provisions of the Clean Water

Act, some members of Congress charged that he might have violated Section 1913 and several other statutes. Although the Interior Department concluded that Perry had not violated federal law, the Fish & Wildlife Service issued guidelines a week later for Service employees who attend a press conference held by an advocacy group to discuss a bill being considered in Congress. If "the forum is considered biased, rather than neutral," statements by Service employees "will likely be interpreted as advocacy rather than information and education."[155]

On December 21, 1995, the General Accounting Office issued its report on the dispute and concluded that Perry's conduct constituted a violation of Section 303 of the Interior appropriations act for fiscal 1995, which contained this language: "No part of any appropriation contained in this Act shall be available for any activity or the publication or distribution of literature that in any way tends to promote public support or opposition to any legislative proposal on which congressional action is not complete." GAO concluded that the Interior Department had misread the legislative history of Section 303.[156] In February 1996, the Interior Department issued new guidelines on prohibited lobbying activities.

In 1996, the House Committee on Government Reform and Oversight held hearings on a bill to tighten statutory prohibitions on the use of appropriated funds by federal agencies for lobbying activities.[157] Although the bill was not enacted, legislative language was adopted later that year to place further restrictions on executive lobbying.[158]

Sanctions against executive lobbying have limited effect because the Justice Department believes that Congress intended Section 1913 to bar "gross solicitations" of public support, and the GAO lacks jurisdiction to determine violations of the criminal code. Judging from the few judicial decisions, it is apparent that the courts are inclined to defer to Congress and the president on the definition of appropriate lobbying activity by executive officials.

Conclusions

Even in the days of patronage and the spoils system, the administration of sanctions and favors by the president was time-consuming and quite likely to irritate and alienate important members of Congress. Civil service reforms and the rise of the welfare state, which automatically dispenses benefits through entitlement programs, have removed much of the leverage previously available to the White House. In addition, since members of Congress are increasingly independent of the White House in their reelection campaigns, they may vote as they please with little worry of presidential retaliation.

The president is left essentially with modest powers of persuasion, bargaining, negotiation, favors, services, flattery, appeals to national interest, and personal loyalty. Success in enlisting the support of a legislator comes at a cost, at least in time and energy; often the price is a specific benefit that the legislator wants, and expects, in return. All these tactics may fail when legislators decide that a presidential request is injurious to their constituents or contrary to their own principles and conscience.[159]

An ambitious program to "care and feed" legislators carries a high risk. If a president extends favors to fence-sitters to secure their votes, other legislators may resent the fact that they routinely support the administration without receiving comparable assistance. Such thoughts might encourage signs of "disloyalty" until the White House takes notice and demonstrates its appreciation. A president's election rarely provides a "mandate" for the administration's program. Legislators successful in the same election usually enter office with mandates of their own, quite different from the values and objectives of the president-elect. Seldom will these legislators depend on the president's "coattail effect." Consequently, they owe the chief executive little. Two-thirds of the senators gained their seats by winning elections two to four years earlier.

Leadership from the White House will always be possible, whether Congress is centralized or decentralized. It is often argued that the decentralization of Congress in the 1970s, which took power from committee heads and dispersed it to House and Senate subcommittees, thwarted the legislative goals of Presidents Ford and Carter. They could not contact a handful of influential committee leaders to push forward the White House program.

This is a convenient excuse, but it ignores the fact that earlier presidents complained that the *centralization* of power in Congress made it impossible to get bills past uncooperative committee heads. Legislative decentralization can be an opportunity, not an obstacle, because it opens up lines of communication. Moreover, the same congressional structure that appeared to obstruct Ford and Carter was remarkably compliant to Reagan's budgetary and tax initiatives in 1981.

It is also said that government cannot function effectively because of "divided government" (one party controlling the White House and the other party controlling Congress). But Reagan functioned well in 1981 with divided government and Carter fared poorly for four years even though his party controlled both branches. Democratic control of Congress in Clinton's first two years did not facilitate his plan to reform the nation's health system.

Part of presidential leadership consists in fashioning a broad coalition of support and remaining capable of adjusting to new circumstances and conditions. It is irresponsible to complain that conditions are not like they used to be (or not like we *thought* they used to be). A good leader makes the best of a situation that is never ideal. President Franklin D. Roosevelt once told an aide: "I am the captain of this ship, but the seas control the captain." He recognized that the strength of forces, impulses, and opinions at any given time would determine what he had to do.[160] A skillful leader can find some margin for action in any situation.

CHAPTER 3

◆

Congress as Administrator

It has become customary to criticize legislators for interfering with administrative matters. Woodrow Wilson chided Congress in 1885 for entering "more and more into the details of administration, until it has virtually taken into its own hands all the substantial powers of government." Despite almost twenty-five years of congressional service, President Ford warned Congress that its attempt to become a "virtual co-administrator" in operational decisions would seriously distract from its proper legislative role.[1]

High on the list of accused congressional "meddling" are these practices: excessive detail in statutes, passage of private bills, the use of "riders" in appropriation bills to direct and confine administrative actions, statutory restrictions on personnel policies, legislative vetoes, directives in committee reports, redundant and intrusive investigations, casework demands that consume agency time, and the creation of independent commissions to perform regulatory tasks that could be carried out by existing executive departments. These congressional initiatives are criticized for undermining the unity of the presidency, violating hierarchical principles of public administration, disrupting the orderly functioning of agencies, and threatening the stability of the constitutional system. Congress is advised to confine itself to legislative duties and leave administration to the president and the executive branch.

In 1986 the Supreme Court claimed that the Constitution "does not contemplate an active role for Congress in the supervision of officers charged with the execution of the laws it enacts." According to the Court, "once Congress makes its choice in enacting legislation, its participation ends. Congress can thereafter control the execution of its enactment only indirectly—by passing new legislation."[2] This is a caricature of Congress. The Court contradicts everything we know about the ability (and determination) of Congress to control the execution of laws through hearings, committee investigations, GAO studies, informal contacts between members of Congress and agency officials, committee subpoenas, the contempt power, and nonstatutory controls.

Members of Congress continue to participate in administration because they have learned time and again that details are the crucial building blocks of policy. No better formula for legislative impotence has ever been devised than to limit Congress to "broad policy questions" and assign "administrative details" to the executive. The administration of a program almost always involves legislative power. Congress cannot restrict itself to broad policy alone.

Constitutional Basis

Administration is not a monopoly of the executive. Congress has a legitimate role and responsibility in supervising the efforts of federal agencies. Little was said at the Philadelphia Convention concerning the president's power as administrator. Certainly the framers were keenly aware of the failings of the Continental Congress, especially its lack of administrative accountability and efficiency.[3] Moreover, Madison discovered in the state legislatures an appetite for usurpation: "The Executives of the States are in general little more than Cyphers; the legislatures omnipotent." James Wilson, Gouverneur Morris, and John Mercer were among the delegates at the Convention who warned against legislative aggrandizement. The delegates rejected the idea of a plural executive, preferring to anchor that responsibility in a single individual. Said John Rutledge: "A single man would feel the greatest responsibility and administer the public affairs best."[4]

It can be argued that congressional participation in administrative matters creates a divided executive, something the framers explicitly rejected. Nevertheless, at the Convention, Roger Sherman considered the executive "nothing more than an institution for carrying the will of the Legislature into effect." Although Alexander Hamilton, Thomas Jefferson, and others had criticized the Continental Congress for meddling in administrative details, the framers were never able to distinguish clearly between legislative and executive duties.[5]

Agencies have a direct responsibility to Congress, the body that creates them. In 1854 Attorney General Caleb Cushing admitted that departmental heads are created by law and "most of their duties are prescribed by law." Congress "may at all times call on them for information or explanation in matters of official duty; and it may, if it see fit, interpose by legislation concerning them, when required by the interests of the Government." The extent to which Congress could direct officials prompted Cushing to warn that Congress might by statute so divide the executive power as to subvert the government "and to change it into a parliamentary despotism, like that of Venice or Great Britain, with a nominal executive chief utterly powerless— whether under the name of Doge, or King, or President."[6]

Not only is the administrative process today open to congressional intervention, but parties from the private sector are invited to participate in agency decisions. The Administrative Procedure Act of 1946 requires public notice and comment in rulemaking and provides for group representation in adjudicatory proceedings. The statutory requirement for boards, committees, and task forces allows interested parties from the private sector to advise federal agencies on the implementation of laws. The Freedom of Information Act, the Sunshine Act of 1976, and funding of public participation in agency proceedings have given citizens and interest groups greater access to the administrative process.[7]

The judiciary is another important participant in the administrative process, reviewing agency decisions to see that they conform to legislative intent, satisfy standards of procedural fairness, and meet the test of constitutionality. Courts are routinely criticized for intervening so deeply in the administrative process that they usurp the policymaking functions of Congress and the agencies.[8]

With participation of this breadth in the administrative process, it seems anomalous to ask Congress to stay out. When members of

Congress believe that an agency has departed from its statutory purpose, they are entitled, if not obligated, to express their views through individual statements on the floor, questions at committee hearings, or direct contact with agency officials. The legislative function does not cease with a bill that creates an agency. Only by monitoring the operation of a law can members uncover statutory defects and correct agency misinterpretations.

In a study sympathetic to congressional supervision of agencies, Frank Neuman and Harry Keaton concluded: "One point seems obvious. Congress goes too far if it spends so much time supervising that not enough time is left for legislating."[9] This attitude presumes that supervision and legislation are distinct duties, whereas it is impossible to legislate intelligently and effectively without close supervision. Only through regular feedback from administrators can laws be perfected. How much time to allocate for supervision is a judgment left solely to Congress.

Instruments of Legislative Control

A number of express or implied constitutional powers allows Congress to direct administrative matters. Congress has the power to create an office, define its powers and duration, and determine the compensation for officials. Additional legislative guidance comes from the process of confirming presidential appointees, advisory participation in the administrative process, the investigatory and appropriation powers, private bills, casework, and nonstatutory controls. One of the prime devices for congressional control—the legislative veto—is discussed later in this chapter.

Personnel Policies

The U.S. Code contains extraordinarily detailed instructions from Congress to cover personnel policies for agencies: examination, selection, and placement of employees; training, performance ratings, and incentive awards; classification of positions, pay rates, and travel expenses; hours of work, leave, and holidays; rights of employees; preferential points in hiring veterans; medical plans and life insurance; and restrictions on political activities by federal employees.[10]

In creating departments, Congress may require that the appointment of certain executive officials be subject to the advice and consent of the Senate. It may stipulate the qualifications of appointees, itemizing in great detail the characteristics a president must consider before submitting a name for Senate action. Congress has the power to delegate the appointment of officers to departmental heads; it may also specify grounds for removal and impose procedural safeguards before administrators suspend or dismiss employees (see pp. 121–23).

During confirmation hearings, senators have an opportunity to explore a nominee's depth of knowledge and policy commitments. Promises may be extracted at that time with regard to keeping the committees informed of proposed actions and even requiring prior approval from the committees on specific issues. In 1972 President Nixon invoked executive privilege to prevent White House aide Peter Flanigan from testifying before the Senate Judiciary Committee. In an adroit countermove, Senator Sam Ervin, Democrat of North Carolina, asked the committee to delay the consideration of Richard Kleindienst's nomination as attorney general until Nixon let Flanigan testify. The tactic worked. Flanigan was permitted to appear before the committee under special procedures.[11]

Participating as Advisers

The Constitution specifically prohibits persons from simultaneously holding federal office and serving as members of Congress. This Incompatibility Clause is one of the supporting structures of the separation of powers doctrine. Nevertheless, some statutes allow members of Congress to take part in the implementation of laws. The Trade Expansion Act of 1962 directed the president, before each negotiation, to select four representatives from the congressional tax committees to be accredited as members of the U.S. delegation. Under the Trade Act, ten members of Congress are accredited by the president as official advisers to U.S. delegations at international conferences, meetings, and negotiation sessions relating to trade agreements.[12] The fast-track procedure in trade statutes anticipates that members of Congress will be closely involved in the negotiation process so that the president's draft-implementing bill can be handled expeditiously (pp. 184–85).

Congress appoints members of various commissions to oversee the implementation of federal policy. In 1976 Congress established a

Commission on Security and Cooperation in Europe to monitor compliance with the Helsinki Agreement on human rights. Congress appoints twelve of its members to the commission. The president appoints three, drawing from the departments of State, Defense, and Commerce. The Speaker of the House designates the chair from among the House members.[13] As if to underscore the mixed executive-legislative nature of this commission, it is funded not from the legislative branch appropriation bill but from the State-Justice appropriation bill. The commission was reconstituted in 1985, retaining the mixed legislative-executive membership but rotating the leadership between the House and the Senate.[14]

Investigations

The power of Congress to conduct investigations, the Supreme Court noted in 1957, "comprehends probes into departments of the Federal Government to expose corruption, inefficiency or waste." Even Joseph Harris, author of a 1965 study critical of congressional involvement in administration, recognized that it is not enough for Congress to enact policies and programs into law. Members of Congress "must check to see how those policies are being executed, whether they are accomplishing the desired results, and, if not, what corrective action the legislature may appropriately prescribe."[15]

The House of Representatives sharpens its investigative power through the use of "resolutions of inquiry." A member may introduce a resolution authorizing a committee to request the information from the heads of executive departments. All resolutions of inquiry must be reported to the House within one week after presentation. Resolutions of inquiry are answered by departmental officials, either directly or through the president.[16] If the executive branch resists the call for certain papers, congressional committees can issue subpoenas for documents or force individuals to testify. The Court has held that the issuance of a subpoena pursuant to an authorized investigation is "an indispensible ingredient of lawmaking."[17] If a subpoena fails to get the attention of the executive branch, Congress can invoke its contempt power to protect legislative privileges and prerogatives.[18] Contempt proceedings produced material from Secretary of Commerce Rogers Morton during the Ford administration and from Secretary of Energy Charles W. Duncan, Jr., during the Carter administration.[19] Similarly, the contempt power was instrumental in prying loose documents from the Reagan and Clinton administrations (see pp. 16–17).

During the Bush administration, Senator Jesse Helms, Republican of North Carolina, blocked the nomination of an ambassador to Guyana because the State Department refused to show him the secret cable traffic regarding a Helms visit to Chile in 1986. The hold on the nomination lasted a record-breaking seventeen months, until the deputy secretary of state showed up at Helms's office and let him read the documents. The internal memos were critical of Helms and his aide. Helms then agreed to lift the hold and permit the nomination to go forward.[20]

Restrictions on the investigative power generally protect private citizens rather than agency officials. Citizens are entitled to First Amendment rights of free speech and association, the Fourth Amendment right to be free of unreasonable searches and seizures, the Fifth Amendment right that protects witnesses against self-incrimination, and certain Sixth Amendment rights of due process. Committee hearings must be properly authorized; the judiciary insists that committee questions must be pertinent and directed toward a legislative purpose.

These limitations do not apply to committee inquiries into agency activities. Agencies are expected to cooperate with legislative efforts to determine the expenditure of taxpayer funds. Presidents may raise the barrier of executive privilege, claiming a constitutional right to withhold information from Congress, but such defenses are rarely employed.[21] President Reagan invoked executive privilege in 1986 to keep from the Senate certain memoranda that Justice William Rehnquist had written while in the Justice Department during the Nixon years, but when it looked as if this action might delay Rehnquist's nomination to be chief justice and therefore prevent the confirmation of Antonin Scalia to be associate justice, the documents were released to the Senate.

The courts have added a few restrictions on congressional investigations into agency affairs. Committees may not intervene in a pending adjudicatory proceeding by focusing on the process used by agency officials to reach a decision; here the congressional interference is not in an agency's "*legislative* function, but rather, in its *judicial* function."[22] The legislative (rulemaking) function of an agency is more open to congressional inquiries than adjudicatory proceedings, but a member may not force an executive official to take into account considerations that Congress had not intended.[23]

For the most part, however, the courts assume that agency officials possess the necessary backbone to withstand searching inquiries by congressional committees.[24] Even when the pressure during a congressional hearing is the direct impetus for a change in agency policy, the courts treat such influence as "part of the give and take of democratic government."[25]

Appropriations

The power of the purse allows Congress to monitor and to control the administration of programs. At the end of each appropriation bill lies a "General Provisions" section that contains dozens of limitations, riders, and restrictions on agency operations. Within each appropriation account are additional restrictions that take the form of "provisos." When Congress felt that the Legal Services Corporation had abused its powers, it resorted to an increasing number of restrictions. For example, the appropriation for fiscal 1986 provided $305.5 million subject to a long list of conditions, prohibiting the corporation from using appropriated funds to lobby the national, state, or local governments; to provide legal assistance for an alien unless certain conditions are met; to support or conduct training programs for the purpose of advocating particular public policies or encouraging political activities; or to take certain other actions proscribed by the appropriation.[26]

Audits by the General Accounting Office (GAO) permit Congress to hold executive officers accountable for the use of public funds. The GAO has the power to disallow an expenditure, thereby making the disbursing officer liable for the funds involved in an illegal transaction. In 1974 the GAO used this power to stop the expenditure of funds for Secret Service protection to Spiro Agnew after he had resigned as vice president.[27]

The power of the purse cannot be protected merely through the authorization and appropriation process. Congress must monitor the *expenditure* of funds to prevent the abuse of discretionary authority by executive officials. Members of Congress find it necessary to exercise statutory and nonstatutory controls over administrative operations such as transfer of funds, reprogramming of funds, year-end buying, deficiency spending, impoundment, carryover balances, and contractor expenses.[28]

Very few constitutional limits operate on the appropriations power. While the flow of federal money is not "the final arbiter of constitutionally protected rights,"[29] only rarely has the judiciary placed restrictions on the power of the purse. For example, Congress may not diminish the compensation of members of the federal judiciary, since this is specifically proscribed by the Constitution.[30] In addition, the Supreme Court, in *United States v. Lovett* (1946), declared invalid a section of an appropriation act that prohibited the payment of federal salaries to three named "subversives." The language in the statute was struck down because it represented a bill of attainder that Article II, Section 3 of the Constitution forbids.[31]

Private Bills

Members of Congress introduce private bills to overcome injustices and inadequacies in the administrative process.[32] The flood of private bills after the Civil War to assist constituents turned down by the Pension Bureau was particularly flagrant. President Grover Cleveland declared open season on such measures, often employing sarcastic language in his veto messages to rebuke these legislative efforts. During the 49th Congress (1885–1887) there were more than twice as many private laws as public laws: 1,031 to 434. The ratio climbed to 3-to-1 by the 56th Congress (1899–1901)—1,498 private laws and 443 public laws. Private bills introduced in the 59th Congress (1905–1907) topped 6,000.[33]

In an effort to reduce the private bill workload, the Legislative Reorganization Act of 1946 prohibited the consideration of any private bill or resolution (including omnibus claims or pension bills) or an amendment to any bill or resolution authorizing or directing (1) the payment of money for property damages, for personal injuries or death for suits that could be instituted under the Federal Tort Claims Act (Title IV of the 1946 act), or for a pension (other than to carry out a provision of law or treaty stipulation); (2) the construction of a bridge across a navigable stream (Title V of the act); or (3) the correction of a military or naval record.[34]

Due to a surge in legislative activity regarding immigration from 1949 through 1955, private laws averaged more than one thousand in each Congress, but from 1971 to 1997 they fell sharply, averaging about one hundred a Congress. The number of private bills continues to decline, with only a few dozen enacted in recent Congresses.

Private bills need not be *enacted* to affect the administrative process. Whenever a senator or representative introduces an immigration bill and the judiciary committees request a report from the Immigration and Naturalization Service, a deportation is delayed until action is taken on the bill. This procedure continues to exist even after the Supreme Court declared the legislative veto unconstitutional in 1983. Although private bills are subject to abuse, they allow Congress to correct mistakes in past legislation or current administration.

Casework

Members of Congress often become aware of administrative deficiencies by attending to "casework"—that is, assisting a constituent's contact with the bureaucracy. Much of the literature on Congress refers disparagingly to casework because it supposedly diverts members from more significant matters, making them "errand runners" instead of legislators. But casework, aside from its importance for reelection, helps educate legislators on the actual workings of a law. It forces them to descend from the lofty and often abstract universe of statutes to the practical world of administration. By responding to constituent requests, legislators obtain information that allows them to perfect laws and improve agency procedures. One member of Congress advised his colleagues: "You should not underestimate the value of constituent work on the legislative process. Don't you get a lot of your ideas about needed changes in the laws from the problems of your constituents? In processing a problem before the VA or a draft problem you gain your best insight into how laws operate, and you discover where they might be changed."[35]

Some studies conclude that casework reinforces the "institutionalized suspicion" that administrators and legislators have about each other. To bureaucrats, legislators and their staffs "appear as special pleaders for the narrow interests of their constituents even when these conflict with the 'national welfare,' which bureaucrats tend to equate with the overall rules and programs of their agency or department to which the senators so often seek exception." Members, in turn, are said to characterize bureaucrats as arbitrary, patronizing, and compulsively attached to their procedures.[36]

These attitudes, while they do exist, are atypical. Most bureaucrats believe that members of Congress should intervene on behalf of constituents. Casework is accepted as a legitimate and healthy input into the administrative process. Administrators find that casework helps them watch over their subordinates, uncover program flaws, and generate improvements in rules and regulations.[37] Much of the congressional liaison apparatus established in agencies and departments is designed to assist members with casework. Departments that are heavily involved in casework—such as the Department of Veterans' Affairs, the Social Security Administration, the Office of Personnel Management, and the military services—maintain offices in the Senate and House office buildings.

Nonstatutory Controls

Simple resolutions (adopted by either house) and concurrent resolutions (adopted by both houses) have been used to direct administrative action. Although these resolutions are not presented to the president and therefore escape the veto power, and are invalid under the legislative veto case of *INS v. Chadha* (1983), they can still be effective means of control. Some statutes allow committees, acting by resolutions, to direct an agency to investigate.[38] Most resolutions are advisory only, to be accepted by agencies as a recommended course of action.[39] They express the "sense of Congress" (or of either house) on some aspect of public policy.

Congress directs administrative action through the use of other nonstatutory controls: language placed in committee reports, instructions issued by members during committee hearings, correspondence from committee and subcommittee heads to agency officials, and various types of agreements worked out between committees and agencies. Under a philosophy of good-faith efforts by administrators, this system makes sense for both branches. Instead of locking legislative policy into a rigid statutory mold, agency officials are given substantial leeway to adjust programs throughout the year in response to changing circumstances. In return for this latitude, administrators are expected to follow the legislative policy expressed in nonstatutory directives.

In some cases the system fails. In 1975 a conference report adopted by the House and Senate directed the Navy to produce as its air combat fighter a derivative of an aircraft to be selected by the Air Force.

Instead of following the directive in the conference report (usually of high priority as legislative history), the Navy picked a different type of aircraft. The comptroller general decided that nonstatutory controls are not legally binding on agencies unless there is some ambiguity in a statute that requires recourse to the legislative history. Agencies follow nonstatutory controls for practical, not legal, reasons.[40] To ignore such controls invites Congress to cut agency budgets and add restrictive statutory language.

Two other disputes highlight the risk of relying on nonstatutory controls to check delegated power. In 1978 the Supreme Court had to decide whether the Tennessee Valley Authority should complete a dam that threatened the existence of a tiny fish called the snail darter. Opponents of the dam claimed that its operation would violate the Endangered Species Act. The Court declined to allow language in the reports of the appropriations committees, urging completion of the dam, to have precedence over a statute, particularly in the circumstances presented by the case.[41] In another dispute two years later, a lower court reviewed language in a conference report stating that Congress did not contemplate the use of authority given in the bill. The court ruled that the report language could not in any way alter the fact that Congress had granted the authority and had done so with unambiguous language in the bill.[42]

For the most part, agencies find it in their interests to adhere closely to nonstatutory controls. They do not want to risk congressional retaliations in the form of spending cuts and other limitations placed in a public law. Nonetheless, OMB Director James C. Miller III decided in 1988 to challenge Congress on its use of report language to control agency activities. The continuing resolution signed by President Reagan the previous December was accompanied by committee reports that earmarked a number of projects favored by legislators. Miller announced that the reports had "no force of law" because they had not been formally approved by Congress and signed by the president. In a memo to Cabinet officers and agency heads, he said they could "redirect funds not legally required to be used for a particular wasteful, unnecessary, or low priority project to a legally authorized and higher priority project."[43]

Members of Congress were quick to respond. The chairman of the House Appropriations Committee, Jamie Whitten, warned the administration that Miller's views were "unsound and must not be followed."[44] The Democratic chairmen of both Appropriations Committees, together with the ranking Republicans on those panels, wrote to President Reagan and reminded him that the continuing resolution he signed contained this language in Section 107: "Amounts and authorities provided by this resolution shall be in accordance with the reports accompanying the bills as passed by or reported to the House and the Senate and in the Joint Explanatory Statement of the Conference accompanying this Joint Resolution." The four leaders asked Reagan to withdraw Miller's memorandum.[45]

Miller did not accept this interpretation of Section 107, but did write a conciliatory letter to the four legislators, explaining that it was not the intention of the administration to ignore the committee reports. Later, he backed away even more by telling federal agencies to follow report language. He reasoned that members of Congress had "relied on what they perceived to be a former practice" of using report language to fund projects, and that compliance with those understandings would be in the interest of "comity between the branches."[46]

Nonstatutory controls are especially binding in the case of secret budgets for the U.S. intelligence community, composed of the Central Intelligence Agency and several other federal units. The classified nature of U.S. intelligence activities prevents the disclosure of budgetary recommendations. Instead, the intelligence committees prepare a classified "Schedule of Authorizations," listing the amounts of dollars and personnel ceilings for all the intelligence and intelligence-related programs authorized by Congress. The intelligence community is expected to comply fully with the limitations, guidelines, directions, and recommendations in the classified schedule prepared by the conference committee.[47]

Limitations on Congress

Members of Congress have many legitimate reasons for participating in the administrative process. In some cases, however, the representative function oversteps legal boundaries and takes on the color of influence peddling, leading to indictments in the courts against members who use their legislative and oversight positions for personal gain.

This kind of activity is controlled largely by two statutes. The bribery statute (18 U.S.C. 201) is directed against public officials—including members of Congress—who seek or accept anything of value in return for an official act. The conflict-of-interest statute (18 U.S.C. 203) makes it a criminal offense for members of Congress to receive or seek compensation for services relating to any proceeding, contract, claim, or other activity of the federal government. Depending on the circumstances, members may seek immunity under the Speech or Debate Clause of the Constitution, which prohibits questioning a senator or representative for any legislative act.

The Supreme Court has repeatedly held that members of Congress may not use the Speech or Debate Clause as a shield for contacts with the executive branch. Representative Thomas Johnson, Democrat of Maryland, tried to influence the Justice Department to drop a pending investigation of a savings and loan institution. He was accused of receiving more than $20,000 for his efforts and found guilty of violating the conflict-of-interest statute. Representative Bertram Podell, Democrat of New York, pleaded guilty in 1974 to conspiracy and conflict-of-interest charges after he had intervened in several federal agency actions to help an airline company obtain a route between Florida and the Bahamas. His family law firm in Manhattan had been collecting monthly legal fees from the airline's parent company. In another action marking the limits of legislative intervention in agency activities, Representative Frank Brasco, Democrat of New York, was found guilty of bribery and conspiracy in a scheme to obtain Post Office contracts for a trucking firm. Representative Joshua Eilberg, Democrat of Pennsylvania, was indicted for receiving compensation for helping a Philadelphia hospital win a $14.5 million federal grant. After a federal court held in 1979 that his contacts with the executive branch were not protected by the Speech or Debate Clause, Eilberg pleaded guilty to a conflict-of-interest charge.[48]

As part of FBI's Abscam operation during the Carter administration, Representative Michael J. Myers, Democrat of Pennsylvania, was charged with conspiracy, bribery, and traveling in interstate commerce to carry on an unlawful act. In defense, Myers argued that congressional independence would be undermined if government agents could entice members with manufactured opportunities to accept bribes. His charge of entrapment was rejected by an appellate court, which pointed out that Congress may at any time protect itself by redefining the statutory meaning of bribery to exclude a legislator's acceptance of bribes offered by government undercover agents.[49]

Aside from criminal prosecutions, members who interfere in agency proceedings are subject to other limitations. Members immune under the Speech or Debate Clause may face disciplinary action by the House or the Senate. As a result of a Supreme Court decision in 1979, members of Congress who publicize agency waste or abuse by issuing press releases and newsletters to their constituents are not protected by the Speech or Debate Clause. The case arose from a "Golden Fleece Award" announced by Senator William Proxmire, Democrat of Wisconsin, in 1975. After more than forty hours of staff research and a hearing by the Senate Appropriations Committee, Proxmire gave the award to the National Science Foundation (NSF), the National Aeronautics and Space Administration (NASA), and the Office of Naval Research for grants they had made to Dr. Ronald Hutchinson for his studies on animal aggression. Proxmire was in a key position to judge agency waste and abuse. He chaired the Senate appropriations subcommittee that funds NSF and NASA and was also a member of the defense and HEW appropriations subcommittees. Hutchinson sued Proxmire, claiming that he had been libeled by Proxmire's press release and newsletter publicizing the award and by Proxmire's appearance on the Mike Douglas television show, where he mentioned the award.

Lower courts decided that the press release (almost identical to Proxmire's floor speech) was protected by the Speech or Debate Clause. The newsletter was considered part of the informing function of Congress and therefore immune, while the television appearance was protected by the First Amendment. However, the Supreme Court held that Proxmire's press release and newsletter were not protected by his constitutional function as a legislator. The curious result of this decision is that a member of Congress may disclose the results of agency waste, fraud, and abuse only in official remarks in the *Congressional Record* or in committee hearings. Once the member seeks to publicize the issue, by informing constituents or the press, there is risk of a lawsuit.[50]

The Growth of Formal Controls

Congress balances a two-pronged strategy: delegating broad grants of power to agencies while insisting on a share in overseeing programs and activities. In the case of appropriations, funds are generally granted to agencies in large, lump-sum accounts, permitting considerable agency discretion throughout the year to withhold spending in some areas (impoundment), shift funds to new programs (reprogramming), and limit the size of the agency workforce (personnel ceilings). In all three areas Congress has begun to abandon its traditional reliance on nonstatutory controls as the instrument for regulating administrative policy. Because of a breakdown in good-faith relations between the branches, over the past two decades Congress has increasingly used statutory controls.

Impoundment

Prior to 1974 several administrations impounded funds, justified either on the basis of statutory authority or on the claim that presidents had inherent authority to withhold funds from obligation. Despite confrontations from time to time, the two branches managed to fashion political accommodations that were acceptable to both sides. Rarely was there a stalemate that required the courts to referee the dispute.

This informal system fell apart during the Nixon administration. Funds were withheld in a manner, quantitatively and qualitatively, that threatened Congress's power of the purse. Budgetary priorities established by Congress through the appropriation process were quickly reshuffled by administrative officials who refused to spend funds the president did not want. As a result, programs were severely curtailed and in some cases terminated. The administration assumed an adamant, even truculent, position, offering extraordinary and often bizarre legal arguments to justify the impoundments. Although the federal courts handed down dozens of decisions against the administration, the lengthy process of litigation meant that program objectives set by Congress could not be achieved.[51]

In response to this unprecedented abuse of presidential power over expenditures, Congress stepped into the administrative process to protect its own prerogatives. The result was the Impoundment Control Act of 1974. When deciding to withhold funds, the president had to submit a report to Congress. If the withholding was temporary (a *deferral*), either house of Congress could disapprove it at any time. The funds then must be released for obligation by the agencies. If the withholding was to be permanent (a *rescission*), the president had to obtain the support of both houses within forty-five days of continuous session. Otherwise, the funds must be released. A process that traditionally had been part of "budget execution and control," and therefore within the president's realm as administrative chief, was now explicitly tied to congressional review and action.

The procedures of the Impoundment Control Act eliminated the stark confrontations between the president and Congress that characterized the Nixon years. The statute explicitly recognized the right of the president to withhold funds but subjected executive decisions to congressional review and disapproval. This accommodation was severely shaken in 1983 when the Supreme Court struck down the legislative veto in *INS v. Chadha* (see pp. 96–99). The one-house veto was no longer available to disapprove deferrals. Nevertheless, as a means of keeping peace, the OMB director, David Stockman, entered into an agreement with the appropriations committees that the Reagan administration would not abuse its veto-free deferral power, now shorn of the legislative veto.

After Stockman left the government in 1985 the administration decided to use the deferral power aggressively, in part because of the need to meet the deficit targets of the Gramm-Rudman-Hollings Act of 1985 (see pp. 236–39). President Reagan's budget for fiscal 1987, submitted on February 5, 1986, proposed huge amounts in deferred funds. Especially hard hit were the housing programs. Members of Congress and urban groups responded by filing suit to invalidate the president's deferral authority. They argued that the Impoundment Act of 1974 depended on the one-house veto to check the president's deferral authority, and that when the legislative veto was declared invalid in 1983, the deferral authority disappeared as well. Congress did not intend, said the suit, that the legislative veto could ever be severed from the authority granted. If one fell, so did the other.

A federal district judge decided that the president's deferral authority under the 1974 law was no longer available. The judge concluded that the history of that statute convinced him that Congress would have preferred no statute to one without the one-house veto provision. Severing the one-house veto while allowing the president to retain impoundment authority would allow the White House to use the authority "in effect, as a 'line-item veto' (which is, of course, anathema to Congress)."[52] That decision was upheld by an appellate court.[53] The effect of these decisions was to limit deferrals to routine managerial actions, a policy that Congress promptly enacted into law.[54] As federal deficits climbed in the 1980s, members of Congress were under pressure to delegate greater authority to the president to curb spending. The result was the Line Item Veto Act of 1996, which authorized the president to cancel spending and certain taxes (pp. 248–50).

Reprogramming

It is the practice of Congress to appropriate large, lump-sum amounts for general purposes. For example, the defense appropriation bill for fiscal 1997 contained the following amounts for research, development, testing, and evaluation: $5.0 billion for the Army, $8.2 billion for the Navy, and $14.5 billion for the Air Force. Other than a few restrictions in each account, the Pentagon is legally free to spend funds for the broad purposes described in the statute. The Defense Department must also adhere to language in authorization bills, but these too are framed in lump-sum amounts.

Administrative discretion of such vast scope is narrowed by the expectation of Congress that agencies will keep faith with the itemized material they submit in their budget justifications. Agencies are expected to spend funds for the precise purposes stated in these justifications (as amended by Congress). Over the course of a fiscal year, however, officials find it desirable or necessary to depart from their original budget submissions in order to respond to unforeseen developments, new requirements, incorrect price estimates, wage-rate adjustments, and legislation enacted after appropriations. To permit these changes, Congress allows agency officials to take funds from one program and "reprogram" them to another within the same appropriation account.

The latitude for reprogramming increased dramatically after 1949, when Congress began to consolidate a number of appropriation accounts. By administering larger accounts, agency officials gained new discretionary authority to reprogram funds. To retain some semblance of control, congressional committees insisted on various types of procedures requiring agencies to notify committees of significant reprogrammings and, in some cases, to seek their prior approval.

The degree of congressional control has gradually become more formalized over the years. At first the appropriations committees asked the Pentagon to keep them advised of major reprogrammings. Next they required semiannual reports. Within a few years the Pentagon had to obtain prior approval from the appropriations committees before proceeding with certain reprogrammings. Shortly thereafter, the armed services committees were added to the system of notification and prior approval for defense reprogrammings.[55]

Similar controls evolved for other agencies. Although these controls are nonstatutory, agencies usually feel bound by them as a means of preserving good relationships with their review committees. As one official told a legislator in 1980: "We are acting under the belief that this is a project of such magnitude that it is necessary for us to appropriately inform the Congress and the committees and to obtain its permission [before reprogramming funds]."[56]

Even with elaborate procedures to govern reprogramming, clearly spelled out in committee reports and agency directives, officials sometimes used reprogramming to bypass congressional control. The next step in legislative supervision was to add statutory controls.

Particularly objectionable to Congress was the Pentagon's practice of requesting funds for a program, being turned down by Congress, and then spending other appropriated funds for the rejected program. Legislation in 1974 specifically prohibited the Pentagon from asking committees for permission to reprogram funds to an item that had been previously submitted to Congress and denied.[57] This language is repeated every year in the defense appropriation bill.

Reprogramming by domestic agencies is now scrutinized with greater care by Congress. The congressional review committees have borrowed some of the controls previously applied to the Defense Department. For example, the Senate Appropriations Committee publishes guidelines in its report on the annual Treasury-Postal Service appropriation bill (see box).

These expectations of Congress have been incorporated in agency manuals, supplying additional formality to the understanding between Congress and the executive branch. The Budget Guidance Manual

Committee Controls on Domestic Reprogramming

The Committee expects the justfications for proposed reprogramming requests to be clear and strongly documented. Furthermore, except in extraordinary circumstances, reprogramming proposals will not be approved by the Committee 45 days prior to the end of the fiscal year, nor will they be approved if the proposed actions would effectively reverse previous congressional directives.

The guidelines to be used to determine whether or not a reprogramming shall be submitted to the committee for prior approval during the fiscal year 1997 are as follows:

(1) For agencies, departments, or offices receiving appropriations in excess of $20,000,000, a reprogramming must be submitted if the amount to be shifted to or from any object class, budget activity, program line item, or program activity involved is in excess of $500,000 or 10 percent, whichever is greater;

(2) For agencies, departments, or offices receiving appropriations less than $20,000,000, a reprogramming must be submitted if the amount to be shifted to or from any object class, budget activity, program line item, or program activity involved is in excess of $50,000 or 10 percent, whichever is greater;

(3) For any actions which would result in a major change contrary to the program or item presented to and approved by the Committee or the Congress;

(4) For any action where the cumulative effect of past reprogramming actions added to the new reprogramming would exceed the dollar threshold mentioned above;

(5) For any actions where funds earmarked for a specific activity are proposed to be used for another activity; and

(6) For any actions where funds earmarked for a specific activity are in excess to meet the project or activity requirement, and are proposed to be used for another activity.

• • •

The Committee is concerned that in the past transfer and reprogramming authority has been overutilized and often used by agencies for reorganizations that have major policy implications. Such transfers and reprogrammings are interpreted by the Committee as circumventing the appropriations process and will not be condoned.

SOURCE: Committee report on the Treasury, Postal Service appropriation bill for fiscal 1997, S. Rept. 104–330, 104th Cong., 2d sess., 1996, pp. 3–4.

for the Defense Department explains the procedures for reprogramming. In some cases the department is obliged only to notify congressional committees. Other types of reprogrammings require prior approval from the House and Senate Committees on Appropriations, the House and Senate Committees on Armed Services, and the House and Senate Committees on Intelligence.

If presidents and departmental officials object to reprogramming procedures, raising questions about the constitutionality of committee vetoes and the propriety of congressional involvement in administrative matters, they may jeopardize the grant of delegated power. Agencies accept committee-review procedures as a necessary condition for the freedom that Congress gives them. Committee review and agency discretion cannot be separated; they are opposite sides of the same coin.

Personnel Ceilings and Floors

To protect legislative priorities, members of Congress find themselves increasingly involved in monitoring personnel levels. While the Office of Management and Budget (OMB) does not actually withhold funds from agencies, as with impoundment, OMB personnel restrictions can prevent agencies from using funds. The agencies have the money but lack the people to spend it.

Committee studies pointed out that OMB used its personnel ceilings to frustrate congressional additions to the president's budget. Congress found that even when it increased the funding of a program and funds were not withheld through the deferral-rescission process, the programs were restricted by OMB ceilings. When the House of Representatives learned in 1980 that OMB had withheld positions from the Immigration and Naturalization Service, Representative Millicent Fenwick, Republican of New Jersey, asked her colleagues:

> I do not know what is going on in this Congress and in our government. How is it the business of OMB to decide whether or not the laws we pass are sensible? They are supposed to execute the laws. Have we no right to impeach people? I thought impoundment was ended, that it was no longer legal. How is it that we have a department of the government that simply defies Congress? What are we

doing here? Have we not the right to pass laws and expect that they shall be obeyed?[58]

Committee investigations discovered that OMB ceilings were sometimes adhered to at the cost of hiring thousands of "temporary" employees (on a thirty-nine-hour week or fifty-one-week year) to work at substantially full-time schedules. Contrivances of this nature led to recruitment difficulties, morale problems, wasteful turnover and retraining, "a watering down in the quality of the staff and the buildup of a caste system with two classes of employees." Another technique of staying within a personnel ceiling was to contract out for services that could have been done less expensively with in-house staff. As part of the "ceiling game," agencies dismissed thousands of employees just before the end of the fiscal year and rehired them when the new year began, thus keeping within end-of-year employment ceilings.

To discourage artificially low personnel ceilings, the House Appropriations Committee began placing the number of authorized permanent positions for each agency in committee reports. Any agency deviations from those figures were to be reported to the committee.[59] The Senate Appropriations Committee insisted that any efforts to restrain agency spending through employment ceilings should be reported to Congress either as a deferral or a rescission.[60]

Nonstatutory directives are usually effective. In the case of the agriculture appropriation bill, however, Congress resorted to *statutory* language to prevent the administration from using personnel ceilings to defeat congressional funding initiatives. The language in a 1977 statute read:

> None of the funds provided in this Act may be used to reduce programs by establishing an end-of-year employment ceiling on permanent positions below the level set herein for the following agencies: Farmers Home Administration, 7,400, Agricultural Stabilization and Conservation Service, 2,473; and Soil Conservation Service, 13,955.[61]

Members of Congress recognize that statutory specifications for personnel and total salary levels can encroach on the executive power of program management. They also realize, however, that legislators bear a responsibility for assuring sound management of the programs they have created and efficient use of taxpayer dollars.[62] The incentive to intervene is all the greater when personnel ceilings become just another form of impoundment.

Congressional efforts to put an end to restrictive personnel ceilings have been unsuccessful partly because of inconsistent legislative policy. When James T. McIntyre, Jr., appeared before the Senate Governmental Affairs Committee in 1978 for his nomination hearing as OMB director, he assured the senators:

> [W]e do not use and will not use personnel ceilings to stop or delay carrying out any program established by the Congress. . . . There are times when it is important to institute some type of personnel ceilings to bring about efficiencies and greater productivity in agencies. . . . But we certainly do not use them to thwart or delay or stop anyone from carrying out the program of the Congress.[63]

This agreement between OMB and Congress was short-lived because of the Civil Service Reform Act that became law later that year. Section 311, known as the "Leach amendment," established a temporary employment limitation on the total federal workforce. Although the language provided some latitude for the president, it also gave OMB a firm statutory foothold to impose personnel ceilings.

On assuming office on January 20, 1981, President Reagan ordered a hiring freeze on federal employees. The order was made retroactive to November 5, 1980, the day after his election, and affected thousands of people who had been offered and had accepted a position with the federal government. An appeals court upheld his action by labeling most of the individuals "federal appointees" rather than "federal employees." They therefore lacked the usual procedural safeguards provided against removal.[64]

Congress continued to place statutory restrictions on the use of personnel ceilings. The agriculture appropriations bill for fiscal 1992 established personnel floors for five agencies, setting specific employment levels below which the agencies could not fall.[65] The Clinton administration, in releasing the "reinventing government" proposals in the 1993 National Performance Review report (the Gore report), opposed personnel floors. The administration argued that these floors complicated the goal of reducing 252,000 federal jobs over five years, a major plank in the Gore report. Congress agreed to remove most of these statutory floors.[66] However, when it appeared that the Clinton reforms would require severe cuts in veterans' hospitals, Congress intervened with statutory language that limited the reductions in the federal workforce at veterans' hospitals over a five-year period.[67]

Legislative Veto

The determination of Congress to share in administrative decisions, and to do so through formal statutory controls, is reflected in the growth of "legislative vetoes." Legislative vetoes are statutory provisions that delay an administrative action, usually for sixty to ninety days, during which time Congress may approve or disapprove without further presidential involvement. Congressional action can take several forms: a one-house veto (by simple resolution of either house), a two-house veto (by concurrent resolution), a committee veto, and even a committee chair's veto. The legislative veto originated in the 1930s but proliferated in the 1970s. In *INS v. Chadha* (1983), the Supreme Court declared the legislative veto unconstitutional because it bypassed the president's veto power.

Origins of the Legislative Veto

The legislative veto emerged in the 1930s as a technique for reconciling two competing interests. The president wanted Congress to delegate additional authority to the White House; Congress wanted to control that authority without having to pass another public law. This accommodation took the form of a statute passed by Congress in 1932 giving President Hoover authority to issue executive orders to reorganize the executive branch. His orders would become law within sixty days unless either house disapproved (further details appear on pp. 116–19). Although the legislative veto in later years appeared to be an invasion of the executive branch, clearly President Hoover gained an important advantage. He could, in effect, "make law" without obtaining the approval of Congress.

The reorganization procedure obviously differed from the regular constitutional process of having Congress pass a bill and present it to the president. The legislative veto turned the process on its head.

The president submitted proposals subject to the veto of Congress. However, this irregular procedure had to be sanctioned by a public law. Was there anything unconstitutional about a public law that included, as a condition, such a process?

No one ever argued that Congress could make law by simple resolution or concurrent resolution. The issue changes once those resolutions are authorized in a bill presented to the president and signed into law. An opinion by the attorney general in 1854 explained the difference. The opinion stated that a simple resolution could not coerce a department head "unless in some particular in which a law, duly enacted, has subjected him to the direct action of each; and in such case it is to be intended, that, by approving the law, the President has consented to the exercise of such coerciveness on the part of either House."[68] Statutes in 1903 and 1905 relied on simple resolutions and concurrent resolutions to direct executive officers to make investigations and issue reports.[69]

Hoover's attorney general, William Mitchell, challenged the constitutionality of the legislative veto in the reorganization statute. He regarded it as a congressional intrusion on the president's administrative duties.[70] Based partly on that opinion, but also reflecting greater trust in President Franklin D. Roosevelt, Congress gave Roosevelt reorganization authority without the check of a legislative veto. This authority lasted two years.[71] When Roosevelt asked for reorganization authority in 1937, he insisted that if Congress wanted a disapproval mechanism, it had to rely on a joint resolution. Unlike a simple or concurrent resolution, a joint resolution must be submitted to the president for signature. The Senate passed legislation in accordance with Roosevelt's directions, but members of the House of Representatives refused to go along. They objected to a joint resolution because if Roosevelt exercised his veto power, Congress would need a two-thirds majority in each house for an override. Realizing that his proposals would not pass the House, Roosevelt agreed to a compromise: Congress could disapprove by a concurrent resolution.[72] Legislation in 1949 made congressional disapproval even easier: by a simple resolution.[73]

The president's reorganization authority was extended every few years until it expired in the 1980s. By that time the disadvantages outweighed the benefits.[74] The legislative veto in the reorganization statute lasted five decades as a classic quid pro quo. Each branch received what it wanted. Although the legislative veto departed from conventional procedures, it was not constitutionally disruptive. Disapproval by one house left the structure of government unchanged. No new law was made; the status quo remained. A president who had constitutional objections to the process could always initiate reorganization through the regular legislative route. However, there were two risks. Congress might not support the administration's bill, or it might amend the bill in ways objectionable to the president. Presidents liked reorganization authority for two reasons. Reorganization plans automatically became law within a certain number of days, unless vetoed by one house, and the plans could not be amended by Congress. They were voted up or down, without opportunity for change. (For further discussion on reorganization authority, see pp. 116–19)

Other Accommodations

The reorganization statute set a precedent for other legislative vetoes. Legislation in 1940 allowed the secretary of labor (and later the attorney general) to suspend the deportation of aliens, subject to a legislative veto.[75] President Roosevelt acquiesced in a legislative veto in the Lend Lease Act of 1941, even though he had to swallow constitutional misgivings. His attorney general, Robert H. Jackson, later revealed Roosevelt's doubts about the legality of that statute.[76]

Committee vetoes had an even earlier history. Some dated back to 1867.[77] They were challenged on constitutional grounds by President Wilson in 1920 and by Attorney General William Mitchell in 1933.[78] Committee vetoes were tolerated in the 1940s because of emergency wartime conditions. It was impractical to expect Congress to pass statutes that authorized each defense installation or public works project, as it had done in the past. Beginning with an informal system in 1942, all proposals for acquisitions of land and leases were submitted in advance to the naval affairs committees for their approval. With that safeguard, Congress passed statutes without specifying the individual projects. Two years later the informal accommodation was converted into law. Additional "coming into agreement" provisions were added in 1949 and 1951, requiring the approval of the armed services committees for land acquisition and real-estate transactions.[79]

In the 1950s, President Eisenhower challenged the constitutionality of these committee-clearance provisions. Attorney General Herbert Brownell advised Eisenhower that the committee veto represented an unconstitutional infringement on executive duties.[80] Congress promptly figured out another procedure that yielded precisely the same control. A bill was drafted to prohibit appropriations for certain real-estate transactions unless the public works committees had first approved the contracts. Eisenhower signed the bill after Brownell assured him that this procedure—based on the authorization-appropriation distinction—was within Congress's power.[81] Congress enacted the same procedure in 1972, which President Nixon accepted as a legitimate exercise of congressional rulemaking power.[82] The new committee vetoes were accepted as valid because they were directed against congressional committees, not against the executive branch. By acting internally within Congress they were constitutionally permissible.

The politics of committee vetoes are brought out vividly in a foreign assistance dispute during the Carter administration. After John Gilligan had been nominated to head the Agency for International Development (AID), he was told by Senator Daniel Inouye, Democrat of Hawaii, that agency-legislative relationships had deteriorated because of AID's penchant for diverting economic aid to military purposes without ever consulting Congress. Inouye, who chaired the appropriations subcommittee that had jurisdiction over AID, told Gilligan that whenever his agency decided to spend funds for purposes not previously justified to Congress, it would have to seek the approval of the House and Senate appropriations subcommittees responsible for foreign operations. Gilligan agreed to this clearance procedure as a way to improve congressional relations. When Inouye asked to have the agreement drawn up as a letter, Gilligan consented to that as well.

As part of the standard procedure within an agency, Gilligan had the draft letter routed through the general counsel's office. Questions were raised there about the legality of allowing congressional committees to participate in administrative decisions. The Justice Department expressly disapproved the arrangement. When Gilligan said he could not send the letter, Inouye countered by placing the agreement in a public law. The foreign assistance appropriation bill for fiscal 1978 contained this language in Section 115: "None of the funds made available by this Act may be obligated under an appropriation account to which they were not appropriated without the written prior approval of the Appropriations Committees of both Houses of the Congress."[83] Carter signed the bill into law without indicating any constitutional objections about the clearance procedure, but on that very day he wrote to Secretary of State Cyrus Vance, stating that Attorney General Griffin Bell had challenged the constitutionality of Section 115. Consequently, Vance was to treat the section not as a legally binding requirement for prior approval but rather as a request by the appropriations committees to be notified, after which Vance and AID could spend the funds as they thought best.[84] The appropriations committees did not learn of Carter's letter to Vance until almost two years later.

Had the legislators attached to an appropriation bill a requirement that all agency officials obtain prior approval from designated committees before obligating funds, Congress would have made an unmistakable intrusion into executive responsibilities. But Section 115 did not involve Congress in the execution of a law. It concerned executive departures from the law. Congress became a party, and properly so, only when the president wanted to obligate funds for a purpose for which Congress had not appropriated.

Carter's letter to Vance suggests that the president successfully repelled a congressional effort to intervene in administrative details. So it was, on the surface. But at the agency level, far below the constitutional principles argued by the White House and the Justice Department, conditions were different. Gilligan consistently sought the prior approval of the appropriations committees before diverting funds. Everyone seemed satisfied. President Carter had defended his prerogatives, Gilligan maintained good relations with Congress, and the review committees continued to exercise their controls.

The executive branch accepted other legislative vetoes. After losing almost all the impoundment cases in court, officials of the Nixon administration were happy to obtain authority in the Impoundment Control Act of 1974 to defer funds, subject to a one-house veto. No one in the Nixon, Ford, or Carter administrations questioned this statute on constitutional grounds. The accommodation survived until 1986, when excessive use of the deferral authority by the Reagan administration provoked an open confrontation with Congress (see pp. 84–85). Legislative vetoes in arms sales and the War Powers Resolution are other areas in which the two branches managed to compromise their differences (see pp. 201–202, 213–14).

The experiment with the legislative veto was of greatest concern to the administration when Congress decided to apply it to agency rules and regulations. In 1976, the House of Representatives voted 265 to 135 for the Administrative Rulemaking Reform Act. Although far in excess of a majority, the vote fell short of the two-thirds needed under the parliamentary procedure used (suspension of the rules). The bill would have permitted Congress, by concurrent resolution, to disapprove agency rules.[85] In 1982 the Senate voted 65 to 27 for a two-house veto over agency regulations.[86]

This generic legislative veto for all agency rules was not enacted, but in 1974 Congress succeeded in adopting a one-house veto over General Services Administration (GSA) regulations concerning Nixon's papers, a two-house veto over regulations issued by the commissioner of education, a two-house veto over passenger restraint rules by the National Highway Traffic Safety Administration, and a one-house veto over regulations by the Federal Election Commission.[87] In 1978 it chose a one-house veto to disapprove incremental pricing regulations issued by the Federal Energy Regulatory Commission (FERC). In 1980 it enacted a two-house veto for Federal Trade Commission rules and renewed that legislative veto two years later.[88]

Invalidation of the Legislative Veto in 1983

A number of early decisions in the federal courts tested the constitutionality of the legislative veto. Initially the courts approached the issue with great caution, deciding only the particular statutory mechanism being challenged. The courts refused to make broad, across-the-board rulings.[89] That pattern was broken in 1982 when an appellate court struck down the one-house veto of FERC regulations, a two-house veto of FTC regulations, and a committee veto of HUD reorganizations. The broad basis of these rulings implied that all legislative vetoes, of whatever character, were unconstitutional because they failed to follow the established course for lawmaking.[90] In one of these cases, the court held that the legislative veto enabled Congress "to expand its role from one of oversight, with an eye to legislative revision, to one of shared administration." This increase in congressional power, said the court, "contravenes the fundamental purpose of the separation of powers doctrine."[91]

The case decided by the Supreme Court in 1983 concerned a one-house veto used by Congress in immigration cases. The Immigration and Nationality Act authorized the attorney general to suspend the deportation of aliens, subject to the disapproval of either house. This procedure had been adopted decades ago as a compromise arrangement. It gave the attorney general greater discretion to relieve some of the harshness in the immigration law, while at the same time protecting the traditional interest of members of Congress (previously exercised through private bills).

The contrast between executive and legislative procedures was striking. The Immigration and Naturalization Service established an adversary hearing procedure for the alien, with an opportunity for cross-examination. The statute required the attorney general to give Congress a complete and detailed statement of the facts and pertinent provisions of law if the deportation was suspended. Congress followed a different course. In recommending that a suspension be disapproved, the judiciary committees did not provide an explanation, nor were reasons offered on the floor. In perfunctory manner the House or the Senate would agree to a resolution of disapproval, without a recorded vote.

An appellate court struck down this procedure in 1980 as a prohibited legislative intrusion on the executive and judicial branches, especially the executive authority to execute the laws faithfully and the judicial power to determine cases or controversies. But the decision was narrowly decided and restricted to adjudicatory (trial-like) questions by the agencies.[92] In 1983 the Supreme Court affirmed this decision by a 7-2 vote. *INS v. Chadha* decided that the legislative veto in the immigration statute was unconstitutional because it violated two constitutional principles. The one-house veto violated the principle of bicameralism, and the legislative veto violated the Presentation Clause, which requires that every order, resolution, or vote "to which the Concurrence of the Senate and House of Representatives may be necessary (except on a question of Adjournment)" shall be presented to the president. The sweeping nature of this decision appeared to invalidate every type of legislative veto.

Chief Justice Warren Burger, joined by five justices, wrote the opinion for the Court. He said that whenever congressional action has the "purpose and effect of altering the legal rights, duties and relations of persons" outside the legislative branch, Congress must act through both houses in a bill presented to the president.[93] Justice Lewis Powell concurred in the judgment, but stated his preference for a more narrowly drawn holding. Justice Byron White delivered a lengthy dissent that supported the legislative veto. Justice William Rehnquist also dissented, but only on the question of severability. The legislative history seemed persuasive to Rehnquist that Congress had delegated the authority to suspend deportations only on the condition that it retain a one-house veto. If the legislative veto fell, so should the attorney general's authority, for they were inseverable. The majority held that it was possible to strike down the legislative veto without losing the delegated authority.

The *Chadha* decision came at the cost of a misreading of history and of congressional procedures. The Court claimed that the mere fact that a law or procedure is "efficient, convenient, and useful in facilitating functions of government, standing alone, will not save it if it is contrary to the Constitution. Convenience and efficiency are not the primary objectives—or the hallmarks—of democratic government."[94] Later in the decision the Court said that although the legislative veto may be a "convenient shortcut" and an "appealing compromise," it is "crystal clear from the records of the Convention, contemporaneous writings and debates, that the Framers ranked other values higher than efficiency." Here the Court played careless with history, for efficiency was highly valued by the framers. The decade prior to the Philadelphia Convention represented an anxious and persistent search for a form of government that would perform more efficiently than that set up by the Articles of Confederation.

The Court suggested that the legislative veto, by evading the president's veto, threatened the independence of the executive and invited ill-considered measures.[95] This argument is misleading because the legislative veto was directed only against measures submitted by the president. The White House sent them up and retained total control over their contents. Congress could not amend them. If exercised, a legislative veto merely restored the status quo. The president did not need the executive veto for purposes of "self-defense." This argument had merit only for proposals that were submitted to

Congress by agencies not directly under the president's control, such as the independent commissions.

The Court also presented a simplistic picture of the legislative process. It said that the framers wanted congressional power exercised "in accord with a single, finely wrought and exhaustively considered, procedure." The records of the Convention and debates in the states preceding ratification provide "unmistakable expression of a determination that legislation by the national Congress be a step-by-step, deliberate and deliberative process."[96] However, both houses regularly use shortcut methods that pose no problems under *Chadha:* suspending the rules, asking for unanimous consent, placing legislative riders on appropriations bills, and even passing bills that have never been sent to committee.

Legislative Vetoes after Chadha

Even with *Chadha,* the need for a quid pro quo between Congress and the executive branch remains. The conditions that spawned the legislative veto a half-century ago have not disappeared. Executive officials still want substantial latitude in administering delegated authority; legislators still insist on maintaining control without having to pass another law. The persistence of these legislative-executive compacts underscores the gap between the Court's decision and the operations of government. Both executive officials and legislators are finding ways to avoid the static model of separated powers advanced by the Court.

For example, it came as a surprise to some observers that Congress continued to place legislative vetoes in bills and President Reagan continued to sign the bills into law. In the sixteen months between *Chadha* and the adjournment of the 98th Congress on October 12, 1984, an additional fifty-three legislative vetoes were added to the books. During subsequent years, Congress enacted still other legislative vetoes. Most of these are of the committee variety.

President Reagan often objected to this practice. When he received the HUD–independent agencies appropriations bill for fiscal 1985, which included eight legislative vetoes, he asked Congress to stop adding provisions that the Supreme Court had held to be unconstitutional. He indicated that the administration did not feel bound by these provisions, many of which required agencies to seek the approval of congressional committees before implementing certain actions.[97]

The House Appropriations Committee responded to Reagan's provocation by reviewing an agreement it had entered into with the National Aeronautics and Space Administration (NASA) four years previously. NASA had been allowed to exceed dollar caps established for various programs, provided the agency obtain the approval of the appropriations committees. Because of Reagan's threat to ignore committee controls, House Appropriations said it would repeal the committee veto and also repeal NASA's freedom to exceed the dollar ceilings.[98] This meant that NASA would need new statutory language if it wanted to go beyond a ceiling. To avoid this kind of rigidity, the administrator of NASA, James M. Beggs, wrote to both appropriations committees on August 9, 1984. His letter reveals the pragmatic sense of give-and-take that is customary between executive agencies and congressional committees. The letter also highlights the impracticality and unreality of the doctrines enunciated in *Chadha:*

> ... We believe that the present legislative procedure could be converted by this letter into an informal agreement by NASA not to exceed amounts for Committee designated programs without the approval of the Committees on Appropriations. This agreement would assume that both the statutory funding ceilings and the Committee approval mechanisms would be deleted from the FY 1985 legislation, and that it would not be the normal practice to include either mechanism in future appropriations bills. Further, the agreement would assume that future program ceiling amounts would be identified by the Committees in the Conference Report accompanying NASA's annual appropriations act and confirmed by NASA in its submission of the annual operating plan. NASA would not expend any funds over the ceilings identified in the Conference Report for these programs without the prior approval of the Committees.[99]

In short, the agency would continue to honor legislative vetoes, but the understanding would be informal rather than statutory. NASA is not legally bound by this agreement. However, a violation could provoke the appropriations committees to place caps in the funding bill and force the agency to lift them only through the enactment of another law.

The NASA agreement describes a world of informal agency-committee accommodations that were solidly in place before *Chadha.*

No doubt these arrangements, such as for reprogramming of funds, will continue despite the Court's strictures on the proper steps of lawmaking. Statutes after *Chadha* may rely more heavily on notification to designated committees before an agency acts. Notification does not raise a constitutional issue, since it falls within the report-and-wait category already sanctioned by prior court rulings.[100] In an informal sense, however, notification can become a code word for committee prior approval. Few agencies will be willing to notify a committee, learn of its opposition, and proceed anyway. The committees have many ways to retaliate, particularly with the next reauthorization or appropriation bill. *Chadha* does not affect these nonstatutory legislative vetoes. Agencies are aware of the penalties that Congress can invoke if they decide to violate understandings and working relationships with their review committees.

What is now prohibited directly by *Chadha* can be accomplished indirectly through House and Senate rules. Each house can stipulate that no funds may be appropriated for a particular purpose unless the authorizing committee has granted its approval by committee resolution. Since this procedure concerns the internal workings of Congress, the "committee veto" is directed at the appropriations committees rather than at the executive branch. To that extent it should create no problem under *Chadha*, even if this type of committee veto is the functional equivalent of the legislative veto declared invalid.

Congress retains the right to place language in an appropriations bill to deny funds for agency activities. Members of both houses find it convenient to attach legislation and limitations to the most available appropriations bill. Since a president is unlikely to veto an appropriations bill simply because it contains an offensive rider, the practical effect is at least a two-house veto. Because of accommodations and comity between the House and the Senate, the reality in many cases is a one-house veto.

Finally, Congress can use a joint resolution as a substitute for the legislative veto. It clearly meets *Chadha*'s requirement of bicameralism and presentment. Depending on the type of joint resolution, the burden shifts to Congress or the president. A joint resolution of disapproval usually weakens legislative control because it requires Congress to act and the resolution is vulnerable to the president's veto. On the other hand, a joint resolution of approval shifts the burden to the president, who would have to obtain the approval of both houses within a set number of days. The results could be ironic. For example, reorganization plans were subject to a one-house veto. If Congress selected a joint resolution of approval, and one house decided to withdraw its support or not to act at all, the practical effect is a one-house veto. Moreover, this new type of "one-house veto" would be effective by *inaction*. The previous one-house veto required Congress to act.[101]

Chadha has not stopped Congress from placing legislative vetoes in public laws. These bills are regularly signed into law, although at times Presidents Reagan, Bush, and Clinton commented on the unconstitutionality of these provisions in light of the Court's ruling. From the day that *Chadha* was issued, on June 23, 1983, to the end of 1997, more than four hundred new legislative vetoes have been enacted into law. For example, the Treasury, Postal Service appropriation act for fiscal 1996 required the General Services Administration (GSA) to obtain advance approval from the appropriations committees before it exceeded 10 percent of the construction costs on new buildings. The GSA may expend funds from the Federal Buildings Fund "when advance approval is obtained from the Committees on Appropriations of the House and Senate."[102] Agencies must seek the approval of the appropriations committees before they use money carried over from one year to the next or before they expend funds for certain travel expenses.[103]

Even if Congress discontinued legislative vetoes and complied fully with *Chadha*, committees would still retain veto power over the agencies. A few examples will illustrate the staying power of the legislative veto.

In 1987, OMB Director James Miller III told the appropriations committees that a provision in the foreign operations appropriations bill violated the constitutional principles of *Chadha*. The statutory language required the Agency for International Development (AID) to obtain the prior, written approval of the Appropriations Committees before transferring funds from one appropriations account to another.

Miller's challenge stirred up a hornet's nest. The appropriations subcommittees handling foreign operations never liked this statutory provision, but not for the reasons cited by Miller. They believed that funds should be spent in the manner authorized, but went along with the transfer authority on the condition that they retained veto power. Then, with Miller rocking the boat, they decided to delete not only the committee veto but also the transfer authority. When AID let out a howl about its loss of administrative flexibility, OMB backed away. The regular language, including the committee veto, was enacted into law.[104]

After Miller left the administration, Congress adopted new statutory language, allowing AID to transfer funds provided that it follow "regular notification procedures."[105] That means that AID must notify the appropriations committees about proposed transfers and wait fifteen days. If the subcommittees on foreign operations object during that period, AID does not proceed. Legally it might be able to, but only at great cost to itself and the possible loss of transfer authority.

An example from the Bush administration illustrates the great variety in which legislative vetoes may appear. The administration wanted non-military funds for the Contras in Nicaragua. Congress, recalling the years that led up to the Iran-Contra affair, was reluctant to supply the funds. Realizing the level of distrust on Capitol Hill, Secretary of State James A. Baker III suggested a compromise. Congress could appropriate the funds and have a portion placed in reserve. If the administration acted in good faith the reserve funds would be released with the approval of four committees of Congress and several congressional leaders.

Although White House counsel C. Boyden Gray and former federal judge Robert H. Bork claimed that Baker's agreement constituted a legislative veto forbidden by *Chadha*, no such violation existed. *Chadha* concerns only legislative vetoes placed in public laws. Baker executed a "side agreement" that was not part of the bill language. It was simply a letter from Baker to the Speaker of the House, Jim Wright, explaining the procedure. This type of informal, nonstatutory agreement is constitutionally permissible. Four members of Congress challenged the "Baker Accord" as unconstitutional, but their suit was dismissed by a federal district court.[106]

Through its misreading of history, congressional procedures, and executive-legislative relations, the Supreme Court has directed the political branches to follow a lawmaking process that is impracticable and unworkable. The inevitable result is a record of noncompliance, subtle evasion, and a system of lawmaking that is now more convoluted, cumbersome, and covert than before. In many cases the Court's decision simply drives underground a set of legislative and committee vetoes that had previously operated in plain sight. No one should be misled if the number of legislative vetoes placed in statutes gradually declines over the years. Fading from view will not mean disappearance. In one form or another, legislative vetoes will remain an important technique for reconciling legislative and executive interests. Administrators want additional discretionary authority; Congress is determined to control that authority without always having to pass another public law.

Conclusions

Despite an accumulation of learned studies and reports that urge Congress to leave administrative duties to the president, legislative involvement persists from one decade to the next. The reason has to be found in something more complex than an obstinate desire on the part of members of Congress to overstep constitutional boundaries. Presidents and their supporters face continued frustration because they ignore, or try to overlook, the legitimate stake and interest of Congress in administrative matters.

When executive officials deny Congress the right to add to presidential budgetary estimates, and subsequently withhold funds or restrict programs by artifices that favor the administration's priorities over those enacted by Congress, they provoke Congress to intervene in the implementation of a statute. Out of frustration, legislators are inclined to place new restrictions in a public law, concluding that flexibility in a statute is used too often by agencies as an excuse for thwarting congressional policy. As Senator Edmund Muskie, Democrat of Maine, told one official in 1973, after discovering that a broad grant of discretionary authority had been used to cut a legislative program in half:

> Having in mind the devious motives that you pursued to undercut the purposes of the Congress, I could now write better language and believe me, I will. Believe me, I will. The clear language and debate was what we were giving you, is what we understood to be legitimate administrative discretion to spend the money, not defeat the purposes. Then to have you twist it as you have, is a temptation to this Senator to really handcuff you the next time.[107]

The growth of agency and congressional staff has placed a heavy strain on traditional techniques of legislative oversight and the dependence on good-faith agency efforts. Congress now has the resources to delve more deeply into administration. As the gap between the branches widens, because of staff build-up and turnover, Congress is less able and less willing to rely on customary methods of control. Oral agreements are being replaced by committee report language, which is giving way to statutory directives.

In studies avowedly cynical of the congressional process, scholars have argued that members of Congress and agency bureaucrats have joined forces to produce a system of expensive programs, complex regulations, and legislative intervention in the administrative process—all for the purpose of helping incumbent legislators return to office with larger vote margins. Programs that automatically appropriate and distribute funds, such as revenue sharing, are opposed in Congress because they reduce the need for members to participate in the administration and allocation of federal resources.[108]

Examples can be found to support this scenario, but it is largely contradicted by the legislative record. Recent decades have witnessed the growth of mechanical, automatic formulas that sharply circumscribe the opportunity for members to intervene in agency decisions. What we have instead is a system run on permanent authorizations, permanent appropriations, entitlements, indexing (adjusting benefits to cover inflation), and assorted "uncontrollables." A more telling criticism of Congress is that it has allowed a substantial part of the executive branch to operate without adequate congressional intervention, judgment, and accountability. Certainly that judgment applies to the decade of the 1980s with its S & L failures, HUD scandals, corruption within the Pentagon, and the Iran-Contra affair. A series of scandals in the Clinton administration—the dismissal of employees from the White House Travel Office, White House access to FBI files, White House aides learning of an investigation by the Resolution Trust Corporation into Whitewater—provoked congressional hearings into executive abuses and wrongdoing.[109]

CHAPTER 4

◆

Bureaucracy: Agent of Congress or the President?

As a source of executive-legislative friction, it would be difficult to pick something more deep-rooted than control of the bureaucracy. For more than two centuries, Congress and the president have battled with one another for the power to regulate the activities of departments and agencies. Both branches have legitimate claims to a general supervisory power.

According to one constitutional model, the president is the chief administrative officer of a unified and hierarchical executive branch, capable of directing the activities and operations of agency personnel. The members of the executive branch serve as the president's agents in seeing that "the Laws be faithfully executed." The other model begins with the premise that Congress creates the departments and may specify how laws are to be implemented. Hierarchical rules are displaced by a system of spreading power and instituting checks. The Constitution empowers Congress to make all laws "which shall be necessary and proper for carrying into Execution" the powers vested "in the Government of the United States, or in any Department or Officer thereof."

The issue becomes one of reconciling two competing models of the Constitution. To allow one model to transcend the other would create a concentration of power within one branch that the framers sought to avoid. Some of the precedents established by the First Congress, in creating the executive departments, set the stage for subsequent patterns of bureaucratic control. Much is left to the play of political forces, leaving in doubt whether Congress or the president controls the executive branch. David Truman aptly pointed out that "a number of key points of decision are established in parallel with no formal, solid basis of hierarchy among them. Informal, extralegal means may provide a measure of superordination and subordination, but the way is always open for an interest group to operate through the Congress or the president alternatively, to play one off against the other, to destroy a fragile hierarchical arrangement and fabricate a transitory substitute."[1]

Creating the Executive Departments

The Constitution authorizes the president to "require the Opinion, in writing, of the principal Officer in each of the executive Departments, upon any Subject relating to the Duties of their respective Offices." Quite undecided, however, was the relationship between the president and the departmental heads. Were they merely staff advisers to the president, to assist in carrying out the chief executive's constitutional responsibilities? Or did they also owe allegiance to Congress? Upon entering office as the nation's first chief executive, George Washington suggested that the departments were agents of the president, not Congress:

> . . . I have, however, been taught to believe, that there is, in most polished nations, a system established, with regard to the foreign as well as the other great Departments, which, from the utility, the necessity, and the reason of the thing, provides that business should be digested and prepared by the Heads of those departments.
>
> The impossibility that one man should be able to perform all the great business of the State, I take to have been the reason for instituting the great Departments, and appointing officers therein, to assist the supreme Magistrate in discharging the duties of his trust.[2]

An even stronger statement in support of presidential responsibility was offered by Senator William Maclay of Pennsylvania, after Congress had taken up the question of creating the executive departments:

. . . There are a number of such bills, and may be many more, tending to direct the most minute particle of the President's conduct. If he is to be directed, how he shall do everything, it follows he must do nothing without direction. To what purpose, then, is the executive power lodged with the President, if he can do nothing without a law directing the mode, manner, and, of course, the thing to be done? May not the two Houses of Congress, on this principle, pass a law depriving him of all powers? You may say it will not get his approbation. But two thirds of both Houses will make it a law without him and the Constitution is undone at once.[3]

The debate on the executive departments began on May 19, 1789, when Elias Boudinot of New Jersey requested that the House of Representatives establish general principles to guide the creation of departments. He believed that the departments under the Articles of Confederation should not be "models for us to form ours upon, by reason of the essential change which has taken place in the Government, and the new distribution of Legislative, Executive, and Judicial powers."[4] Still, the experiences with the departments of foreign affairs, war, and treasury—all of which were created in 1781 by the Continental Congress—had a definite influence on their disposition in 1789. John Jay had taken over as secretary for foreign affairs in 1784 and served throughout the remaining years of the Continental Congress, continuing in that capacity as acting secretary of state in Washington's administration until Jefferson assumed the duties in March 1790. Henry Knox was elected secretary of war in 1785 and remained in that post until the final days of 1794, illustrating vividly the continuity in administrative structures from the confederation to the national government.

The treasury, however, had a different history. The Continental Congress accepted the positions of secretary for foreign affairs and secretary of war as essentially executive in nature. The question of finance proved much more difficult. Congress appointed Robert Morris to be superintendent of finance but denied his request for total control over his subordinates. He was allowed to remove them only for stated cause: incapacity, negligence, dishonesty, or other misbehavior. In cases of removal, he had to report to Congress and give reasons for the dismissal. Moreover, Congress decided to keep a hand on Morris's subordinates. Congress appointed the comptroller rather than allow the superintendent to make that selection. The legislature also named the treasurer, the register, and the auditors.[5] In short, even though Congress agreed to place responsibility in a single executive, it immediately adopted checks through the appointment and removal process.

After the surrender of Cornwallis at Yorktown, the Continental Congress withdrew its support for a single executive in fiscal matters and returned to the board system. An ordinance in 1784 re-created the Board of Treasury, and Congress continued to appoint a comptroller, a treasurer, a register, and the auditors.[6] Significantly, Congress did not change the single executives for foreign affairs and war.

Departmental Heads

Since each department had to be created by statute in 1789, legislators could decide whether to place a department under one individual or establish a board of commissioners. There was some concern that departmental heads might become more important than the legislature, but the experience under the Continental Congress convinced most members that the board system lacked responsibility, energy, and order. The House voted for single executives to head the departments.[7]

Part of this decision rested on the belief that Congress, by statute, could check and restrain the operations of an executive official. James Madison preferred, in all cases of an executive nature, that Congress first consider the powers to be exercised. If the powers were too extensive to be entrusted to a single individual, "proper care should be taken so to regulate and check the exercise, as would give indubitable security for the perfect preservation of the public interest, and to prevent that suspicion which men of integrity were ever desirous of avoiding."[8]

Congress regarded the secretary of foreign affairs and the secretary of war as executive officials, reflecting the experience under the Articles of Confederation. In the words of Representative John Vining of Delaware: "The Departments of Foreign Affairs and War are peculiarly within the powers of the President, and he must be responsible for them."[9] This understanding appears in the statutes creating both departments. On July 27, 1789, Congress established an "Executive department, to be denominated the Department of Foreign Affairs." The secretary of foreign affairs would "perform and execute such duties as shall from time to time be enjoined on or intrusted to him by the President of the United States." The same format and structure were used for the Department of War.[10]

But the House of Representatives regarded the Treasury Department partly as a *legislative* agent, reflecting the mixed record during the Articles of Confederation when the duties shifted back and forth between a superintendent of finance and a Board of Treasury. As a result, the statute creating the Treasury Department in 1789 differed substantially from the statutes for foreign affairs and war. Treasury was not styled an "executive department." Nowhere did the statute direct the secretary of the treasury to perform and execute duties for the president. Instead, the statute included legislative instructions directing the secretary to report and give information to either the House or the Senate, "in person or in writing (as he may be required)," respecting all matters referred to the department by Congress."[11]

Treasury differed in yet another aspect. For the departments of Foreign Affairs and War, Congress identified only the secretary and a chief clerk (to be appointed by the secretary). The clerk would have charge and custody of papers in the event of the secretary's removal by the president or in any other case of vacancy. For the Treasury Department, however, Congress created the office of secretary, a comptroller, an auditor, a treasurer, a register, and an assistant to the secretary. The secretary appointed only the latter. The comptroller would become a "hybrid officer" (see the next section).

Although Congress anticipated that the secretary of the treasury would serve both branches, in practice the secretary performed as an arm of the president, not Congress. No one doubted that Hamilton served as "minister of finance" for President Washington. Senator William Maclay, in a contemporary (if prejudiced) account of Washington's cabinet, voiced his exasperation: "Congress may go home. Mr. Hamilton is all-powerful, and fails in nothing he attempts."[12] Congress eventually drove Hamilton from office.

Four decades later, Congress attempted to treat President Andrew Jackson's secretary of the treasury as a legislative agent, delegating to him, rather than the president, the responsibility for placing government money either in the national bank or in state banks. Jackson removed two secretaries of the treasury before finding someone willing to follow his instructions, rather than those of Congress. A Senate resolution of censure declared that Jackson had assumed "authority and power not conferred by the Constitution and laws, but in derogation of both." In a lengthy and impassioned defense, Jackson answered that the secretary of the treasury was "wholly an executive officer" and could be removed at will by the president. Three years later the Senate ordered its resolution of censure removed from the record.[13]

Hybrid Agencies

When the First Congress created the departments, Madison argued strongly for presidential power to remove the secretaries of foreign affairs, war, and treasury. However, when it came to the tenure of the comptroller, Madison regarded the properties of that office as partly judicial and therefore needing to be insulated from presidential control.[14] Only by understanding the history of the comptroller's office during the Continental Congress could Madison have gained this insight.

Legislation in 1795 made the comptroller's decision on certain claims "final and conclusive."[15] Actions by the comptroller were eventually challenged in court as a violation of due process of law. The case of *Murray's Lessee v. Hoboken Land and Improvement Co.* (1856) involved Samuel Swartwout, a collector of customs for the port of New York from 1830 to 1838. During that period he kept large amounts of revenue for personal speculation. After the government discovered shortages in his account, a "warrant of distress" was issued to recover the funds. Acting under an 1820 statute, the first comptroller of the treasury certified the condition of the account to the agent of the treasury, who then issued the warrant against the delinquent officer. The statute authorized the marshal to execute the warrant by entering into the district of the officer to collect the necessary amount. The marshal could post notices in the town announcing the sale of the officer's goods and property.[16]

Swartwout argued that the statute was unconstitutional because it allowed executive officers to discharge judicial duties. The Supreme Court admitted that the actions against delinquent officers bore some resemblance to judicial power, but, largely on the strength of early British law and congressional legislation in 1798, 1813, and 1815, a unanimous Court concluded that the statute of 1820 satisfied due process.[17]

Legislative prerogatives in financial matters also prompted Congress to treat the Post Office in unique fashion. The statute creating the Post Office in 1789 did not designate it "executive department," even though the postmaster general was "subject to the direction of the President of the United States in performing the duties of his office."[18] During the debates on renewing the statute in 1790, members were divided on the question of whether to delegate the power to designate post roads to the president or the postmaster general or to reserve it for Congress. Those who argued against the first option warned that revenue would be centered in the hands of the executive, combining purse and sword and thus leading to the destruction of liberties in America. They also maintained that such delegation was unconstitutional because the power to establish post roads was expressly reserved to Congress by the Constitution.[19]

By 1792, Congress decided to retain for itself the power to specify post roads. The statute authorized the postmaster general (not the president) to enter into contracts and make appointments. It also deleted language making the postmaster general subject to the direction of the president. Financial autonomy was assured by allowing the Post Office to operate from postal revenues, with the balance to be returned to the Treasury Department.[20]

The location of the Post Office was more than a political struggle between Congress and the executive. Deep divisions existed even within the executive branch. Thomas Jefferson wanted the Post Office in his agency (the Department of State) to keep power from Alexander Hamilton, his rival, who headed the Treasury.[21] Under these circumstances, it was easier for both branches to leave the Post Office floating somewhere outside the executive departments.

Legislation in 1836 put an end to the financial autonomy of the Post Office. All revenues were placed in the Treasury, subject to appropriations by Congress. Beginning with Jackson's administration, the postmaster general became part of the cabinet.[22] By 1935, the Supreme Court said that a postmaster "is merely one of the units in the executive department and, hence, inherently subject to the exclusive and illimitable power of removal by the Chief Executive, whose subordinate and aide he is."[23]

These "inherent" and "illimitable" powers are not as fixed as the Court implied. In 1970 Congress came full circle by abolishing the Post Office Department and replacing it with the U.S. Postal Service, described in the statute as an "independent establishment of the executive branch."[24] Other than the power of the president to nominate members of the Board of Governors and the Postal Rate Commission, subject to the advice and consent of the Senate, the Postal Service is expected to operate in an independent, nonpolitical manner.

Toward the end of his term, President George Bush tried to use his removal and recess appointment powers to gain control over the Postal Service, which was locked in litigation with the Postal Rate Commission. Bush threatened to remove any member of the Board of Governors who refused to withdraw from the lawsuit. The objective was to protect the authority of the Justice Department to litigate, rather than have such decisions exercised by independent agencies like the Postal Service. A bare majority of the governors (five out of nine) rejected his appeal. To gain a majority in his favor, Bush used his recess appointment power to replace someone whose term had expired but remained on the board. That tactic backfired when federal courts held that because of a holdover provision in the statute governing the Postal Service, which allowed governors to serve after the expiration of their term until a successor had taken office, there was no vacancy to fill. Moreover, the Postal Service was allowed to appear in court without Justice Department approval.[25]

The legal status of the General Accounting Office (GAO) raises questions as to whether the comptroller general is an executive or a legislative officer. The issue goes back to the creation of the comptroller's office in the Treasury Department. In the Budget and Accounting Act of 1921, Congress transferred all powers and duties of the comptroller of the treasury, the six auditors of the Treasury Department, and the Division of Bookkeeping and Warrants of the Office of the Secretary of the Treasury to a newly created General Accounting Office, generally recognized as part of the legislative branch.[26] A committee established by President Roosevelt in 1937 (the Brownlow Committee) objected to GAO's interference with expenditure responsibilities, which it called "essentially an executive function." A staff study sponsored by the committee recommended (unsuccessfully) that several GAO functions be returned to the Treasury Department.[27]

Although GAO functions as an agent of Congress when it audits accounts, it carries out "executive" duties by approving payments and settling and adjusting accounts.[28]

This two-hat theory, making the comptroller general both an executive and a legislative officer, has been challenged in recent years. The Competition in Contracting Act of 1984 gave the comptroller general the power to stay the award of a contested contract. When President Reagan signed this bill, he objected that this bid-protest procedure unconstitutionally delegated to the comptroller general, "an officer of Congress, the power to perform duties and responsiblities that in our constitutional system may be performed only by officials of the executive branch." Reagan instructed the attorney general to inform all executive branch agencies how to comply with the bill in a manner consistent with the Constitution.[29] A memorandum prepared by the Office of Legal Counsel in the Justice Department concluded that the stay provisions were unconstitutional and should not be enforced by the agencies. The memo stated that there was "very little difference" between the power of the comptroller general to lift a stay and the legislative veto declared unconstitutional the previous year in *INS v. Chadha*.[30] Attorney General William French Smith notified Congress that the Justice Department had instructed agencies not to execute the bid-protest provisions. The director of OMB, David A. Stockman, followed with a bulletin instructing all agencies to proceed with the procurement process as though no stay provisions were contained in the Competition in Contracting Act.[31] Through this complicated series of maneuvers, President Reagan had exercised the equivalent of an item veto.

The response came from two sources: Congress and the courts. Hearings were held by the House Government Operations Committee to contest the theory that the president could selectively carry out the laws, enforcing some provisions while ignoring others.[32] Shortly thereafter a federal judge upheld the bid-protest powers, accepting the notion that the comptroller general possessed a combination of executive and legislative duties. The judge regarded the stay provision as unlike the legislative veto struck down in *Chadha*, since congressional influence in the bid-protest process "is completely excluded."[33] A few months later the same judge rejected the theory that the president could deliberately disobey portions of a bill passed by Congress and signed into law. The "fundamental role of this Court in stating what the law is has now been challenged by the Executive Branch." He particularly objected to the claim that the executive possessed the power to *decide* that statutes, or parts of them, were unconstitutional. The new attorney general, Edwin Meese III, maintained not only that the president had this power but that there was no necessity to follow a decision by a district judge. Meese, claiming that district judges do not make constitutional law, said the administration would await a decision by an appellate court. Obviously, the district judge could not let Meese's assertion go unchallenged: "Such a position by the Executive Branch, I find, flatly violates the express instruction of the Constitution that the President shall 'take care that the Laws be faithfully executed.' . . . It has been one of the bedrocks of our system of government that *only* the Judiciary has the power to say what the law is."[34]

Attorney General Meese received another incentive to rethink his position when the House Judiciary Committee acted on the authorization bill for the Justice Department. The bill deleted all funds for the Office of Attorney General "unless and until he instructs all executive officials to comply fully with the provisions of the Competition in Contracting Act." At stake was not only the $4.706 million for Meese's office, but also the far larger principle of separation of powers.[35] Meese responded by instructing the agencies to comply with the district court ruling.[36]

The district court's decision was upheld in 1986 by the Third Circuit. The comptroller general "is an independent official with duties involving both the legislative and executive branches of the United States government."[37] The comptroller general, who is appointed by the president in accordance with the Appointments Clause of the Constitution, is not merely an agent of Congress. The fact that the comptroller general "is not under executive control does not necessarily mean that he is under legislative control."[38] GAO is, instead, a "hybrid agency."[39] Circuit Judge Edward Becker, concurring, disagreed with the majority's refusal to place the comptroller general in one branch or another. He said that the Constitution establishes three branches of government, not four. He observed: "Even a living constitution cannot grow a new branch."[40] Becker decided that the comptroller general was in the legislative branch. Moreover, he determined that the bid-protest powers were executive or even quasi-judicial. He then asked whether it was unconstitutional for a legislative officer to carry out these executive or quasi-judicial duties, and concluded that the duties exercised did not threaten executive power or individual liberties.

The Third Circuit's decision seemed shaken by the Supreme Court's ruling in *Bowsher v. Synar* (1986), which struck down a provision in the Gramm-Rudman-Hollings Act that gave executive duties to the comptroller general.[41] The Court held that this provision was unconstitutional because Congress could remove the comptroller general by passing a joint resolution. Although a joint resolution must be submitted to the president for signature or veto, the Court decided that the removal procedure made the comptroller general too subservient to Congress (p. 238).

The Third Circuit reheard the case in light of *Bowsher*. It also looked at another case, handed down the same day as *Bowsher*, in which the Court announced a more flexible interpretation of separated powers.[42] Faced with these two contradictory rulings, the Third Circuit decided to rely on the latter in reaffirming its earlier position. It reviewed the many legitimate methods used by Congress to oversee agency activities and concluded that the comptroller general's role in federal contracting was "entirely justified."[43]

Reorganizing the Bureaucracy

After Congress creates departments and prescribes specific functions and duties for administrators, it may decide to reorganize the departments and abolish or transfer functions. Congress carried out these changes by statute until it delegated reorganization powers to the president in the 1930s.

Hoover received statutory authority in 1932 to reorganize executive departments and independent agencies, but not without raising awkward questions of executive-legislative responsibilities. The legislation provided that the president could propose a reorganization by an executive order, which either house of Congress could disapprove within a sixty-day waiting period (a "legislative veto"). Hoover issued eleven executive orders in December 1932, consolidating some fifty-eight governmental activities. By that time, however, he had been overwhelmingly defeated in the general election. It was evident that the Democratic majority in the House, in the closing hours of a lame-duck session, preferred to leave reorganization changes to Hoover's successor, Franklin D. Roosevelt. The House of Representatives disapproved all the executive orders.[44]

When Congress renewed the president's reorganization authority in 1933, it eliminated the legislative veto.[45] Legislators had abandoned hope that major reorganization could ever be achieved with congressional involvement. As Senator Arthur Vandenberg, Republican of Michigan, remarked: "Let us confront the precise situation and the realities. We now face the necessity for drastic retrenchment and reorganization of the bureaus, departments, and so forth. We have just witnessed the impossibility of achieving even an incidental step in that direction by presidential order so long as Congress, with its diverse interests, retains the veto."[46]

Roosevelt's request to renew reorganization authority in 1937 coincided with his attempt to increase the size of the Supreme Court, giving critics the opportunity to warn that he intended to establish a "presidential dictatorship." The Senate passed a reorganization bill in 1938, requiring Congress to disapprove a reorganization by bill or joint resolution. The Senate's action marked a victory for Roosevelt, since bills and joint resolutions must be presented to the president for signature or veto. Roosevelt announced that a concurrent resolution (which passes both houses but is not presented to the president) could not be used for congressional disapproval. It was "only an expression of congressional sentiment" and could not repeal "executive action taken in pursuance of a law."[47]

This constitutional position had a short life. When Roosevelt realized within a few days that the House of Representatives was adamantly opposed to the requirement of a bill or joint resolution to reject reorganization proposals, he shifted ground. In order to attract sufficient votes in the House, he accepted a two-house veto by concurrent resolution. In 1949, as a way of eliminating a string of exemptions in the reorganization act placed there to protect favored agencies, Congress switched from a two-house to a one-house legislative veto. Disapproval by a simple resolution assured members that they could protect the agencies of special interest to them.[48]

Over the years, Congress continued to renew reorganization authority for the president, keeping the one-house veto. After the Supreme Court declared the legislative veto unconstitutional in 1983, Congress passed legislation to require that all reorganization plans be approved by joint resolution within ninety days. However, this authority was in effect for less than two months before expiring.[49] Because of the need to obtain the approval of both houses within a fixed time period, the Reagan administration did not seek a renewal of this statute. Reorganization must now be achieved through the regular legislative process.

Control of Federal Personnel

After creating executive departments and agencies, Congress continues to exercise control by participating in the appointment power, placing conditions and restrictions on the removal power, establishing a civil service system, and mandating the performance of certain duties.

Appointing Officials

The power to appoint agency officials is an essential tool used by both president and Congress to control the bureaucracy. In his report to President John F. Kennedy in 1960, James M. Landis counseled: "The prime key to the improvement of the administrative process is the selection of qualified personnel. Good men can make poor laws workable; poor men will wreak havoc with good laws."[50] The potential of the appointment power has been narrowed by civil service regulations and other restrictions imposed by Congress. Departmental heads are able to appoint only a handful of senior political executives. Michael Blumenthal, Carter's first secretary of the treasury, estimated that out of 120,000 people in his department he was able to select only about 25.[51] He was probably referring only to Treasury officials appointed with the advice and consent of the Senate. In addition to these officials (currently 31), the secretary of the treasury also appoints 28 members of the Senior Executive Service (SES) who serve in noncareer slots, another 50 "Schedule C" appointments (policymaking positions not subject to the competitive civil service), and 28 noncareer appointments.[52] Many of these appointments are shared with the White House.

While the power to nominate belongs to the president, in creating an office Congress may stipulate in considerable detail the qualifications for appointees. And in practice, if not in theory, the responsibility for recommending nominees often falls to members of Congress. Nominations also depend on recommendations by organizations such as the American Bar Association, farm groups, labor unions, and other organizations. The Senate's advice and consent and "senatorial courtesy" (the power of a single senator to block a nomination) are other counterweights to the president's power to nominate.[53]

The appointment process is taken seriously because it is assumed that "who you get *in* government directly affects what you get *out* of government."[54] The number of Senate rejections cannot be measured by floor votes. Of forty major nominations rejected from 1961 to 1977, only four were rejected on the floor. Nine were rejected by committee vote, while twenty-seven nominees were forced to withdraw.[55] Ernest Lefever, nominated by President Reagan in 1981 for a top post in the State Department, was a casualty of this process. After the Senate Foreign Relations Committee voted 13-4 to disapprove his nomination, Lefever asked Reagan to withdraw his name. A number of recent nominees have experienced the same fate. Victor Stello, Jr., picked by President Bush for a position in the Energy Department, withdrew his name in 1990 after it became clear that the Senate would not confirm him. Other Bush nominees fell by the wayside without a formal Senate vote. Hundreds of potential nominees are never even submitted by the White House because of congressional opposition.

Several Clinton nominees chose to withdraw their names after encountering resistance in the Senate: Zoe E. Baird, nominated for Attorney General; Lani Guinier, selected to head the Justice Department's civil rights division; Stanley Tate, scheduled to head the Resolution Trust Corporation; and Anthony Lake, who abruptly withdrew as nominee for CIA director. Henry W. Foster, Clinton's choice to be surgeon general, withdrew his name in 1995 after running into a Senate filibuster.

Congress has broad powers, under the Necessary and Proper Clause of Article I, Section 8, to place restrictions on the president's powers of removal, appointment, organization, and reorganization.[56] But it may not, by law, designate a person to fill an office.[57] Congress tried to do that, in a circuitous way, in 1974. A statute gave the Commodity Futures Trading Commission the power to nominate its executive director, subject to the advice and consent of the Senate. In signing the bill, President Ford stated that the provision raised "serious constitutional questions, by providing for an executive branch appointment in a manner not contemplated by the Constitution." Recognizing that it had overreached, Congress changed the procedure in 1978 to vest the appointment of the executive director solely in the commission, without submitting the name to the Senate.[58]

This modification followed the Supreme Court's decision two years earlier striking down the method of appointment used by Congress for the Federal Election Commission (FEC). Congress appointed four of the members. All six voting members (including two nominated by the president) required confirmation by the majority of *both* houses. An appellate court justified this procedure by reasoning that Congress possessed adequate authority under the Necessary and Proper Clause, but in 1976 the Supreme Court denied that Congress could appoint members to the FEC, especially since it was created by Congress to discharge more than legislative functions. The FEC, through its duty to exercise an enforcement or prosecutorial power, might have to institute a lawsuit and seek judicial relief. Such actions fell not to Congress but to the president, who is required under the Constitution to "take Care that the Laws be faithfully executed." Administrative functions, said the Court, had to be carried out by "Officers of the United States." The Court limited Congress to one of two constitutional options: letting the president nominate the members, subject to the advice and consent of the Senate, or vesting the appointment power solely in the president, in the courts of law, or in departmental heads.[59] Congress chose the first option when it rewrote the act in 1976.

For agencies that do not have enforcement or prosecutorial powers, Congress can participate in making appointments. For example, President Reagan and Congress fought over who would control the Civil Rights Commission, which has been an investigative agency since 1957. The commission makes findings of fact and presents recommendations to both branches, but has no enforcement authority. Consequently, Congress was able to pass legislation in 1983 that divided the appointment authority between Congress and the president: the White House appoints only four of its eight members; the other four are named by Congress.[60]

Removals

Some members of the First Congress believed that the Constitution permitted only one means of removing executive officers: the impeachment process. Others insisted that since the Senate participated in the appointments process, it must also consent to removals. Most of the debate, however, narrowed to two choices: (1) the president, pursuant to constitutional responsibilities, may remove administrators at will, or (2) Congress, since it creates an office, may attach to it any conditions it decides appropriate, including tenure and grounds for removal. This latter position appears in Connecticut Representative Roger Sherman's statement of June 17, 1789:

> As the officer is the mere creature of the Legislature, we may form it under such regulations as we please, with such powers and duration as we think good policy requires. We may say he shall hold his office during good behavior, or that he shall be annually elected. We may say he shall be displaced for neglect of duty, and point out how he shall be convicted of it; without calling upon the President or Senate.[61]

James Madison led the fight to vest in the president almost total discretion to remove executive officials. He maintained that the power was implied in the Constitution and did not belong to Congress to delegate. Statutory limitations, Madison warned, would undermine presidential responsibility and destroy the unity of the executive branch. He forcefully denied that the Senate was entitled to a role in the removal process. To Madison, the Senate's participation in the appointment process represented an exception to the general rule that reserved executive responsibilities for the president. Madison drew support from the president's constitutional duty to "take Care that the Laws be faithfully executed." To fulfill that purpose, the president had to use all necessary means, including the dismissal of incompetent, corrupt, or unreliable administrators. If anything by nature is executive, Madison said, "it must be that power which is employed in superintending and seeing that the laws are faithfully executed." Others pointed out that while the Senate might be acquainted with the record of a nominee, the president was in a better position to judge the person's *performance* in office.[62]

As enacted into law, the statutes governing the executive departments indirectly treated the removal power. The chief clerk of each department would have the responsibility and custody of all records, books, and papers, "whenever the said principal officer shall be removed from office by the President of the United States." This language left unclear whether Congress had acted by declaration (delegating the power) or by implication (acknowledging that the power was inherent or implied by the Constitution).

According to Chief Justice William Howard Taft, the debates of 1789 meant there was not the "slightest doubt" that the power to remove officers appointed by the president and Senate is "vested in the President alone."[63] Taft reached too far; the debates revealed deep divisions among House members and close votes on the Senate side.[64]

Furthermore, the debate on the removal power focused on the president's power to remove the *secretary of foreign affairs*, who, members conceded, was an agent of the president and executive in nature. It is an error to conclude from that debate that the president's power extends to *all* administrative officials. Much depends on the nature of the office. When the First Congress considered the comptroller's office in the Treasury Department, Theodore Sedgwick said that the office "seemed to bear a strong affinity to this branch [the legislature] of the Government." Madison remarked that the comptroller's settlement of legal claims "partake too much of the Judicial capacity to be blended with the Executive." To Madison the office was neither executive nor judicial: "I think it rather distinct from both, though it partakes of each."[65]

The removal power created an explosive issue for the administration of Andrew Johnson. The Tenure of Office Act in 1867 gave the Senate a role in the suspension and removal of executive officials. Johnson vetoed the bill, claiming that it violated the Constitution, but both houses quickly overrode the veto. Johnson decided to suspend Secretary of War Edwin M. Stanton, a disruptive element in his cabinet. Although the Senate refused to concur in the suspension, Johnson removed Stanton, helping set in motion Johnson's impeachment by the House of Representatives. After another executive-legislative confrontation, this time involving Grover Cleveland and the Senate, Congress repealed the Tenure of Office Act.[66]

Congress, however, continued to place statutory limitations on the removal power. It specified causes for removal such as inefficiency, neglect of duty, and malfeasance in office. The Supreme Court recognized that it is proper for Congress to identify the grounds for removal,[67] especially for independent regulatory commissions (see pp. 160–62). A balance must be struck between the president's removal power and Congress's power under the Necessary and Proper Clause to create an office.[68] The removal power is also limited by procedural rights (sometimes statutory, sometimes adjudicated) that are available to protect employees from arbitrary dismissals.[69]

Congress is deeply engaged in the process of filling vacancies in the executive branch. Positions are found for former members of Congress and their staff assistants. In fact, Congress is often responsible for *creating* vacancies. Studies of executive-legislative relationships estimate that firings and reassignments of executive officials result more from congressional pressure than from presidential action.[70]

Although Congress has been instrumental in driving some office holders out of government, it also intervenes to *protect* executive officials threatened by dismissal, demotion, or reprimand. Because of a fundamental interest in program implementation, the career service, and access to agency information, members of Congress will always be concerned about the suspension and removal of federal employees. Federal workers remain in a kind of twilight zone, pulled between the conflicting desires of the president and Congress. Given the responsibilities of Congress in legislation and program oversight, questions of suspension, removal, demotion, and reassignment can never remain the monopoly or exclusive preserve of the president.[71]

Civil Service Reforms

The civil service system, including the reforms of 1978, imposes other restrictions on the president's power to recruit and discipline federal employees. The civil service merit system rests on an elaborate set of procedures to determine the qualifications needed for entry into the federal workforce; specific safeguards are available to employees who face suspension and removal.[72]

Periodically efforts are made to increase the president's power over the civil service. A report commissioned by President Roosevelt recommmended in 1937 that the Civil Service Commission be reorganized into a Civil Service Administration, led by a single executive officer.

The administrator of this new agency, to be appointed by the president with the advice and consent of the Senate, would serve at the pleasure of the president and act as the president's direct adviser on all personnel matters. The Civil Service Administration was to be "a part and parcel of the Executive Office."[73]

Congress resisted this reform, fearing that presidential control over federal employees would revive political patronage on a grand scale and subvert merit standards and the principle of professionalism. The record of the Nixon administration reinforced this apprehension. The White House personnel operation sought to make the career bureaucracy "responsive" to the president's program. In 1972 the White House created a program to improve "Departmental responsiveness in support of the President's re-election." Career employees were screened by the White House for their political philosophy and sense of loyalty to administration goals. Personnel procedures were often manipulated, with the knowledge of the Civil Service Commission, to provide preferential treatment of politically favored candidates for career appointments.[74]

The Civil Service Reform Act of 1978 replaced the Civil Service Commission with an Office of Personnel Management (OPM). Although OPM is identified in the statute as "an independent establishment in the executive branch," the director of OPM is clearly an agent of the president. The legislative history describes the OPM director as "the president's agent" and "the president's chief lieutenant."[75] Independence is suggested by two features: a four-year term for the director and removal of the Senate's proposed requirement that the term be coterminous with that of the president.[76] However, the director serves at the pleasure of the president and is subject to presidential instructions.

Certainly Donald J. Devine was unabashedly political and partisan during his four years as Reagan's OPM director. His term was marked by a combative personality, low morale among federal employees, and a politicization of the entire civil service. While OPM's workforce fell by almost 20 percent, the number of political appointees within OPM increased from twelve to thirty-four.[77] President Reagan nominated Devine for another four years, but that prospect was dashed when it was revealed that on Devine's last day as OPM director he signed a delegation of authority to the newly created position of "executive assistant," a post he assumed the following day. The comptroller general rendered an opinion that the delegation effectively evaded the four-year statutory term.[78] After this disclosure, Devine asked that his name be withdrawn for reconfirmation.

The Civil Service Reform Act of 1978 also created a new Senior Executive Service (SES) of top-level officials who gave up job security to qualify for substantial bonuses and other benefits. The financial benefits were restricted when Congress later placed caps on the salaries of all federal employees and limited the size of bonuses for SES officials. These officials were regarded as an elite corps to be moved from agency to agency, responding to managerial needs throughout the government. Presidential appointees can control SES officials through reassignments, but the use of these sanctions can be "a two-edged sword which also cuts away at the initiative and candor of career executives. It will deny to appointees of the new administration at crucial points in the decision-making processes substantial knowledge and insights on relevant laws, policies, and programs."[79] A 1983 survey of about two thousand career executives revealed that only 15 percent agreed that reassignments improved managerial and organizational effectiveness; 60 percent disagreed.[80]

The Civil Service Reform Act reserves ten percent of the SES positions for political appointments. That is the allocation for the entire federal government; the percentage may vary from agency to agency. Congress has intervened to protect nonpolitical SES officials from punishment meted out by an administration. The Treasury-Postal Service appropriations act for fiscal 1992 provided: "None of the funds in this Act may be used to reduce the rank or rate of pay of a career appointee in the SES upon reassignment or transfer."[81] The Veterans Affairs Housing appropriations act that year applied this restriction to the Department of Housing and Urban Development: "During fiscal year 1992 . . . the number of individuals employed by the Department . . . in other than 'career appointee' positions in Senior Executive Service shall not exceed 15."[82]

The Civil Service Reform Act of 1978 created two other agencies: the Merit Systems Protection Board (MSPB) and the Federal Labor Relations Authority (FLRA). The members may be removed by the president only for the specific causes listed in the statute. The FLRA, which establishes policies for federal labor-management relations, may have no more than two of its three members belonging to the same political party; members may be removed only on notice and hearing; and their terms are staggered, eventually reaching a length of five years.

The MSPB, which investigates and adjudicates federal employee grievances, has three members, with no more than two belonging to the same political party. As another means of assuring independence from the president, members are given seven-year terms. Moreover, the statute directs the MSPB to submit its budget requests and legislative recommendations concurrently to the president and Congress. Within the board is a special counsel who is responsible for protecting "whistleblowers" (employees who reveal agency wrongdoing). The special counsel has some autonomy from MSPB, so much in fact that in 1980 the head of MSPB went to court charging that the special counsel had ignored a series of directives from the board. This appeared to be the first instance in which one unit of a federal agency sued another unit within the same agency.[83] The suit was dismissed in 1981 after the acting special counsel was replaced by a permanent special counsel.[84]

A major challenge to the civil service system came in September 1993 with the release of the National Performance Review report (popularly known as the Gore report). Although federal employees participated in the study to "reinvent" government, the report sharply condemned waste and inefficiency within the national government. The report predicted that NPR reforms, over a five-year period, would reduce the federal workforce by 252,000 and save an estimated $108 billion. The federal government "is not simply broke; it is broken. . . . It is also as if federal programs were *designed* not to work."[85]

These attacks were tempered with the admonition that the problem "is not lazy or incompetent people. . . . The federal government is filled with good people trapped in bad systems."[86] Nevertheless, the report noted that civil service employees "have virtual lifetime tenure, regardless of their performance," and that federal employees "learn that the goal is not to produce results, please customers, or save taxpayers' money, but to avoid mistakes."[87] Curiously, many of the "success" stories cited in the report concerning initiative, creativity, and innovation came from the federal government. The proposal to reduce the federal workplace by 252,000 (increased by

Congress to 272,900) fell entirely on civil servants. NPR imposed no reductions on political appointees whose numbers have grown substantially in recent decades. The result is a workforce increasingly controlled by short-term political appointees.[88]

Ministerial and Discretionary Duties

The heads of executive departments function only in part as political agents of the president. They also perform legal duties assigned to them by Congress. Even the departments initially labeled as executive in character, such as the State and War departments, served Congress as well as the president.

This dual role surfaced in the controversy over judicial appointments, precipitating *Marbury v. Madison* in 1803. Just before he left office, President John Adams nominated a number of men to serve in the judiciary. The Senate gave its advice and consent, and commissions for the officers were signed by Adams. Even the seal of the United States had been affixed to the commissions to attest to their validity. But after a change in administrations, Jefferson's secretary of state, James Madison, refused to deliver some of the commissions.

Chief Justice John Marshall, writing for the Supreme Court, distinguished between two types of duties for the secretary: ministerial and discretionary. One duty (as a public ministerial officer of the United States) extended to the United States or to its citizens. Here Congress, operating through statutes, could direct the secretary to carry out certain activities. The second duty (as an executive official and adviser) was to the president alone. A secretary of state, performing as an officer of the United States, was bound to obey the laws: "He acts, in this respect, as has been very properly stated at the bar, under the authority of law, and not by the instructions of the President. It is a ministerial act which the law enjoins on a particular officer for a particular purpose." [89] Although in this case Marshall did not issue a writ of mandamus (compelling Madison to deliver the commissions), Marshall's interpretation of a statute opened the door to judicial review of legislation passed by Congress.

The concept of ministerial acts reappears in a case decided in 1838. Amos Kendall, postmaster general in the Jackson administration, refused to pay the claim of an individual who had contracted to carry the mail and sought compensation for his services. Congress directed that the amount be paid, as did the Circuit Court of the District of Columbia. The Supreme Court agreed that the postmaster general could not refuse a payment authorized by law. Payment of the claim constituted a "purely ministerial" act for which there could be no discretion. Neither the president nor the postmaster general possessed any authority to deny or control a ministerial act. Although the executive power is vested in the president, "it by no means follows, that every officer in every branch of that department is under the exclusive direction of the president." It would be an "alarming doctrine," said the Court, that Congress could not impose on any executive officer any duty it thinks proper, "which is not repugnant to any rights secured and protected by the constitution; and in such cases, the duty and responsibility grow out of and are subject to the control of the law, and not to the direction of the president."[90]

Reinforcing this distinction, in 1854 the attorney general stated that when laws "define what is to be done by a given head of department, and how he is to do it, there the President's discretion stops; but if the law require an executive act to be performed, without saying how or by whom, it must be for him to supply the direction." The courts traditionally defer to the president and executive officials when an executive act demands judgment and discretion.[91]

The courts invoked the ministerial-discretionary distinction on a regular basis during the Nixon administration to force the release of impounded funds. In case after case the judiciary found that the allocation or obligation of funds constituted a ministerial action, permitting no discretion or judgment on the part of an administrator. Some decisions pointed out that discretion existed up to a certain point but no further. For example, in 1972 Secretary of Agriculture Earl Butz declared that fifteen counties in Minnesota were eligible for emergency loans. A federal judge announced that although the act of declaration was discretionary, once the secretary designated the counties eligible for assistance it was incumbent upon his department to accept loan applications and process them.[92] At that point the statutory purpose of Congress must be carried out. Ministerial duties also apply to the president. In 1974 an appellate court held that President Nixon had violated the law by refusing to carry out a statute on federal pay.[93]

Autonomy of Agency Proceedings

The Constitution directs the president to "take Care that the Laws be faithfully executed." However, many attorneys general have advised presidents of substantial political and legal constraints that limit their ability to intervene in departmental matters. Even when the president has the *power* to control the decision of a departmental head, such intervention may be inexpedient and of doubtful propriety.[94] While it is theoretically correct that departmental heads shall discharge their administrative duties in such manner as the president may direct, it was conceded by Attorney General Edward Bates that it is "quite impossible for the president to assume the actual direction of the multifarious business of the departments."[95]

On many occasions an attorney general has advised the president that the White House had no *legal* right to interfere with administrative decisions. President James Monroe asked whether he could alter the decisions made by the auditors and comptrollers in the Treasury Department. The advice from Attorney General William Wirt was blunt: "It appears to me that you have no power to interfere. . . . If the laws, then, require a particular officer by name to perform a duty, not only is that officer bound to perform it, but no other officer can perform it without a violation of the law; and were the President to perform it, he would not only be not taking care that the laws were faithfully executed, but he would be violating them himself."[96] The same message appears in many other opinions from attorneys general.[97]

Congress may distribute ministerial functions of government among various bureau chiefs and executive officials, without regard to hierarchical principles of public administration. Neither the president nor any departmental head "could, by any degree of laborious industry, revise and correct all the acts of his subordinates. And if he could, as the law now stands, it would be as illegal as unwise."[98] If a president agreed to take appeals in one case and to review a subordinate's decision, "it is apparent that it would lie in every case and from all Executive Departments, and soon you would be overwhelmed with the details of administration."[99]

Attorneys general have alerted presidents to other problems. If every dissatisfied claimant had a right to appeal to the president and ask that the settlement of a lower official be reversed, the president "would be constrained to abandon the greater national objects which are committed to his peculiar care, and become the accountant general of the government."[100] The president is responsible for seeing that administrative officers faithfully perform their duties, "but the statutes regulate and prescribe these duties, and he has no more power to add to, or subtract from, the duties imposed upon subordinate executive and administrative officers by the law, than those officers have to add or subtract from his duties."[101]

Departmental officers who discharge quasi-judicial functions have had an independent status from the start, whether they are comptrollers and auditors in the Treasury Department or reviewers of pensions and other claims. In a number of instances Congress lodged these responsibilities in a board operating within an executive agency but later transferred the duties to a "legislative court" (to carry out the responsibilities of Congress under Article I of the Constitution). Still later, Congress converted the legislative court to a "constitutional court," conferring on the judges the protections available under Article III of the Constitution, particularly the privilege of holding office during good behavior and receiving a compensation that may not be diminished during continuance in office. As a result of such changes, the identical function would travel from the legislative branch to the executive branch and finally to the judicial branch.

For example, in 1890 Congress established within the Department of Treasury a Board of General Appraisers to review the acts of appraisers of merchandise and collectors of duties. The board's decision on cases submitted to it was final and conclusive within the department, although appeals could be taken to the federal courts. Legislation in 1926 created the United States Customs Court to supersede the board. Although not changing the powers, duties, or personnel of the board, the statute did establish it as an Article I legislative court. Congress made the Customs Court a constitutional judicial body in 1956. Legislation in 1980 replaced the Customs Court with the Court of International Trade.[102]

A similar evolution followed the handling of claims against the United States. This function belongs "primarily to Congress as an incident of its power to pay the debts," but Congress may exercise it directly or delegate the responsibility to other agents.[103] When the burden of private bills became too great for Congress, it created a Court of Claims in 1855, calling on it to give advisory decisions and gradually, over the years, establishing for the court a capacity to make binding judgments. Legislation in 1953 made the Court of Claims an Article III, constitutional court.[104] In 1982, Congress returned the Claims Court to the status of an Article I, legislative court.[105] Its name was changed in 1992 to the U.S. Court of Federal Claims.[106]

The tax court also illustrates how functions can be placed initially in an executive department but eventually migrate to a legislative court. Legislation in 1924 created a Board of Tax Appeals. Although the secretary of the treasury was directed to furnish the board with appropriate quarters, staff, and supplies, the board was described in the statute as "an independent agency in the executive branch of the Government." Congress changed the name in 1942 to the Tax Court of the United States and converted it to a legislative court in 1969.[107]

At certain stages in an agency proceeding, intervention by Congress and the president may violate basic principles of administrative law. Particularly sensitive are adjudicatory proceedings and the activities of independent regulatory agencies (pp. 167–70). Agency employees who handle adjudicatory matters have a special right to independence with their decisions. Departmental heads recognize the limitations that prevent them from interfering with decisions by administrative law judges (ALJs).[108] Congressional interference with an adjudicatory proceeding may be of damaging character and constitute an improper intrusion. Questions by a Senate subcommittee in 1955 were so probing that Edward F. Howrey, chairman of the Federal Trade Commission, announced that he would have to disqualify himself from a pending case.[109]

Intervention by presidential aides in agency rulemaking and adjudication is a subject of serious concern.[110] Efforts by the Office of Management and Budget (OMB) and the White House may seem like reasonable initiatives to "coordinate" the activities of the executive branch and carry out the president's program. But ex parte contacts by presidential staffers permit them to gather information privately from the industries or from state officials and to communicate such information in closed-door sessions with agency decision makers, without the knowledge of other interested parties in the rulemaking process. Responding to this concern, the Justice Department argued in 1979 that there is no prohibition against communications within the executive branch after the close of the comment period on proposed rules, provided that presidential advisers do not serve as a conduit for persons outside the executive branch to have ex parte communications with agency staff.[111]

The Justice Department's guideline depends too much on self-policing and self-constraint by presidential aides who have a reputation for ignoring procedural niceties that stand in the way of White House objectives. There is a strong tradition—expressed in opinions by attorneys general, statutory language, and decisions by the federal judiciary—for agency autonomy in adjudicatory proceedings. The rulemaking process, while less formal and structured than the adjudicatory model, also must be conducted in a manner that observes standards of openness and fairness.

The President's Inner Circle

Fenced in by statutory restrictions and a strong tradition of agency autonomy, presidents turn increasingly to a select "inner circle" for guidance. Political appointments in the departments are made with an eye for controlling the career bureaucracy. A senior adviser in Lyndon Johnson's administration remarked that the separation of power between Congress and the president was not as great "as between a president and those people like subcabinet and bureau officials who become locked into their own special subsystems of self-interested policy concerns."[112]

The Cabinet

Presidents enter office with deep suspicions about the loyalty and motivations of civil servants. Before long they come to distrust even their own cabinet chiefs. After his reelection in 1972, President Nixon commented that "it is inevitable when an individual has been in a Cabinet position or, for that matter, holds any position in Government, after a certain length of time he becomes an advocate of the status quo; rather than running the bureaucracy, the bureaucracy runs him."[113] Carter, in the summer of 1979, asked every member of his cabinet to hand in signed letters of resignation.

In the judgment of a career executive with many years of experience in the White House, presidential aides view cabinet officials as "necessarily living somewhat inflexibly in their worlds of laws, rules, regulations and precedents, and tending to 'go by the book,' whereas in the White House view delicate circumstances often require special sensitivity in interpretation and execution."[114] White House personnel realize that cabinet officials are exposed to substantially greater pressures and entreaties from Congress, interest groups, and independent bureaucrats. They believe that departments have a propensity to leak information that is embarrassing and sometimes politically damaging to the president. Departmental heads are seen as inadequately responsive to the needs of party or campaign officials. In addition to casting the departments in the role of antagonist or protagonist, White House staffers believe that issues of interest to the president cut across so many organizational boundaries that cabinet officials cannot be expected to present well-rounded and comprehensive reports.[115]

Frustration with departmental leaks of agency information resulted in an extraordinary effort in the Carter administration to have top officials sign affidavits saying they were not the source of the leaks. According to press accounts in 1980, Secretary of State Cyrus Vance, CIA Director Stansfield Turner, and National Security Adviser Zbigniew Brzezinski signed the affidavits, along with other high-ranking aides. Brzezinski suspected that the State Department was leaking the material; State Department officials were convinced that most leaks came from Brzezinski's National Security Council."[116] A directive issued by President Reagan in 1985 would have required all government employees with access to highly classified information to submit periodically to polygraph tests. Secretary of State George Shultz threatened to resign, saying, "The minute in this government I am told that I'm not trusted is the day that I leave."[117]

Cabinet officers maintain their own inventory of complaints. They object to White House aides who have the luxury to make policy but need not subject themselves to congressional inquiries. This sours the relationship between protected White House advisers and departmental officials who cannot hide from legislative scrutiny. Cabinet officers find that they have to defend policies, both before the press and the public, that they had vainly argued against within the White House. Moreover, they dismiss the White House claim of superior political judgment, pointing out that departmental employees are regularly in touch with the views of state and local officials, private organizations, local papers, and constituent pressures that are applied to members of Congress.[118]

Just as there is tension between executive departments and the White House, a similar friction exists between the political appointees and career civil servants within a department. In recent decades, there has been a marked increase in the number of noncareer SES and Schedule C employees within executive departments, all of whom can be monitored and controlled by the White House. Short-term political employees have more loyalty to the president than to the departmental policies enacted into law. They have less stake in healthy executive legislative relations. As James Pfiffner notes, political appointees "have enough time to make mistakes, but not enough time to learn from them."[119] The trend toward increased numbers of political appointees within the departments (1) adds a layer of inexperienced policy makers subject to frequent turnover, (2) excludes many career professionals from policy deliberations, (3) contributes to administrative instability and incompetence, and (4) undermines the morale of the career civil service. The result: Congress enacts legislation but has less confidence that it will be carried out faithfully, the quality of service to citizens declines, and cynicism toward government reaches corrosive levels.

Thomas Cronin has distinguished between two types of cabinet offices. An "inner cabinet" (State, Defense, Treasury, and Justice) provides the president with counseling and information on broad national topics, acting closely with White House interests and objectives. An "outer cabinet" (Agriculture, Interior, Labor, and others) pursues a straightforward advocate course, responding to the more specialized needs of their departments.[120] Under this classification, the inner cabinet is oriented toward the president; the outer cabinet stands the risk of being captured by Congress, the agencies, and interest groups.

This is a useful distinction, but some qualifications are needed. The so-called clientele departments (including Agriculture and Labor) have considerable room to maneuver in responding to White House needs and the demands of specialized interests. Moreover, the experiences of Elliot Richardson (attorney general under Nixon),

Michael Blumenthal (treasury secretary under Carter), and Cyrus Vance (secretary of state under Carter) provide telling evidence that even members of the inner cabinet are not always trusted by chief executives. All three left office after acrimonious disputes with the White House. In the early months of the Reagan administration, Secretary of State Alexander Haig clashed sharply with White House aides. Haig lasted little more than a year before being replaced by George Shultz, who proved to be more durable and trusted. Secretary of State William Rogers performed more as an outsider in the Nixon administration, unable to compete successfully with the resources and personality of White House adviser Henry Kissinger. President Nixon was not alone in preferring a White House-centered system to the State Department.[121]

During the Clinton administration, the FBI was rebuked for maintaining a cozy relationship with the White House in such matters as the dismissal of Travel Office employees and the production of FBI files to presidential aides.[122] The Justice Department concluded in 1997 that the FBI general counsel had exercised "very poor judgment" in his contacts with the White House.[123] Also in 1997, the FBI declined to share some information with the White House regarding a Justice Department investigation into possible attempts by China to influence U.S. elections. The reason for withholding some information was the possibility that White House aides might have acted criminally in receiving funds from the Chinese. President Clinton expressed concern about being denied information needed to conduct foreign policy, but recognized that the Justice Department is at times faced with conflicting obligations: "Now, they have dual obligations to share with the State Department—the Secretary of State—where appropriate, information we need to protect and advance national security and to preserve the integrity of criminal investigations. And ultimately, those things almost have to be resolved on a case-by-case basis, where there is a doubt, by the Attorney General."[124] FBI director Louis J. Freeh agreed to brief Clinton's national security adviser about the investigation into Chinese influence, but the session was restricted to a general overview and omitted details about the criminal probe.[125]

It is ironic that the cabinet "insiders," so closely identified with the White House, are generally excluded from political campaign activities. During hearings in 1979, Senator Strom Thurmond, Republican of South Carolina, discussed this issue with the nominee for attorney general, Benjamin Civiletti:

> Senator THURMOND. Three Cabinet officials I feel should be all free from political influence especially, [and] not participate in campaigns.
>
> Last year when I ran for reelection in the U.S. Senate a number of Cabinet officers came down and participated against me in my campaign. Which is all right if they want to do that. On the other hand, the Secretary of State did not come, and the Secretary of Defense did not come. The Attorney General did not come. And those are the three I feel should always be restrained in matters of politics. I presume you would agree with that, would you not?
>
> Mr. CIVILETTI. Yes, sir.[126]

William French Smith, Reagan's first attorney general, resigned in 1984 because he wanted to help in Reagan's reelection campaign. Smith indicated that campaign participation "would not be possible in my present position."[127]

Independent Counsel

After the Watergate revelations, followed by the resignation of Attorney General John Mitchell, legislation was introduced to make the Justice Department an independent agency and to insulate it from political pressures exerted by the White House. In a private study, a committee of attorneys concluded from their search of historical materials that most of the functions of the Justice Department were not purely and inherently executive in nature, to be placed solely under the president. Even during the early years of the presidency, when the attorney general spent more time as a counselor to the president than as the government's representative in court, "it was recognized that much of what he did had quasijudicial characteristics. His vastly expanded powers since that time have been largely in various areas of law enforcement." The committee concluded that Congress could place these investigatory and prosecutorial powers in an independent agency while still retaining the attorney general's political role as adviser to the president.[128]

President Nixon took a small step in that direction in 1973 by agreeing to establish a special prosecutor in the Justice Department to investigate crimes relating to the Watergate break-in and the 1972 presidential campaign. The Justice Department published a regulation stating that the attorney general would not

> countermand or interfere with the Special Prosecutor's decisions or actions. The Special Prosecutor will determine whether and to what extent he will inform or consult with the Attorney General about the conduct of his duties and responsibilities. The Special Prosecutor will not be removed from his duties except for extraordinary improprieties on his part.[129]

This agreement collapsed later in the year when the special prosecutor, Archibald Cox, was fired after insisting that the White House make available the Watergate tapes rather than the tape summaries proposed by Nixon. Attorney General Richardson resigned and Deputy Attorney General William Ruckelshaus was fired for refusing to discharge Cox. That chore fell to Robert Bork as acting attorney general. A district court ruled that Cox had been removed in clear violation of the regulation issued by the Justice Department.[130] The abrupt departures of Cox, Richardson, and Ruckelshaus set in motion a serious effort in Congress to impeach Nixon. The "firestorm" that followed these dismissals, together with the Supreme Court's decision in *United States v. Nixon* (1974) denying Nixon's claim to withhold the tapes, led to his release of incriminating information and his resignation.[131]

The Ethics Act of 1978 established a mechanism for the court appointment of an independent special prosecutor within the Justice Department to investigate charges against the president, the vice president, and specified high-level executive branch employees—including those in the Executive Office of the President, the Justice Department, the Central Intelligence Agency, and the Internal Revenue Service. The special prosecutor has "full power and independent authority to exercise all investigative and prosecutorial functions and powers." Under the 1978 statute, the special prosecutor could be removed from office (other than by impeachment and conviction) only by the personal action of the attorney general and only for extraordinary impropriety, physical disability, mental incapacity, "or any other condition that substantially impairs the performance of such special prosecutor's duties."[132]

The Carter administration supported the ethics bill as a necessary step to restore the reputation of the Justice Department. The provision for a special prosecutor, however, implies that the department cannot be trusted to carry out its responsibilities. Some opponents of the bill remarked: "If an Attorney General cannot be trusted to enforce the law against the Executive, the remedy is impeachment and not the cloning of an additional Attorney General to do the job of the first."[133] The Ethics Act attempted to find a middle-level strategy short of impeachment.

A special prosecutor was first appointed to investigate charges that Hamilton Jordan, Carter's chief of staff, had used cocaine. Jordan was cleared of the charge in 1980. Another special prosecutor was appointed to look into drug charges against Timothy Kraft, a Carter White House aide. Kraft also was exonerated. The length of these investigations, and the financial cost to both in defending themselves, resulted in criticism against this section of the Ethics Act. Moreover, Reagan's first attorney general, William French Smith, expressed constitutional objections to the special prosecutor office because it lodges enforcement responsibilities in an officer who is not appointed by or accountable to the president.[134] The office was also criticized by former Attorney General Civiletti and others for triggering major investigations on the basis of very little evidence.[135]

Congress revised the Ethics Act in 1983 by changing the name of the "special prosecutor" to "independent counsel" and giving the attorney general greater discretion to dismiss allegations that have little merit. The revised statute allowed a court to reimburse a government official for legal fees during the defense, provided the person was not indicted, and changed the grounds for removal of the independent counsel by striking "extraordinary impropriety" and inserting "good cause."[136]

Reagan signed the 1983 reauthorization bill without indicating any constitutional misgiving about the office of independent counsel. When the office was reauthorized in 1987, Reagan once again signed the bill, but this time expressed his belief that the independent counsel violated separation of powers principles by vesting enforcement authority in an officer who was not fully subject to executive branch appointment, review, and removal. Instead of vetoing the bill on these grounds, Reagan signed the measure with the hope that the courts would declare the legislation unconstitutional.[137] Reagan found it politically difficult to exercise his veto power because by 1987 the independent counsel machinery had been turned against Edwin Meese III and the defendants in the Iran-Contra affair.

In a surprising decision in 1988, the Supreme Court voted 7 to 1 to sustain the independent counsel. The margin of victory for Congress was greater than most experts on constitutional law anticipated. It was particularly baffling to discover that the author of the opinion was Chief Justice William Rehnquist, a former assistant attorney general during the Nixon years and someone normally identified with defending presidential power. In his decision, Rehnquist upheld the appointment of the independent counsel by a special panel of federal judges and also supported statutory limits on the power of the attorney general to remove the independent counsel only "for cause." Rehnquist justified those limitations on executive power because the attorney general still had available "several means of supervising or controlling the prosecutorial powers that may be wielded by an independent counsel."[138]

The Court's decision represented a significant setback for presidential power, not only by upholding the independent counsel but by rejecting the "unitary theory" model that the Reagan Justice Department had advocated. All executive powers were to be subordinated to presidential control, a position the Court flatly dismissed. This strict view of separated powers was dealt another blow a year later when the Court upheld by a vote of 8 to 1 the constitutionality of the U.S. Sentencing Commission.[139] The commission, created by Congress in 1984, is an independent body located within the judicial branch and empowered to promulgate binding guidelines for sentencing individuals convicted of offenses. Federal judges serve on the commission and may be removed from the commission by the president, but only for cause. The Court upheld this statutory framework.

The independent counsel statute expired in 1992 after Republicans, angry with the investigation by independent counsel Lawrence E. Walsh into the Iran-Contra affair, blocked the reauthorization bill. But with the election of Bill Clinton that year, Republicans reversed course and advocated reauthorization as a way of investigating

Clinton's involvement in an Arkansas land development venture (Whitewater Development Company). Before that law could be reauthorized, Attorney General Janet Reno relied on her authority on January 20, 1994, to name a special prosecutor, Robert B. Fiske, Jr., to investigate Whitewater and the death of White House aide Vincent Foster. The independent counsel law, reauthorized on June 30, 1994, gave the federal court panel the option of reappointing Fiske or selecting someone else. The panel chose a replacement, former Republican Solicitor General Kenneth W. Starr.

The office of independent counsel remains under heavy fire. The open-ended nature of recent investigations, both in time and money, is one objection (see Table 4-1). Critics also charge that the "hair trigger" in the statute leads to unnecessary appointments. But no one has been able to draft acceptable language for triggering action by the Attorney General and appointment by the court panel.

Executive Office of the President

Presidents are strongly tempted to adopt a fortress mentality, relying on immediate advisers within the White House for loyalty, support, and understanding. The White House staff expands into a counterbureaucracy to control unruly departments and agencies.[140] David Stockman's experience in the Reagan administration led him to conclude: "It'll be the people in the Executive Office versus the cabinet departments like it always is. The cabinet secretaries are getting domesticated by their people, by their permanent bureaucracies."[141]

For reasons of comity between the branches, Congress has been reluctant to probe very deeply into the activities of the Executive Office of the President (EOP). An institution of modest size when created in 1939, the EOP is now staffed by about two thousand people. At present it consists of the White House Office, the Office of Administration, the Office of Management and Budget, the Office of Policy Development, the National Security Council, the Council of Economic Advisers, and a number of smaller units.[142]

The custom of leaving the EOP alone was largely tolerable until a series of misadventures by the Nixon administration provoked Congress to tighten its control. Statutory restrictions in 1978 on confidential White House funds reflect this change in legislative attitudes.[143] Closer controls were also applied to the Office of Management and Budget

TABLE 4-1

Independent Counsel Investigations

COUNSEL	SUBJECT	RESULT	COST
Arthur H. Christy (1979)	Hamilton Jordan (cocaine use)	no charges	$182,000
Gerald J. Gallinghouse (1980)	Tim Kraft (cocaine use)	no charges	$3,300
Leon Silverman (1981)	Raymond J. Donovan (bribery and perjury)	no charges	$326,000
Jacob A. Stein (1984)	Edwin Meese III (financial improprieties)	no charges	$312,000
Alexia Morrison (1986)	Theodore B. Olson (perjury)	no charges	$1.5 million
Whitney North Seymore, Jr. (1986)	Michael K. Deaver (perjury)	convicted	$1.5 million
Lawrence E. Walsh (1986)	Iran-Contra affair	7 guilty pleas, 4 convictions (2 overturned) 6 presidential pardons	$47.9 million
James C. McKay (1987)	Lyn Nofziger and Meese (conflicts of interest)	Nofziger's conviction overturned; no charges against Meese	$2.8 million
James R. Harper (1987)	confidential	no charges	$50,000
Sealed (1989)	confidential	confidential	$15,000
Arlin M. Adams (1990) Larry D. Thompson (1995)	Samuel R. Pierce and others (HUD conspiracy to defraud the United States)	16 convictions	$26.4 million

TABLE 4-1, *continued*

COUNSEL	SUBJECT	RESULT	COST
Sealed (1991)	confidential	confidential	$93,000
Joseph E. deGenova (1992)	Janet G. Mullins and Margaret D. Tutwiler (search of State Department passport files)	no charges	$2.8 million
Robert B. Fiske, Jr. (1994) (appointed by Attorney General Janet Reno)	President Clinton's involvement in Whitewater and death of Vincent Foster	3 plea agreements; ongoing investigation by Kenneth W. Starr	$6.1 million
Kenneth W. Starr (1994)	Continuation of Fiske's investigation plus other assignments	12 convictions, 2 acquittals; ongoing	$22.2 million
Donald C. Smaltz (1994)	Michael Espy and others (Agriculture Department scandal)	6 convictions, 4 acquittals; ongoing	$8.6 million
David M. Barrett (1995)	Henry G. Cisneros (lying to FBI)	ongoing	$2.1 million
Daniel S. Pearson (1995)	Ronald H. Brown and others (financial improprieties)	investigation of Brown ended when he was killed in plane crash in Bosnia; remainder of investigation transferred to Justice Department	$2.6 million

SOURCES: Adapted from *National Journal*, February 1, 1997, p. 216; "Keeping Tabs on Independent Counsels," *Washington Post*, April 4, 1997, p. A19; "Independent Counsel Investigations," *Washington Post*, April 13, 1997, p. A12.

(OMB), long considered a presidential staff agency. When Congress proposed in 1973 to subject the OMB director and deputy director to Senate confirmation, the Nixon administration insisted that Senate scrutiny of appointees should not extend to the "inner circle" of presidential advisers.[144] The director of the OMB, Roy Ash, claimed that the role of the two officers was "clearly that as agents and advisers of the President and therefore clearly inappropriate for Senate confirmation." He described the OMB "as an arm—and if he wants to, a physical arm of the President, more eyes, more ears, more heads, and more arms for the President, and to in some way deprive him of their use is to deprive him of his full faculties to do that with which he is charged."[145] Congress enacted legislation in 1974 to apply the confirmation process to future OMB directors and deputy directors.[146]

In his appeal to anthropomorphism, Ash neglected to say that other presidential advisers within the EOP had been subject to Senate confirmation, including the director and deputy director of the Central Intelligence Agency and the three members of the Council of Economic Advisers. As for the Budget Bureau (forerunner of OMB), it was never solely an agent of the president. In creating it in 1921, Congress imposed on the agency a duty to advise both branches. The statute directed that the bureau "shall, at the request of any committee of either House of Congress having jurisdiction over revenue or appropriations, furnish the committee such aid and information as it may request." This requirement remains part of the law today.[147] The first circular issued by the Budget Bureau described the director as "an advisor of the President and Congress in the matter of correcting business administration."[148]

Even after President Roosevelt transferred the Budget Bureau from the Treasury Department to the newly formed EOP, statutory ties to Congress remained. By 1970, when Nixon proposed abolishing the bureau and replacing it with the OMB, Congress had vested in the bureau at least fifty-eight statutory duties.[149] Sharp opposition materialized in the House to the provision in Nixon's plan that would transfer those statutory functions to the president, who could delegate them to subordinates later. Although the House Government Operations Committee opposed the OMB reorganization plan, the full House favored it by the margin of 193-164. No opposition developed in the Senate.[150]

Other parts of the Executive Office of the President have come under congressional scrutiny. Bills have been introduced to make the president's national security adviser subject to Senate confirmation. The adviser serves as staff director of the National Security Council, established by statute to advise the president regarding the integration of domestic, foreign, and military policies. Although presidential advisers are traditionally immune from congressional questioning, greater congressional oversight is invited when presidential staff, including the national security adviser, assume operational responsibilities and compete with the duties of departmental and agency officials. Recent national security advisers, including Henry Kissinger and Zbigniew Brzezinski, have been especially prominent in competing with the secretary of state, producing what Senator Frank Church, Democrat of Idaho, called a "mini-State Department."[151]

President Reagan's first national security adviser, Richard V. Allen, was given a much lower profile. Allen did not meet alone with the president each morning, as Brzezinski did with Carter, to present a daily intelligence briefing. The briefings occurred, but with others in the room. Allen was also expected to be less visible to the press and to function more as a coordinator than a formulator of policy. Whereas Brzezinski had chaired crisis management in the Carter administration, that assignment was given to Vice President George Bush in the Reagan administration. Allen's successors played a less prominent role than Kissinger and Brzezinski, but Robert McFarlane and John M. Poindexter permitted the National Security Council to become involved in operations in Nicaragua and in arms sales to Iran (pp. 206–13).

When presidential advisers behave as surrogates for departmental heads, it is proper for Congress to call them to account for their actions. The autonomy of White House staff is relative, not absolute. Violations of trust, misapplication of funds, obstruction of legislative programs, and interference with departmental assignments are some of the actions that encourage Congress to circumscribe White House operations. During the Clinton administration, an unprecedented number of White House aides were brought to Capitol Hill to testify on White House–Treasury contacts, Travelgate, Whitewater, and White House access to FBI files.[152] The growing dominance in the White House of aides with little experience other than running a campaign suggests that future White House mishaps, especially during first terms, will remain more the rule than the exception.

Conclusions

Presidents complain about the fragmented nature of the executive branch, which they say makes it impossible to carry out a coherent, effective program. The fragmentation is partly their own making. Often they prefer to set up organizational entities outside the regular departments. Even when agencies are located within the regular departments, they may be relatively immune to White House pressures because of adjudicatory functions or political independence. Organizations such as the Federal Highway Administration, Army Corps of Engineers, National Park Service, and Forest Service "constitute the departmental power centers and are quite capable of making it on their own without secretarial help, except when challenged by strong hostile external forces. Often they can do more for the secretary than he or she can do for them."[153]

Both branches have powerful arguments supporting their efforts to control the bureaucracy. The framers established a single executive for the purpose of assuring responsibility and accountability. They specifically vested in the president the duty to take care that the laws be faithfully executed. But these laws often place administrative duties outside the president's immediate control, reflecting not merely a congressional preference but, in the opinion of attorneys general, an appropriate and expedient course of action.

Many of the administrative duties placed outside the president's control are routine ministerial or adjudicatory decisions, concerned with claims, pensions, and other entitlements. But often whole agencies within an executive department are so independent, because of their institutional history and culture, that they can function with a high degree of autonomy from the president and departmental heads. The erosion of presidential control has continued with the application of statutory restrictions to staff within the Executive Office of the President, but the diffusion of executive power is especially conspicuous with the creation of independent regulatory commissions that represent a mix of legislative, executive, and judicial functions.

CHAPTER 5

◆

The Independent Regulatory Commission: Mahomet's Coffin

The independent regulatory commission differs from the conventional administrative agency in two ways: (1) it is somewhat detached from the operations of the executive branch, and (2) responsibility falls on a group of administrators with essentially equal power instead of on a single executive. This independent status provoked Professor Corwin to ask if a commissioner is not in the executive department, "where is he? In the legislative department; or is he, forsooth, in the uncomfortable halfway situation of Mahomet's coffin, suspended 'twixt Heaven and Earth?"[1]

The Interstate Commerce Commission (ICC), created by Congress in 1887, is the forerunner and prototype of the independent regulatory commission. Congress modeled the ICC after railroad commissions that had been operating in more than twenty states. Reformers believed that commissions could accumulate more easily than legislators the expert knowledge needed to effectively supervise the railroad corporations. With the railroad industry changing rapidly, the commission form seemed a more flexible instrument for regulation than the enactment of fixed statutes to guide an executive agency. Initially the state railroad commissions functioned as fact-finding and advisory bodies, operating as agents of the legislatures. In no sense were they part of the executive branch. Gradually the commissions assumed the character of permanent bodies, discharging duties that might have been entrusted to executive departments.[2]

After the financial panics of 1873 and 1885, many of the small railroad lines went bankrupt. As the lines consolidated they formed *inter*state, not *intra*state, systems. In 1886 the Supreme Court struck down an Illinois railroad statute because it affected, even for the part of the journey within the state, commerce among the states.[3] That decision made national regulation imperative.

The Interstate Commerce Act of 1887, which created the ICC, prohibited railroad practices such as rate discrimination, rebating, pooling, and the charging of unjust and unreasonable rates. Although the ICC had no power to fix railroad rates, it could issue orders against the rates set by railroads and enforce its orders in the courts. Congress debated two approaches to regulation: allowing the Department of Justice to enforce a specific railroad policy enunciated by Congress or creating a commission to carry out a more general charter. Congress favored the latter approach because it would:

- provide flexible and expert administration of the industry;
- serve as an expert body to aid Congress in formulating a railroad policy;
- protect the public and small shippers against the legal talents of the railroad corporations;
- serve as an arbiter for conflicting interests among the railroads;
- provide valuable expert opinion to the courts; and
- build on the successful model of state commissions.

These arguments prevailed over objections that the commission's "flexibility" would actually dilute the force of statutory policy and that the commission would be powerless to withstand the expertise and political influence of the railroads.[4]

The ICC was followed by other independent regulatory commissions: the Federal Reserve System (the "Fed") in 1913, the Federal Trade Commission (FTC) in 1914, and the Federal Power Commission (FPC) in 1920. Five other agencies appeared in the 1930s: the Securities and Exchange Commission (SEC), the Federal Communications Commission (FCC), the Civil Aeronautics Board (CAB), the National Labor Relations Board (NLRB), and the Federal Maritime Commission (FMC), although the latter had antecedents dating back several decades. More recent additions include the Consumer Product Safety Commission (CPSC) and the Commodity Futures Trading Commission (CFTC); the latter performs functions previously placed in the Department of Agriculture. The Federal Energy Regulatory Commission (FERC), established in 1977, is successor to the Federal Power Commission. The Nuclear Regulatory Commission (NRC), created in 1974, inherited some of the functions of the now defunct Atomic Energy Commission (see Table 5-1).

Conflicting Assessments

Ever since their creation, independent regulatory commissions have inspired contradictory evaluations. One of the harshest indictments came from the Brownlow Committee in 1937, which excoriated the commissions as "a headless 'fourth branch' of the Government, a haphazard deposit of irresponsible agencies and uncoordinated powers." According to the committee, the independent agencies violated the "basic theory of the American Constitution that there should be three major branches of the Government and only three."[5]

Far more tolerant was a study by an equally distinguished group, a task force of the 1949 Hoover Commission. It described the independent regulatory commission as a "useful and desirable agency where constant adaptation to changing conditions and delegation of wide discretion in administration are essential to effective regulation." The independent commission provided a means of "insulating regulation from partisan influence or favoritism, for obtaining deliberation, expertness and continuity of attention, and for combining adaptability of regulation with consistency of policy so far as practical." The task force found that the potential for conflict and inadequate coordination between the commissions and other executive agencies, although a theoretical possibility, had been "limited in extent and generally avoided by cooperation."[6]

These two studies appear to be discussing entirely unrelated organizations. In fact, they focus on different aspects of the same phenomenon. The Brownlow Committee, preoccupied with the theory

TABLE 5-1

Independent Regulatory Commissions[a]

AGENCY	YEAR ESTABLISHED
Interstate Commerce Commission[b]	1887
Board of Governors of the Federal Reserve System	1913
Federal Trade Commission	1914
Federal Power Commission	1920
Federal Communications Commission	1934
Securities and Exchange Commission	1934
National Labor Relations Board	1935
Federal Maritime Commission	1936
Civil Aeronautics Board[c]	1938
Atomic Energy Commission	1946
Board of Governors of the U.S. Postal Service	1970
Consumer Product Safety Commission	1972
Nuclear Regulatory Commission[d]	1974
Commodity Futures Trading Commission	1975
Federal Energy Regulatory Commission[e]	1977
Social Security Administration[f]	1994

[a] This table includes only the major independent regulatory commissions. The list could be extended to include the Equal Employment Opportunity Commission, Federal Deposit Insurance Corporation, Federal Election Commission, Federal Home Loan Bank Board, and Occupational Safety and Health Review Commission. Other regulatory bodies are generally considered within the executive branch, such as the Environmental Protection Agency.

[b] Terminated in 1995 but some ICC functions were transferred to a new independent board (Surface Transportation Board) in the Department of Transportation. 109 Stat. 803 (1995).

[c] Under the Airline Deregulation Act of 1978 (P.L. 95-504), the CAB went out of existence in 1985. Some of its functions were transferred to the Department of Transportation in 1984 (P.L. 98-443).

[d] Inherited some of the functions of the Atomic Energy Commission.

[e] Successor to the Federal Power Commission.

[f] Originally located within the Department of Health and Human Services as an independent agency, the Social Security Administration became a separate entity in 1994. 108 Stat. 1464 (1994).

and structure of government, found the commissions repugnant because they did not fit squarely within one of the three branches. The task force of the Hoover Commission concentrated on functions and administrative experience. After studying the operations of nine commissions and boards, the task force identified these advantages of the independent commission:

1. *Resistance to pressures.* The extensive powers given to regulatory agencies and the administrative flexibility required for their effective use obviously open the door to favoritism, unfairness, political influence, and even corruption. The independent commission, with its multiple membership, shared responsibility, and security of tenure, is in a favorable position to resist partisan control and to expose pressures and improper actions.
2. *Collective policy formation.* The commission, by requiring collective policy making and decision, provides a barrier to arbitrary or capricious action and secures decisions based on different points of view and experience. This process has definite advantages where the problems are complex, the relative weight of various factors affecting policy not clear, and the range of choice wide.
3. *Expertness.* Regulated industries are complex and highly technical. Their problems need constant study and continuous attention. While expertness must be supplied in large part by the staff, the commission form is designed to assure expertness or at least familiarity with the problems of the regulated field on the part of the commissioners, who have fixed terms and a good chance of reappointment. Devoting full time to the particular industry, the commissioners become fully familiar with the technical aspects of the industry and its basic problems through day-to-day contacts.
4. *Continuity of policy.* In order to enable private industry to plan ahead, the regulatory agency must seek to

achieve as much stability in policy and methods as is consistent with continuous adaptation of regulation to meet changing conditions.[7]

Because the commissions are administrative bodies established to carry out a number of judicial duties, they require a hybrid form. Adjudicatory decisions are typically made independently from Congress and the White House. The judicial function also explains why commissions are multimember (or "collegial") bodies, instead of being headed by a single administrator: "Just as we want appellate courts to be made up of plural members, to protect against the idiosyncracies of a single individual, we want agencies that exercise judicial power to be collegial."[8]

Much of the criticism directed at independent commissions is rooted in fundamental misconceptions. Commissions are routinely attacked for being unresponsive to popular pressures, but they were made independent precisely to avoid abrupt policy swings that might otherwise occur from one election to another. It is inconsistent—indeed inconceivable—to expect a commission to be both independent and politically responsive. Moreover, for agencies that decide judicial questions such as licensing and ratemaking, independence from political pressures is entirely compatible with the standards and values expected of the courts. Commissions are not structured to accommodate each shift in the political winds.

Critics argue that the independent commissions have been "captured" by the industries they are charged to regulate. First, the regular executive departments are vulnerable to the same critique. Second, the capture theory conflicts with the chorus of protests heard from the regulated community. Agriculture, business, and labor are not monoliths capable of controlling a commission. Truckers and railroads were at cross-purposes in their pleadings before the ICC. AT&T and other segments of the communications industry compete for FCC's favors. Local broadcast stations appeal to the FCC to limit the growth of cable television. Other commissions are faced with similar dissension. The ferocity of this conflict ("cutthroat competition") in the latter half of the nineteenth century created the demand for government regulation in the first place. The private sector tried unregulated free enterprise and found the risk and pain unbearable.[9]

Commissions are not created as independent bodies simply because they perform "regulatory" functions. A large number of executive agencies carry out regulatory duties. Consumer protection, for example, is a responsibility not only of the FTC but also of the Food and Drug Administration (located within the Department of Health and Human Services). Antitrust actions are pursued by the FTC as well as by the Department of Justice. The Agricultural Marketing Service, operating within the Agriculture Department, regulates practices in livestock and processed meat markets.[10]

Nor are commissions independent solely because their tasks are complex and technical. Tax and housing issues, exceedingly complex and technical, are left to the Treasury Department and the Housing and Urban Development Department.

Many of the commissions began as part of an executive department, or were closely associated with a department, and only later gained autonomy. For example, when the ICC was established in 1887, it had various ties to the secretary of the interior. The commission could employ and fix the compensation of employees, subject to the approval of the secretary, and expenditures were approved by the head of the commission and the secretary of the interior. The commission also reported to the secretary each year. Those ties were severed two years later.[11] The "arm of Congress" concept did not surface until much later, after the ICC had been strengthened by the Hepburn Act of 1906 and the Mann-Elkins Act of 1910.[12]

The Federal Reserve Board originally consisted of seven members, including the secretary of the treasury and the comptroller of the currency as ex officio members. Legislation in 1935 terminated their membership on the board, while the "Accord of 1951" helped free the board from Treasury Department policy demands. When the Department of Commerce and Labor was established in 1903, Congress created within it the Bureau of Corporations to investigate business practices in interstate and foreign commerce. The bureau was abolished in 1914, at which point all pending investigations and proceedings were transferred to the newly created FTC.

Other independent commissions had their start within the executive branch. As established in 1920, the Federal Power Commission (FPC) was composed of the secretary of war, the secretary of the interior, and the secretary of agriculture. The president named the head of the commission. A decade later the FPC acquired its independent status. A reorganization act in 1930 changed the FPC to consist of five commissioners with staggered terms. After the original term of the commissioner designated as chair by the president had expired, future heads were to be elected by the commission itself. In 1977 the FPC was renamed the Federal Energy Regulatory Commission (FERC) and located within the newly created Department of Energy. However, FERC retained its status as an independent regulatory organization.

Techniques of Executive-Legislative Control

The "independence" of regulatory commissions is secured in three ways: (1) the terms of commissioners are staggered to insulate them from presidential transitions; (2) the president's power to remove commissioners is limited by specific statutory grounds; and (3) restrictions are placed on the number of commissioners who may belong to the same political party. This third restriction may be neutralized to some degree by selecting nominal members of a political party or members who identify their political affiliation as independent.

Regulatory commissions are subject to the control of Congress, the president, and the courts. They have been aptly described as "stepchildren whose custody is contested by both Congress and the executive, but without very much affection from either one."[13] The struggle for influence has been largely defensive, "with each elected branch seeking to prevent the other from exercising active control, but with neither consistently wanting to do so itself."[14]

Congress and the president have at their disposal a number of techniques for controlling the independent commissions. Congress creates the commissions, defines their duties, specifies qualifications for commissioners, and provides appropriations. Although presidents designate the heads of the commissions, statutory restrictions have severely limited their power to remove commissioners. The president relies on the executive establishment, especially the Justice Department and the Office of Management and Budget, to control the commissions' litigation, review their budget requests and legislative recommendations, and monitor their requests for information from the business community. The appointment of commissioners is formally shared by the president and the Senate, and yet members of both houses have had impressive success in seeing their own staff selected as commissioners.

The Creative Act

Independent commissions are creatures of Congress. Called into existence by statute, they may be modified, circumscribed, or abolished by statute. Congress controls their jurisdiction, purpose, structure, and funding. The standards established by Congress to guide commissions are characteristically more vague than for the executive agencies. The judiciary has been satisfied by general guidelines such as "public convenience, interest, or necessity" for the FCC, "unfair methods of competition" for the FTC, and "public interest" for the ICC.[15]

The Federal Reserve System is often regarded as the very model of independence, autonomous from congressional as well as presidential interference. But the Fed is not legally independent, for this would represent not a delegation but a clear abdication of legislative power. At the time of William McChesney Martin's nomination as chairman of the Fed, Senator Paul Douglas, Democrat of Illinois, lured the nominee into this dialogue:

> Senator DOUGLAS: Let me turn to a general question. Do you regard the Federal Reserve Board as the agent of the Executive or the agent of Congress?

> Mr. MARTIN: I regard it as an independent agency of the government.

> Senator DOUGLAS: To whom is it responsible? To the executive or the Congress?

> Mr. MARTIN: It is responsible to Congress. I will give you my concept as I see it.

> Senator DOUGLAS: If you will just say that you regard it as responsible to Congress, that is all I want. . . .

• • •

Senator DOUGLAS: Mr. Martin, I have had typed out this little sentence which is a quotation from you: "The Federal Reserve is an agency of the Congress." I will furnish you with scotch tape and ask you to place it on your mirror where you can see it as you shave each morning, so that it may remind you.

Mr. MARTIN: I will be glad to comply.[16]

The mere threat of statutory action and the uncertainty about what Congress might do has occasionally caused the Fed to adjust its policy. When Arthur Burns served as Fed chairman during the Nixon administration, he expended considerable time and energy in lobbying Congress—meeting with members for breakfast and testifying before committees.[17] As a result of a concurrent resolution passed in 1975, followed by statutes in 1977 and 1978, the Fed now meets with the House and Senate banking committees twice a year to discuss monetary targets. Members of the Reagan administration announced that they would feel free to advise the Fed on appropriate policies. As a top official in the Treasury Department remarked in 1981: "I think the Federal Reserve has long felt free to advise the administration on what they thought was appropriate fiscal policy. . . . I think the major difference is that we're going to feel free to advise them on what we think is an appropriate monetary policy."[18]

Appointing Commissioners

Through their power to nominate commissioners, presidents are able to alter the composition and orientation of independent agencies. Within a matter of a couple of years, and in some cases a few months, presidents have used their appointment power to create majorities of their own choosing. By the time of Nixon's resignation in 1974, after five and a half years in office, he had nominated *every* commissioner of these agencies: CAB (5 commissioners), FCC (7), FMC (5), FPC (5), NLRB (5), SEC (5), and CPSC (5).[19]

The opportunity to select commissioners with particular policy orientations gives the president an advantage in the legislative process. During the 1976 presidential campaign, Jimmy Carter committed himself to airline deregulation and, once in office, appointed Alfred Kahn and Elizabeth Bailey to the CAB. Both had made statements favoring deregulation. Under their influence, the agency took several steps to make the industry more competitive. Those initiatives helped build a favorable climate for passing airline deregulation legislation in 1978.[20] Presidents are usually not so purposeful with their appointments.

A 1978 study of the FCC concluded that "the President has never used the appointments power to shape communications policy in any distinctive fashion. The ability to shape policy has been frittered away largely through presidential indifference."[21] However, a determined use of the appointment power during the Reagan years had a dramatic impact on the FCC. By appointing free-marketeers, President Reagan pushed the agency toward a deregulatory agenda and the repeal of the fairness doctrine (requiring radio stations to provide a variety of viewpoints). The result: fierce collisions between the administration and congressional committees. President Bush soothed FCC-congressional relations by appointing less confrontational, less ideological nominees.[22]

Even though statutes are drafted to protect the nonpartisan nature of commissions, presidents are able to circumvent the restrictions. For example, the six-member Tariff Commission was structured so that no more than three commissioners could be from the same political party. But with Democrats identified nationally as advocates of lower tariffs, and Republicans labeled as protectionists, President Wilson could easily pick a Republican free-trader while Presidents Harding and Coolidge could search for protectionist Democrats. When President Nixon had to name a Democrat to the SEC, he chose A. Sydney Herlong, Jr., a conservative identified with the business community.[23]

Both branches have received poor marks for their records in appointing high-quality people to the independent commissions.[24] The Senate tended to approve nominations routinely; its rejection of Leland Olds, nominated in 1949 to a third term to the FPC, stands as a rare exception.[25] Floor votes to reject a nominee are rare. Committees prefer to let the White House know that they will not support a candidate, forcing the president to withdraw the nomination.

In the last three decades, the Senate has examined nominations more closely. In 1973 it rejected Robert Morris for the FPC after deciding that the agency was already top-heavy with commissioners oriented toward industry and that Morris, despite his qualifications, could not be counted on to represent the consumer's point of view.[26] In 1977 the Senate Environment and Public Works Committee rejected the nomination of Kent F. Hansen to the Nuclear Regulatory Commission. The opposition reflected concern about his limited experience in policy matters and possible conflict-of-interest issues.[27] Also in 1977, opposition by the Senate Commerce Committee forced President Carter to withdraw his nomination of Donald L. Tucker to be vice chairman of the Civil Aeronautics Board.

Senate committees are examining more carefully the financial backgrounds of nominees to commissions, looking for potential conflict-of-interest. The committees also create a public record of the nominee's depth of knowledge, previous policy commitments, and regulatory philosophy.

This committee capability defeated a number of Reagan nominees. In 1981 the Senate Labor and Human Resources Committee rejected the nomination of John R. Van de Water as chairman of the NLRB. He received a recess appointment, but when his name was resubmitted in 1982, the Senate refused to act on it. William M. Bell's name was withdrawn in 1982 as chairman of the Equal Employment Opportunity Commission (EEOC); F. Keith Adkinson pulled out as nominee in 1982 after the Senate Commerce Committee opposed his appointment to the FTC; and in 1986 the Senate Labor and Human Resources Committee killed Reagan's nomination of Robert E. Rader, Jr., to the Occupational Safety and Health Review Commission. The Senate Labor and Human Resources Committee rejected Jeffrey I. Zuckerman in 1986 as general counsel of the EEOC. In 1989 Heather J. Gradison, chair of the ICC, resigned rather than face a tough reconfirmation fight against the Senate Commerce Committee.

Senior staffers from Congress stand a good chance to become commissioners of the independent agencies. John R. Evans went from the Senate Banking Committee to the SEC as commissioner in 1973 and was reappointed to another term in 1979. John Vernon Rainbolt II, an aide to Democratic Representative Graham Purcell, Jr., of Texas and counsel to the House Agriculture Committee, became commissioner of the Commodity Futures Trading Commission in 1975. Charles Ferris, for many years director of the Senate Democratic Policy Committee and later general counsel for House Speaker Tip

O'Neill, was picked to head the FCC in 1977. Charles B. Curtis, counsel to the House Commerce Committee from 1971 to 1976, became chair of the FPC in 1977 and was reappointed in 1979 to chair the successor agency, the Federal Energy Regulatory Commission (FERC).

This pattern continued under President Reagan. In 1981 he selected Charles M. Butler III, an aide to Senator John Tower, Republican of Texas, to chair the FERC. Robert P. Hunter, chief counsel and chief of staff of the Senate Labor and Human Resources Committee, became a member of the NLRB in 1981. Fowler C. West, staff director of the House Agriculture Committee, was selected to serve on the Commodity Futures Trading Commission (CFTC) in 1982. In 1988 he was reappointed to the CFTC. Charles L. Marinaccio left the Senate Banking Committee in 1984 to become a commissioner with the SEC. James R. Curtiss, after serving seven years with the Senate Committee on Environment and Public Works, became a member of the Nuclear Regulatory Commission in 1988. Also in 1988, James M. Stephens was named chair of the NLRB after spending three years with the Board and almost a decade before that with House and Senate committees.

Similar examples can be taken from the Bush administration. In 1989 President Bush named Deborah Kaye Owen a Federal Trade Commissioner after she had served years with the House and Senate Judiciary Committees. In the same year, he appointed William D. Hathaway, for many years a member of Congress, to be a Federal Maritime Commissioner. These patterns are more difficult to track in the Clinton administration because it does not release detailed biographies with nominations.

Congressional staffers are sometimes instrumental in creating the agencies on which they will serve. Stuart Statler was special assistant to the chair of the National Commission on Product Safety, which made recommendations leading to the creation of the Consumer Product Safety Commission (CPSC). After serving as chief counsel to the minority for the Senate Permanent Subcommittee on Investigations and counsel to Republican Senator Charles Percy of Illinois, in 1979 Statler was selected to become a commissioner of the CPSC.

The Senate Commerce Committee has a particularly good record in placing its staff on the independent regulatory commissions. A. Daniel O'Neal, transportation counsel to the committee, became a member of the ICC in 1973 and was designated chairman in 1977. Joseph R. Fogarty, after thirteen years as a committee staffer, joined the FCC as commissioner in 1976. David A. Clanton served eight years as assistant to Senator Robert Griffin, Republican of Michigan, and as minority staff counsel to the Senate Commerce Committee before becoming a commissioner of the FTC in 1976. President Reagan named him acting chair in 1981. Michael Pertschuk, staff director of the committee, became chair of the FTC in 1977, while Richard Daschbach, maritime counsel to the committee, was named commissioner of the Federal Maritime Commission that same year. President Reagan selected Mary Ann Weyforth Dawson to be a commissioner of the FCC in 1981. She had previously served with Democratic representatives James W. Symington and Richard Ichord of Missouri, but during her service as an assistant to Senator Bob Packwood of Oregon, a Republican, she had special responsibility for the Senate Commerce Committee, chaired by Packwood. In 1982 Malcolm M. B. Sterrett went from the Senate Commerce Committee to be an Interstate Commerce commissioner. In 1988 he was replaced on the commission by Karen Borlaug Phillips, who had worked six years with the Senate Committee on Finance and the Senate Committee on Commerce.

Designating Commission Heads

When Congress created the Federal Reserve Board in 1913, it gave the president the power to designate the governor. Similarly, the statute creating the Federal Power Commission in 1920 authorized the president to choose its chair. In other agencies, the members of the commissions named their chiefs. The Interstate Commerce Commission had rotating chairs, elected annually by the membership.

In 1949 a task force of the Hoover Commission recommended that the head of each regulatory commission be designated from among its members by the president, to serve at the pleasure of the president. The task force also recommended that administrative duties be centralized in the chair.[28] The full commission did not endorse the task force's suggestions and remained noncommittal on the issue.[29]

Beginning in 1950, a succession of reorganization plans submitted by presidents implemented the recommendations of the task force.[30] To assure that new presidents could appoint their own chiefs of the

Federal Reserve System, former Fed chairs Thomas McCabe and William McChesney Martin both favored making the four-year tenure coterminous with that of the president. The Commission on Money and Credit made the same suggestion in 1961, and President Kennedy included the recommendation in his 1962 economic report.[31] Despite repeated support over the years, this proposal has never been adopted. The political leverage and significance of designating the chair is well appreciated by Congress. Instead of the president having sole power to designate the chair and vice chair of the Fed, Congress passed legislation in 1977 to make those selections subject to the advice and consent of the Senate.[32]

Most of the heads of the independent regulatory commissions serve at the pleasure of the president, but upon removal as chair the individual remains a member of the commission. For example, when President Carter removed Joseph Hendrie from his position as chair of the NRC, Hendrie retained his seat on the commission.

Despite the commissions' role as "arms of Congress," the chairs sometimes perform political chores for the White House. During the 1972 presidential campaign, three commission heads campaigned actively for Richard Nixon: William Casey of the SEC, Helen Delich Bentley of the FMC, and John Nassikas of the FPC.[33]

Removals

President Franklin D. Roosevelt tested the scope of his removal power by dismissing William Humphrey, a business-oriented FTC commissioner appointed by Coolidge and reappointed by Hoover. Roosevelt removed him for policy reasons rather than the statutory grounds for removal (inefficiency, neglect of duty, or malfeasance in office). The Justice Department argued that the statute served to guide but not limit the president's discretion in exercising the removal power. The grounds were not meant to be exclusive, according to Justice Department officials, unless Congress specified that there were three grounds "and no other." No such language appeared in the FTC statute.[34]

The Justice Department argued that if Congress could limit the president to three grounds for removal, it could set the limit at one, such as malfeasance in office or neglect of duty. The result of such reasoning, said the Justice Department, "would be that the President would have no power, even with the aid of the Senate, to remove an admittedly inefficient officer in the executive branch of the Government." Moreover, the president's faithful execution of the laws "may require more than freedom from inefficiency, neglect of duty, or malfeasance in office."

In a unanimous and remarkably brief opinion for the Supreme Court, Justice Sutherland held in *Humphrey's Executor v. United States* (1935) that an FTC commissioner could be removed only for one or more of the causes specified in the statute. Sutherland tried to distance the FTC from executive agencies by describing it as "charged with the enforcement of no policy except the policy of the law. Its duties are neither political nor executive, but predominantly quasijudicial and quasi-legislative." Anticipating this argument, the Justice Department had pointed out that the regular executive departments also performed judicial and legislative functions, as indeed they did.[35]

Sutherland offered a strained and unrealistic view of the doctrine of separated powers: "The fundamental necessity of maintaining each of the three general departments of government entirely free from the control or coercive influence, direct or indirect, of either of the others, has often been stressed and is hardly open to serious question."[36] Yet there is very little that one branch of government can do without being controlled, directly or indirectly, by another branch. To bolster his opinion, Sutherland had to misrepresent the views of James Wilson and Justice Joseph Story, implying that they believed in a strict separation between the branches when in fact they emphasized mutual dependency.[37]

During his last year on the bench, Sutherland expressed confusion about the location of independent commissions in the scheme of three branches of government. Upon hearing someone argue that the U.S. Shipping Board (forerunner of the Federal Maritime Commission) was not in the executive branch, he asked the legal basis for such an assertion. The counsel replied, "Why, in your Honor's opinion in the Humphrey case." Sutherland pressed further. If not in the executive branch, then where was it? The legislative branch, came the answer. Justice Sutherland "shook his head, as though he disagreed, and seemed to be thinking the question over as the discussion went on to other points."[38]

Although *Humphrey's Executor* has been reinforced by other decisions,[39] we still lack a satisfactory theory on the removal power as applied to the independent commissions. What we have is largely what Sutherland called a "field of doubt" that occupies the territory between *Myers* (for executive officers) and the independent commissions covered by *Humphrey*.[40] *Humphrey* could have been avoided had Roosevelt based his removal on one of the three statutory grounds specified for FTC commissioners. It is doubtful that the Court would have questioned his judgment, and future commissioners of the independent agencies would have been sensitive to the potential intervention of the president. But even with *Humphrey*, presidents are able to put pressure on commissioners to resign. The Ford White House applied steady pressure on Robert Timm until he finally resigned from the Civil Aeronautics Board. In 1980 the Court of Claims rejected Timm's argument that he had been forced to resign and was entitled to back pay.[41]

Reviewing Budget Estimates

The Budget and Accounting Act of 1921 authorized the president, supported by the Bureau of the Budget, to review and revise budget estimates submitted by all departments and establishments, *including* independent commissions. Despite the clarity of the statutory language, a number of independent regulatory commissions and boards insisted that the provisions for budgetary review did not apply to them. To remove all doubts, Congress had to add Title II to the Reorganization Act of 1939. The reorganization statute amended the Budget and Accounting Act by adding the words "any independent regulatory commission or board" to the list of government agencies whose budgets were subject to review and revision by the Budget Bureau.[42]

Agency budget estimates and supporting material submitted to the Budget Bureau (now Office of Management and Budget) can be disclosed to Congress *after* the president's budget is transmitted.[43] Because of a long train of abuses by the Nixon administration, members of Congress wanted to receive certain agency estimates *before* the president transmitted the budget. In most cases Congress settled on the submission of agency estimates simultaneously to Congress and the OMB, but in a few cases the estimates bypassed the OMB and the president altogether.

The Consumer Product Safety Commission, established in 1972, is required to submit its budget concurrently to Congress and to OMB.[44] Congress followed the same approach in 1973 for the National Railroad Passenger Corporation; in 1974 for the U.S. Railway Association, the Federal Election Commission, the Commodity Futures Trading Commission, and the Privacy Protection Study Commission; in 1975 for the National Transportation Safety Board; and in 1976 for the Interstate Commerce Commission.[45] When the secretary of energy seeks funds from Congress, he must show the amount requested by the Federal Energy Regulatory Commission in its budgetary presentation made to the secretary and to the OMB.[46] Legislation in 1978 directed the Merit Systems Protection Board to submit its budget concurrently to the president and to Congress.[47]

More serious, from the standpoint of the principles of the Budget and Accounting Act, are prohibitions that deny the president and OMB the right to revise agency estimates. The Senate made a concerted effort in 1972 to have the appropriation requests of independent regulatory agencies submitted directly to Congress rather than to OMB. Commissioners of the agencies complained that OMB review and reductions prevented Congress from appreciating the agency's own assessment of its budgetary needs. As a commissioner of the FTC, Paul Rand Dixon, told a Senate committee in 1972: "There is no area more sensitive to formulation of policy than the budget of an agency. You simply cannot do what you cannot afford to do." He complained that five commissioners had their request reviewed by OMB staffers: "Here are five presidential appointees, subject to the advice and consent of the Senate, and we go down there and plead with a bunch of low-grade staff people. I have done everything except play the request on a violin."[48]

The Trade Act of 1974 provides that the estimated expenditures and proposed appropriations for the International Trade Commission shall be included in the president's budget "without revision."[49] Also, as a result of legislation passed in 1974, the requests of the Postal Service for "public service costs" (rural delivery) and "foregone revenue" (subsidies for third-class mail) have to be included in the president's budget "with his recommendation but without revision."[50] Other budgets not subject to OMB review include the legislative branch, the judiciary, the Milk Market Orders Assessment Fund, the International Trade Commission, the Federal Reserve System Board of Governors, and the budgets of a number of privately-owned, government-sponsored enterprises.[51]

Some of the banking institutions are immune from OMB control because they do not depend on appropriations. The Federal Reserve System, for example, generates income in the form of interest on securities held in its investment portfolio. The Board of Governors also levies upon the Federal Reserve banks an assessment sufficient to pay estimated expenses. These funds are not "appropriated moneys," although legislation enacted in 1978 permits the GAO to conduct limited audits of the Federal Reserve Board.[52]

A determined president backed by an electoral mandate to retrench federal programs can cut deeply into agency budgets, including those of the independent commissions. These conditions prevailed in 1981 when President Reagan submitted revisions to Carter's budget. Substantial cuts were made in the budgets of the independent regulatory commissions, particularly the CPSC and the FTC.

Reviewing Legislative Recommendations

As part of its central clearance function, the OMB reviews legislative recommendations and testimony prepared by the independent commissions, but there are exceptions to this general principle. To strengthen the hand of independent commissions, Congress enacted other exemptions. Whenever the Commodity Futures Trading Commission transmits any legislative recommendations, testimony, or comments on legislation to the president or to the OMB, it concurrently forwards copies to the House and Senate agriculture committees.[53] A similar provision in 1974 covers the SEC, the Board of Governors of the Federal Reserve System, the Federal Deposit Insurance Corporation, the Federal Home Loan Bank Board, and the National Credit Union Administration.[54] In 1976 Congress authorized the ICC to transmit to Congress legislative recommendations prepared for congressional hearings, or comments on legislation, at the same time that it sends the information to the OMB. Legislation the following year extended the same authority to the FERC. The Merit Systems Protection Board (created in 1978) submits its legislative recommendations concurrently to Congress and to the president. Whenever requested by a committee or subcommittee of Congress, the board may transmit reports, testimony, information, and views "without review, clearance, or approval by any other administrative authority."[55]

Control of Litigation

With certain exceptions, independent agencies must channel their requests for litigation through the Department of Justice when they petition the Supreme Court for review.[56] The ICC had statutory authority to appear independently when its orders were being challenged. Commissioners from other agencies have complained that the review by Justice diminishes their independence and effectiveness.[57]

Congress added another exception in 1973 when it authorized the FTC to appear in court in its own name after formally notifying the attorney general. President Nixon signed the bill reluctantly, stating that the FTC's authority "would dangerously decentralize the general control and coordination over federal litigation which has traditionally been exercised by the Department of Justice."[58] In 1974 the Department of Justice opposed legislation designed to authorize the independent commissions in any civil action, including appeals to the Supreme Court, to act in their own names and through their own attorneys.[59] Congress did not pass this legislation, but a combination of heavy caseload and an inadequate number of attorneys in the Justice Department has resulted in the delegation of litigating authority to a number of executive agencies and independent commissions.[60]

The Bush administration went to court to challenge the authority of the U.S. Postal Service and the Postal Rate Commission to litigate without first obtaining the permission of the Justice Department. After President Bush tried to use his removal and appointment powers to regain control, a federal court decided that the Postal Service was allowed to appear in court without Justice Department approval.[61] Control over litigation has also precipitated a number of collisions between the Justice Department and the FCC.[62]

Federal Reports

During World War II, as part of a campaign to reduce the burden of excessive paperwork on business enterprises, Congress passed the Federal Reports Act of 1942. The responsibility for implementing this statute fell to the Bureau of the Budget (BOB). Federal agencies, including the independent regulatory commissions, were required to seek approval from the BOB (later the OMB) before collecting information from the private sector. The commissions objected that their investigative functions were being hampered by this procedure, adversely affecting their independence and their ability to carry out statutory missions.[63]

In 1973, at the height of congressional furor over presidential and OMB arrogance, Senator Philip Hart, Democrat of Michigan, successfully offered an amendment to the trans-Alaska oil pipeline bill to exempt the independent regulatory agencies from OMB review under the Federal Reports Act. The responsibility for reviewing these agencies was transferred to the General Accounting Office, although the agencies would make the final determination as to what information they needed to carry out statutory duties.[64]

When President Nixon signed the bill, he remarked that the provision "will unfortunately eliminate present safeguards against bureaucratic harassment of business and industry by permitting endless duplication of requests by regulatory agencies." The GAO was not happy about its new assignment and three years later admitted its limited success in stemming the paperwork requirements imposed on the public by the regulatory agencies. In 1980, following the GAO's recommendation, Congress returned the responsibility for information clearance to the OMB. In a peculiar "agency veto," a majority of commissioners can vote to override the OMB's decision.[65]

Legislative Vetoes

Of all the independent commissions, none fared quite so badly in the 1970s as the Federal Trade Commission. It became a lightning rod for the frustrations, complaints, and lamentations directed at federal regulation. Some of its proposed rules—on mobile homes, the cereal industry, insurance businesses, children's television advertising, and the funeral industry—helped trigger attacks from the private sector and Congress. For several years it had to survive without an authorization by Congress, kept alive by continuing resolutions and special appropriations.

Much of the delay in authorizing the FTC resulted from a conflict within Congress. Members of the House of Representatives wanted a legislative veto over FTC rules; senators opposed this form of congressional control. The deadlock was eventually broken by the Federal Trade Commission Improvements Act of 1980. The statute required the FTC, after promulgating a final rule, to submit the rule to Congress, where it was referred to the Senate and House commerce committees. The rule became effective after ninety days unless both houses adopted a concurrent resolution of disapproval. The statute also provided for expedited treatment in the federal courts to handle challenges to the constitutionality of this procedure.[66]

The Natural Gas Policy Act of 1978 allowed Congress, by a one-house veto, to disapprove rules issued by the Federal Energy Regulatory Commission regarding the pricing of natural gas. In 1980 Congress exercised this one-house veto against the FERC's proposed rule, and two years later it exercised its two-house veto to disapprove the FTC's rule designed to regulate the used-car industry. Both congressional actions were held unconstitutional in the aftermath of *INS v. Chadha* (1983).[67]

Although Congress no longer attempts to use one-house or two-house vetoes to control agency regulations, in the years following *Chadha* it continues to use hundreds of committee vetoes to exercise directions over agency activities (pp. 99–104). Through the use of the power of the purse, it can at any time prohibit the use of appropriated funds to carry out a particular regulation. For independent commissions, such as the FTC, Congress has available a number of other tools to exercise close legislative control.[68]

More Power to the President?

For more than six decades there have been efforts to place the independent commissions under the control of the president. In 1937 the Brownlow Committee recommended that the commissions be placed within the regular executive departments, with their work divided into an administrative section and a judicial section. The chief of the administrative section would be directly responsible to the head of the department, while the judicial section would be wholly independent of the secretary and the president. The Hoover Commission, in 1949, proposed that the "purely executive functions of quasi-legislative and quasi-judicial agencies" be brought within the regular executive departments. The Ash Council in 1971 recommended that rulemaking functions of the independent commissions be placed directly under the president and their adjudicatory functions transferred to a new institution called the Administrative Court of the United States.[69] The Reagan administration made a concerted effort to fold the commissions into the executive departments.

All of these proposals recognize that certain functions of the independent commissions—judicial or adjudicatory activities—need to be isolated from direct presidential control. The prospect of organizational reform is even more complex when one realizes that the work of independent commissions does not divide so crisply between "rulemaking" and "adjudicatory." In a 1960 study, Emmette Redford doubted that the "regulatory scrambled egg can be cleanly separated into an executive-policy determining yellow and a quasi-judicial white."[70] Indeed, agencies have substantial discretion in choosing between rulemaking and adjudication.[71]

Federal judges and specialists in administrative law have not been comfortable with the dichotomy between rulemaking and adjudication. "Unhappily," Chief Judge David Bazelon has remarked, "no such bright line can be drawn between rulemaking and adjudicatory proceedings."[72] Agencies, discovering that adjudication of each case results in huge backlogs, turn increasingly to rulemaking in order to expedite their operations.[73] To further complicate matters, Congress and the courts have developed a hybrid type of administrative proceeding that combines adjudicatory safeguards with informal rulemaking.[74]

Placing independent commissions within the executive departments is neither practical nor desirable. Less drastic reforms, however, are available to subject the commissions to presidential review and direction. Beginning in 1961, after Kennedy entered the White House, all regulatory commissions were requested to send monthly reports on their activities to the president. The reports covered general policy and administrative actions, not specific decisions pending before the commissions.[75] Presidents may also submit to Congress specific proposals to monitor the activities of the regulatory agencies. Kennedy's message to Congress on April 13, 1961, is one example.[76]

Presidents have met with the heads of independent commissions to describe administration goals and seek the commissions' support. In one such meeting Lyndon Johnson summed up the curious relationship between the president and the commissions with this tantalizing sentence, suggesting that the commissions are agents carrying out presidential duties: "I want to convey my deep sense of reliance upon you and your agencies in discharging the responsibilities which have been thrust upon me."[77]

President Ford met with commissioners from the independent regulatory agencies in 1975 and urged them to scale down their activities. At a news conference a few days later he told reporters that he expected to make headway with regulatory reform: "If we don't we will change some of the commissions." However, neither Ford nor his White House staff called other conferences or proposed specific recommendations.[78]

In 1977, regarding a proposed executive order to improve government regulations, President Carter asked for public comment on the question of whether the procedures outlined in the order should apply to the independent regulatory agencies. Thirteen senators wrote to him a month later, stating their "unqualified view" that the order could not cover the independent agencies without an express statutory basis. When the final order was published, on March 24, 1978, it exempted the independent regulatory agencies.[79] Although the Justice Department had advised Carter that most of the order could bind the independent agencies, he decided that a confrontation with Congress "would only detract from the important reform steps being taken" and therefore asked the heads of the independent agencies to apply on a voluntary basis the policies and procedures of the order.[80]

Carter's executive order was revoked in 1981 by President Reagan, who issued his own order to direct the OMB to monitor the cost of agency rules. However, the order specifically excluded the following agencies: the Board of Governors of the Federal Reserve System, CAB, CFTC, CPSC, FCC, FERC, FMC, FTC, ICC, NLRB, NRC, SEC, and several other banking corporations and safety commissions.[81]

An influential study by Lloyd Cutler and David Johnson in 1975 advocated legislation authorizing the president to modify or direct certain actions by the regulatory agencies, subject to a one-house legislative veto and expedited judicial review.[82] A study commission of the American Bar Association (ABA) considered this proposal and suggested a similar approach, but without the legislative veto. The commission recommended that Congress enact a statute authorizing the president to direct certain regulatory agencies, "both within and outside the executive branch," to consider or reconsider the issuance of "critical regulations." Before the presidential order became effective, Congress would have a specified number of days to react to the order. Based on this reaction, the president could modify or withdraw the order and issue a new one. The commission preferred this approach over legislative vetoes, which it believed were constitutionally suspect and politically inefficient.[83] The commission's recommendation did not cover agency actions that were "adjudicatory" or "quasi-judicial." A majority of the commission believed that presidential orders should apply to the regulations of most independent agencies.[84]

The constitutionality of the Federal Reserve System has been challenged several times. A suit filed by Senator John Melcher in 1986 claimed that the statutory procedure governing the appointment of the five Reserve Bank members of the Federal Open Market Committee violates the Appointments Clause of the Constitution because they are not appointed by the president with the advice and consent of the Senate. The five members are chosen by the boards of directors of the several Federal Reserve banks and are private individuals. A federal district court upheld the appointment process by noting that Congress, since 1791, had decided that monetary policy should be administered by a mix of public and private interests.[85] A federal court agreed.[86] The Federal Reserve has survived other legal challenges.[87]

The concept of a "fourth branch" was the subject of repeated attacks by members of the Reagan administration. In a speech in 1985, Attorney General Edwin Meese III interpreted *INS v. Chadha* as an "important breakthrough" in clarifying the boundaries between Congress and the executive. In the interest of accountability, he said it "should be up to the President to enforce the law, and to be directly answerable to the electorate for his success or failure in carrying out this responsibility." In a tripartite government, power delegated by Congress "should be properly understood as power granted to the Executive." He concluded that "we should abandon the idea that there are such things as 'quasi-legislative' or 'quasi-judicial' functions that can be properly delegated to independent agencies or bodies."[88]

Litigation on the Gramm-Rudman-Hollings Act raised additional questions about the constitutionality of independent commissions.

On February 7, 1986, a three-judge federal court held the statute unconstitutional because it vested executive power in the comptroller general, who is removable by Congress (p. 238). The issue was disposed of on that ground, but the court nevertheless indulged in some dicta about the commissions. The court, no doubt with the guiding hand of Judge Antonin Scalia (now a Supreme Court justice), claimed that Justice Sutherland's decision in *Humphrey's Executor* (1935):

> is stamped with some of the political science preconceptions characteristic of its era and not of the present day—if not stamped as well, as President Roosevelt thought, with hostility towards the architect of the New Deal. It is not as obvious today as it seemed in the 1930s that there can be such things as genuinely "independent" regulatory agencies, bodies of impartial experts whose independence from the President does not entail correspondingly greater dependence upon the committees of Congress to which they are then immediately accountable; or, indeed, that the decisions of such agencies so clearly involve scientific judgment rather than political choice that it is even theoretically desirable to insulate them from the democratic process.[89]

Of course, the independent commissions did not originate in the 1930s, or with the New Deal, even if some writers enjoy making that connection. Perhaps the purpose is guilt by association. If an idea had its birth with the New Deal, apparently that is prima facie evidence to forever blacken its reputation and destroy its credibility.

The preoccupation with *Humphrey's Executor* is misguided. Defenders of presidential power usually harken back to Chief Justice Taft's decision in *Myers v. United States* (1926),[90] which made sweeping assertions that the president needed full removal powers to maintain responsibility over the actions of subordinates. But Taft recognized that Congress could insulate some executive officers from presidential control. Although the president should be able to remove officers who are negligent and inefficient, "there may be duties so peculiarly and specifically committed to the discretion of a particular officer as to raise a question whether the President may overrule or revise the officer's interpretation of his statutory duty in a particular instance." Taft was *not* referring to quasi-judicial officers, like the comptroller.

He was talking about officers who carry out executive duties. In the very next sentence he stated: "Then there may be duties of a quasi-judicial character imposed on executive officers and members of executive tribunals whose decisions after hearing affect interests of individuals, the discharge of which the President cannot in a particular case properly influence or control."[91] Taft was familiar with the variety of administrative and adjudicatory functions that Congress had assigned to executive officers who operated free of presidential interference.

In its brief in the Gramm-Rudman case, the Justice Department attacked the status of the independent commissions. The brief argued that the commissions are inconsistent with the framers' deliberate choice of "a unitary Executive in order to promote a sense of personal responsibility and accountability to the people in the execution of the laws—and thereby to ensure vigorous administration of the laws and protection of the liberty, property, and welfare of the people."[92]

There is much truth in this, but the framers were not ideologues or single-minded zealots about executive responsibility. It was not the only value of administration they espoused. From the creation of an independent comptroller in 1789 to the establishment of legislative courts within executive departments, hierarchical values were regularly violated. The president was not made responsible for every action that occurred within the administration.[93]

When the Gramm-Rudman case was argued before the Supreme Court, attorneys defending the statute warned the Justices that the Reagan administration wanted to invalidate all the independent regulatory agencies. Solicitor General Charles Fried dismissed these contentions as just "scare tactics." The courtroom filled with laughter when Justice Sandra Day O'Connor replied: "Well, Mr. Fried, I'll confess you scared me with it."[94]

Chief Justice Burger assigned himself the task of writing the majority opinion in the Gramm-Rudman case. He was advised by other Justices not to cast any doubt about the constitutionality of the independent commissions, and yet his first draft did precisely that, prompting the Justices to insist that the final opinion steer clear of posing any challenge to *Humphrey's Executor*.[95] When the Court handed down its decision in *Bowsher v. Synar*, it specifically stated in a footnote that it did not intend to unravel the tangled skein of the independent commissions. In affirming the three-judge court ruling, it denied that its action "requires casting doubt on the status of 'independent' agencies because no issues involving such agencies are presented here."[96] The concurrence by Justice John Paul Stevens, in which Justice Thurgood Marshall joined, said that it was "well settled" that Congress may delegate legislative power to independent agencies. In his dissent, Justice Byron White criticized the majority's "distressingly formalistic" view of separation of powers and concluded that Congress could vest a broad range of executive functions to officers who "are free from the partisanship that may be expected of agencies wholly dependent upon the President." Justice Harry Blackmun's dissent interpreted *Humphrey's Executor* to allow executive powers to be carried out by officers who do not serve "at the President's pleasure."

On the same day that the Court decided the Gramm-Rudman case, which broadcast such a doctrinaire view of separated powers, it offered a much more pragmatic ruling in a case involving the Commodity Futures Trading Commission. The issue was whether the agency's adjudication of counterclaims violated the judicial powers vested in Article III of the Constitution. A typical dispute involved a customer bringing a claim against a broker, charging that a debit in the customer's account resulted from the broker's violations of the Commodity Exchange Act. The broker would then file a counterclaim, charging that the debit resulted from the customer's lack of success in the market.

With a 7-2 majority, the Court upheld the commission and refused to adopt "formalistic and unbending rules" to decide the separation of powers issue. Such rules might "unduly constrict Congress' ability to take needed and innovative action pursuant to its Article I powers." The Court avoided a doctrinaire insistence that every adjudicatory function be discharged by an Article III court. A number of factors were weighed "with an eye to the practical effect that the congressional action will have on the constitutionally assigned role of the federal judiciary."[97]

Theodore B. Olson, former head of the Office of Legal Counsel in the Reagan administration, filed a suit that challenged the constitutionality of the FTC. The suit argued that the commission's enforcement functions must be carried out by officers who are subject to the supervisory control of the president and who serve at the president's pleasure.[98] The merits of the case were not addressed because of procedural questions of jurisdiction and ripeness.[99] In a subsequent case, a federal appellate court upheld the Securities and Exchange Commission against a challenge that its exercise of civil enforcement actions violated separation of powers. The litigants argued that the president is given sole and exclusive control over the execution of the laws. That thesis was firmly rejected by the court:

> It is a matter of fundamental law that the Constitution assigns to Congress the power to designate duties of particular officers. The President is not obligated under the Constitution to exercise absolute control over our government executives. The President is not required to execute the laws; he is required to take care they be executed faithfully.[100]

This decision relied on the Supreme Court's ruling in *Morrison v. Olson* (1988), which upheld the independent counsel.[101] The status of independent commissions was further strengthened when the Court a year later sustained another independent body, the U.S. Sentencing Commission.[102]

Conclusions

Are independent commissions and independent officers such an anomaly? Are they mere aberrations that violate the framers' decision to create a unitary executive, which they hoped would secure accountability by making all executive functions subject to the supervision and control of the president? Beginning with the First Congress, this principle of presidential accountability was tempered by statutes that placed certain administrative decisions outside the reach of the president. Congress refused to concentrate all executive powers in the president.

Delegating additional powers to the president will not necessarily yield greater expertise and coordination of regulatory policy, nor will it assure freedom from the "special interests" that supposedly dominate Congress. Organized groups from the private sector are not fastidious about their source of assistance. They influence whatever branch of government, including executive, is in a position to help. Most powers transferred to the president will slide past the chief executive and be exercised by various assistants of uncertain experience, skill, and judgment. An observation by Judge Henry J. Friendly offered in 1962 is still on target:

> ... it is indulging in fantasy to speak of "the President" as formulating policy pronouncements for the agencies himself. The spectacle of a chief executive, burdened to the limit of endurance with decisions on which the very existence of mankind may depend, personally taking on the added task of determining to what extent newspapers should be allowed to own television stations or whether railroads should be allowed to reduce rates only to or somewhat below the truck level, is pure mirage.[103]

Writing in 1979, however, Judge Friendly supported the ABA commission's recommendation for closer presidential control over regulatory activities, including those in the independent agencies. ABA's proposed grant of power to the president seemed to Friendly narrow in scope and highly structured. If abused, Congress could withdraw the authority.[104]

There is considerable doubt about how the process would work. The initial task of identifying issues and bringing them to the attention of the president must fall to the White House staff. These staff members have no unique claim to be operating in the "national interest." Like the executive agencies and independent commissions, these staffers too have a special interest: protecting the president. As has been demonstrated more than once in recent decades, the political interests of the president are not necessarily synonymous with the national interest. Those who have contributed financially to the president or to the president's party will have greater access to the White House staff, and will be able at that point to specify the regulations they want overturned or modified. Requirements can be established for a public record of these ex parte contacts, but the special status of White House staff does not allow Congress or the courts the same degree of review they can exercise over executive agencies or independent commissions.

American administrative and constitutional history does not support the idea of making the president responsible—in both a political and a legal sense—for all agency actions. The Constitution does not call for, let alone require, a monolithic executive branch. Congress has a legitimate interest in seeking administrative arrangements that provide continuity and expertise from one administration to the next. It has the authority to devise structural checks and procedural safeguards for agencies that discharge a combination of executive, legislative, and judicial duties.

CHAPTER 6

◆

War Powers
and Foreign Affairs

During the twentieth century, advocates of presidential power have argued strongly for executive independence in matters occurring outside the U.S. borders. With great force they claim that the Constitution assigns questions of foreign affairs, the use of military force, and diplomacy primarily (if not exclusively) to the chief executive. However, the Constitution does *not* allocate foreign policy to a single branch. It assigns portions to Congress, to the president, and to the president working jointly with the Senate. The framers deliberately dispersed political functions, including foreign affairs, to avoid concentrating too much power in a single branch.

Critics object that this parceling of authority, while perhaps appropriate for the eighteenth century, makes it impossible to achieve coherence or consistency in foreign policy. However, it could be argued equally well that coherence and consistency are impossible when presidents act rashly, with single-handed ventures, and are forced back into line by public pressures and legislative restrictions. Over the long run, coherence and consistency are more likely when the two branches act jointly to produce foreign policy.

The Constitution gives Congress the power to declare war but makes the president the commander in chief; in this way the war power is divided. Although the president commands the armed forces, the Constitution empowers Congress to raise and support armies, provide and maintain a navy, and make regulations for the military forces. The power of the purse is vested solely in Congress. The Constitution gives Congress the power to regulate foreign commerce. Recalling the political climate in 1787 and the fear that commercial conflicts among nations could precipitate war, this grant of power makes Congress a major participant in foreign policy.

The president is empowered to make treaties and appoint ambassadors, with both powers subject to the advice and consent of the Senate. Because treaties generally require appropriations before they can be implemented, the House of Representatives helps determine the scope of treaty commitments. This allocation of power over foreign policy puts a heavy premium on consultation, coordination, and cooperation by the two branches.

Foreign and Domestic Affairs

In a landmark decision in 1936, Justice Sutherland claimed that foreign and domestic affairs were different "both in respect of their origin and their nature."[1] His decision in *United States v. Curtiss-Wright* elaborated on "this vast external realm" of international affairs, "with its important, complicated, delicate and manifold problems." According to his reasoning, legislation over this domain must accord to the president "a degree of discretion and freedom from statutory restriction which would not be admissible were domestic affairs alone involved."[2]

The issue in *Curtiss-Wright* should have been a narrow one: Had Congress delegated too broadly in authorizing the president to prohibit the shipment of arms or munitions to any country in South America if he determined that the materials would promote domestic violence? The power was clearly *legislative*, not executive. Could Congress delegate *its* power to the president? The Court needed only to decide that legislation in foreign affairs may give the president greater discretion than would be permissible for domestic legislation. Instead, Sutherland went far beyond the issue of delegation, adding pages of obiter dicta (comments extraneous to the issue before the Court) that assigned to the president a number of powers not found in the Constitution.

Sutherland borrowed heavily from his own private writings and personal views advanced during his earlier career with the U.S. Senate. According to his biographer, Sutherland advocated a "vigorous diplomacy which strongly, even belligerently, called always for an assertion of American rights."[3] As Justice Jackson later observed, the most that can be drawn from *Curtiss-Wright* is the intimation "that the President might act in external affairs without congressional authority, but not that he might act contrary to an Act of Congress."[4] Jackson noted that "much of the [Sutherland] opinion is dictum."[5] In 1981, a federal appellate court cautioned against placing undue reliance on "certain dicta" in Sutherland's opinion: "To the extent that denominating the President as the 'sole organ' of the United States in international affairs constitutes a blanket endorsement of plenary Presidential power over any matter extending beyond the borders of this country, we reject that characterization."[6]

The "sole organ" concept comes from Sutherland's use of a statement made by John Marshall in 1800 during Marshall's service in the House of Representatives: "The President is the sole organ of the nation in its external relations, and its sole representative with foreign nations."[7] The manner in which Sutherland used this quote implied that Marshall promoted an exclusive, independent power for the president in foreign affairs. When the 1800 House debate is read in full, however, it is evident that Marshall merely argued that the president carries out national policy *after* it has been established by statute or by treaty. The two branches work in concert. Marshall never claimed that the president made foreign policy single-handedly.

Marshall uttered his remarks during a House debate regarding President John Adams's decision to turn over to England a person charged with murder. Because the case was already pending in court, some members of Congress recommended that Adams be impeached for encroaching upon the judiciary. Marshall defended Adams by pointing out that the president was carrying out a treaty with England. The "sole organ" remark appears in a passage emphasizing that foreign policy is exercised jointly by Congress and the president:

> The case was in its nature a national demand made upon the nation. The parties were the two nations. They cannot come into court to litigate their claims, nor can a court decide on them. Of consequence, the demand is not a case for judicial cognizance.

The President is the sole organ of the nation in its external relations, and its sole representative with foreign nations. Of consequence, the demand of a foreign nation can only be made on him.

He possesses the whole Executive power. He holds and directs the force of the nation. Of consequence, any act to be performed by the force of the nation is to be performed through him.

He is charged to execute the laws. A treaty is declared to he law. He must then execute a treaty, where he, and he alone, possesses the means of executing it.[8]

Marshall clearly understood that foreign policy is made jointly by the president and the Senate (for treaties) or by the president and Congress (for statutes). Only after the two branches establish national policy does the president operate as the "sole organ" in implementing national policy.

Sutherland insisted that foreign and domestic affairs were different "both in respect of their origin and their nature." He claimed that the states "severally never possessed international powers" and that, upon separation from England in 1776, "the powers of external sovereignty passed from the Crown not to the colonies severally, but to the colonies in their collective and corporate capacity as the United States of America."[9] By transferring external or foreign affairs directly to the national government and then linking foreign affairs to the executive, Sutherland supplied a powerful but deceptive argument for presidential power.

Sutherland's history is inaccurate, however. External sovereignty did not circumvent the colonies and the states and pass directly to an independent executive. In 1776, no president or separate executive branch existed. Only one branch of government functioned at the national level: the Continental Congress. It discharged all governmental duties, including legislative, executive, and judicial. Furthermore, from 1774 to 1788 the colonies (or states) operated as sovereign entities, not as parts of a collective body known as the United States of America. The American states acted freely and independently of one another. Following the break with England, they exercised the sovereign power to make treaties, borrow money, solicit arms, lay embargoes, collect tariff duties, and conduct separate military campaigns.[10]

In other cases, the Supreme Court has acknowledged that the states retained sovereign power immediately after independence from England.[11] Even if the power of external sovereignty had somehow passed intact from the Crown to a unified United States, the simple fact is that the Constitution allocates the power of foreign affairs to both Congress and the president.

Curtiss-Wright retains a secure foothold in Supreme Court rulings, especially those involving the delegation of legislative power to the executive branch. Chief Justice Rehnquist, although generally an opponent of broad delegations, is more sympathetic when the delegation concerns external affairs. He believes that Congress need not include specific guidelines when delegating for international crises, "the nature of which Congress can hardly have been expected to anticipate in any detail."[12] In the same way, when a statute governs military affairs, Rehnquist has stated that Congress "is permitted to legislate both with greater breadth and with greater flexibility."[13] In other cases, the Court cites *Curtiss-Wright* to justify broad delegations of legislative power to the president for international policy and even to justify the existence of independent, implied, and inherent powers for the president.[14]

Sutherland's distinction between external and internal affairs survives to some extent in the contemporary theory of "two presidencies," which analyzes executive power as applied to domestic and foreign affairs. In an influential study published in 1966, Aaron Wildavsky concluded that presidents are more likely to prevail in policy struggles against Congress when the issue involves foreign affairs. Looking at the period from 1948 to 1964, he wrote that presidents since World War II had "much greater success in controlling the nation's defense and foreign policies than in dominating its domestic policies."[15]

Eight years after Wildavsky's publication, Donald Peppers discovered a different state of affairs. The years of Johnson and Nixon had narrowed the gap between presidential power in the domestic and foreign sectors. For Wildavsky, presidential power in foreign policy derived from the immediacy of the Cold War. By 1974, many of the Cold War tensions had subsided and Congress was in the process of reasserting itself by passing such statutes as the War Powers Resolution of 1973.[16] Court decisions and other legislative actions regarding executive agreements, freedom of information, the U.S. intelligence community, and electronic surveillance placed new limits on the president.[17]

This period highlighted the close interaction between domestic and foreign affairs. The American public learned that as the dollar declines abroad, prices rise at home. With stunning speed the Arab oil embargo of 1973 to 1974 doubled the price of gasoline and created long lines at the neighborhood service stations. Grain sales to Russia produced prosperity for American farmers. After the Carter administration's embargo on those sales created hard times for grain companies, grain elevators, and farmers, it was abandoned by President Reagan in 1981. Scholars (with some apologies) coined the word "intermestic" to describe events that represent a blend of international and domestic.[18]

When it suits their purposes, executive officials will concede that it is artificial to distinguish between external and internal affairs. For example, officials in the Nixon administration wanted full freedom to wiretap both foreign agents and domestic organizations. The government insisted that foreign and domestic affairs are "inextricably intertwined and that any attempt to legally distinguish the impact of foreign affairs from the matters of internal subversive activities is an exercise in futility."[19] In 1991, President Bush encountered strong opposition for his travels abroad. He was seen as being more interested in international problems than domestic problems, more interested in the Soviet Union than in southern California. He answered that efforts to promote trade agreements with other nations would benefit U.S. exports: "I guess my bottom line . . . is you can't separate foreign policy from domestic."[20] President Clinton offered this comment in 1993: "There is no longer a clear division between what is foreign and what is domestic."[21]

The Treaty-Making Power

According to the standard annotated version of the Constitution, the process of drafting and negotiating a treaty is a "presidential monopoly."[22] Edward S. Corwin, in his classic study on the presidency, promoted the same theory. Corwin said the president "alone has the power to negotiate treaties with foreign governments."[23] With that sentiment he followed the well-known position of Justice Sutherland, who claimed that the president alone negotiates: "Into the field of negotiation the Senate cannot intrude; and Congress itself is powerless to invade it."[24]

This strict reading of the negotiation process ignores the constitutional text, the intention of the framers, and practical politics. The Constitution does not confer upon the president an exclusive role in negotiations. The president "shall have Power, by and with the Advice and Consent of the Senate, to make Treaties." That language differs markedly from the constitutional process for making appointments, in which the president "shall nominate, and by and with the Advice and Consent of the Senate, shall appoint Ambassadors." The duty to make nominations is clearly set apart and reserved for the president, followed by Senate action. No such two-step division of labor (negotiation by the president and ratification by the Senate) exists for treaties.

George Washington believed that the Constitution intended joint executive-legislative action on treaties. He advised the Senate that oral communications with the Senate regarding treaties "seem indispensably necessary; because in these a variety of matters are contained, all of which not only require consideration, but some of them may undergo much discussion; to do which by written communications would be tedious without being satisfactory."[25] It was his intention to send treaty "propositions" to the Senate, clearly implying that senators could make changes and offer recommendations to treaty drafts rather than simply saying "yes" or "no" to the finished product.[26]

Washington's meeting with the Senate in August 1789, concerning an Indian treaty, is often misinterpreted. Senator William Maclay of Pennsylvania kept detailed notes on President Washington's frustration in trying to negotiate face-to-face with senators.[27] Although Washington never again resorted to personal consultation with the Senate on treaties, he continued to seek the advice of senators through *written* communications. Over the years, senators have been asked to approve the appointment of treaty negotiators and even to advise on their negotiating instructions.[28]

The negotiation of treaties is frequently shared with the Senate to secure legislative understanding and support.[29] Of the eight members of the U.S. delegation who attended the conference at San Francisco to hammer out the details of the United Nations Charter, four were members of Congress: Senators Tom Connally (Democrat of Texas) and Arthur H. Vandenberg (Republican of Michigan) and Representatives Sol Bloom (Democrat of New York) and Charles A. Eaton (Republican of New Jersey). After World War II, Senators Connally and Vandenberg participated in more than two hundred meetings with Secretary of State James F. Byrnes in the negotiations that resulted in the peace treaties with Italy and the satellite states in 1947.[30] During hearings in 1971, former Secretary of State Dean Acheson said that while it was possible to divide the treaty process into negotiation by the president and approval by the Senate, "anybody with any sense would consult with certainly some of the members of the ratifying body before he got himself out on the very end of a limb from which he could be sawed off." He recalled that during the negotiations of the North Atlantic Treaty in 1949, Senators Connally and Vandenberg "were with me all the time," while Senator Walter George actually wrote one of the provisions of the treaty.[31]

Members of both houses of Congress are now formal participants in a multitude of international boards and commissions. They attend international conferences and serve as delegates to the North Atlantic Assembly, the Interparliamentary Union, and other interparliamentary groups. They are also appointed as U.S. representatives to the U.N. General Assembly. During 1977 and 1978, twenty-six senators went to Geneva as official advisers to the SALT II negotiating team to help produce an arms-control agreement.[32]

A president, like Woodrow Wilson, may exclude the Senate from the negotiation stage, but the results can be calamitous. The failure of the Senate to ratify the Treaty of Versailles is the most conspicuous casualty of a presidential determination to negotiate unilaterally.[33] A healthier model of executive-legislative collaboration is the North Atlantic Treaty, developed by the State Department in close cooperation with the Senate Foreign Relations Committee.

Contemporary trade legislation gives Congress a direct role in the negotiation process. In recent decades, it has been the practice of Congress to offer the president a "fast-track" legislative procedure for implementing trade agreements with other nations. After negotiations are over, the president drafts an implementing bill and it is automatically introduced in Congress. Committees must act on the bill within a specific number of days, Congress must complete action within a limited time, and amendments to the president's bill are prohibited either in committee or on the floor. Leaders of foreign governments are thus assured that Congress will act expeditiously on the trade pact.

In return for this expedited procedure, the president assures members of Congress that they will be closely involved in the negotiations that produce the implementing bill. The president knows that Congress cannot be expected to pass a bill within a fixed time period unless it knows ahead of time what is in the bill and how it got there. After President Bush asked Congress in 1991 to extend the fast track for a trade pact with Mexico, U.S. Trade Representative Carla A. Hills told the Senate Finance Committee that the fast track "is a genuine partnership between the two branches." Because Congress retains the power to defeat the implementing bill, Hills emphasized that Congress "has a full role throughout the entire process in formulating the negotiating objectives in close consultation as the negotiations proceed."[34] President Bush gave Congress his "personal commitment to close bipartisan cooperation in the negotiations and beyond."[35]

Role of the House of Representatives

Although the president and the Senate have the exclusive power to make treaties, their need for funds to implement treaties opens the door to participation by the House of Representatives. Throughout history the House has asserted its prerogatives whenever international agreements affect either the power of the purse or the responsibilities of the House over foreign commerce and tariffs. As early as 1796, when President Washington notified the House of Representatives that the Jay Treaty had been ratified, the House debated at length its constitutional role in the implementation of treaties. Congressman Edward Livingston insisted that the House possessed "a discretionary power of carrying the Treaty into effect, or refusing it their sanction."[36] Congressman Albert Gallatin argued that certain powers delegated specifically to Congress by the Constitution, including the authority to regulate trade, might clash with the treaty-making powers. In such cases the House did not have to accept the policies agreed to by the president and the Senate through the treaty process.[37] The House later adopted a 54-to-37 resolution stating that it did not claim any agency in making treaties,

• • •

but that when a Treaty stipulates regulations of any of the subjects submitted by the Constitution to the power of Congress, it must depend, for its execution, as to such stipulations, on a law or laws to be passed by Congress. And it is the Constitutional right and duty of the House of Representatives, in all such cases, to deliberate on the expediency or inexpediency of carrying such Treaty into effect, and to determine and act thereon, as, in their judgment, may be most conducive to the public good.[38]

On several occasions the House has withdrawn its support from treaties that required appropriations to be implemented. Two examples are the Gadsden purchase treaty with Mexico in 1853 and the Alaskan purchase treaty with Russia in 1867. The need to have the support of both houses for certain treaties was acknowledged in a reciprocity treaty with the Hawaiian Islands in 1876. A proviso made the treaty dependent on the consent of both houses.[39]

In 1880, the House declared that the negotiation of a commercial treaty, fixing the rates of duty to be imposed on foreign imports, would be "an infraction of the Constitution and an invasion of one of the highest prerogatives of the House of Representatives."[40] To protect House prerogatives over matters of foreign commerce and tariffs, Congress uses the regular statutory process—not the treaty process— to delegate to the president authority to enter into reciprocal trade agreements with other nations.[41]

When the president is unable to secure a two-thirds majority in the Senate to ratify a treaty, he may turn to both houses of Congress and accomplish the same result by statute or joint resolution, which requires only a majority in each house. After the Senate failed to ratify a treaty for the annexation of Texas, President John Tyler advised the House of Representatives: "The power of Congress is, however, fully competent in some other form of proceeding to accomplish everything that a formal ratification of the treaty could have accomplished. . . . [42] Texas joined the Union after simple majority votes from both houses.[43] Hawaii was annexed in 1898 by joint resolution after the Senate opposed the treaty of annexation. The St. Lawrence Seaway plan between the United States and Canada passed Congress in 1954 as a regular bill after being rejected in treaty form by the Senate in 1934.[44]

The House of Representatives continues to exercise its prerogatives over matters that conceivably might be handled by treaty. The Spanish Bases Treaty of 1976 ran into a number of problems, initially limited to conflicts between the Senate and the president. The Ford administration maintained that a treaty represented an authorization to have funds appropriated, thus bypassing the jurisdictional interests of the Senate Committee on Foreign Relations and the House Committee on Foreign Affairs. In response to these disputes, the Senate Resolution of Advice and Consent contained a declaration that the sums referred to in the Spanish treaty "shall be made available for obligation through the normal procedures of the Congress, including the process of prior authorization and annual appropriations." Not only both houses would be involved, but the authorizing and appropriating committees within each house would also. Congress enacted legislation in 1976 to authorize the appropriation of funds needed to implement the treaty.[45]

Although the Spanish Bases Treaty was replaced by an executive agreement in 1982, Congress must still act through the regular legislative process before Spain receives any assistance. The agreement stipulates that the supply of defense articles and services are subject to "the annual authorizations and appropriations contained in United States security assistance legislation. . . ."[46] The actual level of assistance depends entirely on congressional action.

Treaty Termination and Reinterpretation

The Constitution describes the process for making a treaty, but says nothing about how to terminate a treaty. Over the years, treaties have been terminated by statute, by Senate resolutions, by new treaties, and by presidential action without prior congressional authorization.[47] The constitutional issue ripened in 1978 when President Carter announced his intention to terminate a defense treaty with Taiwan. Under the terms of the treaty, termination would become effective a year later.

The Senate debated the issue at length, including several proposals to require Senate approval or the approval of both houses of Congress before terminating a defense treaty. However, none of those recommendations reached a final vote.[48] The failure to complete action on measures to challenge Carter's authority proved fatal to congressional interests. A federal appellate court rejected a suit by Senator Barry Goldwater, Republican of Arizona, who claimed that President Carter had acted unconstitutionally. The court pointed out that Congress possessed powerful legislative tools to protect its interests but "simply did not take those measures" and therefore failed "to confront the President directly on the treaty termination."[49]

A similar response came from the Supreme Court, although it splintered in many directions as justices wrote a variety of concurring and dissenting opinions. Justice Powell concluded that Goldwater's suit should be dismissed because it was not ripe for judicial consideration, pointing out that the judiciary should not decide executive-legislative conflicts until the two branches reached an impasse. Powell remarked that if Congress "chooses not to confront the President, it is not our task to do so."[50] Rehnquist, joined by Burger, Stewart, and Stevens, regarded the dispute as a nonjusticiable political question that should never be considered by the courts. Brennan, rejecting that conclusion, would have accepted the president's authority to terminate treaties as an incident of his power to recognize foreign governments.

The medley of opinions in this case makes it impossible to predict how the Court will rule again on this issue, but future disputes probably depend on the willingness of Congress to use the legislative tools at its disposal. Senator Goldwater and other members of Congress have introduced legislation to define the process for terminating defense treaties, but Congress has yet to act on these proposals.

Another area of controversy concerns the manner in which presidents may interpret and reinterpret a treaty. Treaty interpretation is normally an executive function, although federal courts also interpret treaties and may reach conclusions that reject executive interpretations.[51] Without a check from Congress or the courts, presidents could "reinterpret" a treaty and arrive at a meaning contrary to what the Senate understood when it granted approval.

That was the issue during the Reagan administration. In 1983, President Reagan advocated a sophisticated anti-missile defense shield consisting of satellites armed with laser weapons. His proposal, called the Strategic Defense Initiative (SDI), was dubbed "Star Wars" by the press. Members of Congress became concerned that deployment or even testing of the SDI would violate the Antiballistic Missile (ABM) Treaty of 1972 with the Soviet Union. A traditional or restrictive interpretation of that treaty permitted only research and development on SDI. Officials within the Reagan administration believed in a broader interpretation that would allow testing and deployment.[52] The conflict became more acrimonious when advocates of the broader interpretation claimed that it was justified by the treaty negotiation record that was classified and not shared with the Senate.

After a full-scale confrontation between the branches, President Reagan limited SDI to research and development and shared with the Senate the administration's study of the negotiation record.[53] Senators objected when executive officials regarded their own representations to the Senate on the meaning of a treaty as not binding. Senator Arlen Specter, Republican of Pennsylvania, asked: "Can we function in a system where the Senate cannot rely on representations made by executive officers?"[54]

Congress retained the power of the purse to restrict the broader interpretation. For example, in 1987 legislation stated that the secretary of defense "may not deploy any anti-ballistic missile system unless such deployment is specifically authorized by law after the date of the enactment of this Act."[55] However, the Senate also wanted to establish the principle that executive officials are accountable for their representations of the meaning of a treaty. Secretary of State George Shultz acknowledged that the testimony of all executive branch witnesses and any submissions for the hearing record by the executive branch can be regarded by the Senate as authoritative.[56] White House Counsel Arthur B. Culverhouse, Jr., wrote to the Senate, stating that the president, as a matter of domestic law, is required "to adhere to the interpretation of a treaty authoritatively shared with, and clearly intended, generally understood and relied upon by the Senate at the time of its advice and consent to ratification."[57] Those clarifications helped, but Culverhouse's language contained potential loopholes that executive officials could exploit.

In 1988, as an amendment to the Intermediate-Range Nuclear Forces (INF) Treaty, the Senate stated that treaties shall be interpreted "in accordance with the common understanding of the Treaty shared by the President and the Senate at the time the Senate gave its advice and consent to ratification."[58] The term "common understanding" was defined to include the text of the treaty, the provisions of the resolution of ratification, and the authoritative representations provided by the president and his representatives to the Senate. Any interpretation that differed with the common understanding would require joint action by Congress and the president either by treaty or by statute. The amendment to the INF Treaty passed 72 to 27.[59]

President Reagan sent a letter to the Senate expressing some concern about the amendment. He acknowledged that in accordance with U.S. law the president "must respect the mutual understanding reached with the Senate during the advice and consent process," but added that executive statements "should be given binding weight only when they were authoritatively communicated to the Senate by the Executive and were part of the basis on which the Senate granted its advice and consent to ratification." Nevertheless, Reagan did agree that the administration "does not take the position that the Executive branch can disregard authoritative Executive statements to the Senate."[60]

Executive Agreements

Presidents also enter into "executive agreements" with foreign nations. Executive agreements are not submitted to Congress or the Senate for approval, but they are generally entered into on the basis of congressional authority. For example, in 1792 Congress passed legislation to authorize the postmaster general to make arrangements with foreign postmasters for the receipt and delivery of letters and packets.[61] Although such agreements lack what the Supreme Court calls the "dignity" of a treaty, they are considered to be valid international compacts.[62] Treaties, too, are a source of authority for executive agreements. To implement treaties, executive officials must enter into agreements with other nations.

More disturbing to Congress are international agreements entered into without any statutory or treaty authority ("sole executive agreements"). These agreements have been upheld by the Supreme Court when the president operates on an implied constitutional power, such as the power to recognize foreign governments.[63] The State Department concedes, however, that an executive agreement cannot be "inconsistent with legislation enacted by Congress in the exercise of its constitutional authority."[64] If an executive agreement contravenes an existing statute in a field delegated to Congress, such as foreign commerce, it can be struck down by the courts.[65] Executive agreements may not violate rights secured by the Constitution, such as just compensation under the Fifth Amendment and the right to trial by jury.[66]

As a result of hearings by the Senate Foreign Relations Committee in 1969 and 1970, Congress discovered that the Johnson administration had entered into a number of secret executive agreements that promised U.S. funds to foreign countries willing to give token support to the Vietnam War. Congress responded in 1972 by passing legislation to require the secretary of state to transmit to Congress within sixty days the text of "any international agreement, other than a treaty," to which the United States is a party. Congress later learned that some agreements had been reported after the sixty-day period or not at all. The problem stemmed largely from late reports from agencies to the Department of State. Legislation passed in 1977 now requires departments and agencies to transmit to the Department of State the text of any international agreement not later than twenty days after its signing.[67]

There are still ways for an administration to circumvent Congress. One is called "parallel policy statements." On September 23, 1977, ten days before expiration of the SALT I arms-control agreement, the United States and the Soviet Union issued statements that they would adhere to SALT I ceilings. Since the statements were issued separately and unilaterally, the State Department argued that they did not constitute an "agreement" and therefore required no report to Congress.[68] In 1994, President Clinton entered into an agreement with North Korea to assist in the replacement of graphite-moderated reactors with light-water reactor power plants. The goal was to prevent North Korea from developing nuclear weapons. By regarding the agreement as a "political agreement" that was nonbinding, the administration argued that there was no need to report the agreement to Congress under the Case Act. The agreement was considered to be a political and moral—not legal—commitment.[69]

The War Power

The war power, originally grounded in Congress as the representative branch, has in recent times gravitated more and more to the executive branch. As commander in chief, the president always had the potential for putting troops in harm's way and provoking military action. But it is only in the last half-century, beginning with President Truman's unilateral action in introducing American troops into Korea, that presidential power has expanded to such an extent that it threatens the original allocation of power designed by the framers.

At the time that America declared its independence from England in 1776, the leading theorists of government placed the power of foreign affairs and war solely with the executive. Even after a civil war in the 1640s that gave the English Parliament the power of the purse to restrain the king, the prerogatives to make treaties, appoint ambassadors, go to war, and engage in other foreign pursuits remained with the executive.

John Locke's *Second Treatise of Government* (1690) separated government into basic powers: legislative, executive, and federative. The latter consisted of "the power of war and peace, leagues and alliances, and all the transactions with all persons and communities without the commonwealth." For Locke the federative power was "almost always united" with the executive.[70] He warned that placing the executive and federative powers in separate hands would invite "disorder and ruin."[71] Sir William Blackstone, the eighteenth-century English jurist whose writings greatly influenced the American framers, placed foreign policy squarely with the executive. The king had the absolute right to send and receive ambassadors, make treaties and alliances, make war or peace, coin money, issue letters of marque and reprisal, command the military, raise and regulate fleets and armies, and represent the nation in its dealings with foreign nations.[72]

The framers rejected this model of government. The national government that existed immediately after the Declaration of Independence had no executive at all. It consisted of a single branch: the Continental Congress. Later, when the framers met at Philadelphia to draft a new constitution, they transferred many of Locke's federative powers and Blackstone's royal prerogatives either to Congress exclusively or allocated them on a shared basis to Congress and the president. The repudiation of the British model was made clear by all. Alexander Hamilton explained in *Federalist* 69 that the president had "concurrent power with a branch of the legislature in the formation of treaties," whereas the British king is "the *sole possessor* of the power of making treaties."[73] Hamilton also explained why the

American president was less threatening to individual liberties than the king of England. Among other differences, he pointed out that the power of the king "extends to the *declaring* of war and to the *raising* and *regulating* of fleets and armies."[74] The Constitution vests those powers in Congress alone. The Constitution specifies a number of other important foreign powers for Congress: the power to "lay and collect" duties and imposts, to provide for the common defense, to declare war, to make rules concerning captures on land and water, to grant letters of marque and reprisal (authorizing private agents to engage in military expeditions), to raise and support armies and to provide and maintain a navy, to make regulations for the land and naval forces, to provide for the calling forth of the militia, and to provide for organizing, arming, and disciplining the militia.

The congressional power to "declare" war reflects a change in language at the Philadelphia convention. The initial draft empowered Congress to "make" war. Charles Pinckney objected that legislative proceedings might be "too slow" for the safety of the country in an emergency. He assumed that Congress would be a part-time body, meeting but once a year. Madison and Elbridge Gerry suggested that "declare" be substituted for "make," thereby "leaving to the Executive the power to repel sudden attacks." Their motion carried.[75]

Although the president retained the implied power to take defensive actions, the framers anticipated that the decision to wage offensive war would be reserved for Congress. At the Pennsylvania ratification convention in 1787, James Wilson said that the system of checks and balances "will not hurry us into war; it is calculated to guard against it. It will not be in the power of a single man, or a single body of men, to involve us in such distress; for the important power of declaring war is vested in the legislature at large."[76] In a similar vein, Madison explained the purpose of keeping the legislative power of the purse separate from the executive power of the commander in chief:

> Those who are to *conduct a war* cannot in the nature of things, be proper or safe judges, whether *a war ought* to be *commenced, continued,* or *concluded.* They are barred from the latter functions by a great principle in free government, analogous to that which separates the sword from the purse, or the power of executing from the power of enacting laws.[77]

Madison's philosophy was widely shared by his contemporaries. Thomas Jefferson praised the transfer of the war power "from the executive to the Legislative body, from those who are to spend to those who are to pay"[78] At the Philadelphia convention, George Mason declared that the "purse & the sword ought never to get into the same hands *whether Legislative or Executive.*"[79]

Early Precedents

Although Congress is empowered to declare war, it has done so only on five occasions: the War of 1812, the Mexican War, the Spanish American War, World War I, and World War II. Over the past two centuries, American forces have fought in several hundred military actions. That presidents used force in an undeclared war does not mean that they circumvented Congress. Many of those actions were authorized by Congress, including the "quasi war" with France in 1798–1800. Congress passed a number of statutes that put the country on a war footing. Members of Congress knew that they had authorized war against France, even if war was never formally declared. Congressman Edward Livingston considered the country "now in a state of war; and let no man flatter himself that the vote which has been given is not a declaration of war."[80]

The Supreme Court recognized the legitimacy of undeclared wars. A decision in 1800 said that military conflicts could be "limited," "partial," and "imperfect," without the need of declaring war.[81] A year later the Court underscored the fact that the war with France had been authorized by Congress: "The whole powers of war being, by the constitution of the United States, vested in congress, the acts of that body can alone be resorted to as our guides in this inquiry."[82] Wars authorized by statute are within the constitutional scheme; soon there would be executive wars without congressional authority.

A presidential war came in 1846. President Polk ordered General Zachary Taylor to occupy disputed territory on the Texas-Mexico border. His initiative created a clash between American and Mexican soldiers, prompting Polk a few weeks later to tell Congress that "war exists." Although Congress eventually declared war against Mexico, in 1848 the House of Representatives censured Polk because the war had been "unnecessarily and unconstitutionally begun by the President of the United States."[83] Abraham Lincoln, at that time a member of Congress, supported the censure vote against Polk, telling a friend:

> Allow the President to invade a neighboring nation, whenever *he* shall deem it necessary to repel an invasion, and you allow him to do so *whenever he may choose to say* he deems it necessary for such purpose and you allow him to make war at pleasure. . . . This, our Convention understood to be the most oppressive of all Kingly oppressions; and they resolved to so frame the Constitution that *no one man* should hold the power of bringing this oppression upon us.[84]

This critique from Lincoln may appear ironic because during his own years as president, during the Civil War, he used military force without first obtaining congressional authorization. In April 1861, while Congress was in recess, he issued proclamations calling forth the state militia, suspending the writ of habeas corpus, and placing a blockade on the rebellious states. However, it would be incorrect to say that Lincoln behaved like a dictator. Instead of claiming that he had full authority to act as he did, he admitted that his actions were legally suspect and needed the sanction of Congress. He told Congress that his actions, "whether strictly legal or not, were ventured upon under what appeared to be a popular demand and a public necessity, trusting then, as now, that Congress would readily ratify them."[85] After extensive debate, Congress passed legislation "approving, legalizing, and making valid all the acts, proclamations, and orders of the President, etc., as if they had been issued and done under the previous express authority and direction of the Congress of the United States."[86]

Lincoln's most controversial action concerned his suspension of the writ of habeas corpus, which permits a federal judge to demand of governmental officials their legal authority for holding someone in jail. Under Article I, Section 9, of the Constitution, the privilege of the writ of habeas corpus "shall not be suspended, unless when in Cases of Rebellion or Invasion the public Safety may require it." Lincoln acknowledged that the authority to suspend the writ appeared in Article I, which defines the powers of Congress, but told Congress in his message of July 4, 1861, that it was necessary for him during the emergency to exercise both Article I and Article II powers. It was for that reason that he needed the sanction of Congress.

Lincoln's authority to suspend the writ was challenged by Chief Justice Taney, sitting as a circuit judge in Baltimore. Taney issued a writ that directed the military to deliver John Merryman to him. Merryman had been arrested and charged with secessionist activities. The military refused to produce him to Taney, who wrote an opinion stating that he had "exercised all the power which the constitution and laws confer upon me, but that power has been resisted by a force too strong for me to overcome."[87] The Court was no match for Lincoln, particularly after Congress passed legislation supporting his actions. A few years later Congress specifically authorized Lincoln to suspend the writ of habeas corpus.[88]

Lincoln's dilemma was unique. Instead of exercising the war power against a foreign nation, or inviting war as Polk did with Mexico, Lincoln used force to put down an internal rebellion. No president has ever faced a comparable situation. He took the emergency actions he thought necessary and called upon Congress to provide the legal sanctions by statute.

Other presidents have used military force without first obtaining authorization from Congress. Anyone inspecting this list of several hundred incidents would reach the conclusion of presidential scholar Edward S. Corwin, who said that the list consists largely of "fights with pirates, landings of small naval contingents on barbarous or semibarbarous coasts, the dispatch of small bodies of troops to chase bandits or cattle rustlers across the Mexican border, and the like."[89]

Two undeclared wars are of an entirely different dimension: President Harry Truman's initiative in June 1950 to involve the nation in war in Korea, and the combined efforts of Presidents John F. Kennedy and Lyndon B. Johnson to widen the war in Vietnam. U.S. involvement in Vietnam generated such political division within the country that Johnson announced he would not run for reelection and Congress passed the War Powers Resolution in 1973 to place constraints on presidential war power.

The Korean and Vietnam Wars

On June 27, 1950, President Truman announced to the country that the U.N. Security Council had requested all members to provide assistance to implement its resolution ordering North Korea to cease hostilities and withdraw to the 38th parallel. As part of American assistance, he ordered air and sea forces to South Korea. Later, ground troops were sent in. Truman never asked Congress for authority. Is a Security Council resolution sufficient authority for presidents to engage in offensive war?

Article 43 of the U.N. Charter establishes the procedures for using armed force. In accordance with "special agreements," members of the United Nations agreed to supply specific numbers and types of military troops. Article 43 states that the special agreements shall be ratified by each nation "in accordance with their respective constitutional processes." Congress passed the United Nations Participation Act of 1945 to define those constitutional processes. Section 6 of that statute requires that the agreements "shall be subject to the approval of the Congress by appropriate Act or joint resolution." Responding by act or joint resolution requires both houses of Congress to pass legislation approving the use of military force.

The legislative history of the U.N. Participation Act of 1945 makes it very clear that congressional approval was an essential principle. The League of Nations Covenant foundered on that very issue, and the framers of the U.N. Charter knew that the constitutional interests of Congress had to be protected.[90] When Under Secretary of State Dean Acheson appeared before the House Committee on Foreign Affairs to testify on the bill, he told the legislators that only after the president receives the approval of Congress is he "bound to furnish that contingent of troops to the Security Council; and the President is not authorized to furnish any more than you have approved of that agreement."[91] In other remarks, Acheson assured the committee that Congress had total control in approving or disapproving special agreements.[92] The Senate and House legislative record reflects that understanding.[93] An amendment in the Senate to permit approval of special agreements by the treaty process, rather than by the full Congress, was decisively rejected, 57 to 14.[94]

The statutory restrictions on presidential war power were underscored by amendments to the U.N. Participation Act in 1949. Presidents were permitted to provide military forces to the United Nations on their own initiative for "cooperative action." However, the statute subjected presidential action to three key conditions: military forces could serve only as observers and guards, they could perform only in a noncombatant capacity, and they could not exceed one thousand.[95]

Despite that explicit legislative history, Truman acted under the U.N. umbrella without any congressional approval. There is even substantial doubt that he acted in accordance with the Security Council resolution. The first resolution, passed on June 25, 1950, merely called on North Korea to cease hostilities and to withdraw their forces. It did not call for military assistance. That request came two days later, when Truman ordered U.S. air and sea forces. On June 29, Secretary of State Acheson announced that all actions by the United States in Korea had been taken under "the aegis of the United Nations" and that Truman's actions were "in conformity with the resolutions of the Security Council of June 25 and 27."[96]

Acheson neglected to mention that Truman had committed U.S. forces on June 26, one day before the Security Council called for military action. Acheson later admitted that "some American action, said to be in support of the resolution of June 27, was in fact ordered, and possibly taken, prior to the resolution."[97] Truman wrote to Acheson a few weeks later, praising him for immediately calling the Security Council: "Had you not acted promptly in that direction we would have had to go into Korea alone."[98] After he left the presidency, Truman was asked whether he was prepared to fight in Korea without U.N. backing. His response: "No question about it."[99]

Truman could skirt Congress and the procedures of the U.N. Participation Act because he never entered into special agreements with the Security Council. In fact, those agreements have never been used in any international crisis. The very safeguards inserted into law to protect the constitutional prerogatives of Congress became nullities under Truman and the presidents who followed him.[100]

Truman did receive one rebuff on his military policy in Korea, but it came from the Supreme Court, not from Congress. In 1952, he ordered his Secretary of Commerce to seize the steel mills to help prosecute the war in Korea. In court, the Justice Department argued that the judiciary had no power to constrain the president. According to the Department's theory, the president was restrained only by impeachment and the ballot box. That reading of the Constitution was repudiated by a federal district court and by the Supreme Court, which voted 6 to 3 to declare Truman's action invalid.[101]

President Dwight D. Eisenhower regarded Truman's initiatives in Korea as a mistaken exercise of presidential power. Eisenhower believed that the country was on sounder constitutional footing when the president acts in concert with Congress. To accomplish that goal, Eisenhower asked for "area resolutions" from Congress to give him statutory authority before using military force in specific areas of the world. He received area resolutions for Formosa in 1955 and for the Middle East in 1957.[102] Eisenhower thought that joint action by Congress and the president was the best method of convincing both allies and enemies of the depth of an American commitment to use armed force. He reminded members of Congress "that the Constitution assumes that our two branches of government should get along together."[103]

Unlike Eisenhower, President John F. Kennedy was prepared to act solely on his constitutional authority when he confronted the Soviet Union during the Cuban missile crisis in 1962. He claimed that he had full authority as commander in chief to take whatever actions he considered necessary to prevent the Soviet Union from placing missiles in Cuba. Congress did pass the Cuba Resolution of 1962, and superficially it looks like the area resolutions favored by Eisenhower. But the resolution of 1962 did not provide congressional authority for presidential action. It merely expressed the sentiments of Congress.[104]

The next area resolution was the ill-fated Southeast Asia Resolution of 1964 (the Gulf of Tonkin Resolution). President Lyndon Johnson reported that North Vietnam had attacked American vessels on August 2 and 4. He requested the resolution on August 4. Without verifying his reports, the Senate began debate on August 6 and passed the resolution the next day, 88-2. The House passed the measure the next day, voting 414-0. The legislation represented a careless abdication of congressional power to the president, for it approved and supported "the determination of the President, as Commander in Chief, to take all necessary measures to repel any armed attack against the forces of the United States and to prevent further aggression." The United States was "prepared, as the President determines, to take all necessary steps, including the use of armed force. . . . "[105] Four years later, after heavy American casualties in a war that seemed to have no end and no possible victory, Johnson was driven from office.

War Powers Resolution of 1973

The acrimony over the Vietnam War sparked a national debate over the appropriate roles of Congress and the president in exercising the war power. Hearings were conducted by both houses to determine what might be done to resolve the competing claims of the two branches. Congress recognized that the president might have legitimate and constitutional reasons in an emergency to use military force without prior legislative action. The Senate wanted to specify by statute the situations in which a president could act militarily without advance legislative sanction. The House doubted that it was possible to define with that kind of precision the president's war powers.[106]

The measure that eventually became law in 1973 borrowed features from the Senate and House bills. The basic thrust of the War Powers Resolution, as expressed in Section 2(a), is "to assure that the collective judgment" of both branches will apply to the introduction of U.S. forces into hostilities. The president is to consult with Congress "in every possible instance," language that obviously leaves substantial discretion to the president as to the form and timing of consultation.

The War Powers Resolution requires that the president, after introducing forces into hostilities, report to Congress within forty-eight hours. Precisely what conditions require a report, and what type of report is required, is unclear from the legislation. If the report is delayed for any reason, so are the mechanisms for congressional control. For example, the resolution states that military action must terminate within sixty days after a report unless Congress (1) declares war or enacts a specific authorization, (2) extends by law the sixty-day period, or (3) is physically unable to meet as a result of an armed attack on the United States. The president may extend the period by an additional thirty days if force is needed to protect and remove American troops. If Congress fails to support the military operation during the sixty- to ninety-day period, the president is supposed to withdraw the troops.

One problem with the War Powers Resolution is that the 60–90 day clock does not actually begin to tick unless the president reports to Congress under a very specific provision: Section 4(a)(1). Not surprisingly, presidents do not report under that section. They usually report "consistent with the War Powers Resolution." Only President Ford reported under Section 4(a)(1) when he authorized military force to rescue the U.S. merchant ship *Mayaguez*, which had been seized by Cambodians. However, by the time Ford reported to Congress the operation was over. The only other time Section 4(a)(1) started the clock was in 1983 when Congress passed a statute authorizing military action in Lebanon, and in this case Congress authorized a period of eighteen months.[107]

Although the War Powers Resolution has not operated as the framers expected, with presidential initiatives limited by a strict 60–90 day clock, in effect it has largely worked out that way. Presidents from Ford to Bush have all used military force without seeking congressional authority. Each operation, however, was of a short-term nature: Ford's rescue of the *Mayaguez*; Carter's attempted rescue of American hostages in Iran; Reagan's invasion of Grenada and his air strikes against Libya; and Bush's intervention in Panama in 1989. More extensive operations, such as the commitment of troops to Lebanon in 1983 and to the Persian Gulf in 1991, have been authorized by statute.

The War Powers Resolution also relies on another procedure to limit the president. The statute allows Congress to pass a concurrent resolution at any time to direct the president to remove forces engaged in hostilities. The two-house veto appears to be unconstitutional as a result of *INS v. Chadha* (1983), in which the Supreme Court declared that any action by Congress intended to affect the legal rights, duties, and relations outside the legislative branch must satisfy two constitutional conditions: action by both houses and presentation of the measure to the president. A concurrent resolution meets the first condition but not the second.

Nevertheless, the overriding factor is the political force of a concurrent resolution telling the president to cease military action. It is difficult to conceive of a situation in which a president would persist with a military operation that is specifically opposed by a majority of legislators from each house. Whether for political or legal reasons, a president is most likely to comply with a concurrent resolution. The problem with acting by joint resolution, which would comply with *Chadha*, is that the president can veto a joint resolution and Congress could prevail only with a two-thirds majority in each house. In other words, the president could continue military operations merely by maintaining a margin of one-third plus one in a single chamber. That cannot be the meaning of the Constitution.

The War Power Resolution, by giving a green light to presidential wars during the 60–90 day period, concedes a measure of authority to the president that would have astonished the framers. The authors of the Resolution claimed that they had restricted presidential power;

in fact they widened it. There are good reasons for concluding that the resolution, seriously compromised from the start and weakened over time, should be repealed. Members of Congress would then have to rely on their own institutional powers to check the president.

The Persian Gulf War

On August 2, 1990, President Saddam Hussein of Iraq invaded Kuwait. President Bush immediately began deploying U.S. forces to Saudi Arabia, which it appeared that Hussein might also invade. The mission of the American presence at that point was purely defensive (to deter further Iraqi aggression), but in November Bush doubled the size of U.S. forces and by then had the military capacity to wage offensive war. The constitutional issue was clearly drawn: Could President Bush shift from his defensive posture to an offensive operation without first obtaining congressional approval?

Instead of seeking congressional support, Bush directed his energies into obtaining the backing of other nations and encouraging the U.N. Security Council to authorize the use of force against Saddam Hussein. On November 29, 1990, the Security Council authorized member states to take all necessary means, including armed force, to implement Security Council resolutions directed against Iraq. The November 29 resolution did not *require* the United States to use force. That decision depended on its constitutional processes.

Some administration officials maintained that Bush did not need congressional authority. Secretary of Defense Dick Cheney testified before the Senate Armed Services Committee on December 3 that President Bush did not require "any additional authorization from the Congress" before attacking Iraq.[108] The Justice Department presented the same argument in a case brought by fifty-four members of Congress, who challenged the president's constitutional authority to initiate war in the Persian Gulf. On December 13, a federal district judge dismissed the case on the ground that it was not ripe for judicial determination. At the same time, he forcefully rejected many of the sweeping claims for presidential authority advanced by the Justice Department. The judge noted that if the president:

had the sole power to determine that any particular offensive military operation, no matter how vast, does not constitute war-making but only an offensive military attack, the congressional power to declare war will be at the mercy of a semantic decision by the Executive. Such an "interpretation" would evade the plain language of the Constitution, and it cannot stand.[109]

On January 8, 1991, driven perhaps in part by this decision, President Bush asked Congress to pass legislation supporting his policy in the Persian Gulf. He was asked by reporters the next day whether he needed a resolution from Congress. He replied: "I don't think I need it. . . . I feel that I have the authority to fully implement the United Nations resolutions."[110] The constitutional standoff lifted on January 12 when Congress, after several days of intense debate, authorized Bush to take offensive actions against Iraq. President Bush signed the legislation two days later.[111] In signing the bill, he claimed that he could have acted without congressional authority:

> As I made clear to congressional leaders at the outset, my request for congressional support did not, and my signing this resolution does not, constitute any change in the long-standing positions of the executive branch on either the President's constitutional authority to use the Armed Forces to defend vital U.S. interests or the constitutionality of the War Powers Resolution.[112]

Bush's signing of the statement does not alter the language of this public law; it clearly authorized him to act. What governs is the law, not what Bush said during a signing ceremony. In the end, Bush acted pursuant to congressional authority, even if he claimed it was not required. For both political and legal reasons, presidents need congressional authority when waging war of the magnitude contemplated in the Persian Gulf. Authority is needed for funds and to sanction the loss of American lives. The Security Council resolutions were never a substitute for congressional action. The U.N. Charter did not strip Congress of its constitutional responsibilities over war and peace.

Clinton's Initiatives

During his first term, Bill Clinton used military force a number of times without ever seeking, or obtaining, congressional authority. Like President Bush, he relied on resolutions adopted by the Security

Council rather than statutes passed by Congress. Moreover, he looked for authority to votes taken by the North Atlantic Council.

Clinton first used military force on June 26, 1993, when he ordered air strikes against Iraq as retaliation for the attempted assassination of former President Bush during a visit to Kuwait. Clinton called the assassination attempt "an attack against our country and against all Americans," citing the right of self-defense recognized in Article 51 of the UN Charter.[113] Two attorneys of constitutional law noted: "calling the U.S. bombing of Iraq an act of self-defense for an assassination plot that had been averted two months previously is quite a stretch."[114] White House officials, however, appreciated the value of the bombings in building Clinton's image as a strong and decisive leader.[115]

The next military involvement came in Somalia. Shortly before leaving office, President Bush sent U.S. troops to Somalia as part of a multinational effort to avert widespread starvation. The humanitarian mission turned bloody in June 1993 when twenty-three Pakistani peacekeepers were killed. U.S. warplanes launched a retaliatory attack against Mohamed Farah Aideed, a Somali political leader blamed for the deaths. In August 1993, four U.S. soldiers were killed when a land mine blasted apart their Humvee vehicle. Earlier conflicts had killed four other American soldiers. Congress included language in an appropriations bill to provide that no funds for the operations of U.S. armed forces in Somalia could be used for expenses after March 31, 1994, unless Clinton requested an extension and Congress provided explicit authority.[116] Under those legislative pressures, U.S. troops were removed from Somalia.

Throughout 1993 and 1994, Clinton threatened the use of military force against Haiti in an effort to have its military leaders leave and restore the deposed government of President Jean-Bertrand Aristide. When the military leaders refused to depart, the UN Security Council on July 31, 1994, adopted a resolution "inviting" all states, particularly those in the region of Haiti, to use "all necessary means" to remove the military leadership on that island. This opened the door to a U.S.-led invasion. At a news conference on August 3, Clinton denied that he needed authority from Congress for the operation: "Like my predecessors of both parties, I have not agreed that

I was constitutionally mandated" to obtain the support of Congress.[117]

On September 15, in a nationwide televised address, Clinton told the American public that he was prepared to use military force to invade Haiti, referring to the UN resolution of July 31 and his willingness to lead a multinational force "to carry out the will of the United Nations."[118] No word about carrying out the will of Congress. Although the public and a substantial majority of legislators assailed the planned invasion, Clinton seemed to glory in the idea of taking an unpopular stand. Regardless of the opposition, he was determined to proceed because "this is what I believe is the right thing to do. I realize it is unpopular. I know it is unpopular. I know the timing is unpopular. I know the whole thing is unpopular. But I believe it is the right thing."[119] Apparently no consideration was given to whether it was the legal thing, the authorized thing, or the constitutional thing.

An invasion proved unnecessary. Former President Jimmy Carter was able to negotiate with the military leaders, who agreed to step down to permit the return of Aristide. House and Senate debates were strongly critical of Clinton's insistence that he could act militarily against Haiti without legislative authority, but statutory restrictions were never enacted. After the matter was resolved, both Houses passed legislation stating that "the President should have sought and welcomed Congressional approval before deploying United States Forces to Haiti."[120]

The major military activity came in Bosnia, torn apart by age-old rivalries among Serbs, Croats, and Muslims. Initially, Clinton worked in concert with the UN and NATO, participating in humanitarian airlifts and helping to enforce a "no-fly zone" (a ban on unauthorized flights over Bosnia-Herzegovina). In several statements during 1993, Clinton indicated that he would have to seek authorization from Congress before ordering any air strikes.[121] However, he also objected to legislative efforts to restrict his military options.[122]

By 1994, Clinton was threatening air strikes against Serbian militias without stating any need to seek authority from Congress. Decisions to use air power would be taken in response to UN Security Council resolutions, operating through NATO's military command. Clinton explained: "the authority under which air strikes can proceed, NATO acting out of area pursuant to U.N. authority, requires the common agreement of our NATO allies."[123] In other words, he would seek the agreement of England, France, Italy, and other NATO allies, but not Congress.

NATO air strikes began in February 1994 and were followed by additional strikes in April, August, and November. NATO continued to conduct limited air strikes during the first half of 1995, but in July the war took a more serious turn when Bosnian Serb forces overran the UN-designated "safe area" of Sbrebrenica. At the end of August, NATO carried out the war's biggest air raid.

Clinton consistently looked for authority not from Congress but from the North Atlantic Council (NAC) or from Security Council resolutions. In messages to Congress and to the country, he explained that NAC had "approved" a number of measures and that the air strikes were "authorized" by the United Nations.[124] When it came to introducing ground troops to Bosnia, Clinton sought the support and approval of Congress but not its authority.[125] U.S. troops were dispatched to Bosnia for an initial one-year commitment, but on December 17, 1996, Clinton extended the troop deployment for another eighteen months. The expenditures for this military commitment are expected to exceed $6 billion.

The framers assumed that in a system of separation of powers, each branch would protect its prerogatives and fight against encroachments. The framers' design has worked well on many fronts, but not in the use of military force. Presidents advance ambitious theories of executive prerogative without triggering a serious check from Congress or the judiciary. It is not merely a matter of Congress being weakened. Public control and democratic values, operating through Congress as the representative branch, are also degraded.

Covert Operations

The Iran-Contra affair burst on an incredulous nation in November 1986. The public learned that the Reagan administration had sold arms to Iran (which for years had held Americans hostage) and had sent weapons to the Contras in Nicaragua (despite a congressional ban). New details on these bizarre transactions appeared almost daily, explaining the scope of a complex covert operation conducted by a mix of executive officials and private citizens. In addition to violating public policy as announced by Reagan officials, the covert operation failed to comply with the procedures established in the Intelligence Oversight Act of 1980. As a result, Congress enacted new controls in the intelligence authorization bill in 1991.

Statutory Controls on Covert Actions

Following disclosures in the 1970s of abuses by the Central Intelligence Agency, Congress created intelligence committees in each house to review and authorize CIA operations. Congress passed legislation in 1980 to regulate the president's power to engage in covert operations. The Intelligence Oversight Act of 1980 required the director of Central Intelligence and the heads of all other agencies or entities of the United States involved in intelligence activities to keep the intelligence committees "fully and currently informed" of all intelligence activities. If the president determined that it was essential to limit prior notice to meet "extraordinary circumstances affecting vital interests of the United States," he could limit notice to eight members of Congress—the chair and ranking minority members of the intelligence committees, the speaker and minority leader of the House, and the majority and minority leaders of the Senate. This so-called "Gang of Eight" was never notified of the Iran-Contra operations. Under the 1980 statute, if the president did not give notice to Congress, he had to "fully inform" the intelligence committees "in a timely fashion" and explain the failure to provide notice. In the case of Iran-Contra, timely notice for Congress meant never being informed until the facts spilled out ten months later in Lebanese and U.S. newspapers.

Congress and President Reagan had battled for years over the proper policy to pursue in the civil war in Nicaragua, where the Contra rebels were in armed revolt against the leftist Sandinista government. The Reagan administration pushed hard for congressional funding to supply the Contras with military assistance. Congress voted some assistance but included a number of statutory restrictions. After several years of ongoing tension between the two branches, Congress decided that the administration had acted in bad faith and prohibited any military assistance to the Contras. The Boland Amendment, enacted in October 1984 and continued until October 1986, prohibited the use of any appropriated funds to give direct or indirect U.S. assistance to the Contras.

With regard to the Middle East, the Reagan administration repeatedly told the nation and our allies that it remained neutral on the war between Iran and Iraq and opposed the sending of weapons to either country (Operation Staunch). The Reagan administration said it was steadfastly opposed to giving any concessions to terrorists, much less providing them arms in exchange for hostages. After the Boland Amendment was enacted in October 1984, an executive official testified before congressional committees in March 1985 and again in April 1985 that the administration would comply fully with the amendment and would not solicit funds from private sources or foreign governments to assist the Contras.[126] When President Reagan signed the statute including the Boland Amendment, he made no statement suggesting that the amendment interfered with his constitutional duties. The constitutionality of the amendment was never challenged by the attorney general, the Justice Department, or the White House.

Iran-Contra

At the very moment the Reagan official was testifying to Congress on the propriety of the Boland Amendment, other officials within the administration were busy soliciting funds from private individuals and foreign governments to assist the Contras militarily. The Reagan administration sold arms to Iran and hoped through that leverage to effect the release of American hostages. When the story broke in November 1986, Reagan initially denied that he had traded arms for hostages.

Once the story was out, Reagan took three steps to provide the public with information about Iran-Contra. He established a Special Review Board on December 1, 1986, headed by former Senator John Tower. The board's report, released the following February, underscored the collapse of accountable government. The National Security Council (NSC) within the White House became the center of an operation that seemed to run outside the control of such agencies as the Departments of Defense and State. The sale of weapons to Iran violated a number of U.S. policies that those departments had articulated: neutrality in the Iran-Iraq war, an embargo on arms sales to Iran, isolation of Iran and other countries associated with terrorism, and the policy of not paying ransom to hostage-takers.

President Reagan next directed Attorney General Edwin Meese III to go to a special panel of federal judges and request that they appoint an independent counsel to investigate the Iran-Contra affair. As a result of those investigations and prosecutions over the next five years, key figures in private life and public service were indicted and convicted or pleaded guilty. The private citizens included Carl R. "Spitz" Channell, Richard Miller, Richard V. Secord, and Albert Hakim. The public officials involved in the scandal included Robert C. McFarlane, former national security adviser to President Reagan; Alan D. Fiers, former CIA official; and Elliot Abrams, former assistant secretary of state.

In addition, former NSC staff member Lt. Col. Oliver L. North was convicted of three felonies: obstructing the investigation of Congress, mutilating government documents, and taking an illegal gratuity (a home security system). The charges were later dismissed because of procedural complications resulting from his testimony to Congress, where he received limited immunity. John M. Poindexter, another national security adviser to President Reagan, was convicted of lying to Congress, obstructing Congress, and conspiring with North and others to obstruct Congress. His conviction was also reversed because of his immunized testimony to Congress.

Finally, President Reagan invited Congress to investigate the Iran-Contra affair and make recommendations to minimize the chance of comparable scandals in the future. Congress held joint hearings for months during 1987 and issued its final report in November of that year. Many of its proposals became law in 1991.

Reforms for Covert Actions

The Intelligence Oversight Act of 1980 required presidents to make a "Finding" on the necessity for a covert operation. In the course of the Iran-Contra affair, President Reagan issued an "oral" Finding on one occasion and at another point issued a Finding that tried to retroactively authorize what the CIA had done. After receiving the Tower Board report, President Reagan issued National Security Decision Directive (NSDD) 266 on March 31, 1987. The NSDD prohibited the staff of the National Security Council from undertaking covert operations. Reagan later issued NSDD 286, which required written Findings (although permitting oral authorizations for short emergencies) and prohibited retroactive Findings.

The congressional report on Iran-Contra supported written Findings and the prohibition on retroactive Findings. It also objected to such vague phrases as "timely notice" included in the 1980 intelligence oversight law. It recommended that Congress be notified prior to the commencement of a covert action "except in certain rare instances and in no event later than 48 hours after a Finding is approved."[127] The Senate passed legislation in 1988 requiring the president to notify Congress of a covert operation within forty-eight hours, but the House failed to act on the bill. Administration officials testified that the restriction violated the president's constitutional powers.[128]

When President Bush took office in 1989, he tried to work out an informal accommodation that would avoid statutory action. On October 30, 1989, he wrote a letter to Senator David L. Boren, chair of the Senate Intelligence Committee. Bush agreed that in "almost all instances" he would give the intelligence committees prior notice of a covert action. In "rare instances" he would provide notice "within a few days." Any failure to inform Congress within those periods would be based not on statutory interpretations of the oversight act but on "my assertion of the authorities granted this office by the Constitution."

Congress decided it wanted the procedures spelled out in law. In 1990, the intelligence authorization bill established new statutory procedures for reporting covert actions. Bush vetoed the bill, in part because he objected to language in the conference report that accompanied the bill. He claimed that the language undermined the understanding expressed in his October 30 letter.[129] After additional negotiations, the two branches finally reached an accommodation the next year. The intelligence authorization bill in 1991 revised the Intelligence Oversight Act of 1980 by requiring a number of reforms for presidential Findings of covert actions: they must be in writing, they cannot have retroactive effect, they may not authorize any action that violates federal law or the Constitution, and they must identify any third party (foreign nation) that is involved in the covert action. Those Findings are submitted to the intelligence committees.[130]

Mixing Purse and Sword

One of the most extraordinary theories of executive power to surface from the Iran-Contra affair was the claim that presidents, denied funds by Congress, could nevertheless finance their foreign policy by using nonappropriated funds obtained from private citizens and foreign governments. To continue military assistance to the Contras, officials in the Reagan administration sought funds from private individuals and from Saudi Arabia, and approached other countries for money. At the congressional hearings, both Poindexter and North defended the constitutionality of these initiatives, claiming that these practices did not violate the Boland Amendment because the amendment applied only to appropriations.[131]

There are two principal problems with the Poindexter-North theory: one is constitutional, the other political. The framers deliberately avoided combining the legislative purse with the presidential sword. They did not want a single branch to both make and fund war. In *Federalist* 69, Hamilton reasoned that the president was less threatening than the king of England because the monarchical power "extends to the *declaring* of war and to the *raising* and *regulating* of fleets and armies."[132] The American Constitution vests those powers solely in Congress. Madison counseled against any mixing of the power to go to war with the power of commander in chief. Those who conduct a war should not judge whether a war ought to be "*commenced, continued,* or *concluded.*" Presidents are barred from the latter functions "by a great principle in free government, analogous to that which separates the sword from the purse. . . . "[133]

Using nonappropriated funds to finance presidential policies carries other risks. Accepting money from foreign governments to fund U.S. foreign policy invites corruption within the executive branch. In return for their contributions, foreign governments will expect executive officials to provide arms sales, foreign assistance, military assistance, or trade concessions. Public policy becomes less what Congress legislates and more what conspires from these deals. Government goes underground.

Congress passed legislation to stop these quid pro quos. The "Pell Amendment" in 1985 prohibited the use of any foreign assistance or military assistance to provide "assistance of any kind, either directly or indirectly, to any person or group engaging in an insurgency or other act of rebellion against the Government of Nicaragua." The purpose was to prevent recipients of U.S. funds and materials from giving assistance to the Contras as a condition, or quid pro quo, for obtaining aid.[134]

After the disclosure of the Iran-Contra affair, members of Congress worked on statutory language to prohibit all quid pro quos (also referred to as "leveraging"). In 1989, President Bush vetoed a foreign assistance authorization bill because it contained a provision that attempted to use criminal sanctions to punish quid pro quos. Bush said that the statutory language was too vague to justify criminal penalties. Moreover, he considered the language an impermissible interference with the constitutional duty of executive officials to communicate with other nations.[135]

Also in 1989, Bush vetoed the foreign operations appropriations bill, which would have prohibited the obligation or expenditure of funds appropriated by the bill "for the purpose of furthering any military or foreign policy activity which is contrary to United States law." The bill would have prohibited the use of appropriated funds "to solicit the provision of funds by any foreign government (including any instrumentality or agency thereof), foreign person, or United States person, for the purpose of furthering any military or foreign policy objective which is contrary to United States law." Although the bill contained no criminal penalties, Bush concluded that it was "sufficiently ambiguous to present an unacceptable risk that it will chill the conduct of our Nation's foreign affairs."[136]

Congress continued to rework the language and eventually reached an accommodation with the executive branch in 1989. The purpose was to prevent quid pro quos that attempt to circumvent statutory prohibitions. The statutory language states that appropriated funds for foreign assistance may not be provided to "any foreign government (including any instrumentality or agency thereof), foreign person, or United States person in exchange for that foreign government or person undertaking any action which is, if carried out by the United States Government, a United States official or employee, expressly prohibited by a provision of United States law."[137] The statute also says it is not the intent of Congress to limit the ability of executive officials to make statements or express their views to foreign governments. In signing the bill, President Bush said it was his intent to construe the statutory language "narrowly" but agreed that the section prohibited quid pro quo transactions "in which U.S. funds are provided to a foreign nation on the express condition that the foreign nation provide specific assistance to a third country, which assistance U.S. officials are expressly prohibited from providing by U.S. law."[138]

The Need for Comity

As the people's branch, Congress must debate and authorize all major military, political, and economic commitments, including the decision to go to war. To fight a war successfully, the president needs the support and cooperation of Congress. In 1975, at the conclusion of the Vietnam War, Secretary of State Henry Kissinger made this observation:

> Comity between the executive and legislative branches is the only possible basis for national action. The decade-long struggle in this country over executive dominance in foreign affairs is over. The recognition that the Congress is a coequal branch of government is the dominant fact of national politics today. The executive accepts that the Congress must have both the sense and the reality of participation: foreign policy must be a shared enterprise.[139]

To conduct foreign policy and wage war on a sustained basis, the president needs to build support within Congress. This fact of constitutional life is evident in such areas as foreign assistance, treaties, foreign commerce, tariff and nontariff barriers, military spending, and arms sales. The latter illustrates the constant give-and-take between the two branches.

The infusion of arms into a particular region, as in the Middle East, can tilt the balance of power and embroil America in a military conflict. Because of those risks, Congress has involved itself closely in the decision to sell weapons to other countries. Under the terms of legislation enacted in 1974, a letter of offer to sell defense equipment beyond a certain dollar level could not be issued if Congress, within thirty calendar days, adopted a concurrent resolution of disapproval.

Congress never exercised a legislative veto over arms sales, but the threat of disapproval forced the president a number of times to make compromises that restricted the use of weapons.[140] In 1978, when President Carter announced his opposition to the legislative veto, Attorney General Griffin Bell was asked whether Carter's position meant that he was prepared to proceed with an arms sale if Congress disapproved it by concurrent resolution. Bell replied that Carter would not be legally bound by such a vote, "but we have to have comity between the branches of government, just as we have between nations. And under a spirit of comity, we could abide by it, and there would be nothing wrong with abiding by it. We don't have to have a confrontation every time we can." At that same briefing, White House domestic adviser Stuart Eizenstat commented that "with certain of these issues where we think the Congress has a legitimate interest, such as the War Powers Act, as a matter of comity, we are willing to forgo the specific legal challenge and abide by that judgment because we think it is such an overriding issue."[141]

In response to *INS v. Chadha* (1983), Congress revised the arms sales legislation in 1986 to provide for a joint resolution of disapproval.[142] A joint resolution satisfies the two requirements identified by the Court: action by both houses and presentment of a measure to the president for his signature or veto. In 1986, President Reagan's proposal to sell $354 million worth of missiles to Saudi Arabia was defeated in both chambers by wide margins—well above the two-thirds needed to override a veto. Here the branches entered into a creative compromise. Reagan decided to veto the joint resolution but also had to respect the congressional opposition to sending two hundred Stinger missiles (shoulder-fired, anti-aircraft weapons) to Saudi Arabia. On the same day that he vetoed the joint resolution he sent a letter to Senate Majority Leader Robert Dole, explaining that if Congress sustained his veto he would proceed with the sale to Saudi Arabia but only after excluding the Stinger missiles and six hundred missile reloads. That letter enabled Reagan to avoid an override in the Senate, which sustained his veto by a vote of 34-66. The 34 votes represented the absolute minimum needed to sustain the president: one-third plus one of the Senate's one hundred members.

The stronger role for Congress in foreign affairs reflects domestic realities. The president's position in foreign affairs has been constantly diluted by domestic considerations and the economics and physical interdependence of nations. The Murphy Commission in 1975 noted that "problems of interdependence will sharply affect the domestic economy of this country and therefore merge with domestic political issues, but the processes of our foreign policy making are still too much designed as though foreign and domestic policy are distinct."[143]

Until recent years, foreign leaders met only with the president and high executive officials (except for occasional ceremonial addresses before Congress). Contacts with congressional committees and members over substantive issues are now made directly. In 1975 King Hussein of Jordan wrote to one hundred senators and fifty key representatives concerning the sale of missiles to his country. Prime Minister Desai of India went to both House and Senate committees in 1978 to persuade them to allow President Carter to sell India enriched nuclear fuel. In both cases the administration supported these contacts as a way to prevent Congress from disapproving the proposals.[144]

Conclusions

Critics of congressional involvement in foreign affairs sometimes point to localism and ethnic group pressures as undesirable ingredients in the legislative process. But high-sounding and perhaps even high-minded programs pursued by the administration abroad need the support of people at home. Programs must be authorized; they must be funded. As an assistant secretary of state observed: "For this we need Congress to refine, to legitimate and to help sell effective international policies."[145]

The executive branch benefits by spending more time and energy in understanding domestic pressures. Presidents should not isolate themselves from Congress and the general public, dismissing their involvement as narrow, local, or parochial. Patsy T. Mink, after careers in both Congress and the State Department, warned that it "is folly to believe, as many in the top echelons of State and White House staff sincerely do, that good foreign policy necessarily stands above the pressures of domestic politics and constituent interests. Politics is the art of reconciling and educating, not of avoiding, those interests."[146]

Congressional review of administrative decisions in foreign affairs and national security is supported by a strong institutional base within the committee structure, personal staffs, and service organizations of Congress, including the General Accounting Office, the Congressional Research Service, and the Congressional Budget Office. Instead of periodic and idiosyncratic interventions, Congress now has the institutional capacity to monitor foreign policy on an informed, sustained basis. Congress is better prepared to challenge assertions and premises from the administration and less willing to show deference to claims of expertise and authority.

Even if there were no Congress to "meddle" in foreign affairs, it is unrealistic to expect the executive branch to prepare and implement a coherent policy. Any administration is torn in different directions by rivalry among the executive departments and by concessions made to domestic interests, foreign governments, and multilateral corporations. In 1989, when the Bush administration debated whether to apply sanctions to Japan as an "unfair" trader, the U.S. trade representative, the secretary of commerce, and the secretary of agriculture wanted to adopt strong measures. They were opposed by the secretary of defense, the director of the Office of Management and Budget, and the chairman of the president's Council of Economic Advisers.[147]

If the executive branch could ever develop a coherent foreign policy, it would begin to unravel as soon as a new administration cleaned house at the top level of the departments and placed its own political appointees into posts for which they are often poorly prepared by experience and aptitude. Foreign policy remains fluid and subject to fluctuation, constantly juggling domestic and international pressures. Congress is fully equipped politically and constitutionally to participate in this process.

Executive dominance in foreign affairs is not healthy for Congress, the country, or even the president. We know from Watergate and the Iran-Contra scandals that executive officials have great capacity for self-inflicted injuries. The loyalty that political appointees have to the president gives them little stake in the long-term operations of government. They are quick to bridle at the frustrations of orderly procedures. Shortcuts seem attractive; officials can circumvent laws with what they think are clever interpretations. Political appointees can initiate actions that injure Congress, the president, and the political system. They may be so eager for results, and so ignorant of constitutional processes, that they seek immediate payoffs despite long-term damage. The task of cleaning up the debris is left to careerists and professionals in Congress and the executive branch. Breaking faith is costly. Afterwards there is less trust and confidence between the branches—qualities that are essential in a government of divided powers, general grants of constitutional authority, and statutes that require mature judgment and discretion.

CHAPTER 7

◆

Budgetary Control

The Constitution vests in Congress the ultimate power of the purse: the power to appropriate and the power to tax. Yet a combination of political, historical, and bureaucratic forces have shifted a substantial amount of budgetary powers to the executive branch. From 1789 to 1921 the nation lacked a formal budgeting system. Agencies bundled up their budget requests in what was called a "Book of Estimates." There was no systematic or centralized effort to relate total expenditures to total revenues. Part of the purpose of the Budget and Accounting Act of 1921 was to place upon the president the responsibility for preparing and submitting a national budget. For its part, Congress retained the prerogative to alter the shape and size of the president's budget by simple majority vote. It consciously rejected a parliamentary model that would have subordinated Congress to the executive branch.

The Congressional Budget and Impoundment Control Act of 1974 marked an effort by Congress to reassert its budgetary power, but this statute weakened executive responsibility for submitting a budget. The 1974 Budget Act produced an irresponsible process in which neither branch can be held politically accountable. The Gramm-Rudman-Hollings Act of 1985 attempted to force the two branches to adhere to a statutory schedule for reducing the federal deficit. In 1986 the Supreme Court invalidated a key mechanism, forcing Congress and the executive branch to discover alternative ways to control the budget deficit. Gramm-Rudman was revised in 1987 and replaced in 1990 by the Budget Enforcement Act; neither statute controlled the deficit. Additional statutes were enacted in 1993 and 1997 in an effort to control federal spending and reduce the size of deficits. Congress also passed an "item veto" statute in 1996 as another method for reducing spending and the deficit.

Evolution of National Structures

Article I, Section 9 of the Constitution provides that "No Money shall be drawn from the Treasury, but in Consequence of Appropriations made by Law." The Constitution does not mention appropriations committees, nor does it distinguish between appropriations and authorizations. It was not until the Civil War period that Congress established appropriations committees. Previously it had relied on its tax committees to handle both appropriations bills and revenue measures.

In 1789 the House appointed a ten-member Committee on Ways and Means to report on supplies and revenues. The committee was disbanded within a few weeks after Congress created the Treasury Department. In 1794, during Alexander Hamilton's last year as secretary of the treasury, the House revived the Ways and Means Committee.[1] The Senate continued to refer general appropriations bills to select committees until 1816, when it established the Committee on Finance as a standing committee. Several decades passed before the Senate consolidated all appropriations bills in that committee.

Executive agencies transmitted their budget requests to Congress in a "Book of Estimates." Neither the secretary of the treasury nor the president was formally responsible for the contents of this document, but such presidents as John Quincy Adams, Martin Van Buren, John Tyler, James K. Polk, James Buchanan, Ulysses S. Grant, and Grover Cleveland intervened to revise budget estimates before they were sent to Congress. A number of secretaries of the treasury assisted them in that task. Some of the presidents entered office with exceptional qualifications for this responsibility. Polk, for example, had chaired the House Ways and Means Committee.[2]

For most of this period, Congress handled the nation's finances with little difficulty. An abundance of customs revenues easily covered the modest expenses of the national government. Under the strain of Civil War financing, the two tax committees found it increasingly difficult to retain their jurisdiction over appropriations. In 1865 the House reduced the jurisdiction of the Ways and Means Committee to revenue bills. Its other responsibilities were parceled out to two new committees: an Appropriations Committee and a Committee on Banking and Currency. The Senate adopted a similar reform two years later. Further fragmentation of the congressional structure occurred over the next few decades as a number of authorizing committees gained the power to report appropriations.[3]

In the years following the Civil War, the president emerged as the more trusted guardian of the purse. Congress came under attack for its handling of rivers and harbors bills. In one of his veto measures, President Chester A. Arthur explained that these bills, through the process of log-rolling, secured additional support as they became more objectionable. Although Congress overrode his veto, he received favorable publicity for his effort. A cartoon by Thomas Nast shows Arthur, armed with a rifle, watching an oversized vulture perched upon the Capitol consume his veto message. At the bottom of the cartoon appear words of encouragement: "President Arthur, hit him again! Don't let the vulture become our national bird."[4]

President Cleveland achieved a similar reputation by resisting veterans' benefits passed by Congress. Many of his vetoes were leveled at private and general pension bills for those who had served in the military. Another Thomas Nast cartoon captures the president exercising his role as protector of the purse: Cleveland manfully blocks the door to the U.S. Treasury while thwarted pension agents slink from his presence.[5]

National expenditures increased sharply at the end of the nineteenth century. In addition to pension bills and rivers and harbors measures, federal outlays rose because of the Spanish-American War and construction of the Panama Canal. After twenty-eight uninterrupted years of budget surpluses, from 1866 to 1903, the nation encountered deficits for the next six years.

Congress had already begun to encourage studies of more efficient administration. The Cockrell Committee (1887–1889) and the Cockrell Dockery Commission (1893–1895) investigated wasteful methods in the executive agencies. President Theodore Roosevelt appointed the Keep Commission in 1905 to make recommendations on more economical and effective practices by the agencies. To prevent agencies from spending their funds before the end of the fiscal year, Congress passed legislation in 1905 requiring appropriations to be apportioned by monthly or other allotments "as to prevent undue expenditures in one portion of the year that may require deficiency or additional appropriations to complete the service of the fiscal year."[6]

In response to a new rash of deficits, Congress directed the secretary of the treasury in 1909 to estimate revenue for the coming year. If a deficit appeared likely, the secretary was to recommend reductions in appropriations. If the secretary considered that impracticable, it was the secretary's responsibility to recommend loans or new taxes to cover the deficiency. At the same time, President Taft directed his departmental heads to keep their estimates as low as possible. He reinforced his control over the agencies by issuing Executive Order 1142, which prohibited bureau officers or division chiefs from applying to Congress for legislation or appropriations except with the consent and knowledge of the head of the department.[7]

At Taft's request, Congress appropriated $100,000 in 1910 to encourage research into more efficient ways of conducting the government's business. Taft used the money to set up a five-member Commission on Economy and Efficiency. Over the next two years the commission prepared comprehensive reports on the management of the executive departments. In June 1912, Taft submitted to Congress the commission's proposal for a national budget. The president would be made responsible for reviewing departmental estimates and organizing them into a coherent document. The president's budget would then serve as the basis for intelligent legislative action. The commission said that the budget was the "only effective means whereby *the Executive* may be made responsible for getting before the country a definite, well considered, comprehensive program with respect to which *the legislature* must also assume responsibility either for action or inaction."[8]

On June 10, 1912, Taft directed departmental heads to prepare two sets of estimates: one for the customary Book of Estimates and a second for the national budget recommended by his commission. Since the budgetary situation had improved and there was little likelihood that Taft would be reelected that year, Congress moved to block his plans. An act of August 23 directed administrative personnel to prepare estimates and to submit them to Congress only in the form required by law.[9] Congress considered the budget format to be part of its spending prerogative. Taft regarded the form in which he transmitted recommendations to Congress as purely an executive matter. He went ahead by telling department chiefs to prepare two sets of estimates:

> Under the constitution the President is entrusted with the executive power and is responsible for the acts of heads of departments and their subordinates as his agents, and he can use them to assist him in his constitutional duties, one of which is to recommend measures to Congress and to advise it as [to] the existing conditions and their betterment. . . . If the President is to assume a responsibility for either the manner in which business of the government is transacted or result obtained, it is evident that he cannot be limited by Congress to such information as that branch may think sufficient for his purposes. In my opinion, *it is entirely competent for the President to submit a budget,* and Congress can not forbid or prevent it.[10]

Congress could not forbid Taft from submitting the budget, but neither did members have to pay attention to it. His model budget was almost completely ignored. After leaving office, Taft lamented that dust was accumulating on the reports of his commission.[11]

Budget and Accounting Act

Just as the financing of the Civil War prompted major changes in the congressional committee system, so did World War I trigger action on national budget reforms. Federal expenditures rose to record levels—from about $700 million before the war to $12.7 billion by 1918 and $18.5 billion by 1919. The national debt, slightly over $1 billion in 1916, jumped to over $25 billion by 1919. Members of Congress realized that debt-management problems after the war would require modernization of the budget process and an increased financial responsibility for the executive branch.

In 1919 the House of Representatives created the Select Committee on the Budget to discover not what was theoretically desirable but what was feasible, "keeping in mind at all times that to it had been committed the problem of recommending a system that would be in complete harmony with our constitutional form of government." Action was needed in three areas: formulation of the budget, congressional action on the budget, and supervision and control of the execution of the budget. The first and third reforms required statutory action. The second could be accomplished by altering the rules of the House and the Senate.[12]

In reviewing the budgetary process, the select committee identified a number of defects: expenditures were not considered in connection with revenues; Congress did not require of the president a carefully thought-out financial program; the estimates of expenditure needs submitted to Congress represented only the desires of the individual departments, establishments, and bureaus; and these requests were not revised by a superior officer to bring them into harmony, eliminate duplication, or make them conform to the needs of the nation. The committee condemned the lack of accountability in the system: "Practically everyone familiar with its workings agrees that its failure lies in the fact that no one is made responsible for the extravagance. The estimates are a patchwork and not a structure. As a result, a great deal of the time of the committees of Congress is taken up in exploding the visionary schemes of bureau chiefs for which no administration would be willing to stand responsible."[13]

To secure increased economy and efficiency, the committee decided to place definite responsibility on the president to subject bureau and departmental estimates to "scrutiny, revision, and correlation." If duplication, waste, extravagance, and inefficiency existed within the executive branch, "the President will be responsible for them if he includes in his budget an estimate for their continuance." In fixing executive responsibility, however, the select committee did not intend to subordinate Congress to the president. The plan provided for executive initiation of the budget, "but the President's responsibility ends when he has prepared the budget and transmitted it to Congress." Only in that sense was it an "executive budget." His proposal did not change "in the slightest degree the duty of Congress to make the minutest examination of the budget and to adopt the budget only to the extent that it is found to be economical."[14] Increases could be made in committee or on the floor by simple majority vote.

Thus Congress explicitly rejected the proposal of a number of reformers who wanted to copy the British parliamentary model. They hoped to concentrate power in the executive and limit the opportunity for legislators to add funds to the president's budget. Representative John J. Fitzgerald, Democrat of New York, had announced in 1915 his support for restrictions on Congress's power of the purse. As chairman of the House Appropriations Committee, he believed that Congress should be prohibited from appropriating any money "unless it has been requested by the head of the department, unless by a two-thirds vote, or unless it was to pay a claim against the government or for its own expenses." In 1920 David Houston, as secretary of the treasury under President Wilson, asked Congress to refrain from adding to the president's budget unless the increase was requested by the secretary of the treasury or approved by a two-thirds vote of Congress.[15]

Charles Wallace Collins, whose studies on budget reform sparked part of the momentum for the Budget and Accounting Act, argued explicitly for the British model. "Our institutions," he said, "being more nearly akin to those of England, it is to the English budget system that we more naturally look for the purpose of illustration." He noted that Parliament had long ago yielded the initiative in financial legislation to the cabinet. Parliament usually passed the budget without alteration. Budget reform in America, according to Collins, required "the relinquishing of the initiative in financial legislation to the executive by the Congress. . . . The President would possess the functions of a Prime Minister in relation to public finance."[16]

Congress rejected this version of an executive budget. The budget was executive only in the sense that the president was responsible for the estimates submitted. It was legislative in the sense that Congress had full power to increase or reduce the president's estimates. The bill was not meant to "impair either the authority or the responsibility of Congress."[17]

The Budget and Accounting Act created a Bureau of the Budget, to be located in the Treasury Department, and authorized the president to appoint the budget director. The statute authorized the Budget Bureau to "assemble, correlate, revise, reduce, or increase the estimates of the several departments or establishments," except estimates for Congress and the Supreme Court, which are included in the budget without revision.[18] This legislation prompted both houses of Congress to centralize their own controls over the budget. In 1920, immediately after passage of the bill on the House side, that chamber acted to consolidate jurisdiction over all appropriations in a single committee. In 1922 the Senate adopted the same reform.

Although the appropriations committees retained formal control over all appropriations, their actual jurisdiction was undercut by the growth of "backdoor spending" recommended by authorization committees. The two major forms were borrowing authority and contract authority. Borrowing authority allows a federal agency to enter into financial obligations and make payments from borrowed monies. Agencies could borrow either from the Treasury Department or from the public. The amounts involved were vast. From January 22, 1932—when Congress initiated borrowing authority for the Reconstruction Finance Corporation—through June 30, 1973, the amount of authority to spend from debt receipts exceeded $133 billion. Of that amount, only $17 billion passed through the appropriations committees. The balance was handled by other committees.[19]

The other backdoor was contract authority, which allowed agencies to enter into obligations before they received an appropriation. For example, the Clean Water Act of 1972 authorized states to enter into obligations up to $18 billion over a three-year period. Once an obligation existed, the appropriations committees had to provide the necessary funds to liquidate it.

Authorization committees also passed mandatory entitlements in the form of veterans' benefits, social security, revenue sharing, and other social programs. Once these benefit levels are set by authorization bills, the United States government is obligated to make payments to eligible individuals or state governments. Most of these entitlements bypass the appropriations committees. Funds usually become available from a permanent appropriation each year without any current action by Congress. To an increasing extent, the federal budget has become uncontrollable from year to year. By the 1960s, a large portion of the budget was uncontrollable within a given year because of various open-ended entitlements and fixed costs.

The congressional budget process was vulnerable to other criticisms. Congress divided the president's budget into thirteen separate appropriations bills, few of which were enacted by the start of the fiscal year. Government then had to be funded by stop-gap measures called "continuing resolutions." The combined effect of appropriations, backdoors, and entitlement legislation was never coordinated with congressional actions on revenue measures.

During the autumn months of 1972, President Nixon and Congress were locked in a prolonged and bitter struggle over a spending ceiling. The president wanted a limit of $250 billion for fiscal 1973, with complete discretion to cut whenever needed to preserve the ceiling. Congress refused to grant him such broad discretion, but the confrontation created a legislative momentum that produced the Congressional Budget and Impoundment Control Act of 1974.

In his message of July 26, 1972, calling for a spending ceiling, Nixon claimed that the budget crisis resulted from the "hoary and traditional procedure of the Congress, which now permits action on the various spending programs as if they were unrelated and independent actions." After Congress denied Nixon the spending ceiling and the discretion to cut programs to preserve the ceiling, the administration imposed a ceiling anyway. Secretary of the Treasury George Shultz announced that the president had reviewed the budget and "now feels sure that he can hold the outlays in the fiscal 1973 budget to $250 billion, and he is determined to do so."[20] The administration proceeded to impound huge amounts for housing, agriculture, and water pollution programs.[21] Nixon had asked Congress for authority to cut spending. Rebuffed, he announced through his treasury secretary that he had the power to do so anyway. Speaker of the House Carl Albert reacted angrily by saying that the president had made a "monkey out of the legislative process."[22]

Although Nixon repeatedly criticized Congress for profligacy, the record does not support his charge of legislative irresponsibility. From fiscal 1969 through fiscal 1973, appropriations bills were $30.9 billion below the president's requests. Over the same five-year period, back-door and mandatory entitlements exceeded the president's budget by $30.4 billion.[23] Through its own informal and decentralized system, Congress had managed to stay within the aggregates proposed by the president. Other studies reinforce the conclusion that Congress had been able to remain within the president's totals while altering the administration's priorities.[24]

Budget Act of 1974

Under President Nixon's goading, Congress passed the Congressional Budget and Impoundment Control Act of 1974. The impoundment provision has been discussed earlier in this book (pp. 83–85). The rest of the statute made major changes in the congressional budget process. Budget committees were established in the House and the Senate to report at least two budget resolutions a year. The budget resolutions allowed Congress to act on the budget as a whole instead of on individual pieces. The resolution contained five aggregates: total outlays, total budget authority, total revenues, the deficit or surplus, and the public debt. Outlays and budget authority were organized in major functional categories (such as national defense, agriculture, and transportation) to permit debate on budget priorities. The first resolution, to be passed by May 15, served as a target for congressional action on appropriations bills and other legislation. The second resolution, scheduled for September 15, acted as a binding ceiling on spending and a floor on revenues. If a mismatch existed between the totals in the fall resolution and the individual actions by Congress on appropriations bills, tax bills, and entitlements, a "reconciliation" bill could be passed to direct committees to report additional savings. The reconciliation process was later moved to the spring to permit cuts in entitlement programs.

The Budget Act established the Congressional Budget Office (CBO) to give legislators technical support. The statute changed the fiscal year to begin October 1 rather than July 1 to give Congress additional time to pass all the appropriations bills before the fiscal year and avoid reliance on continuing resolutions. Other sections of the statute placed restrictions on backdoors and set new deadlines for authorizing committees.

The legislative history of the Budget Act of 1974 contains sharp disagreements about its objectives. The dominant sentiment, however, was the need to restrain the growth of federal spending. The political backdrop included the acrimonious struggle between Nixon and Congress over a spending ceiling. Representative Bob Giaimo, Democrat of Connecticut, testifying as the chairman of the House Budget Committee, offered this perspective in 1978: "We don't need a Budget Act to enable us to spend more. We need a Budget Act in order to impose a discipline on ourselves, which was the very purpose of the Budget Act, to establish and change priorities, but within an overall discipline, within overall limitations."[25]

The history of impoundment legislation underscores his point. Each house passed legislation in 1973 to limit the president's ability to impound funds. Members were nevertheless reluctant to enact an impoundment control bill because they feared its "pro-spending" reputation. Voters might interpret the congressional effort to release impounded funds as evidence of uninhibited legislative spending appetites. Impoundment control would be politically safe only if attached to a measure that promised greater congressional control over spending. That union was achieved by making the Impoundment Control Act the final title (Title X) of the Budget Act. As Giaimo noted: "The Budget Act of 1974 was basically a contract whereby Congress agreed to curb its undisciplined spending habits and the president gave up his impoundment powers."[26]

Some of the provisions of the Budget Act have been worthwhile. Title IV helped restrict new backdoors and CBO established itself as a useful agency for estimating the cost of pending legislation, performing scorekeeping functions, and making macroeconomic projections. Despite those gains, the congressional budget process functions worse than in 1974. Appropriations bills are enacted later than ever, if at all. Before the Budget Act, it was highly unusual for all twelve months of a fiscal year to go by without Congress passing the regular appropriations bills. It is now a common practice. From fiscal 1968 through fiscal 1975, only two appropriations bills operated under a continuing resolution for an entire fiscal year. From fiscal 1976 through fiscal 1985, that figure jumped to twenty-seven.[27] For both fiscal 1986 and fiscal 1987, the fiscal year began without a single appropriations bill being enacted into law.

Deficits were larger, far larger, than they were before passage of the Budget Act. In the ten years from fiscal 1966 through fiscal 1975, deficits averaged $21.2 billion a year. From fiscal 1976 through fiscal 1996 the average annual deficit increased to about $157 billion a year

TABLE 7-1

Budget Deficits

FISCAL YEAR	DEFICIT ($ BILLIONS)	FISCAL YEAR	DEFICIT ($ BILLIONS)
1960	+0.3	1980	73.8
1961	3.3	1981	78.9
1962	7.1	1982	127.9
1963	4.8	1983	207.8
1964	5.9	1984	185.4
1965	1.4	1985	212.3
1966	3.7	1986	221.2
1967	8.6	1987	149.8
1968	25.2	1988	155.2
1969	+3.2	1989	152.4
1970	2.8	1990	221.2
1971	23.0	1991	269.3
1972	23.4	1992	290.4
1973	14.9	1993	255.0
1974	6.1	1994	203.1
1975	53.2	1995	163.9
1976	73.7	1996	107.3
[a]	14.7	1997 est.	23.0
1977	53.7		
1978	59.2		
1979	40.7		

[a] Transition Quarter (from changing the fiscal year).

(Table 7-1). Budgets submitted by presidents and budget resolutions passed by Congress have been chronically unreliable and deceptive. They regularly underestimate spending and overestimate revenues, producing deficits far beyond presidential and congressional projections. The second budget resolution for fiscal 1981 projected a deficit of $27.4 billion. The actual deficit was $78.9 billion. The second budget resolution for fiscal 1982 predicted a $37.65 billion deficit. It came to $127.9 billion. The estimated deficit for fiscal 1983 was $103.9 billion, compared to an actual deficit of $207.8 billion. Projections for recent years have also underestimated deficits (see Table 7-3).

There are other problems with the congressional process. Because continuing resolutions can serve as huge vehicles for general legislation, less is done on authorizing and appropriating bills. The deadlines imposed by the Budget Act have been routinely ignored. Congress found it so difficult to pass the second budget resolution that it figured ways to automatically spring it into place. If Congress failed to pass the second resolution by October 1, the first resolution automatically became binding as the second resolution. Eventually Congress eliminated the second resolution. Adoption of the first budget resolution has been chronically late (Table 7-2).

Did the Budget Act fail? Observers and participants were reluctant to admit failure, in part because there was a felt need for a "process." Even members of Congress who voted consistently against budget resolutions praised the process while condemning the product. Representative Herman Schneebeli, Republican of Pennsylvania, voting against the first budget resolution for fiscal 1977, voiced strong support for the act: "This budget process must work—we cannot allow it to fail. To fail is to admit to our constituents that we cannot control our wild Federal spending."[28] Senator Robert Packwood, Republican of Oregon, took a similar position that year: "Although I can commend the process wholeheartedly, it is with reluctance that I cannot support the result."[29] What logic supports a process that yields deplorable results? Representative Trent Lott, Republican of Mississippi, explained in 1985 why the Budget Act survived: "The primary reason is that it is worthwhile politically. Members of Congress use the budget process to give the appearance that they are doing something about the deficits or dealing with the budget. In my judgment, they are using it as political cover so that they can continue to be fiscally irresponsible."[30]

There are other justifications for the Budget Act. For the first few years it seemed that even if results were disappointing, the process should be given time to prove itself. As time went by, this appeal grew stale. Congress seemed to have a promising process that kept making promises. Years later a different defense emerged. When budget totals became too dreadful for anyone to condone, the results were explained not by the process but by external political and economic events. Defenders of the Budget Act said the process is not the problem; the problem is the problem. But if that is the case, why bother to change the process in 1974 or again in 1985 with the Gramm-Rudman bill? Obviously processes do count and they are expected to deal with events, both internal and external.

The Budget Act of 1974 produced two consequences of immense importance for executive-legislative relations. First, under very unique

TABLE 7-2

Dates for Adopting Budget Resolutions

FISCAL YEAR	FIRST BUDGET RESOLUTION (MAY 15 DEADLINE)	SECOND BUDGET RESOLUTION (SEPTEMBER 15 DEADLINE)
1976	May 14	December 12
1977	May 13	September 16
1978	May 17	September 15
1979	May 17	September 23
1980	May 24	November 28
1981	June 12	November 20
1982	May 21	December 10[a]
1983	June 23	[b]
1984	June 23	[b]
1985	October 1	[b]
1986	August 1 (April 15 Deadline)[c]	[b]
1987	June 27	
1988	June 24	
1989	June 6	
1990	May 18	
1991	October 9	
1992	May 22	
1993	May 21	
1994	April 1	
1995	May 12	
1996	June 29	
1997	June 13	
1998	June 5	

[a] The second resolution merely reaffirmed the figures in the first resolution.

[b] No second resolution was adopted for these years. The first resolution automatically became binding as the second resolution on October 1.

[c] The Gramm-Rudman-Hollings Act of 1985 (P.L. 99-177) changed the deadline of the budget resolution to April 15 and eliminated the second budget resolution.

circumstances the availability of a budget resolution can permit greater presidential control over the legislative process. As explained in the next section, that is what happened in 1981. The second consequence, however, has been just as important and, in some ways, contradicts the first point. The willingness of Congress to adopt budget resolutions has reduced the president's incentive to submit a responsible budget. The overall effect, then, is to weaken presidential responsibility, except in highly unusual conditions.

The Risks of Comprehensive Action: Reagan in 1981

Budget resolutions are highly regarded as vehicles that permit centralized, systematic, and coherent legislative action. The Budget Act assumed that members of Congress would behave more responsibly if they had to vote explicitly on budget aggregates and face up to totals, rather than vote piecemeal on a series of appropriations and legislative bills. In 1974, as now, it was difficult to defend fragmentation, splintering, and decentralization when reformers pressed eagerly for "coordination" and a "unified budget process."

The model of the executive budget looked appealing. The Budget and Accounting Act correctly assumed that presidential control and responsibility are enhanced by centralizing the budget process in the executive branch. However, advantages for the president are not necessarily transferable to Congress. The risks are high when Congress, possessing different institutional qualities, tries to emulate the executive branch. The president heads the executive branch, which is fortified by a central budget officer. There is no head in Congress and there are no comparable powers for CBO. Congress is inherently decentralized and no amount of procedural innovation can disguise that reality.

No one anticipated in 1974 that, given the right president and the right time, the budget resolution could be used as a weapon to advance executive goals. Those conditions materialized in 1981 to produce a radical change in budgetary policies, an explosion in the budget deficit, and the necessity for a major overhaul of the Budget Act. By seizing control of the legislative process in 1981, President Reagan was able to retrench domestic programs, increase military spending, and cut taxes.

Rudolph Penner, former CBO director, asked in 1985: "Would the dramatic actions of 1981 have been possible without the process? It is a question that no one will ever be able to answer with certainty. I believe, however, that it would have been difficult to achieve these results using the old, muddled way of formulating budgets."[31] Penner concluded that Reagan's objectives would have been much harder to accomplish had he been forced to negotiate with a decentralized power structure in Congress. Reagan's program would have been chopped to bits by successive committee and subcommittee action. The budget resolution gave him the centralizing vehicle he needed. Allen Schick makes the same point:

> Historically, the president has been at a disadvantage vis-à-vis Congress in their periodic budget conflicts. Congress excels as an institution that fragments issues and avoids decisions on overall objectives. Before installation of the congressional budget process, this fragmented behavior characterized legislative consideration of the president's budget. Appropriations were splintered into more than a dozen bills, tax legislation was walled off from spending decisions, and Congress did not have to vote on the totals. Members were able to profess support for the president's objectives while "nickel and diming" the budget in their action on appropriations and other spending measures.[32]

Whereas the politics of incrementalism under the old process operated as a brake on radical proposals, the Budget Act of 1974 strengthened Reagan's hand by requiring Congress to vote on an overall budget policy. Once the White House gained control of the budget resolution, which announced the basic policies on spending and taxation, it was in a position to increase defense spending, cut taxes, and use reconciliation to reduce entitlements and domestic spending. David Stockman, Reagan's OMB director from 1981 to 1985, explained how the congressional budget process became a convenient handle to pursue administration goals. The constitutional prerogatives of Congress "would have to be, in effect, suspended. Enacting the Reagan Administration's economic program meant rubber stamp approval, nothing less. The world's so-called greatest deliberative body would have to be reduced to the status of a ministerial arm of the White House."[33]

Some of the preconditions for this control had been supplied by the

1980 elections. The Republicans gained a majority in the Senate, and Reagan's massive popularity produced extraordinary party discipline in that body. Although the House of Representatives remained Democratic, the White House was able to stitch together a majority by combining Republicans with "Boll Weevils" (southern conservative Democrats). This coalition supported the administration's version of the budget resolution: Gramm-Latta I, named after Representative Phil Gramm, a Democrat from Texas, and Representative Del Latta, a Republican from Ohio. Gramm-Latta I incorporated the Reagan budget policy: increases for defense, decreases for domestic programs, and a huge tax cut. Because the tax cut would never be matched by comparable spending cuts, the result was an astonishing string of budget deficits. When Reagan entered office, the total national debt was about one trillion dollars, accumulated over a period of almost two centuries. Within five years the national debt had doubled and approached three trillion dollars by the end of Reagan's second term. After leaving office Stockman admitted that "a plan for radical and abrupt changes required deep comprehension—and we had none of it."[34]

The administration's victory in Gramm-Latta I led to Gramm Latta II: the reconciliation bill that changed benefit levels and benefit criteria in social welfare programs. Although the administration did not get everything it wanted, the omnibus measure was more of an advantage to the executive branch than to Congress. By packaging all the cuts in a single bill, the White House was able to build a majority for final passage. Members could announce that they objected to specific cuts but supported the bill "on balance."

The immense size of the reconciliation bill, its complexity, the confusion, and the lack of adequate information meant that most members had to vote largely with their eyes closed, trusting in the White House. The reconciliation bill was drafted mainly by OMB and the Reagan administration.[35] Senator Lowell Weicker, Republican from Connecticut, voted against the reconciliation process in 1981 "because of the precipitate, injudicious way the President's spending reduction package has been considered in the body. We are supposed to be a deliberative body but, instead, we have been a mirror to the administration's program."[36]

The House Appropriations Committee explained how the reconciliation process played into the hands of the president: "It is much easier for the Executive Branch to gain support for its program when it is packaged in one bill rather than pursuing each and every authorization and appropriation measure to insure compliance with the Executive's program. This device tends to aid the Executive Branch in gaining additional control over budget matters and to circumvent the will of Congress."[37] The results of 1981 exposed serious weaknesses within Congress. Instead of following CBO's projections or substituting an economic forecast of its own, Congress accepted the administration's flawed assumptions. Although the Budget Act has been praised because it gives Congress an independent technical capability, in 1981 Congress chose to adopt the administration's false premises.

Undercutting Presidential Responsibility

Although President Reagan successfully exploited the congressional budget process in 1981, the overall effect of the Budget Act of 1974 has been to undermine the president's budget. Prior to 1974 there was only one budget: the president's. The performance of Congress could be measured by comparing committee actions with presidential requests. The Joint Committee on Reduction of Federal Expenditures prepared "scorekeeping reports" and circulated them on a regular basis. These reports were printed in the *Congressional Record.* Members of Congress therefore knew, from month to month, how legislative actions compared to the president's budget. Through informal techniques, Congress managed to coordinate its actions and change the shape of the president's budget without exceeding its size.

The Budget Act of 1974 changed these dynamics. The use of a single budget—the president's—to serve as a visible benchmark disappeared. There was now the president's budget, the first budget resolution, the second budget resolution, the second budget resolution revised (passed the following spring), and a dizzying number of other budgets to reflect changing baselines, re-estimates, and updates. The phrases "below budget" and "above budget" lost meaning.

As a result, the public found it more difficult to keep the two branches accountable. Increasingly, the congressional budget seemed to overshadow the presidential budget. During debate on an appropriations bill in 1983, House Majority Leader Jim Wright made this statement: "This bill is not over the budget; the amounts proposed in this amendment are well within the budgeted figures. The amounts that we have agreed to and have discussed are not in excess of the congressional budget resolution. That, of course, is the budget. Now they may be in excess of certain amounts requested by the President in his budget request of last January. But that, of course, is not the budget. Congress makes the budget; the President does not."[38]

Instead of staying within the president's aggregates, members of Congress could vote on generous ceilings in a budget resolution and then announce to their constituents that they had "stayed within the budget." Representative Tom Steed, Democrat of Oklahoma, managing the Treasury-Postal Service appropriations bill for fiscal 1977, stated during floor debate: "Although we are over the President's budget, we are under the legislative budget. . . . This particular bill will be well within the limit set by the Committee on the Budget of the Congress."[39] Far from being offended by such statements, presidents invite Congress to take more responsibility. In 1985 President Reagan said that he "would accept appropriations bills, even if above my budget, that were within the limits set by Congress' own budget resolution."[40] Representative Barber Conable, Republican from New York, objected to budget resolutions because they sanctioned higher numbers for programs, giving them "an aura of responsibility they would not otherwise have had."[41]

The White House evidently finds it convenient to relieve the president of the personal responsibility for submitting a national budget, given the magnitude of current deficits. But the country pays a price. The decline in presidential responsibility for budget estimates has been dramatic. After his signal victory in 1981, President Reagan submitted budgets that were almost totally ignored by both houses. He remained a player by opposing tax increases and pushing for increased military spending, but he did not present a budget that he was willing to defend. The task of putting together a national budget fell to Congress. The problem with this process is that it is more difficult to hold accountable an inherently decentralized legislative body than it is to fix responsibility on a single president.

Gramm-Rudman-Hollings

The astonishing growth of budget deficits after 1981, combined with Reagan's refusal to offer constructive proposals, paved the way for the Gramm-Rudman-Hollings Act of 1985. This statute symbolizes many things: an admission that the congressional budget process created in 1974 could not deal with deficits of this size; a recognition that the political stalemate between President Reagan and Congress required a statutory framework with strong sanctions; and an unwillingness to delegate any additional authorities or powers to the executive branch.

Gramm-Rudman created a statutory schedule to eliminate deficits by fiscal 1991. Beginning with a deficit of $171.9 billion for fiscal 1986, the statute directed a decrease in that level by about $36 billion each year over a five-year period. In an effort to create a compact between the two branches, the president's budget and the congressional budget resolution were supposed to adhere to those targets. If in any fiscal year the projected deficit exceeded the statutory allowance by more than $10 billion, a "sequestration process" was triggered to make across-the-board cuts to meet the statutory target. Half of these cuts were to come from defense; a number of social programs were exempted.

As contemplated by Gramm-Rudman, the sequestration process depended ultimately on actions by the comptroller general. OMB and CBO would estimate the amount of deficit for the upcoming fiscal year. If their deficit exceeded the statutory target by more than $10 billion, each agency would calculate the budget reductions necessary on a program-by-program basis. The OMB and CBO reports would then go to the comptroller general. After reviewing the reports, the comptroller general would make whatever adjustments he considered necessary and report the conclusions to the president. The president was required to issue this sequestration order without change, mandating spending reductions throughout the government.

Recognizing that this process was subject to constitutional challenge, Congress provided for a "fallback" procedure in the event the courts invalidated the role of the comptroller general. Under the substitute process, the OMB and CBO reports would go to a specially created Temporary Joint Committee on Deficit Reduction consisting of the full membership of both budget committees. The joint committee would report the sequestration bill for floor action, and, if passed by both houses, it would go to the president to be signed or vetoed.

Gramm-Rudman provided for an expedited process to test the constitutionality of the bill. In 1986, a three-judge court held the comptroller general's role unconstitutional, and the Supreme Court sustained that decision five months later. Both decisions concluded that the sequestration process violated the separation of powers doctrine by vesting executive functions in an officer removable by Congress. Although appointed by the president with the advice and consent of the Senate, the comptroller general is removable only by a joint resolution of Congress or by impeachment. This does not mean that the comptroller general serves at the pleasure of Congress, since the joint resolution must be sent to the president for a signature or veto. However, the court considered the relationship between Congress and the comptroller general too close to satisfy constitutional standards.[42]

Gramm-Rudman suffered from many deficiencies. By focusing primarily on a deficit number for a particular year, it encouraged both branches to play games, making a number of short-run calculations that aggravated long-run problems. The one-year preoccupation inspired a variety of accounting tricks, such as shifting costs from a current year to a previous one (or to the next), or raising revenue for a current year at the cost of losing much larger amounts in future years.[43] Also, deficit targets nearly ensured that appropriations bills would be held to the last minute, awaiting the most recent deficit projection. Gramm-Rudman thus supplied one more incentive for delaying the annual appropriations bills and relying to an even greater extent on continuing resolutions. Eventually, crucial decisions were shifted to "budget summits" held at the White House or other locations, excluding most members of Congress and preventing "the normal give and take of congressional deliberations."[44]

The crutch of Gramm-Rudman made it easier for the political branches to avoid the painful decisions needed to rein in the deficit. Their task was relatively simple: offer budget *projections* that met the Gramm-Rudman deficit targets. If actual deficits soared beyond the projections, the statutory mission was nonetheless fully satisfied. Because the public believed that the deficit crisis was being addressed, Congress and the president were under less political pressure to do something real. Senator Jim Sasser, chair of the Senate Committee on the Budget, summed up the issue in 1989:

> We have ended up with two sets of books. . . . First, we keep a set
> for the Gramm-Rudman game—and this is a useful fiction manipu-

lated to give the illusion of progress—and second, we keep a set of books that are the real books. That is the real deficit. And we neglect getting around to doing something about the real deficit because of the Gramm-Rudman set of books we keep.[45]

Representative Marty Russo, member of the House Committee on the Budget, made a similar point in 1990. He explained how the two branches practiced deceit with budget deficits: "The President submits a budget that relies on very optimistic economic and technical assumptions and questionable savings proposals to meet the Gramm-Rudman deficit target. Congress attacks the assumptions and proposals as phony, but uses them in the budget resolution anyway."[46] Congress accepted the president's phony figures because honest figures (which were available) would have increased the projected deficit and made Congress look like the "big spender." Once the president ducked responsibility by submitting a dishonest budget, politics required Congress to embrace the same mistaken assumptions.

When it became obvious that the deficit targets of Gramm-Rudman could not be reached, the two branches enacted a law in 1987 known as Gramm-Rudman II. The new statute anticipated a zero deficit by fiscal 1993, but that too was fantasy. Deficits continued to climb. Gramm-Rudman I called for a zero deficit by fiscal 1991. Gramm-Rudman II's target for that year was $64 billion. The actual deficit in 1991 was $269.3 billion (Table 7-3).

Budget Enforcement Act of 1990

The experience with the Budget Act of 1974 and the two Gramm-Rudman Acts convinced leaders from both branches to try another tack. Under the 1987 version of Gramm-Rudman, the deficit target for fiscal 1991 was $64 billion. However, projections in 1990 indicated a deficit of at least $150 billion, requiring an unacceptable $86 billion in sequestered cuts. Rather than enact Gramm-Rudman III and promise a zero deficit a few years later, President Bush and congressional leaders abandoned deficit targets and turned toward spending limits. The Budget Enforcement Act of 1990 marked an effort to reduce federal deficits by $500 billion over a five-year period.

As part of the effort to enforce spending limits, the Budget Enforce-

TABLE 7-3

Gramm-Rudman Targets
(in billions of dollars)

FISCAL YEAR	1985 LAW	1987 LAW	1990 LAW	ACTUAL DEFICIT
1986	$171.9			$221.2
1987	144.0			149.8
1988	108.0	$144.0		155.2
1989	72.0	136.0		152.4
1990	36.0	100.0		221.2
1991	0	64.0	$327.0	269.3
1992		28.0	317.0	290.4
1993		0	236.0	255.0
1994			102.0	203.1
1995			83.0	163.9

ment Act of 1990 established spending caps for three categories: defense, international, and domestic. The caps for those categories applied only to fiscal years 1991 through 1993. The last two years were governed by a limit on total discretionary spending. To prevent violations of the spending caps, the new law permitted sequesters several times a year for discretionary programs and once a year for entitlements and taxes. The statute authorized the two branches to designate "emergency funding" that would be exempt from the spending caps.

Institutionally, the executive branch gained important powers. OMB's authority to estimate the costs of legislation and perform scorekeeping functions (crucial for spending control) was clearly greater than under the Gramm-Rudman statutes. Establishing caps for three categories helped shield the Defense Department from hasty congressional cuts motivated by the end of the Cold War. Congress could still reduce defense spending, but "fire walls" between the three categories prevented Congress from taking money from defense and giving it to international or domestic programs. Thus, the statute severely limited the traditional prerogative of Congress to alter budget priorities. Finally, the president was in the driver's seat in designating emergency funding.

Three basic political goals were embedded in the 1990 statute. The two political branches wanted to avoid fixed deficit targets that had embarrassed them in the past. They agreed to protect the defense budget from legislative raids. And they hoped to finesse the budget crisis at least through the 1992 presidential election year. On those three counts the drafters largely failed. Federal deficits remained a prominent issue in the 1992 election, while political pressures mounted to push funds from the Defense Department to domestic programs. Early in 1992, Senate Majority Leader George Mitchell, Democrat from Maine, said that the "first step is to change the 1990 budget agreement. The Cold War is over. It's time to take down the artificial budget walls which prevent us from shifting our priorities from abroad to here at home."[47] The Bush administration agreed to cut military spending, but proposed that the reductions finance a variety of tax proposals aimed at stimulating the economy.[48] There would be no free ride for politicians in 1992. The statutory creature of 1990 offered them no shelter from intense national debate over the budget. President Bush's agreement to raise taxes as part of the 1990 package was a major factor in his defeat in 1992.

In 1993, President Clinton proposed a package of spending cuts and revenue increases to control deficits. The resulting budget resolution provided for about $500 billion in net deficit reduction over five years. Not a single Republican in either the House or the Senate voted for the budget in committee or on the floor. The 1993 initiative, combined with the actions taken in 1990, started the first downward trend in federal deficits (Table 7-1).

Standing on the steps of the U.S. Capitol on September 27, 1994, more than three hundred Republican candidates for the House of Representatives voiced their support for a "Contract with America." The remarkable victories by Republicans in the November elections converted the Contract into a blueprint for legislative action, part of which called for a balanced budget amendment. Congress was never able to pass this constitutional amendment, but the House and Senate Budget Committees reported budget resolutions in 1995 designed to balance the budget by fiscal year 2002.

In the 1996 elections, Republicans retained control of Congress and pressed for a balanced budget by fiscal year 2002. In an accord on May 2, 1997, President Clinton and Congress agreed to a deficit-cutting package that combined $85 billion in net tax cuts, $115 billion of savings in Medicare, and \$34 billion in new spending over five years. The general goals embodied in this plan must be translated into specific legislative language, to be enacted not just in 1997 but in subsequent years. Any economic downturn (or even slowdown) over the five-year period would derail the plan. Most of the budgetary constraints are "backloaded," meaning that about two-thirds of the deficit reduction measures would come after the elections in 2000. President Clinton described the agreement as "the first balanced budget in a generation."[49] In fact, it was merely a *projection* of a balance *five years out*, precisely the sort of "balanced budget" promised by Gramm-Rudman I in 1985 and Gramm-Rudman II in 1987.

The Item Veto

Having lost confidence in its internal budgetary process, Congress turned to automatic mechanisms in Gramm-Rudman and other bills in an effort to control spending and deficits. Among the reform ideas debated is the item veto, which would permit the president to veto individual items within an appropriations bill. This proposal has been offered numerous times since 1876 as a constitutional amendment, but prior to 1984 the only floor action occurred in 1938 when the House of Representatives voted to give the president item-veto authority by statute.[50]

There the matter rested until 1984 and 1985, when Senator Mack Mattingly, Republican from Georgia, proposed that the president be given item-veto authority by statute. His first attempt was rejected by the Senate as an unconstitutional amendment to a pending bill.[51] The next year his bill was withdrawn after a lengthy filibuster.[52] In the midst of these debates the Reagan administration made a strong move to obtain item-veto authority. Other presidents had recommended the item veto, but Reagan was unusually insistent. Having requested this power in previous addresses, he told Congress in his State of the Union message in 1986: "[T]onight I ask you to give me what 43 Governors have: Give me a line-item veto this year. Give me the authority to veto waste, and I'll take the responsibility, I'll make the cuts, I'll take the heat."[53]

Although the states have served as laboratories for developing social programs, there are special problems in trying to borrow the item veto from the states and engraft it onto the national government. The item veto is sustained by a unique culture in the states and cannot be severed from it. The state analogy, in fact, suffers from a number of serious deficiencies. State constitutions differ dramatically from the federal Constitution, especially in their distribution of executive and legislative powers. There is a much greater bias against legislatures in the states than at the national level. State budget procedures are also substantially different from congressional procedures. Appropriations bills in the states are structured to facilitate item vetoes by governors, whereas appropriations bills passed by Congress contain few items. Finally, state judges have experienced severe problems in developing a coherent and principled approach to monitoring the scope of item-veto power. Many of these conceptual pitfalls would be duplicated and possibly compounded at the national level.

The "item veto" is generally discussed as though it represents a single concept. In fact, it can take a number of forms. The first and most basic form is the authority to veto individual items in appropriations bills, but even this power is controversial when used to strike not merely appropriation (dollar) amounts but substantive law (conditions and qualifications) as well. Second, ten states allow their governors to reduce the level of an item. This is called "item-reduction" power. A third type of power is called the "amendatory veto," which allows a governor to condition approval of an enacted bill by returning it to the legislature with suggestions for change. Seven states authorize some form of the amendatory veto.

The Reagan administration advocated a broad interpretation of item-veto authority. An OMB study characterized it as "vital" and urged that the president be given the power to veto substantive provisions (riders) attached to appropriations bills.[54] The importance of the latter authority is underscored by examining decisions in the state courts.

For almost a century, state judges have struggled with the question of whether governors may veto conditions in an appropriations bill while keeping the funds. Could governors, through the item veto, convert a conditional appropriation into an unconditional appropriation? Could they strike the legislative language, or was it inseverable from the dollar amount? A Mississippi court in 1898 decided that the governor should not have the power to veto objectionable conditions on appropriations. Allowing the governor to strike the condition would produce a law that had never received the legislature's assent:

> ... the executive, in every republican form of government, has only a qualified and destructive legislative function and never creative legislative power. If the governor may select, dissect, and dissever, where is the limit of his right? Must it be a sentence or a clause, or a word? Must it be a section, or any part of a section, that may meet with executive disapprobation? May the governor transform a conditional or contingent appropriation into an absolute one in disregard and defiance of the legislative will? That would be the enactment of law by executive authority without the concurrence of the legislative will and in the face of it.[55]

These themes surfaced repeatedly in later years: the legislature may place conditions on appropriations; the veto is destructive and not creative; the governor may not use the item veto to dissect a bill and distort the legislative will. However, state judges found it a difficult matter to distinguish appropriate conditions from those that were inappropriate, to separate the act of destruction from that of creation, and to determine (much less preserve) the legislative will.

A 1915 Illinois case illustrates the ingenuity of some item vetoes. The governor struck the words "per annum" from the phrase "$2,500 per annum" in a biennial appropriation, reducing a two-year amount from $5,000 to $2,500 and giving the governor what amounted to item reduction power. The court held that he had exceeded his authority.[56] Another governor, also without success, attempted to exercise item-veto authority by striking the digit "2" from a $25 million bond authorization.[57]

Some judges decided that a governor may sever sections from a bill if the veto is merely "negative" in effect.[58] Other judges regarded these actions as "affirmative" because they created "a result different from that intended, and arrived at, by the legislature."[59] A Virginia court in 1940 invoked an intriguing medical analogy in a strained effort to distinguish between severable and inseverable items. It defined an "item" as something that could be taken out of a bill without affecting its other purposes or provisions: "It is something which can be lifted bodily from it rather than cut out. No damage can be done to the surrounding legislative tissue, nor should any scar tissue result therefrom."[60] If a provision or condition was "intimately interlocked" with the other portions of the bill, however, the veto was unauthorized.[61] Such tests proved to be too abstract and subjective to apply.

State judges in recent years have become increasingly skeptical about their ability to distinguish between negative and affirmative vetoes. They fear that such tests involve the courts in "disingenuous semantic games" and are unworkable in practice no matter how appealing in theory.[62] However, governors have shown themselves adept in wielding the item veto. In 1988, the Supreme Court of Wisconsin upheld the governor's decision to strike phrases, digits, letters, and word fragments.[63] In response to that decision, Wisconsin amended its constitution in April 1990 to provide: "In approving an appropriation bill in part, the governor may not create a new word by rejecting individual letters in the words of the enrolled bill."[64]

In addition to conceptual difficulties in defining the proper reach of the item veto, there is little analogy between Congress and the state legislatures. State constitutions are filled with detailed prescriptions and proscriptions on the authorization-appropriation process. Many states direct that general appropriations bills shall embrace nothing but appropriations, thereby prohibiting the addition of substantive legislation to funding measures. A court has ruled that a state legislature should not use appropriations bills to create, amend, or repeal substantive legislation.[65] The Louisiana constitution requires that the general appropriations bill "shall be itemized."[66] Some state constitutions even prescribe the format and style of bills.[67]

These provisions are intended to protect the governor's item-veto authority. By contrast, the U.S. Constitution is virtually silent on such matters. It does not contain directives on the style and form of appropriations bills. There are no requirements for itemization, nor is there any effort to prohibit legislation on appropriations bills. These issues are left solely to the rules of the House and the Senate.

State appropriations bills are structured with a high degree of specificity. Individual projects are identified, giving the governor a clear opportunity to exercise the item veto. In contrast, it is the practice of Congress to appropriate in lump sums. Specific projects and activities are not included in the bill presented to the president. They are placed in committee reports as part of the nonstatutory system of controls. Executive agencies prefer this system because it gives them substantial discretion in allocating lump-sum amounts, provided they keep faith with their review committees.

This point must be constantly underscored: item-veto authority would give the president little additional power under the present system, for the simple reason that appropriations bills do not contain items. For example, the energy and water development appropriation for fiscal 1996 included $804 million for the general construction account for the Corps of Engineers. The individual projects are not mentioned in the public law. They are located in the committee reports and the agency budget justification documents.[68] The only "item" is the lump sum of $804 million.

When President Reagan gave his State of the Union address in January 1988, he seemed unaware of the fundamental difference between lump sums in a public law and details in a committee report. He told the nation that item-veto authority would have allowed him to eliminate from a continuing resolution he signed in December such wasteful projects as "cranberry research, blueberry research, the study of crawfish, and the commercialization of wildflowers."[69] Reagan was badly misinformed. Those four projects were never identified in the continuing resolution he signed. Even with an item veto he could not have deleted them since the projects are mentioned only in the conference report.[70] The veto power applies to bills, not reports.

If Congress decided to pattern itself after the states by resorting to line itemization, the consequences may not be attractive. An item veto could make Congress more irresponsible. To satisfy constituent demands, even of the most indefensible nature, a member need only add extraneous material to a bill with the understanding among colleagues that the president will probably strike the offending amendment. The adoption of an item veto could make the problem of log-rolling worse. The availability of an item veto, in fact, would trigger a new round of budgetary legerdemain and political unaccountability.

Nor is it clear that the president would use this authority to curb spending. Presidents, White House aides, and agency officials would possess an additional weapon to influence members of Congress. As Senator Mark Hatfield, Republican of Oregon, remarked in 1984:

The line-item veto has wide-ranging ramifications on the gamut of decisions made by the Congress. We have all witnessed the power of the President when he lobbies Congress by telephone. It does not take much imagination to consider how much more persuasive he would be if his words were buttressed with a veto stamp over individual projects and activities within our States or districts.[71]

The threat of an item veto could force legislators to scale back the size of a program, but that can be done now with the regular veto. On the other hand, consider this scenario: White House lobbyists advise members of Congress that certain projects in their district or state are being considered for an item veto. Members are asked how they plan to vote on the administration's bill scheduled for the following week. Perhaps a minor project would survive in return for a legislator's willingness to support a costly administration program. Both sides would prevail in this accommodation, pushing budget totals upward. A specific project could also be held hostage in return for a member's support for a nominee, treaty, or some other presidential objective.

The item veto has significance beyond the particular budgetary savings that may, or may not, be realized. At stake are the power relationships between the executive and the legislative branches, the exercise of Congress's historic power of the purse, and the relative abilities of each branch to impose its version of budgetary priorities. A radical restructuring of constitutional power could flow from what might appear to be a relatively minor reform proposal.

The item veto would clearly magnify the stature of the president's budget. As originally conceived under the Budget and Accounting Act, the executive budget could be amended, up or down, as Congress decided. The final judgment lay with Congress, subject to presidential veto of the entire bill. The item veto would upset that balance. The president could strike what Congress had added to the White House budget, and rarely could Congress attract a two-thirds majority in each house to override.

Administration officials have been remarkably candid in admitting that the item veto would be used to delete congressional initiatives and add-ons. In 1957 the budget director, Percival Brundage, told the House Judiciary Committee that the authority to veto an appropriation item "would include authority to reduce an appropriation—

but only to the extent necessary to permit the disapproval of amounts added by the Congress for unbudgeted programs or projects, or of increases by Congress of amounts included in the budget."[72] The Economic Report of the President issued in 1985 explains that the adoption of the item veto "may not have a substantial effect on total Federal expenditures" but may be used by the president "to change the composition of Federal expenditures—from activities preferred by the Congress to activities preferred by the President."[73]

Officials in the Reagan and Bush administrations toyed with the novel idea that the president already *has* the item veto. The basic reasoning: "Omnibus bills passed by the contemporary Congress violate the framers' intent that the president receive individual bills containing discrete items. To restore the original scope of the veto power, the president should exercise an item veto."[74] That line of argument is based on a false understanding of what the framers intended and the kind of bills that the early Congresses passed and submitted to the president.[75] In any event, Presidents Reagan and Bush did not follow the advice of some of their aides who encouraged an item veto to test the issue in court.

President Bush admitted in 1992 that he lacked constitutional authority to exercise line-item veto authority. He received that legal advice from his attorney general, William Barr, and White House Counsel C. Boyden Gray.[76] Instead of provoking a court test, he relied on existing statutory authority to propose rescissions to Congress under the procedures of the Impoundment Control Act of 1974.

The Republican "Contract with America" called for an item veto for the president. A version of this budgetary reform, enacted in 1996, created much confusion. Many citizens, as well as legislators, thought that the bill would give the president the same type of item veto exercised by governors (striking some items from a bill and letting the balance become law). In fact, whatever version of the "item veto" became law, President Clinton would have the same choice that he and other presidents have had in the past: either sign the whole bill or veto the whole bill.

What the Republicans passed, and Clinton signed, is more accurately called "enhanced rescission." Under the Impoundment Control Act of 1974, presidents could recommend the cancellation (rescission) of funds but needed the approval of both the House and the Senate within forty-five days of continuous session. Otherwise, the funds would have to be released for obligation by agencies. The Line Item Veto Act of 1996, instead of requiring the president to obtain the support of both houses within a specified time period, shifted the burden. Within five days of signing a bill into law, a president could propose the cancellation of certain items and the proposal would automatically take effect. Congress would have thirty days to disapprove, but the disapproval bill would have to go to the president and could be vetoed. After the expected veto, Congress would need a two-thirds majority in each chamber to override the president and reestablish the priorities decided by Congress. Along with rescission of discretionary appropriations, the 1996 statute also subjects any new item of direct spending (entitlement) and certain limited tax benefits to cancellation by the president.

The president is not limited to dollar amounts identified in a bill or joint resolution. Given the lump-sum nature of most appropriations, the president would be unable to reach specific items. The statute overcomes that problem by allowing the president to cancel any dollar amount represented separately in any table, chart, or explanatory text included in the statement of managers or the governing committee report accompanying such law. That is, the president can cancel items that are located in nonstatutory sources such as committee reports. The scope of the president's discretion therefore depends on the level of detail that Congress chooses to place in committee reports. Details (tables, charts, etc.) might be removed from the report and placed on plain paper, with the understanding that agencies will comply with this nonstatutory control at the risk of sanctions being imposed in subsequent legislation.

Senator Robert C. Byrd and several other legislators challenged the constitutionality of the Line Item Veto Act. A district judge in 1997 held that the procedures established in the statute—allowing the president to sign a bill but then, within five days, canceling parts of it— violated the procedures set forth in the Constitution for enacting legislation. "The President's cancellation of an item unilaterally effects a repeal of statutory law such that the bill he signed is not the law that will govern the Nation. That is precisely what the Presentment Clause was designed to prevent."[77] On June 26, 1997, the Supreme Court held that Senator Byrd and his colleagues lacked standing to bring the suit. The result was to reinstate the law and return item-veto authority to President Clinton.

Conclusions

The Budget Act of 1974 led to a preoccupation with the internal mechanics and technicalities of the congressional budget process: authorizations, appropriations, tax bills, budget resolutions, and reconciliations. Through this process we lost sight of the need for a budget system that connects the legislative branch to the executive. To be effective, a legislative budget process must work in tandem with the White House. The total process must take advantage of the institutional strengths of Congress and the president. For the last two decades we have played on institutional weaknesses rather than institutional strengths.

When Congress ushered in the modern budget system in 1921 by enacting the Budget and Accounting Act, it did a good job of understanding the special roles of the two branches. It placed on the president the responsibility for submitting an annual budget. The statute held the administration accountable for the budget estimates prepared by the agencies. As a single executive officer assisted by a central budget bureau, the president was ideally qualified for that task. At the same time, Congress looked to its own institutional strengths and retained full freedom to modify the president's estimates. Through its decentralized system, both between the House and the Senate and within each chamber, Congress could represent national and local interests that had been excluded from the president's budget. The system held each branch accountable. The president took responsibility for the aggregates, and Congress lived within those totals while rearranging the priorities. In short, each branch did what it was well suited for.

The Budget Act of 1974 offered an entirely different model. Not only did Congress change its internal procedures, but it claimed that it could make the budget. As a consequence, the president is no longer responsible for the budget submitted, at least not to the same degree as between 1921 and 1974. The current system allows a president to submit estimates and deficit projections for which the White House does not assume responsibility. The political system, by no longer holding the president accountable for the budget, has excused the chief executive from the political leadership role that the nation needs. Automatic, statutory mechanisms are less reliable than a dependence on the strengths and attributes natural to each institution and the initiatives that must come from political leaders.

EPILOGUE

We use words to communicate thought. They are supposed to clarify, refine, and enrich. Some words, however, obscure thought and discourage inquiry. Much of the vocabulary used to discuss Congress and the executive becomes an impediment to learning and exploration. Abstract concepts, especially when derogatory, prevent us from appreciating the subtle interactions between the branches and the opportunities for constructive compromise.

Slogans, always tempting, can backfire in unexpected ways. In 1959 President Eisenhower admonished legislators who called foreign aid a "giveaway" program. It would be tragic, he said, "to allow a valuable program to be shot down by a slogan!" Later, however, he resorted to the term "pork barrel" to justify his veto of a public works appropriation bill. Members of Congress were quick to point out the administration's inconsistency in championing dams and reclamation projects abroad while deploring similar efforts at home. Both houses overrode the veto, the first time in seven years that an Eisenhower veto had not been sustained.[1]

Scholars and jounalists describe in rich detail the defects and liabilities of Congress. The federal bureaucracy receives harsh treatment as well, criticized for being "unresponsive" and "resistant to change." Yet despite the failings of individual occupants of the Oval Office, there appears to be a different standard for the presidency.

Legislators seem to travel the low road of "localism" while the president is associated with such lofty qualities as rationality, accountability, and a commitment to the public interest.

High principles, as Willmoore Kendall suggested some years ago, can be a euphemism for empty platitudes. He believed that as a constituency increased in size—from the congressional district to the national forum for a president—"there is greater and greater danger that the persons concerned will find themselves talking about *nothing*, not *something*, and will also find themselves talking about situations and problems that are too large, too complicated, for them to understand." Presidents are not more rational than legislators. They simply draw from different sources, and different levels, of information.[2]

In 1975 I participated in an all-day conference held in Washington, D.C., to analyze the tension between the executive and legislative branches. Throughout the morning and the afternoon, we were joined by members of Congress while senior editors and writers from a national magazine observed. That evening, at the Kennedy Center, we continued the conference over cocktails and dinner. Again the writers and editors listened. After I finished a conversation with one senator, several senior staffers from the magazine approached me and asked, visibly shaken, "Are *other* members of Congress this bright?" I wondered what stereotypes of Congress they had harbored over the years, how much they had miseducated their readers, and whether this exposure to members who were demonstrably informed, thoughtful, and articulate would change their image of Congress. Probably not.

The literature on Congress and the executive is filled with words that are a stumbling block to careful analysis and deeper probing. Why say that Congress, in the legislative process, practices "delay" instead of "deliberation" or "conscientious review"? Is the delay justified? Is there, in fact, a need for the legislation at all? Honest answers would require careful investigation into an individual case, but this kind of search takes time, homework, and persistence beyond the appetite of many analysts.

On a particular issue was Congress "obstructive" or did it merely reject an unworthy presidential proposal? Did Congress "gut," "mangle," "cripple," "mutilate," or "emasculate" a president's bill, or was it necessary to add amendments to a bill imperfectly drafted by the administration? Answers to these questions do not come easily. A researcher must master the original bill and its motivations, anticipate its impact on the public sector, comprehend the purpose behind the amendments, and take into account other considerations of a social, economic, and political nature.

Studies accuse Congress of "parochialism," "localism," and the pursuit of "particularistic" goals, all of which supposedly differentiate Congress from the president. But surely the White House is receptive to special interests. Indeed, it is inconceivable to think of a genuinely democratic political system that would prohibit intervention by special or local interests. What is gained by calling Congress an "assembly of special interests" instead of an institution that allows access, expression, and participation by the voters?

In what has degenerated into a tiresome and trite ritual, presidents try to score points by calling Congress the servant of special interests. When the House of Representatives rejected a standby gasoline rationing plan in 1979, President Carter announced that a majority of the House had followed local or parochial interests, allowing "political timidity [to] prevent their taking action in the interests of our Nation." In a subsequent address he charged that Congress "has yielded to the narrow interest on energy issues time and time again."[3]

Special interest groups, however, do not spend all their time and resources on Capitol Hill. They also seek representation inside the administration. In fact, the White House has been organized for some time to respond to special interests. After World War II, White House assistants were recruited to represent the aged, youth, women, blacks, Jews, labor, Hispanic Americans, the business community, governors and mayors, artists, and citizens of the District of Columbia. As one scholar noted: "Where once the White House had been a mediator of interests, it now had become a collection of interests."[4]

At each point along the legislative journey a bill is exposed to delay and adjustment as it passes through executive agencies, subcommittees, committees, the floor of the House and Senate, and conference committee. The complexity of this process has been criticized as "open season" for lobbyists and special interests to work their will. Would we find greater comfort in a more closed system, or would not that give rise to complaints about autocracy and centralization? At least with the present system we have an opportunity to see interests at work. And since legislation has a major impact on society, we should encourage a process that permits intervention by affected parties.

"Parochialism" can be attributed to any group: Congress, the White House, the bureaucracy, or the judiciary. Although it may be true that members of Congress are more likely than executive officials to be recruited from small towns and local politics, this background enables Congress to perform its representational role and to offset the particular perspective of federal agencies. As one study notes, parochialism "may exist in various forms. If the experiences of congressmen incline them toward local parochialism, those of bureaucrats may incline them toward functional and agency parochialisms."[5]

Specialists in the agencies may attach undue importance to their areas of responsibility. Francis Wilcox recalled that during his service in the State Department, the assistant secretary in charge of European affairs "vigorously defended the interests of his clients in Western Europe, often presenting their views with greater clarity and conviction than the Europeans themselves." Reflecting on his own responsibilities for United Nations affairs, Wilcox conceded that he "probably attached more significance to the role of the United Nations in American foreign policy than it merited."[6]

The different "parochialisms" of Congress and the president are essential in a system of checks and balances. Proposals to have members of Congress elected at large in the nation, for the purpose of bringing the two branches closer, would jeopardize the constitutional system. Checks and balances are not negative instruments designed to frustrate government. They exist because of the propensity of public officials (like the rest of us) to make mistakes and abuse privileges. Checks and balances allow these mistakes to surface so they can be corrected before the damage becomes too great.

Legislators are criticized for acting in "piecemeal" fashion through a "splintered" process. There appears to be a built-in preference for action that is "comprehensive" and "united," and yet every organization, public or private, legislative or executive, depends on a division of labor and allocation of responsibilities to subgroups. Congress cannot decide everything on the floor in general assembly. Nor can it create, with any success, supercommittees to represent every interest. It tried that in 1946 with a joint budget committee consisting of

102 members from the taxing and appropriations committees of each house. After three ineffectual efforts the committee disbanded in 1949.

Recent proposals for a joint committee on national security encountered the same problems. If all of the legislative interests were represented, the committee would be far too large, suffer from poor attendance, and eventually delegate authority to subunits, defeating the original objective of comprehensiveness. An administration must be willing to work with ad hoc legislative groups of shifting memberships, varying with the particular issue.

Criticism of Congress and the executive will not always be tempered, balanced, and fair. However, we can at least recognize when it is contradictory and even irrational. A newspaper account in 1980 referred to an "ossified bureaucracy." Yet the same article managed to describe agency employees who somehow possessed the energy and skills to work assiduously in their schemes to sabotage the White House.[7] "Entrenched bureaucracy" is a sensational label that covers what would otherwise be quite ordinary: civil servants protected from political dismissals. White House officials complain about bureaucrats "blocking" programs, but investigation usually reveals that bureaucrats simply carry out the laws enacted by Congress rather than presidential proposals that are not yet public law. Do we want bureaucrats to behave differently?

Presidents are criticized first for one thing and then another: Johnson for wheeling and dealing, Carter for failing to compromise and bargain, Carter for being too immersed in details, Reagan for remaining arms-length from the operations of government. If legislators do not act quickly enough they are condemned for delay. If they act too quickly they are called a rubber stamp. In the midst of polemics and conflict, members of all three branches need to remember that they share a common task: searching for accommodations that permit government to operate effectively for the common good within constitutional limits. Upon his retirement from the Senate, Charles McC. Mathias, Jr., spoke perceptively in 1986 about the breakdown in executive-legislative relations: "We're losing track of a very essential word in the whole federal system, which is coordinate: the separate, equal, *coordinate* branches of government. . . . There's a lack of that spirit of coordination that is really the heart of the whole constitutional scheme."[8]

NOTES

◆

Chapter 1. Constitutional Underpinnings

1. Woodrow Wilson, *Congressional Government* (Boston: Houghton Mifflin, 1885), p. 309.

2. Richard E. Neustadt, *Presidential Power* (New York: John Wiley & Sons, 1960), p. 33. Emphasis in original.

3. Louis Fisher, *President and Congress* (New York: Free Press, 1972), pp. 6–17.

4. Gaillard Hunt, ed., *The Writings of James Madison*, 9 vols. (New York: G. P. Putnam's Sons, 1900–1910), 2:339–40.

5. Max Farrand, ed., *The Records of the Federal Convention of 1787*, 4 vols. (New Haven: Yale University Press, 1937), 2:80–83.

6. Ibid., 2:183.

7. Ibid., 2:35 (Madison), 1:107 (Wilson), 2:52 (Morris), 2:298 (Mercer).

8. Ibid., 1:108. See also 1:105, 139; 2:77.

9. *Youngstown Co. v. Sawyer*, 343 U.S. 579, 635 (1952).

10. M. J. C. Vile, *Constitutionalism and the Separation of Power* (New York: Oxford University Press, 1967), p. 153.

11. *Annals of Congress*, 1st Cong., May 19, 1789, p. 383.

12. Ibid., June 8, 1789, pp. 453–54, and Aug. 18, 1789, pp. 789–90. For action by the Senate, see U.S. Senate, *Journals, 1789–1794*, 5 vols. (Washington, D.C.: Gales & Seaton, 1820), 1:64, 73–74.

13. Frederick Green, "Separation of Governmental Powers," *Yale Law Journal* 29 (1920): 369, 371.

14. *United States v. Nixon*, 418 U.S. 683, 704 (1974).

15. Farrand, *Records of the Federal Convention*, 1:379–81, 383–90.

16. *Ex parte Garland*, 71 U.S. 333, 381 (1866); United States v. Lovett, 328 U.S. 303 (1946).

17. See *United States v. Johnson*, 383 U.S. 169, 179 (1966).

18. *Powell v. McCormack*, 395 U.S. 486 (1969).

19. *Marbury v. Madison*, 5 U.S. 137, 155 (1803).

20. 13 Op. Att'y Gen. 516 (1871).

21. For example, 5 U.S.C. 3317–18 (1994).

22. Louis Fisher, *Constitutional Conflicts between Congress and the President* (Lawrence: University Press of Kansas, 1997), p. 30.

23. *United States Law Week* 49 (Mar. 24, 1981): 2604.

24. *Minnesota Chippewa Tribe v. Carlucci*, 358 F. Supp. 973, 975–76 (D.D.C. 1973).

25. 96 Stat. 806, sec. 502 (1982).

26. 109 Stat. 803 (1995).

27. Ward Sinclair, "USDA Drops Maine Senators' Hot Potato," *Washington Post*, June 4, 1986, p. A21.

28. Howard Kurtz, "Manion's Nomination Survives," *Washington Post*, June 27, 1986, p. A1.

29. Howard Kurtz, "Democrats Settle Score with Gorton on Judgeship," *Washington Post*, Oct. 11, 1986, p. A10.

30. Fisher, *President and Congress*, pp. 62–66.

31. The resolution is cited in *Annals of Congress*, 5th Cong., 1799, p. 2489; 1 Stat. 613.

32. Detlev F. Vagts, "The Logan Act: Paper Tiger or Sleeping Giant?" *American Journal of International Law* 60 (1966): 268.

33. *Public Papers of the Presidents*, 1979, p. 1861.

34. *Digest of United States Practice in International Law, 1975* (Washington, D.C.: Government Printing Office), pp. 749–50.

35. *Digest of United States Practice in International Law, 1976*, pp. 75–76.

36. 122 *Congressional Record* 4216, 4919 (1976); *Washington Post*, Feb. 26, 1976, p. A7.

37. *Public Papers of the Presidents*, 1980–1981 (II), p. 1087.

38. *Public Papers of the Presidents*, 1984 (II), p. 990.

39. 142 *Congressional Record* H1700 (daily ed. Mar. 5, 1996).

40. Louis Fisher, *Presidential War Power* (Lawrence: University Press of Kansas, 1995), p. 30.

41. *Guaranty Trust Co. v. United States*, 304 U.S. 126, 137–38 (1938).

42. W. W. Humbert, *The Pardoning Power of the President* (Washington, D.C.: American Council on Public Affairs, 1941), p. 22.

43. *Knote v. United States*, 95 U.S. 149, 153–54 (1877). On the primacy of the appropriations power when pitted against the pardon power, see *Hart v. United States*, 118 U.S. 62 (1886); 8 Op. Att'y Gen. 281, 282 (1857); 23 Op. Att'y Gen. 360, 363 (1901).

44. *The Laura*, 114 U.S. 411 (1885); 8 Op. Att'y Gen. 281, 282 (1857).

45. Humbert, *The Pardoning Power of the President*, pp. 43–45.

46. *Ex parte Garland*, 71 U.S. 333, 380. See 12 Stat. 502 (1862) and 13 Stat. 424 (1865).

47. *United States v. Klein*, 13 Wall. 128 (1872).

48. House Judiciary Committee, *Pardon of Richard M. Nixon and Related Matters* (hearings), 93d Cong., 2d sess., 1974, pp. 87–158.

49. *Ex parte Garland*, 71 U.S. 333, 380, 1 Op. Att'y Gen. 341, 343 (1820); *Murphy v. Ford*, 390 F. Supp. 1372 (W.D. Mich. 1975).

50. 2 Op. Att'y Gen. 275 (1825); 6 Op. Att'y Gen. 20 (1853).

51. *Burdick v. United States*, 236 U.S. 79, 94 (1915).

52. *Weekly Compilation of Presidential Documents* 10 (Sept. 8, 1974): 1110.

53. *Public Papers of the Presidents*, 1977 (II), pp. 1409–10. See 91 Stat. 114, sec. 306; 91 Stat. 444, sec. 706.

54. James J. Brosnahan, "Pardoning Weinberger Belittles Democracy," *National Law Journal*, Jan. 18, 1993, pp. 17–18.

55. *Springer v. Philippine Islands*, 277 U.S. 189, 211 (1928).

56. Fisher, *President and Congress*, pp. 1–27, 241–70.

57. Joseph Story, *Commentaries on the Constitution of the United States*, 2 vols. (Boston: Little, Brown, 1905), 1:396.

58. *Myers v. United States*, 272 U.S. 52, 293 (1926) (dissenting opinion).

59. Fisher, *Constitutional Conflicts between Congress and the President*, Chap. 6.

60. *United States v. AT&T,* 419 F. Supp. 454, 461 (D.D.C. 1976).
61. *United States v. AT&T,* 551 F.2d 384, 394 (D.C. Cir. 1976).
62. *United States v. AT&T,* 567 F.2d 121, 126 (D.C. Cir. 1977).
63. Ibid., at 127.
64. House Select Committee on Congressional Operations, *Court Proceedings and Actions of Vital Interest to the Congress, Current to December 31, 1978,* 95th Cong., 2d sess., 1978, p. 50.
65. 128 *Congressional Record* 31746–76 (1982).
66. *United States v. House of Representatives,* 556 F. Supp. 150 (D.D.C. 1983).
67. 142 *Congressional Record* H1959–1964 (daily ed. Mar. 7, 1996).
68. "Panel Moves to Gain Travel Office Files," *New York Times,* May 10, 1996, p. A26; "White House Gives Committee More Papers in Dismissal Case," *New York Times,* May 31, 1996, p. A20.
69. "Legal Experts Uncertain on Prospects of Clinton Privilege Claim," *Washington Post,* Dec. 14, 1994, p. A14; "Compromise on Notes Rejected," *Washington Post,* Dec. 15, 1995, p. A2.
70. "Whitewater Notes Being Surrendered," *Washington Post,* Dec. 22, 1995, p. A1.
71. "Congress Is Denied Report on Bosnia," *New York Times,* Apr. 17, 1996, p. A1; "Clinton Keeps Papers on Haiti from House," *Washington Post,* Sept. 26, 1996, p. A20; "White House Claims Privilege on Drug Memo," *Washington Post,* Oct. 2, 1996, p. A15.
72. *Kennedy v. Sampson,* 364 F. Supp. 1075, 1084 (D.D.C. 1973).
73. *Kennedy v. Sampson,* 511 F.2d 430, 438 (D.C. Cir. 1974). See also *Wright v. United States,* 302 U.S. 583, 596 (1938), and *The Pocket Veto Case,* 279 U.S. 644 (1929).
74. 122 *Congressional Record* 11202 (1976). See also the announcement by Representative John Rhodes, 121 *Congressional Record* 41884 (1975).
75. *Public Papers of the Presidents,* 1981, p. 1208.
76. *Barnes v. Carmen,* 582 F. Supp. 163 (D.D.C. 1984); *Barnes v. Kline,* 759 F.2d 21 (D.C. Cir. 1985).
77. *Burke v. Barnes,* 479 U.S. 361 (1987).
78. H. Rept. 417 (part 1), 101st Cong., 2d sess. (1990); H. Rept. 417 (part 2), 101st Cong., 2d sess. (1990).
79. *Public Papers of the Presidents,* 1992–93 (11), pp. 472–73.

Chapter 2. President as Legislator

1. There are political benefits as well as liabilities in convening Congress for special session. See Wilfred E. Binkley, "The President as Chief Legislator," *The Annals* 307 (1956): 92, 99–100; Joseph E. Kallenbach, *The American Chief Executive* (New York: Harper and Row, 1966), pp. 324–33.
2. *Youngstown Co. v. Sawyer,* 343 U.S. 579, 587 (1952).
3. *Hinds' Precedents of the House of Representatives,* 5 vols. (Washington, D.C.: Government Printing Office, 1907), 5:6629; *Cannon's Precedents of the House of Representatives,* 11 vols. (Washington, D.C.: Government Printing Office, 1935), 8:3333; Kallenbach, *The American Chief Executive,* pp. 333–36.
4. James D. Richardson, ed., *A Compilation of Messages and Papers of the Presidents,* 20 vols. (New York: Bureau of National Literature, 1897–1925), 4:1864.
5. H. Wayne Morgan, *From Hayes to McKinley* (Syracuse, N.Y.: Syracuse University Press, 1969), pp. 274–319.

6. Donald F. Anderson, *William Howard Taft: A Conservative's Conception of the Presidency* (Ithaca, N.Y.: Cornell University Press, 1973), p. 299.

7. Richard E. Neustadt, "Presidency and Legislation: Planning the President's Program," *American Political Science Review* 49 (1955): 980, 1015.

8. For a detailed analysis of the Clinton health-care bill, see Haynes Johnson and David S. Broder, *The System* (Boston: Little, Brown & Co., 1996).

9. *Missouri Pac. Ry. Co. v. Kansas*, 248 U.S. 277 (1919). A president may sign a bill after Congress recesses; see *La Abra Silver Mining Co. v. United States*, 175 U.S. 423 (1899). The president may also sign a bill after a final adjournment of Congress; see *Edwards v. United States*, 286 U.S. 482 (1932).

10. Anonymous "William Penn" writing in the Philadelphia *Independent Gazetteer*, Jan. 3, 1788, cited in *The Antifederalist Papers*, ed. Morton Borden (East Lansing: Michigan State University Press, 1965), p. 210.

11. Max Farrand, ed., *The Records of the Federal Convention of 1787*, 4 vols. (New Haven: Yale University Press, 1937), 1:139. See also 2:74, 586–87; 4:81.

12. *Annals of Congress*, 15th Cong., 1st sess., 1817, pp. 18, 451–52.

13. Richardson, *Messages and Papers of the Presidents*, 9:4475, 4488, 4494 (April 29, May 29, and June 23, 1879); T. Harry Williams, ed., *Hayes: The Diary of a President* (New York: David McKay, 1964), pp. 193–234.

14. Louis Fisher, "The Authorization-Appropriation Process in Congress: Formal Rules and Informal Practices," *Catholic University Law Review* 29 (1979): 51.

15. Richard A. Watson, "The President's Veto Power," *The Annals* 499 (1988): 37. For other analyses of the factors behind vetoes and congressional overrides, see Albert C. Ringelstein, "Presidential Vetoes: Motivations and Classification," *Congress and the Presidency* 12 (1985): 43; Jong R. Lee, "Presidential Vetoes from Washington to Nixon," *Journal of Politics* 37 (1975): 522.

16. Cited in Raoul Berger, *Government by Judiciary* (Cambridge, Mass.: Harvard University Press, 1977), pp. 117, 407. See also Raoul Berger, *Executive Privilege* (Cambridge, Mass.: Harvard University Press, 1974), pp. 57–58.

17. Patrick W. Duff and Horace E. Whiteside, "Delegata Potestas Non Potest Delegari: A Maxim of American Constitutional Law," *Cornell Law Quarterly* 14 (1929): 168; and Horst P. Ehmke, "'Delegata Potestas Non Potest Delegari,' A Maxim of American Constitutional Law," *Cornell Law Quarterly* 47 (1961): 50.

18. *Wayman v. Southard*, 10 Wheat. 1, 46 (1825).

19. *Hampton & Co. v. United States*, 276 U.S. 394. 406 (1928). See also *Field v. Clark*, 143 U.S. 649, 692 (1891).

20. *Sunshine Coal Co. v. Adkins*, 310 U.S. 381, 398 (1940). See also the discussion in Fisher, *Constitutional Conflicts between Congress and the President*, 4th ed., pp. 87–106.

21. *Panama Refining Co. v. Ryan*, 293 U.S. 388 (1935); *Schechter Corp. v. United States*, 295 U.S. 495 (1935).

22. 84 Stat. 799 (1970).

23. *Amalgamated Meat Cutters & Butcher Work. v. Connally*, 337 F. Supp. 737, 750 (D.D.C. 1971).

24. *California Bankers Assn. v. Shultz*, 416 U.S. 21, 90–93 (1974) (Justices Douglas and Brennan dissenting); *Arizona v. California*, 373 U.S. 546, 624–27 (1963) (Justice Harlan dissenting); *Zemel v. Rusk*, 381 U.S. 1, 21–22 (1965) (Justice Douglas dissenting).

25. *Industrial Union v. American Petroleum*, 448 U.S. 607 (1980).

26. *United States v. Eliason*, 41 U.S. 291, 301 (1842).
27. 6 Op. Att'y Gen. 10 (1853).
28. *Lincoln Electric Co. v. Commissioner of Int. Rev.*, 190 F.2d 326, 330 (6th Cir. 1951). See James Hart, *The Ordinance Making Powers of the President of the United States* (1925; reprint, New York: Da Capo Press, 1970).
29. *Manhattan Co. v. Commissioner*, 297 U.S. 129, 134 (1936). See also *Ernst & Ernst v. Hochfelder*, 425 U.S. 185, 213–14 (1976).
30. 127 *Congressional Record* 781 (1981).
31. *Citizens to Save Spencer Cty. v. EPA*, 600 F.2d 844 (D.C. Cir. 1979).
32. *Weekly Compilation of Presidential Documents* 16 (1980): 583, 768, 841, 901.
33. Ibid., 575, 922.
34. Proclamation 4744, *Federal Register* 45 (1980): 22864, as amended by Proclamations 4748 and 4751; *Independent Gasoline Marketers Council, Inc. v. Duncan*, 492 F. Supp. 614 (D.D.C. 1980).
35. House Ways and Means Committee, *Oil Import Fees: The Administration of the Program and Its Impact* (hearings), 96th Cong., 2d sess., 1980.
36. *United States v. Yoshida Intern., Inc.*, 526 F.2d 560 (Ct. Cust. & Pat. App. 1975); Fisher, *Constitutional Conflicts between Congress and the President*, p. 109.
37. *Carl Zeiss, Inc. v. United States*, 76 F.2d 412 (Ct. Cust. & Pat. App. 1935); *Schmidt Pritchard & Co. v. United States*, 167 F. Supp. 272 (Cust. Ct. 1958).
38. See John L. Blackmun, Jr., *Presidential Seizure in Labor Disputes* (Cambridge, Mass.: Harvard University Press, 1967).
39. 90 *Congressional Record* 6022 (1944); 58 Stat. 387, sec. 213 (1944); 31 U.S.C. 1347 (1988). See also 31 U.S.C. 1346 (1988).
40. 49 Comp. Gen. 59 (1969); 42 Op. Att'y Gen. 405 (1969); *Contractors Assn. of Eastern Pa. v. Secretary of Labor*, 442 F.2d 159, 171 (3d Cir. 1971), *cert. denied*, 404 U.S. 854 (1971).
41. 118 *Congressional Record* 21063–64 (1972). See Fisher, *Constitutional Conflicts between Congress and the President*, pp. 112–13. See also Joel L. Fleishman and Arthur A. Aufses, "Law and Orders: The Problem of Presidential Legislation," *Law and Contemporary Problems* 40 (1976): 1.
42. *Cole v. Young*, 351 U.S. 536 (1956); *Youngstown Co. v. Sawyer*, 343 U.S. 579 (1952); *Panama Refining Co. v. Ryan*, 293 U.S. 388, 433 (1935); *United States v. Symonds*, 120 U.S. 46 (1887); *Little v. Barreme*, 2 Cr. 170 (1804). See Louis Fisher, "Laws Congress Never Made," *Constitution* 5 (1993): 59–66.
43. H. Rept. No. 100-498, 100th Cong., 1st sess. (1987), p. 943.
44. *Rust v. Sullivan*, 500 U.S. 173 (1991).
45. *National Family Planning and Reproductive Health Ass'n, Inc. v. Sullivan*, 979 F.2d 227 (D.C. Cir. 1992).
46. 58 Fed. Reg. 7455 (1993).
47. Executive Order 12954, 60 Fed. Reg. 13023 (1995).
48. *Chamber of Commerce of U.S. v. Reich*, 74 F.3d 1322 (D.C. Cir. 1996). See also *Chamber of Commerce of U.S. v. Reich*, 886 F.Supp. 66 (D.D.C. 1995); *Chamber of Commerce of U.S. v. Reich*, 57 F.3d 1099 (D.C. Cir. 1995); *Chamber of Commerce v. Reich*, 897 F.Supp. 570 (D.D.C. 1995).
49. *Public Papers of the Presidents*, 1981, p. 104.
50. Morton Rosenberg, "Beyond the Limits of Executive Power: Presidential Control of Agency Rulemaking under Executive Order 12,291," *Michigan Law Review* 80 (1981): 193.

51. Judith Havemann, "'Defunding' OMB's Rule Reviewers," *Washington Post,* July 18, 1986, p. A17.
52. H. Rept. 723, 99th Cong., 2d sess., 1986, p. 47.
53. "Office of Management and Budget Influence on Agency Regulations," S. Prt. 156, 99th Cong., 2d sess., May 1986.
54. S. Rept. 347, 99th Cong., 2d sess., 1986, pp. 14–15.
55. Julie Rovner, "Senators Hail OMB Decision to Open Rule Review Process," *Congressional Quarterly Weekly Report,* June 21, 1986, p. 1409.
56. S. Rept. 406, 99th Cong., 2d sess., 1986, p. 35.
57. OMB Watch and Public Citizens' Congress Watch, "All the Vice President's Men: How the Quayle Council on Competitiveness Secretly Undermines Health, Safety, and Environmental Programs," Sept. 1991; Dana Priest, "Competitiveness Council under Scrutiny," *Washington Post,* Nov. 26, 1991, p. A19.
58. Charles Tiefer, *The Semi-Sovereign Presidency: The Bush Administration's Strategy for Governing without Congress* (Boulder, Colo.: Westview Press, 1994), pp. 86–87.
59. Robert J. Duffy, "Regulatory Oversight in the Clinton Administration," *Presidential Studies Quarterly* 27 (1997): 71.
60. John C. Fitzpatrick, ed., *Writings of Washington,* 39 vols. (Washington, D.C.: Government Printing Office, 1931–1944), 30:394.
61. Ibid., 369–70, 375, 393–94. See also Washington's letter to Senator Pierce Butler, Aug. 10, 1789, p. 379.
62. Ibid., Washington's letter to Senator Pierce Butler, p. 373.
63. Richardson, *Messages and Papers of the Presidents,* 1:64–65, 68–69, 71–72, 81ff., 110, 115 (Feb. 9, 1790, to Mar. 8, 1792).
64. For information on the Knox incident, see James Hart, *The American Presidency in Action* (New York: Macmillan, 1948), p. 77. For 1790 and 1792 actions, see Leonard D. White, *The Federalists* (New York: Macmillan, 1948), p. 57.
65. William Maclay, *Sketches of Debate in the First Senate of the United States* (Frederick Ungar, 1965), pp. 135, 172, 201, 251.
66. *Annals of Congress,* 1st Cong., June 25, 1789, pp. 592–93.
67. 1 Stat. 65 (1789); White, *The Federalists,* p. 118n.
68. Maclay, *Sketches of Debate in the First Senate* (1965 ed.), pp. 185, 373, 374, 376, 399. For Hamilton's other activities to influence Congress, see pp. 377, 397–98.
69. *Annals of Congress,* 2d Cong., 1st–2d sess., Nov. 20, 1792, pp. 703–708. On the 1793 and 1794 investigations, see ibid., Feb. 28 to Mar. 1, 1793, pp. 899–963; ibid., 3d Cong., 1st–2d sess., Feb. 19, 1794, p. 458; ibid., Feb. 24, 1794, pp. 463–66, and Dec. 2, 1794, p. 954. See also Broadus Mitchell, *Alexander Hamilton,* 2 vols. (New York: Macmillan, 1957–1962), 2:245–86. For some strategic errors that caused Hamilton political problems, see James Willard Hurst, "Alexander Hamilton, Law Maker," *Columbia Law Review* 78 (1978): 483.
70. On Jefferson to Gallatin, see Henry Adams, ed., *The Writings of Albert Gallatin,* 3 vols. (New York: Antiquarian Press, 1960), 1:380. On Representative Giles, see Ralph Volney Harlow, *The History of Legislative Methods in the Period before 1825* (New Haven: Yale University Press, 1917), p. 168, citing the *Washington Federalist* of Feb. 17, 1802. On Jefferson to Nicholas, see *The Writings of Thomas Jefferson* (Memorial Ed., 1904), 11:162.
71. Harlow, *The History of Legislative Methods,* p. 175.

72. Dice Robins Anderson, *William Branch Giles* (Menasha, Wis.: George Banta, 1914), p. 82.

73. Robert M. Johnstone, Jr., *Jefferson and the Presidency* (Ithaca, N.Y.: Cornell University Press, 1978), p. 140.

74. Charles Francis Adams, ed., *Memoirs of John Quincy Adams*, 12 vols. (Philadelphia: J. B. Lippincott, 1874–1877), 1:447.

75. Henry Adams, *The Life of Albert Gallatin* (New York: Peter Smith, 1943), pp. 302–303. See also Johnstone, *Jefferson and the Presidency*, pp. 140–43.

76. James Sterling Young, *The Washington Community: 1800–1828* (New York: Columbia University Press, 1966), pp. 16, 162.

77. Ibid., p. 168.

78. Stephen Horn, *The Cabinet and Congress* (New York: Columbia University Press, 1960), pp. 55–59.

79. Ibid., pp. 63–71.

80. Ibid., pp. 78–92. See also Gamaliel Bradford, "Congress and the Cabinet," *Annals of the American Academy of Political and Social Science* 2 (Nov. 1891): 289–90.

81. 34 Stat. 454 (1906).

82. 40 *Congressional Record* 8810–11 (1906).

83. Ibid., p. 8812.

84. James W. Garner, "Executive Participation in Legislation as a Means of Increasing Legislative Efficiency," proceedings of the annual meeting of the American Political Science Association (Washington, D.C., Dec. 30, 1913–Jan. 1, 1914), 10:183–84.

85. Estes Kefauver, "Executive-Congressional Liaison," *The Annals* 289 (1953): 108; Horn, *The Cabinet and Congress*, pp. 136–75; Lee H. Hamilton and Michael H. Van Dusen, "Making the Separation of Powers Work," *Foreign Affairs* 57 (1978): 17, 37–38.

86. Bureau of the Budget, Circular No. 49 (Dec. 19, 1921); Stephen J. Wayne, *The Legislative Presidency* (New York: Harper & Row, 1978), pp. 96–97 n.1.

87. Richard E. Neustadt, "Presidency and Legislation: The Growth of Central Clearance," *American Political Science Review* 48 (1954): 641, 643.

88. On executive orders and proclamations, see Executive Order 8247, *Federal Register* 4 (1939): 3864, sec. II.2(f); Horace W. Wilkie, "Legal Basis for Increased Activities of the Federal Budget Bureau," *George Washington Law Review* 11 (1943): 265, 273. See also Carl R. Sapp, "Executive Assistance in the Legislative Process," *Public Administration Review* 6 (1946): 10. On reviewing testimony, see John H. Reese, "The Role of the Bureau of the Budget in the Legislative Process," *Journal of Public Law* 15 (1966): 63, 77–78; and Neustadt, "Presidency and Legislation," pp. 649–50.

89. Allen Schick, "The Budget Bureau That Was: Thoughts on the Rise, Decline, and Future of a Presidential Agency," *Law and Contemporary Problems* 35 (1970): 519, 527. See also Robert S. Gilmour, "Central Legislative Clearance: A Revised Perspective," *Public Administration Review* 31 (1971): 150.

90. Wayne, *The Legislative Presidency*, pp. 70–100. For other studies on central clearance, see James W. Davis and Randall B. Ripley, "The Bureau of the Budget and Executive Branch Agencies: Notes on Their Interaction," *Journal of Politics* 29 (1967): 749; and Larry Berman, *The Office of Management and Budget and the Presidency, 1921–1979* (Princeton, N.J.: Princeton University Press, 1979), pp. 116–25.

91. Woodrow Wilson, *Congressional Government* (Boston: Houghton Mifflin, 1885), p. 297.

92. Stephen Kemp Bailey, *Congress Makes a Law* (New York: Columbia University Press, 1950), pp. 9, 41.

93. Robert A. Dahl, *Congress and Foreign Policy* (New York: Harcourt Brace Jovanovich, 1950), p. 58.

94. Francis O. Wilcox, *Congress, the Executive, and Foreign Policy* (New York: Harper & Row, 1971), p. 14.

95. See James A. Robinson, *Congress and Foreign Policy-Making* (Homewood, Ill.: Dorsey Press, 1967); and David Baldwin, "Congressional Initiative in Foreign Policy," *Journal of Politics* 28 (1966): 754. Studies crediting Congress with significant voice include: James A. Robinson, *The Monroney Resolution: Congressional Initiative in Foreign Policy Making* (New York: Henry Holt, 1959); Thomas M. Franck and Edward Weisband, *Foreign Policy by Congress* (New York: Oxford University Press, 1979); and Cecil V. Crabb, Jr., and Pat M. Holt, *Invitation to Struggle: Congress, the President and Foreign Policy*, 4th ed. (Washington, D.C.: CQ Press, 1992).

96. Charles Tiefer, *The Semi-Sovereign Presidency*, pp. 89–136; Louis Fisher, "President Clinton as Commander in Chief," in *Rivals for Power: Presidential-Congressional Relations*, ed. James A. Thurber (Washington, D.C.: CQ Press, 1996), pp. 214–31.

97. Robinson, *Congress and Foreign Policy-Making*, pp. 44–46.

98. For thoughtful analyses by John R. Johannes, see his *Policy Innovation in Congress* (Morristown, N.J.: General Learning Corporation, 1972); "Where Does the Buck Stop—Congress, President, and the Responsibility for Legislative Initiation," *Western Politics Quarterly* 25 (1972): 396; "Congress and the Initiation of Legislation," *Public Policy* 20 (1972): 281; and "The President Proposes and the Congress Disposes, But Not Always: Legislative Initiation on Capitol Hill," *Review of Politics* 36 (1974): 356. See also David E. Price, *Who Makes the Laws?: Creativity and Power in Senate Committees* (Cambridge: Schenkman, 1972); and Gary Orfield, *Congressional Power: Congress and Social Change* (New York: Harcourt Brace Jovanovich, 1975).

99. George B. Galloway, *The Legislative Process in Congress* (New York: Thomas Y. Crowell, 1953), p. 38; Samuel P. Huntington, "Congressional Responses to the Twentieth Century," *The Congress and America's Future*, ed. David B. Truman (Englewood Cliffs, N.J.: Prentice-Hall, 1965), p. 23.

100. Lawrence H. Chamberlain, *The President, Congress and Legislation* (New York: Columbia University Press, 1946), pp. 23, 454; Ronald C. Moe and Steven C. Teel, "Congress as Policy-Maker: A Necessary Reappraisal," *Political Science Quarterly* 85 (1970): 443. See also Nelson W. Polsby, "Policy Analysis and Congress," *Public Policy* 18 (1969): 61.

101. *Public Papers and Addresses of Franklin D. Roosevelt*, 13:491, 497; 53 Stat. 565 (1939).

102. Edwin E. Witte, "The Preparation of Proposed Legislative Measures by Administrative Departments," President's Committee on Administrative Management, *The Exercise of Rule-Making Power and the Preparation of Proposed Legislative Measures by Administrative Departments* (Washington, D.C.: Government Printing Office, 1937), pp. 52, 57, 57n. See also O. Douglas Weeks, "Initiation of Legislation by Administrative Agencies," *Brooklyn Law Review* 9 (1940): 117;

and Edwin E. Witte, "Administrative Agencies and Statute Lawmaking," *Public Administration Review* 2 (1942): 116.

103. Harold W. Stoke, "Executive Leadership and the Growth of Propaganda," *American Political Science Review* 35 (1941): 490, 491.

104. On General Persons, see Bryce Harlow, "Text of Address at Nashville Symposium, October 21, 1973," *Center House Bulletin of the Center for the Study of the Presidency* 4 (Winter 1974), cited by Maura E. Heaphy in "Executive Legislative Liaison," *Presidential Studies Quarterly* 5 (1975): 42. On the legal counselor in 1950, see Earl D. Johnson, "Legislative-Executive Relationships in the Formulation of Public Policy as Viewed by the Executive," in *Legislative-Executive Relationships in the Government of the United States*, ed. O. B. Conway (Washington, D.C.: Graduate School of the U.S. Department of Agriculture, 1954), p. 30. See also Abraham Holtzman, *Legislative Liaison* (Chicago: Rand McNally, 1970), p. 11; and Thomas P. Murphy, "Congressional Liaison: The NASA Case," *Western Politics Quarterly* 25 (1972): 192.

105. House Select Committee on Lobbying Activities, *Legislative Activities of Executive Agencies (Part 10)* (hearings), 81st Cong., 2d sess., 1950, pp. 9–10.

106. Holtzman, *Legislative Liaison*, pp. 231–33, 236, 259.

107. Ibid., p. 233.

108. Heaphy, "Executive Legislative Liaison," pp. 42, 43.

109. Holtzman, *Legislative Liaison*, pp. 232–37.

110. Dwight D. Eisenhower, *Mandate for Change* (Garden City, N.Y.: Doubleday, 1963), p. 298; see also Chaps. 8, 12.

111. Holtzman, *Legislative Liaison*, p. 239. For additional criticism of Kennedy liaison staffers, characterized as young and arrogant, see Meg Greenfield, "Why Are You Calling Me, Son?" *The Reporter*, Aug. 16, 1962, pp. 29–31.

112. G. Russell Pipe, "Congressional Liaison: The Executive Branch Consolidates Its Relations with Congress," *Public Administration Review* 26 (1966): 14, 21.

113. Interview with Lawrence F. O'Brien, "From White House to Capitol . . . How Things Get Done," *U.S. News & World Report* (Sept. 20, 1965): 73.

114. Lawrence F. O'Brien, *No Final Victories* (Garden City, N.Y.: Doubleday, 1974), p. 176.

115. Mary McGrory, "GOP Dream Still Unfulfilled," *Washington Star*, Feb. 11, 1969, p. A7.

116. *Public Papers of the Presidents*, 1971, pp. 23–25.

117. *New York Times*, July 3, 1972, p. 15; *The Washington Lobby* (Washington, D.C.: Congressional Quarterly Press, 1971), p. 142.

118. *New York Times*, July 7, 1972, p. 10.

119. *New York Times*, June 30, 1973, p. 16; *Christian Science Monitor*, Feb. 26, 1974, p. 1; *Washington Star*, Apr. 13, 1974, p. A2.

120. *Washington Post*, Jan. 2, 1975, p. A28.

121. "Hill Democrats Unhappy with Carter's Emissary," *Washington Post*, Nov. 5, 1976, p. A1; "Hill Leaders Ask Carter to Improve Consultation," *Washington Post*, Jan. 28, 1977, p. A4. See also *Christian Science Monitor*, Jan. 28, 1977, p. A4. See also *Christian Science Monitor*, Jan. 27, 1977, p. 3; and *New York Times*, Jan. 27, 1977, p. 1.

122. Speaker Tip O'Neill, *Man of the House* (New York: Random House, 1987), p. 311. For other analyses of Carter's relations with Congress, see Q. Whitfield Ayres, "The Carter White House Staff," and Tinsley E. Yarbrough, "Carter and

the Congress," in *The Carter Years,* ed. M. Glenn Abernathy et al. (New York: St. Martin's Press, 1948).

123. 127 *Congressional Record* 18765–67 (1981). The author of the amendment was Patricia Schroeder, Democrat of Colorado.

124. James R. Dickinson, "Breaking Rules, Flying High: Iowa's Grassley Seems to Cross Reagan with Impunity," *Washington Post,* Mar. 25, 1985, p. A5.

125. Richard E. Cohen, "The Gloves Are Off," *National Journal,* Oct. 14, 1989, pp. 2508–12; Burt Solomon, "No-Nonsense Sununu," *National Journal,* Sept. 1, 1991, pp. 2248–52.

126. Jennifer Senior, "White House Liaison Fights Irrelevance," *The Hill,* Jan. 10, 1996, p. 1; Burt Solomon, "Bill Who?" *National Journal,* Apr. 15, 1995, pp. 910–14.

127. 38 Stat. 212.

128. 50 *Congressional Record* 4409 (1913).

129. James L. McCamy, *Government Publicity: Its Practices in Federal Administration* (Chicago: University of Chicago Press, 1939), p. 7.

130. For statement of Representative James Good, see 58 *Congressional Record* 403 (1919).

131. Two early restrictions appeared in 1949 in the appropriations acts of the Agriculture Department and the Interior Department (63 Stat. 342, 765). Another restriction appeared in 1962 (76 Stat. 739). More examples, from fiscal 1995, cover Commerce, Justice, and State (108 Stat. 173, sec. 601); Defense (108 Stat. 2616, sec. 8001); Foreign Operations (108 Stat. 1646, sec. 554); Treasury-Postal Services (108 Stat. 2409, sec. 508); District of Columbia (108 Stat. 2584, sec. 113); Interior (108 Stat. 2536, sec. 303); and Labor-Health and Human Services (108 Stat. 2572, sec. 505).

132. J. Leiper Freeman, *The Political Process: Executive Bureau-Legislative Committee Relations* (New York: Random House, 1966), p. 39; Richard L. Engstrom and Thomas G. Walker, "Statutory Restraints on Administrative Lobbying— 'Legal Fiction,'" *Journal of Public Law* 19 (1970): 89.

133. Ancher Nelsen, "Lobbying by the Administration," in *We Propose: A Modern Congress,* ed. Mary McInnis (New York: McGraw-Hill, 1966), p. 145.

134. 92 Stat. 1217, sec. 7211 (1978). This provision originally appeared at 37 Stat. 555, sec. 6 (1912).

135. *Washington Post,* Oct. 10, 1980, p. A3. See also Elmer E. Cornwell, Jr., *Presidential Leadership of Public Opinion* (Bloomington: Indiana University Press, 1965).

136. *Legislative Activities of Executive Agencies (Part 10),* pp. 24–25, 31–33.

137. H. Rept. 2474, 80th Cong., 2d sess., 1948, pp. 2–4.

138. Ibid., pp. 7, 9.

139. Nelsen, "Lobbying by the Administration," p. 149.

140. 77 Stat. 827 (1963). See also H. Rept. 355, 88th Cong., 1st sess., 1963, pp. 28–29; S. Rept. 497, 88th Cong., 1st sess., 1963, p. 23; and H. Rept. 1088, 88th Cong., 1st sess., 1963, p. 10.

141. Mike Causey, "Administration Supplies One Liners," *Washington Post,* Apr. 6, 1973, p. D17.

142. On Staats, see 119 *Congressional Record* 11872, 13060, 14484 (1973). See also *Public Citizen, Inc. v. Clawson,* Civil Action No. 759-73 (D.D.C. July 30, 1973).

143. *New York Times,* Dec. 19, 1975, p. 23.

144. 122 *Congressional Record* 3022–25 (1976). See also "Turning Screws: Winning Votes in Congress," *Congressional Quarterly Weekly Report,* Apr. 24, 1976, 947–54.

145. 125 *Congressional Record* 29739–40 (1979); and Kenneth L. Adelman, "Raf-shooning the Armageddon: The Selling of SALT," *Policy Review* 9 (Summer 1979): 85–102.

146. On Indian Health Services, see S. Rept. 363, 96th Cong., 1st sess., 1979, p. 94. On the Commission on Civil Rights, see S. Rept. 706, 96th Cong., 2d sess., 1980, pp. 9–11; and 126 *Congressional Record* 11721–22 (1980). On the Office of Juvenile Justice, see H. Rept. 96-946, 96th Cong., 2d sess., 1980, pp. 78–80. On the Maritime Administration, see *Washington Post*, Jan. 28, 1979, p. A5. On the Office of Surface Mining, see 126 *Congressional Record* 6834–45 (1980).

147. On the Legal Services Corporation, see 93 Stat. 422 (1979); 126 *Congressional Record* 11509–10, 12758–60, 14687–95, 14711–27 (1980). See also House Committee on Appropriations, *Department of State, Justice, and Commerce, the Judiciary, and Related Agencies Appropriations for 1981 (Part 9)* (hearings), 96th Cong., 2d sess., 1980, pp. 142, 153–54. On ACTION, see H. Rept. 164, 96th Cong., 1st sess., 1979, pp. 6, 29–30, 49–51, 69–96; and 125 *Congressional Record* 15654–56 (1979).

148. *Legal Times of Washington*, Oct. 29, 1979, p. 1.

149. *American Conservative Union v. Carter*, Civil Action No. 79-2495 (D.D.C. Dec. 14, 1979).

150. See House Committee on Armed Services, *Allegations of Improper Lobbying by Department of Defense Personnel of the C-5B and B-1B Aircraft and Sale to Saudi Arabia of the Airborne Warning and Control System*, 97th Cong., 2d sess. (Committee Print 24, Dec. 30, 1982).

151. Senate Committee on Governmental Affairs, *Uniform Lobbying Cost Principles Act of 1984* (hearings), 98th Cong., 2d sess., 1984.

152. 128 *Congressional Record* 17173–76 (1982); H. Rept. 579, 98th Cong., 1st sess., 1983.

153. Letter from Harry R. Van Cleve, for Comptroller General of the United States, to Congressmen Jack Brooks and Dante B. Fascell, Sept. 30, 1987, B-229069.

154. R. Jeffrey Smith, "DOE Violated Rules on Lobbying, GAO Says," *Washington Post*, Oct. 8, 1987, p. A58.

155. Memorandum to All Fish and Wildlife Service Employees from the Office of Legislative Services, "General Guidance on Contacts with Congress and Expressing Views on Pending Legislation," May 12, 1995, p. 3.

156. Letter from the Comptroller General of the United States [signed by Robert P. Murphy, General Counsel] to the Honorable Bud Shuster, Chairman, House Committee on Transportation and Infrastructure, Dec. 21, 1995, B-262234.

157. House Committee on Government Reform and Oversight, *H.R. 3078, Federal Agency Anti-Lobbying Act* (hearing), 104th Cong., 2d sess. (1996).

158. 110 Stat. 3009-362, sec. 631 (1996) ("No part of any funds appropriated in this or any other Act shall be used by an agency of the executive branch, other than for normal and recognized executive-legislative relationships, for publicity or propaganda purposes, and for the preparation, distribution or use of any kit, pamphlet, booklet, publication, radio, television or film presentation designed to support or defeat legislation pending before the Congress, except in presentation to the Congress itself.")

159. George C. Edwards III, *Presidential Influence in Congress* (San Francisco: W. H. Freeman, 1980), pp. 116–202.

160. *The White House: Organization and Operations* (New York: Center for the Study

of the Presidency, 1971), p. 94. Recollection of Thomas Corcoran, former FDR adviser.

Chapter 3. Congress as Administrator

1. Woodrow Wilson, *Congressional Government* (Boston: Houghton Mifflin, 1885), p. 45; *Public Papers of the Presidents, 1976–1977* (II), p. 1483.
2. *Bowsher v. Synar*, 478 U.S. 714, 722, 733–34 (1986).
3. Louis Fisher, *President and Congress* (New York: Free Press, 1972), pp. 1–27, 253–70.
4. On Madison, see Max Farrand, ed., *The Records of the Federal Convention of 1787*, 4 vols. (New Haven: Yale University Press, 1937), 2:35. On Wilson, Morris, and Mercer, see ibid., 1:107; 2:52, 298. On Rutledge, see 1:65.
5. On Sherman, see ibid., 1:65; see also Harold C. Syrett, ed., *The Papers of Alexander Hamilton* (New York: Columbia University Press, 1961–), 2:404; and Julian P. Boyd, ed., *The Papers of Thomas Jefferson* (Princeton: Princeton University Press, 1950–), 11:679.
6. 6 Op. Att'y Gen. 326, 344 (1854); 7 Op. Att'y Gen. 453, 469–70 (1855).
7. Advisory Commission on Intergovernmental Relations, *Citizen Participation in the American Federal System* (Washington, D.C.: Government Printing Office, 1979), pp. 99–179.
8. Louis L. Jaffe, *Judicial Control of Administrative Action* (Boston: Little, Brown, 1965); Martin Shapiro, *The Supreme Court and Administrative Agencies* (New York: Free Press, 1968); Nathan Glazer, "Should Judges Administer Social Services?" *Public Interest* 50 (Winter 1978): 64. See also the chapter "Administration by Judiciary," in *Politics, Position, and Power*, ed. Harold Seidman and Robert Gilmour (New York: Oxford University Press, 1986).
9. Frank C. Neuman and Harry J. Keaton, "Congress and the Faithful Execution of Laws—Should Legislators Supervise Administrators?" *California Law Review* 41 (1953–1954): 565, 571.
10. See Title 5 of the U.S. Code; see also Joseph P. Harris, *Congressional Control of Administration* (Garden City, N.Y.: Doubleday, 1965), pp. 180–225.
11. Robert C. Randolph and Daniel C. Smith, "Executive Privilege and the Congressional Right of Inquiry," *Harvard Journal on Legislation* 10 (1973): 621, 649.
12. On the Trade Expansion Act, see 76 Stat. 878, sec. 243 (1962). On the Trade Act, see 19 U.S.C. 2211(a) (1994).
13. 90 Stat. 661 (1976).
14. 99 Stat. 18 (1985).
15. *Watkins v. United States*, 354 U.S. 178, 187 (1957); Harris, *Congressional Control of Administration*, p. 1.
16. *Hinds' Precedents of the House of Representatives* (Washington, D.C.: Government Printing Office, 1907), 3:1908–10.
17. *Eastland v. United States Servicemen's Fund*, 421 U.S. 491, 505 (1975).
18. *Anderson v. Dunn*, 6 Wheat. 204, 228 (1821).
19. House Committee on Interstate and Foreign Commerce, *Contempt Proceedings against Secretary of Commerce Rogers C. B. Morton* (hearings), 94th Cong., 1st sess., 1975; 121 *Congressional Record* 40768–69 (1975); *Congressional Quarterly Weekly Report*, May 17, 1980, pp. 1352–53.

20. Al Kamen, "Ambassador to Guyana Is Appointed after 17-Month Standoff," *Washington Post*, Nov. 29, 1991, p. A40.

21. Louis Fisher, *Constitutional Conflicts between Congress and the President* (Lawrence: University Press of Kansas, 1997), pp. 181–95.

22. *Pillsbury Co. v. FTC*, 354 F.2d 952, 964 (5th Cir. 1966). Emphasis in original.

23. *D.C. Federation of Civic Associations v. Volpe*, 459 F.2d 1231, 1247 (D.C. Cir. 1971), *cert. denied*, 405 U.S. 1030 (1972).

24. *Gulf Oil Corp. v. FPC*, 563 F.2d 588, 610–12 (3d Cir. 1977).

25. *United States ex rel. Parco v. Morris*, 426 F. Supp. 976, 982 (E.D. Pa. 1977).

26. 99 Stat. 1162–65 (1985).

27. 53 Comp. Gen. 600 (1974).

28. Louis Fisher, *Presidential Spending Power* (Princeton: Princeton University Press, 1975). See also Arthur W. Macmahon, "Congressional Oversight of Administration: The Power of the Purse," *Political Science Quarterly* 58 (1943): 161, 380; Lucius Wilmerding, Jr., *The Spending Power* (New Haven: Yale University Press, 1943); and Elias Huzar, *The Purse and the Sword: Control of the Army by Congress through Military Appropriations, 1933–1950* (Ithaca, N.Y.: Cornell University Press, 1950).

29. *Clark v. Board of Education of Little Rock Sch. Dist.*, 374 F.2d 569, 571 (8th Cir. 1967). See also *Califano v. Westcott*, 443 U.S. 76, 92–93 (1979).

30. *United States v. Will*, 449 U.S. 200 (1980); *Will v. United States*, 478 F. Supp. 621 (N.D. Ill. 1979); *Booth v. United States*, 291 U.S. 339 (1934); *O'Donoghue v. United States*, 289 U.S. 516 (1933).

31. 328 U.S. 303 (1946).

32. See G. Lowell Field, "Administration by Statute—The Question of Special Laws," *Public Administration Review* 6 (1946): 325; Note, "Private Bills and the Immigration Law," *Harvard Law Review* 69 (1956): 1083; Note, "Private Bills in Congress," *Harvard Law Review* 79 (1966): 1684.

33. On Cleveland, see James D. Richardson, ed., *A Compilation of the Messages and Papers of the Presidents*, 20 vols. (New York: Bureau of National Literature, 1897–1925), 10:5001–5002 (May 8, 1886), and 10:5020–40 (June 21–23, 1886). For statistics on private laws, see Library of Congress, Congressional Research Service, *Private Bills and Federal Charters*, Marc D. Yacker, Report No. 79-110 GOV, 22.

34. 60 Stat. 831, sec. 131 (1946); 2 U.S.C. 190(g) (1994), repeated in House Rule XXII, clause 2.

35. Charles L. Clapp, *The Congressman: His Work as He Sees It* (Garden City, N.Y.: Doubleday, 1964), pp. 88–89. On the range of casework and its relationship to legislative duties, see Kenneth E. Gray, "Congressional Interference in Administration," in *Cooperation and Conflict*, ed. Daniel J. Elazar (Itasca, Ill.: F. E. Peacock, 1969); and Kenneth G. Olson, "The Service Function of the United States Congress," in *Congress: The First Branch of Government*, ed. Alfred de Grazia (Washington, D.C.: American Enterprise Institute, 1966).

36. Donald R. Matthews, *U.S. Senators and Their World* (New York: Vintage Books, 1960), p. 225.

37. John R. Johannes, *To Serve the People: Congress and Constituency Service* (Lincoln: University of Nebraska Press, 1984). A critique of congressional casework is by Robert Klonoff, "The Congressman as Mediator between Citizens and

Government Agencies: Problems and Prospects," *Harvard Journal on Legislation* 16 (1979): 701. For a broader and I think more understanding account, see Morris S. Ogul, *Congress Oversees the Bureaucracy* (Pittsburgh: University of Pittsburgh Press, 1976), pp. 162–75; and Frank E. Smith, *Congressman from Mississippi* (New York: Capricorn Books, 1967), pp. 235–57.

38. Resolutions adopted by either tax committee can compel the International Trade Commission to investigate whether an article imported into the United States injures a domestic industry; 19 U.S.C. 2252(b) (1994). The Board of Engineers for Rivers and Harbors shall, on request by resolution of the Senate Committee on Environment and Public Works and the House Committee on Transportation and Infrastructure, examine and review the report of any examination or survey made pursuant to any statute or resolution of Congress. 33 U.S.C. 542 (1994).

39. *F.H.E. Oil Co. v. Commissioner of Internal Revenue*, 150 F.2d 857 (5th Cir. 1945).

40. 55 Comp. Gen. 319, 325–26 (1975). See also 55 Comp. Gen. 812 (1976).

41. *TVA v. Hill*, 437 U.S. 153 (1978).

42. *National Small Shipments v. CAB*, 618 F.2d 819 (D.C. Cir. 1980).

43. Paul Blustein, "Review of 'Pork' Projects Ordered by Budget Chief," *Washington Post*, Mar. 19, 1988, p. A4; Memorandum for Cabinet Officers and Agency Heads from James C. Miller III, Mar. 15, 1988.

44. Letter of Mar. 23, 1988 to James C. Miller, OMB Director, from Jamie L. Whitten, chair of the House Appropriations Committee.

45. Letter of Mar. 23, 1988 to President Reagan from John Stennis, chair of the Senate Appropriations Committee, Jamie L. Whitten, chair of the House Appropriations Committee, Mark O. Hatfield, ranking Republican of the Senate Appropriations Committee, and Silvio O. Conte, ranking Republican of the House Appropriations Committee.

46. Letter of Apr. 19, 1988 from OMB Director Miller to Representative Jamie L. Whitten and Silvio O. Conte and Senators John C. Stennis and Mark O. Hatfield; Memorandum for Cabinet Officers and Agency Heads from OMB Director Miller, July 8, 1988, M-88-25; "Miller Acts to End Feud with Hill over Funding," *Washington Post*, July 12, 1988, p. A20.

47. 110 Stat. 3463, sec. 102 (1996).

48. See *Congressional Ethics* (Washington, D.C.: Congressional Quarterly Press, 1980), pp. 172–75; *United States v. Johnson*, 383 U.S. 169 (1966); *Gravel v. United States*, 408 U.S. 606, 625 (1972); *United States v. Eilberg*, 465 F. Supp. 1080, 1083–84 (E.D. Pa. 1979). Often a legislative act becomes mixed with a member's intervention in an agency. For example, Representative John Dowdy, a Democrat of Texas, was indicted for bribery, conspiracy, and perjury stemming from his intervention as subcommittee chair into a Justice Department investigation. He was charged with accepting $25,000 in return for assisting a home-improvement firm threatened with prosecution. The charges of bribery and conspiracy were dropped eventually because of the Speech or Debate Clause immunity, particularly in view of his status as subcommittee chair, but after a new trial he was found guilty of perjury. See *United States v. Dowdy*, 479 F.2d 213 (4th Cir. 1973).

49. *United States v. Myers*, 635 F.2d 932, 939 (2d Cir. 1980).

50. *Hutchinson v. Proxmire*, 443 U.S. 111 (1979). Proxmire agreed to pay $10,000 from his own funds as an out-of-court settlement; see *Washington Post*, Mar. 25, 1980, p. A3; and 126 *Congressional Record* 6271–72 (1980).

51. Fisher, *Presidential Spending Power*, pp. 147–201; and James P. Pfiffner, *The President, the Budget, and Congress: Impoundment and the 1974 Budget Act* (Boulder, Colo.: Westview Press, 1979).

52. *New Haven v. United States*, 634 F. Supp. 1449, 1458 (D.D.C. 1986).

53. *New Haven v. United States*, 809 F.2d 900 (D.C. Cir. 1987).

54. 101 Stat. 785, sec. 206 (1987).

55. Fisher, *Presidential Spending Power*, pp. 75–98.

56. House Committee on Appropriations, *Supplemental Appropriation Bill, 1980 (Part 4)* (hearings), 96th Cong., 2d sess., 1980, p. 395.

57. 87 Stat. 1046, sec. 745 (1974).

58. 126 *Congressional Record* 18011 (1980).

59. H. Rept. 1218, 94th Cong., 1st sess., 1976, pp. 4–5.

60. S. Rept. 276, 95th Cong., 1st sess., 1977, p. 35. See also H. Rept. 392, 95th Cong., 1st sess., 1977, p. 13.

61. 91 Stat. 828, sec. 609 (1977).

62. S. Rept. 1058, 95th Cong., 2d sess., 1978, p. 9.

63. Senate Committee on Governmental Affairs, *Nomination of James T. McIntyre, Jr.* (hearings), 95th Cong., 2d sess., 1978, pp. 76–77.

64. *National Treasury Employees Union v. Reagan*, 663 F.2d 239 (D.C. Cir. 1981).

65. 105 Stat. 913, sec. 724 (1991).

66. *From Red Tape to Results: Creating a Government That Works Better and Costs Less*, Report of the National Performance Review, Vice President Al Gore, Sept. 7, 1993 (Washington, D.C.: Government Printing Office), pp. 19–20; "Administration Asks Congress to Ease Way for Personnel Cuts," *Washington Post*, Sept. 16, 1993, p. A27; "Hill Panels Remove Obstacles to Job Cuts," *Washington Post*, Oct. 8, 1993, p. A25.

67. Albert J. Kliman and Louis Fisher, "Budget Reform Proposals in the NPR Report," *Public Budgeting and Finance* 15 (1995): 34; 108 Stat. 4680-81, sec. 1101-02 (1994).

68. 6 Op. Att'y Gen. 680, 683 (1854).

69. 32 Stat. 829, sec. 8 (1903); 33 Stat. 1147, sec. 2 (1905).

70. 37 Op. Att'y Gen. 56, 63–65 (1933).

71. 47 Stat. 1518, sec. 403(c) (1933); 48 Stat. 16 (1933).

72. 83 *Congressional Record* 4487, 5004–5005 (1938); 53 Stat. 561 (1939).

73. 63 Stat. 203 (1949).

74. Louis Fisher and Ronald C. Moe, "Presidential Reorganization Authority: Is It Worth the Cost?" *Political Science Quarterly* 96 (1981): 301.

75. Harvey C. Mansfield, "The Legislative Veto and the Deportation of Aliens," *Public Administration Review* 1 (1940): 281.

76. Robert H. Jackson, "A Presidential Legal Opinion," *Harvard Law Review* 66 (1953): 1353.

77. 14 Stat. 469 (1867).

78. H. Doc. 764, 66th Cong., 2d sess., 1920; 37 Op. Att'y Gen. 56 (1933).

79. Virginia A. McMurtry, "Legislative Vetoes Relating to Public Works and Buildings," in House Committee on Rules, *Studies on the Legislative Veto*, 96th Cong., 2d sess., 1980, pp. 432–514.

80. 41 Op. Att'y Gen. 230 (1955). See also 41 Op. Att'y Gen. 300 (1957).

81. Joseph P. Harris, *Congressional Control of Administration* (Washington, D.C.: Brookings Institution, 1964), pp. 230–31.

82. 86 Stat. 217, sec. 7(a) (1972); *Public Papers of the Presidents, 1972*, p. 1076.

83. 91 Stat. 1235, sec. 115 (1977).

84. 91 Stat. 1235, sec. 115 (1977); letter from President Carter to Secretary of State Vance, Oct. 31, 1977. For testimony on this issue by AID officials, the Senate legal counsel, and the author, see Senate Committee on Appropriations, *Foreign Assistance and Related Programs Appropriations, Fiscal Year 1981 (Part 1)* (hearings), 96th Cong., 2d sess., 1980, pp. 53–170.

85. 122 *Congressional Record* 31668 (1976).

86. 128 *Congressional Record* 5081–30 (1982). The bill, containing the two-house veto, passed the Senate 94-0; 128 *Congressional Record* 5297 (1982).

87. GSA: 88 Stat. 1697, sec. 104(b) (1974); Education: 88 Stat. 566, sec. 509 (1974); NHTSA: 88 Stat. 1482, sec. 109 (1974); FEC: 88 Stat. 1287, sec. 209 (1974) and 90 Stat. 486, sec. 110 (1976).

88. FERC: 92 Stat. 3372, sec. 202(c) (1978); FTC: 94 Stat. 393, sec. 21(a) (1980) and 96 Stat. 1870 (1982).

89. *Buckley v. Valeo*, 424 U.S. 1, 140 n.176, 284–86 (1976); *Clark v. Valeo*, 559 F.2d 642 (D.C. Cir. 1977), aff'd sub nom. *Clark v. Kimmitt*, 431 U.S. 950 (1977); *Atkins v. United States*, 556 F.2d 1028, 1063–65 (Ct. Cl. 1977), *cert. denied*, 424 U.S. 1009 (1978); *Chadha v. INS*, 634 F.2d 408, 433 (9th Cir. 1980).

90. *Consumer Energy Council of America v. FERC*, 673 F.2d 425 (D.C. Cir. 1982); *Consumers Union, Inc. v. FTC*, 691 F.2d 575 (D.C. Cir. 1982); *AFGE v. Pierce*, 697 F.2d 303 (D.C. Cir. 1982).

91. *Consumer Energy Council of America v. FERC*, at 474.

92. *Chadha v. INS*, at 408.

93. *INS v. Chadha*, 462 U.S. 919, 952 (1983).

94. Ibid. at 944.

95. Ibid. at 946–48.

96. Ibid. at 951, 958–59.

97. *Public Papers of the Presidents, 1984* (II), pp. 1056–57.

98. H. Rept. 916, 98th Cong., 2d sess., 1984, p. 48.

99. Letter of Aug. 9, 1984, to Congressman Edward P. Boland, chair, subcommittee on HUD-Independent Agencies, House Committee on Appropriations, from James M. Beggs, NASA Administrator.

100. *Sibbach v. Wilson & Co.*, 312 U.S. 1, 14–15 (1941); *INS v. Chadha*, at 935 n.9.

101. For more details, see Louis Fisher, "Judicial Misjudgments about the Lawmaking Process: The Legislative Veto Case," *Public Administration Review* 45 (Special Issue, Nov. 1985): 705–11.

102. 109 Stat. 482, 484–85 (1995).

103. 109 Stat. 493, secs. 518 and 519.

104. 101 Stat. 1329-155, sec. 514 (1987). See "OMB Objection Raises House Panel's Hackles," *Washington Post*, Aug. 13, 1987, p. A13.

105. 103 Stat. 1219, sec. 514 (1989).

106. *Burton v. Baker*, 723 F. Supp. 1550 (D.D.C. 1990). For the positions of Gray and Bork, see *Washington Post*, Mar. 26, 1989, p. A5, and 135 *Congressional Record* S3885 (daily ed. Apr. 13, 1989). See Louis Fisher, "The Legislative Veto: Invalidated, It Survives," *Law and Contemporary Problems* 56 (1993): 273.

107. Senate Committee on Government Operations and Committee on the Judiciary, *Impoundment of Appropriated Funds by the President* (hearings), 93d Cong., 1st

sess., 1973, p. 411. The official was William D. Ruckelshaus, administrator of the EPA.

108. Morris P. Fiorina, *Congress: Keystone of the Washington Establishment* (New Haven: Yale University Press, 1977), pp. 71–74. See also R. Douglas Arnold, *Congress and the Bureaucracy* (New Haven: Yale University Press, 1979), and his article, "The Local Roots of Domestic Policy," in *The New Congress*, ed. Thomas E. Mann and Norman J. Ornstein (Washington, D.C.: American Enterprise Institute, 1981), pp. 281–84.

109. Louis Fisher, "White House Aides Testifying before Congress," *Presidential Studies Quarterly* 27 (1997): 145–50.

Chapter 4. Bureaucracy

1. David B. Truman, *The Governmental Process* (New York: Alfred A. Knopf, 1964), p. 401.

2. John C. Fitzpatrick, ed., *Writings of Washington*, 39 vols. (Washington, D.C.: Government Printing Office, 1931–1944), 30:334.

3. William Maclay, *Sketches of Debate in the First Senate of the United States, 1789–91* (Harrisburg, Pa.: Lane S. Hart, 1880), p. 107.

4. *Annals of Congress*, 1st Cong., May 19, 1789, p. 383.

5. *Journals of the Continental Congress, 1774–1789*, 34 vols. (Washington, D.C.: Government Printing Office, 1904–1937). See particularly 19:290–91, 326–27, 337–38, 429, 431–33; 21:949–50.

6. Ibid., 27:437–42.

7. *Annals of Congress*, 1st Cong., May 20, 1789, pp. 384–96.

8. Ibid., p. 392.

9. Ibid., June 17, 1789, p. 512.

10. 1 Stat. 28–29, 49–50.

11. 1 Stat. 65–67.

12. Maclay, *Sketches of Debate in the First Senate*, p. 376.

13. James D. Richardson, ed., *A Compilation of the Messages and Papers of the Presidents*, 20 vols. (New York: Bureau of National Literature, 1897–1925), 3:1288–1312; *Register of Debates*, 24th Cong., 2d sess., 1837, pp. 379–418, 427–506; *Senate Journal*, 24th Cong., 2d sess., Apr. 15, 1837, pp. 123–24.

14. *Annals of Congress*, 1st Cong., June 27, 1789, pp. 611–12.

15. 1 Stat. 441–42 (1795).

16. 3 Stat. 592 (1820).

17. 18 How. 272 (1856). For earlier statutes, see 1 Stat. 602, sec. 16 (1798); 3 Stat. 33, sec. 8 (1813); 3 Stat. 176–77, sec. 33 (1815).

18. 1 Stat. 70 (1789).

19. Leonard D. White, *The President's Cabinet* (New Haven: Yale University Press, 1912), pp. 232–35. 200. 1 Stat. 232–234 (1792). 21. White, *The Federalists*, pp. 226–27. The basic provisions of the statute of 1792 were repeated in 1794; 1 Stat. 354–66. 22. 5 Stat. 80, sec. 1–2 (1836); Learned, *The Federalists* (New York: Macmillan, 1948), pp. 77–78; Henry Barrett Learned, *The President's Cabinet*, pp. 220, 244–52. See also Gerald Cullinan, *The United States Postal Service* (New York: Praeger, 1973), pp. 48–64.

23. *Humphrey's Executor v. United States*, 295 U.S. 602, 627 (1935).

24. 84 Stat. 720, sec. 201 (1970); 39 U.S.C. 201 (1994).
25. *Mail Order Ass'n v. U.S. Postal Service*, 986 F.2d 509 (D.C. Cir. 1993); *Mackie v. Clinton*, 827 F.Supp. 56 (D.D.C. 1993); *Mackie v. Bush*, 809 F.Supp. 144 (D.D.C. 1993); Neal Devins, "Tempest in an Envelope: Reflections on the Bush White House's Failed Takeover of the U.S. Postal Service," *UCLA L. Rev.* 41 (1994): 1035.
26. 42 Stat. 24, sec. 304 (1921).
27. Louis Fisher, *Presidential Spending Power* (Princeton: Princeton University Press, 1975), pp. 41–42.
28. *United States ex rel. Brookfield Const. Co., Inc. v. Stewart*, 234 F. Supp. 94, 99–100 (D.D.C. 1964), aff'd, 339 F.2d 754 (D.C. Cir. 1964). See also *Staats v. Lynn* (D.D.C. Civil Action No. 75-0551), "Opposition of Plaintiff to Defendants' Motion to Dismiss," July 28, 1975, pp. 18–48.
29. *Weekly Compilation of Presidential Documents* 20 (July 18, 1984): 1037.
30. Office of Legal Counsel, Department of Justice, Memorandum for the Attorney General, "Implementation of the Bid Protest Provisions of the Competition in Contracting Act" (October 17, 1984): 15.
31. Office of Management and Budget, Bulletin No. 85-8 (Dec. 17, 1984): 2.
32. House Committee on Government Operations, *Constitutionality of GAO's Bid Protest Function* (hearings), 99th Cong., 1st sess., 1985.
33. *Ameron, Inc. v. U.S. Army Corps of Engineers*, 607 F. Supp. 962, 973 (D. N.J. 1985).
34. *Ameron, Inc. v. U.S. Army Corps of Engineers*, 610 F. Supp. 750, 755 (D. N.J. 1985). Emphasis in original.
35. H. Rept. 113, 99th Cong., 1st sess., 1985, p. 11.
36. Myron Struck, "Meese Averts Showdown on GAO Contract Power," *Washington Post*, June 5, 1985, p. A21.
37. *Ameron, Inc. v. U.S. Army Corps of Engineers*, 787 F.2d 875, 878 (3d Cir. 1986).
38. Ibid. at 885.
39. Ibid. at 886.
40. Ibid. at 892.
41. 478 U.S. 714 (1986).
42. *Commodity Futures Trading Com'n v. Schor*, 478 U.S. 833 (1986).
43. *Ameron, Inc. v. U.S. Army Corps of Engineers*, 809 F.2d 979 (3d Cir. 1986). The comptroller general's powers were also upheld in *Lear Siegler, Inc. Energy Products Div. v. Lehman*, 842 F.2d 1102 (9th Cir. 1988).
44. 47 Stat. 413–15 (1932). On Hoover's orders, see 76 *Congressional Record* 233–54 (1932). On the House disapproval, see 76 *Congressional Record* 2125–26.
45. 47 Stat. 1518, sec. 403(c) (1933).
46. 76 *Congressional Record* 2587 (1933).
47. 83 *Congressional Record* 4487 (1938).
48. S. Rept. 232, 81st Cong., 1st sess., 1949, p. 15; 95 *Congressional Record* 6227 (1949).
49. 98 Stat. 3192 (1984).
50. Senate Committee on the Judiciary, *Report on the Regulatory Agencies to the President-Elect*, 86th Cong., 2d sess., 1960, p. 66.
51. W. Michael Blumenthal, "Reflections of a Businessman in Washington," *Fortune* (Jan. 29, 1979).
52. *Policy and Supporting Positions*, House Committee on Government Reform and Oversight, 104th Cong., 2d sess., Nov. 13, 1996, pp. 152–59.

53. Louis Fisher, *Constitutional Conflicts between Congress and the President* (Lawrence: University Press of Kansas, 1997), pp. 26–38.

54. G. Calvin MacKenzie, *The Politics of Presidential Appointments* (New York: Free Press, 1981), p. xx.

55. Ibid., p. 177.

56. William W. Van Alstyne, "The Role of Congress in Determining Incidental Powers of the President and of the Federal Courts: A Comment on the Horizontal Effect of the Sweeping Clause," *Law and Contemporary Problems* 40 (1976): 102.

57. *United States v. Ferreira*, 54 U.S. 39, 50–51 (1852).

58. 88 Stat. 1390, sec. 5 (1974); *Public Papers of the Presidents*, 1974, p. 189; 92 Stat. 865 (1978); S. Rept. 850, 95th Cong., 2d sess., 1978, p. 28.

59. *Buckley v. Valeo*, 424 U.S. 1, 134–43 (1976). See also *Buckley v. Valeo*, 519 F.2d 821, 890–92 (D.C. Cir. 1975); Note, "Congressional Power under the Appointments Clause after Buckley v. Valeo," *Michigan Law Review* 75 (1977): 627.

60. 97 Stat. 1301 (1983).

61. *Annals of Congress*, 1st Cong., June 17, 1789, p. 492.

62. Ibid., pp. 496, 500, 534 (Representative Goodhue).

63. *Myers v. United States*, 272 U.S. 52, 114 (1926).

64. Fisher, *Constitutional Conflicts between Congress and the President*, pp. 50–54.

65. *Annals of Congress*, 1st Cong., June 29, 1789, pp. 613, 614.

66. Louis Fisher, "Grover Cleveland against the Senate," *Congressional Studies* 7 (1979): 11.

67. *Shurtleff v. United States*, 189 U.S. 311 (1903), recognized the potential that Congress has to restrict the president's removal power to specified causes. See also the dissenting opinions by Justices McReynolds and Brandeis in *Myers v. United States*, at 181–82, 262–64.

68. Edward S. Corwin, *The President's Removal Power under the Constitution* (New York: National Municipal League, 1927).

69. For example, see 37 Stat. 555, sec. 6 (1912). Current procedures are found at 5 U.S.C. 7501–14, 7532 (1994). The courts frequently overturn the removal of federal employees who lack elementary procedures to challenge assertions that they were disloyal. See *Peters v. Hobby*, 349 U.S. 331 (1955); *Cole v. Young*, 351 U.S. 536 (1956); *Service v. Dulles*, 354 U.S. 363 (1957); *Vitarelli v. Seaton*, 359 U.S. 535 (1959); *Greene v. McElroy*, 360 U.S. 474 (1959); and *Cafeteria Workers v. McElroy*, 367 U.S. 886 (1961).

70. Harold Seidman and Robert Gilmour, *Politics, Position, and Power* (New York: Oxford University Press, 1986), p. 51.

71. Louis Fisher, "Congress and the Removal Power," *Congress and the Presidency* 10 (1983): 63.

72. 5 U.S.C. 7503, 7513, 7532 (1994).

73. The President's Committee on Administrative Management, *Administrative Management in the Government of the United States* (Washington, D.C.: Government Printing Office, 1937), pp. 5–6, 10; see also pp. 7–11.

74. House Committee on Post Office and Civil Service, *Final Report on Violations and Abuses of Merit Principles in Federal Employment*, 94th Cong., 2d sess. (Committee Print 94-28, Dec. 30, 1976).

75. H. Rept. 1403, 95th Cong., 2d sess., 1978, p. 6; S. Rept. 969, 95th Cong., 2d sess., 1978, p. 5.

76. S. Rept. 1272, 95th Cong., 2d sess., 1978, p. 132.

77. Bernard Rosen, "Crises in the U.S. Civil Service," *Public Administration Review* 46 (1986): 209.

78. Ibid., p. 211.

79. Bernard Rosen, "Uncertainty in the Senior Service," *Public Administration Review* 41 (Mar./Apr. 1981): 203, 204.

80. House Committee on Post Office and Civil Service, *Senior Executive Service* (hearings), 98th Cong., 1st–2d sess., 1984, pp. 122–23 (statement of Bernard Rosen). See also William J. Lanouette, "SES—From Civil Service Showpiece to Incipient Failure in Two Years," *National Journal,* July 18, 1981, p. 1296.

81. 105 Stat. 866, sec. 526 (1991).

82. 105 Stat. 756 (1991).

83. "MSPB Carries Special Counsel Battle to Court," *Federal Times,* Dec. 8, 1980, p. 1. See also statements by Representative Patricia Schroeder, Democrat of Colorado, in 126 *Congressional Record* 33697–98, 34066–67 (1980); *Governors of U.S. Postal Service v. U.S. Postal Rate Commission,* 654 F.2d 108 (D.C. Cir. 1981).

84. *MSPB v. Eastwood,* 516 F. Supp. 1297 (D.D.C. 1981).

85. *From Red Tape to Results: Creating a Government That Works Better and Costs Less,* Report of the National Performance Review, Sept. 7, 1993, pp. iii, 1. Emphasis in original.

86. Ibid., p. 2.

87. Ibid., pp. 3, 4.

88. Ronald C. Moe, "The 'Reinventing Government' Exercise: Misinterpreting the Problem, Misjudging the Consequences," *Public Administration Review* 54 (Mar./Apr. 1994): 116; James D. Carroll, "The Rhetoric of Reform and Political Reality in the National Performance Review," *Public Administration Review* 55 (May/June 1995): 306.

89. 5 U.S. 137, 157, 162 (1803).

90. *Kendall v. United States,* 37 U.S. 522, 610 (1838). For other ministerial duties directed by the courts, see *United States v. Schurz,* 102 U.S. 378 (1880); *Butterworth v. Hoe,* 112 U.S. 50 (1884); *United States v. Price,* 116 U.S. 43 (1885); *United States v. Louisville,* 169 U.S. 249 (1898); and *Clackamus County, Ore. v. McKay,* 219 F.2d 479, 496 (D.C. Cir. 1954), *vacated as moot,* 349 U.S. 909 (1955).

91. 6 Op. Att'y Gen. 326, 341 (1854). See also *Decatur v. Paulding,* 39 U.S. 497, 516 (1840); *Reeside v. Walker,* 52 U.S. 272, 290 (1850); *United States v. Guthrie,* 58 U.S. 284 (1854); and *Panama Canal Co. v. Grace Line Inc.,* 367 U.S. 309, 317–18 (1958).

92. *Berends v. Butz,* 357 F. Supp. 143, 151 (D. Minn. 1973). See also Bruce Ledewitz, "The Uncertain Power of the President to Execute the Laws," *Tennessee Law Review* 46 (1979): 757, 787–93.

93. *National Treasury Employees Union v. Nixon,* 492 F.2d 587 (D.C. Cir. 1974).

94. 10 Op. Att'y Gen. 526 (1863).

95. Ibid. at 527–28.

96. 1 Op. Att'y Gen. 624, 625 (1823).

97. 1 Op. Att'y Gen. 636 (1824); 1 Op. Att'y Gen. 678 (1824); 1 Op. Att'y Gen. 705 (1825); 1 Op. Att'y Gen. 706 (1825); 2 Op. Att'y Gen. 480 (1831); 2 Op. Att'y Gen. 507 (1832); 2 Op. Att'y Gen. 544 (1832); 4 Op. Att'y Gen. 515 (1846); 5 Op.

Att'y Gen. 287 (1851); 11 Op. Att'y Gen. 14 (1864); and 13 Op. Att'y Gen. 28 (1869).

98. 11 Op. Att'y Gen. 14, 15 (1864).

99. 18 Op. Att'y Gen. 31, 32 (1884).

100. 1 Op. Att'y Gen. 624, 629 (1823).

101. 19 Op. Att'y Gen. 685, 686–87 (1890).

102. 26 Stat. 131, 136–38, sec. 12–15 (1890); 44 Stat. 669 (1926); 70 Stat. 532 (1956); 94 Stat. 1727 (1980).

103. *Ex parte Bakelite Corp.*, 279 U.S. 438, 452 (1929).

104. 10 Stat. 612 (1855); 12 Stat. 765 (1863); 14 Stat. 9 (1866); 22 Stat. 485 (1883); 23 Stat. 283 (1885); 24 Stat. 505 (1887); 67 Stat. 226 (1953).

105. 96 Stat. 27 (1982). The judges serve for a term of fifteen years; judges of constitutional courts serve for life.

106. 106 Stat. 4516 (1992).

107. 43 Stat. 336–38 (1924); 56 Stat. 957 (1942); 83 Stat. 730 (1969).

108. *Nash v. Califano*, 613 F.2d 10 (2d Cir. 1980).

109. *Pillsbury Company v. FTC*, 354 F.2d 952, 954–56, 963–64 (5th Cir. 1966). On also limiting Congress in its contacts with executive officials, see *D.C. Federation of Civic Associations v. Volpe*, 459 F.2d 1231, 1245–48 (D.C. Cir. 1971), *cert. denied*, 405 U.S. 1030 (1972).

110. Paul R. Verkuil, "Jawboning Administrative Agencies: Ex Parte Contacts by the White House," *Columbia Law Review* 80 (1980): 943; Senate Committee on Environment and Public Works, *Executive Branch Review of Environmental Regulations* (hearings), 96th Cong., 1st sess., 1979, pp. 191–230; *Legal Times of Washington*, Jan. 29, 1979, p. 34; House Committee on Energy and Commerce, *Role of OMB in Regulation* (hearings), 97th Cong., 1st sess., 1981; House Committee on Energy and Commerce, *EPA's Asbestos Regulations*, 99th Cong., 1st sess. (Committee Print, 1985); *Environmental Defense Fund v. Thomas*, 627 F. Supp. 566 (D.D.C. 1986). See also *Sierra Club v. Costle*, 657 F.2d 298, 400–408 (D.C. Cir. 1981).

111. *Legal Times of Washington*, Jan. 29, 1979, p. 32.

112. Adviser is quoted in Thomas E. Cronin, *The State of the Presidency* (Boston: Little, Brown, 1980), p. 232.

113. *Public Papers of the Presidents*, 1972, p. 1150.

114. Bradley H. Patterson, Jr., *The President's Cabinet: Issues and Questions* (Washington, D.C.: American Society for Public Administration, 1976), pp. 52–53.

115. Ibid., pp. 52–67.

116. "Carter Given Oaths on 'Leaks,'" *Washington Post*, July 16, 1980, p. A1.

117. "President Sharply Restricts Polygraph Tests for Officials," *Washington Post*, Dec. 21, 1985, pp. A1, A8.

118. Patterson, *The President's Cabinet*, pp. 70–72.

119. James P. Pfiffner, "Political Appointees and Career Executives: The Democracy-Bureaucracy Nexus in the Third Century," *Public Administration Review* 47 (1987): 57, 63. See also Patricia W. Ingraham, "Building Bridges or Burning Them? The President, the Appointees, and the Bureaucracy," *Public Administration Review* 47 (1987): 425; and National Commission on the Public Service [Volcker Commission], *Leadership for America* (1989), pp. 158–90.

120. Cronin, *The State of the Presidency*, pp. 276–86.

121. I. M. Destler, *Presidents, Bureaucrats, and Foreign Policy* (Princeton: Princeton

University Press, 1972); Graham Allison and Peter Szanton, *Remaking Foreign Policy: The Organizational Connection* (New York: Basic Books, 1976), pp. 120–40.

122. *Investigation of the White House Travel Office Firings and Related Matters*, report by the House Committee on Government Reform and Oversight, H. Rept. No. 104-849, 104th Cong., 2d sess., 1996, p. 93; *Investigation into the White House and Department of Justice on Security of FBI Background Investigation Files*, report by the House Committee on Government Reform and Oversight, H. Rept. No. 104-862, 104th Cong., 2d sess., 1996, p. 3.

123. "Report Says F.B.I. Aide Acted Unwisely in Files Case," *New York Times*, Mar. 29, 1997, p. 11; "Justice Department Criticizes Shapiro for 'Poor Judgment,'" *Washington Post*, Mar. 29, 1997, p. A6.

124. *Weekly Compilation of Presidential Documents* 33 (Mar. 26, 1997): 413.

125. "Freeh Briefs Clinton Aide on China Probe," *Washington Post*, May 1, 1997, p. A6.

126. Senate Committee on the Judiciary, *Confirmation of Benjamin R. Civiletti, Nominee, Attorney General* (hearings), 96th Cong., 1st sess., 1979, p. 16.

127. *Congressional Quarterly Almanac*, 1984, p. 248.

128. *The Record*, Association of the Bar of the City of New York, No. 5-6, 29 (1974): 492. See also Senate Committee on the Judiciary, *Removing Politics from the Administration of Justice* (hearings), 93d Cong., 2d sess., 1974.

129. 38 *Federal Register* 14688 (1973).

130. *Nader v. Bork*, 366 F. Supp. 104 (D.C. Cir. 1973).

131. *United States v. Nixon*, 418 U.S. 683 (1974).

132. 92 Stat. 1869, sec. 594, 596 (1978).

133. H. Rept. 1307, 95th Cong., 2d sess., 1978, p. 22.

134. "Attorney General Questions Prosecutor Law," *Washington Post*, Apr. 21, 1981, p. A3; "Attorney General Urges Repeal of Prosecutor Act," *Washington Post*, May 22, 1981, p. A4.

135. "Special Prosecutor Investigations Called 'Enormous Waste,'" *Washington Post*, May 21, 1981, p. A20.

136. 96 Stat. 2039 (1983).

137. *Public Papers of the Presidents*, 1987 (II), p. 1524.

138. *Morrison v. Olson*, 487 U.S. 654, 696 (1988).

139. *Mistretta v. United States*, 488 U.S. 361 (1989).

140. Richard P. Nathan, *The Plot That Failed: Nixon and the Administrative Presidency* (New York: John Wiley & Sons, 1975).

141. David A. Stockman, *The Triumph of Politics* (New York: Harper & Row, 1986), p. 103.

142. See Harold C. Relyea, *The Executive Office of the President: A Historical, Biographical, and Bibliographical Guide* (Westport, Conn.: Greenwood Press, 1997).

143. Louis Fisher, "Confidential Spending and Governmental Accountability," *George Washington Law Review* 47 (1979): 347, 373–82.

144. House Committee on Government Operations, *Confirmation of the Director and Deputy Director of the Office of Management and Budget* (hearings), 93d Cong., 1st sess., 1973, p. 164.

145. Ibid., pp. 51, 53.

146. 88 Stat. 11 (1974).

147. 42 Stat. 23, sec. 212 (1921); 31 U.S.C. 1113(a)(1) (1994).

148. Bureau of the Budget, Circular No. 1, June 29, 1921, para. 2.

149. H. Rept. 1066, 91st Cong., 2d sess., 1970, p. 6.
150. Fisher, *Presidential Spending Power*, pp. 46–51.
151. Senate Committee on Foreign Relations, *The National Security Adviser: Role and Accountability* (hearings), 96th Cong., 2d sess., 1980. See "Beyond the Vance-Brzezinski Clash Lurks an NSC under Fire," *National Journal*, May 17, 1980, p. 814; and Kevin V. Mulcahy, "The Secretary of State and the National Security Adviser: Foreign Policymaking in the Carter and Reagan Administrations," *Presidential Studies Quarterly* 16 (1986): 280. For criticism of the national security adviser, see articles by I. M. Destler, "A Job That Doesn't Work," *Foreign Policy* 38 (1980): 80, and "Can One Man Do?" *Foreign Policy* 5 (1971–1972): 28.
152. Louis Fisher, "White House Aides Testifying before Congress," *Presidential Studies Quarterly* 27 (1997): 139.
153. Seidman and Gilmour, *Politics, Position, and Power*, p. 168.

Chapter 5. Independent Regulatory Commission

1. Edward S. Corwin, *The President: Office and Powers, 1787–1957* (New York: Oxford University Press, 1957), p. 93.
2. Robert E. Cushman, *The Independent Regulatory Commissions* (New York: Oxford University Press, 1941), pp. 21–34.
3. *Wabash &c., Railway Co. v. Illinois*, 118 U.S. 557 (1886).
4. Cushman, *The Independent Regulatory Commissions*, pp. 45–54.
5. President's Committee on Administrative Management, *Administrative Management in the Government of the United States* (Washington, D.C.: Government Printing Office, 1937), p. 36.
6. Commission on Organization of the Executive Branch of the Government (Hoover Commission), *Task Force Report on Regulatory Commissions* [Appendix N] (Washington, D.C.: Government Printing Office, 1949), p. viii.
7. C. Herman Pritchett, "The Regulatory Commissions Revisited," *American Political Science Review* 43 (1949): 978, 982.
8. Kenneth Culp Davis, *Administrative Law of the Seventies* (Rochester, N.Y.: Lawyers Co-operative Publishing Co., 1976), p. 15.
9. Richard A. Posner, "Theories of Economic Regulation," *Bell Journal of Economics and Management Science* 5 (1974): 335.
10. For an inventory of federal regulatory organizations, see *The Challenge of Regulatory Reform*, a report to the president from the Domestic Council Review Group on Regulatory Reform (Washington, D.C.: Government Printing Office, 1977), pp. 50–57.
11. 24 Stat. 386, 387, sec. 18, 21 (1887); 25 Stat. 861–62, sec. 7, 8 (1889).
12. Cushman, *The Independent Regulatory Commissions*, pp. 100–102.
13. William L. Cary, *Politics and the Regulatory Agencies* (New York: McGraw-Hill, 1967), p. 4.
14. Lloyd N. Cutler and David R. Johnson, "Regulations and the Political Process," *Yale Law Journal* 84 (1975): 1395, 1410.
15. Henry J. Friendly, *The Federal Administrative Agencies: The Need for Better Definition of Standards* (Cambridge, Mass.: Harvard University Press, 1962); *Federal Communication Comm. v. Pottsville Broadcasting Co.*, 309 U.S. 134, 137–38 (1940); *Federal Trade Comm. v. Gratz*, 253 U.S. 421, 427, 436–37 (1920); *N.Y. Central Securities Co. v. United States*, 287 U.S. 12, 24–25 (1932).

16. Ralph K. Huitt, "Congressional Organization and Operation in the Field of Money and Credit," *Fiscal and Debt Management Policies* (Englewood Cliffs, N.J.: Prentice-Hall, 1963), pp. 470–71.

17. John T. Woolley, "Congress and the Conduct of Monetary Policy in the 1970s" (Paper delivered at the annual meeting of the Midwest Political Science Association, Chicago, Apr. 22–24, 1980), pp. 1, 14.

18. *Washington Post*, Feb. 4, 1981, p. E1.

19. *Guide to Congress* (Washington, D.C.: Congressional Quarterly Press, 1976), 186. See also David M. Welborn, "Presidents, Regulatory Commissioners and Regulatory Policy," *Journal of Politics* 15 (1966): 3; Glen O. Robinson, "On Reorganizing the Independent Regulatory Agencies," *Virginia Law Review* 57 (1971): 947, 951 n.14. For individual studies see Seymour Scher, "Regulatory Agency Control through Appointment: The Case of the Eisenhower Administration and the NLRB," *Journal of Politics* 23 (1961): 667.

20. Bradley Behrman, "Civil Aeronautics Board," in *The Politics of Regulation*, ed. James Q. Wilson (New York: Basic Books, 1980), pp. 110–20.

21. Glen O. Robinson, "The Federal Communications Commission: An Essay on Regulatory Watchdogs," *Virginia Law Review* 64 (1978): 169, 184.

22. Neal Devins, "Congress, the FCC, and the Search for the Public Trustee," *Law and Contemporary Problems* 56 (1993): 145.

23. On the Tariff Commission, see Philip G. Wright, *Tariff-Making by Commission* (Washington, D.C.: Rawleigh Tariff Bureau, 1930), pp. 17–29; Catherine Hackett, "The Failure of the Flexible Tariff: 1922–1927," *New Republic* (July 27, 1927): 244–47; E. Pendleton Herring, "The Political Context of the Tariff Commission," *Political Science Quarterly* 49 (1934): 421. On Nixon, see *New York Times*, Jan. 14, 1970, p. 26.

24. Senate Committee on Commerce, *Appointments to the Regulatory Agencies*, 94th Cong., 2d sess. (Committee Print, Apr. 1976); Senate Committee on Government Operations, *Study on Federal Regulations: The Regulatory Appointments Process*, vol. 1, 95th Cong., 1st sess. (Committee Print, Jan. 1977).

25. Joseph P. Harris, "The Senatorial Rejection of Leland Olds: A Case Study," *American Political Science Review* 45 (1951): 674.

26. 119 *Congressional Record* 19492–508 (1973).

27. *Congressional Quarterly Almanac 1977* (Washington, D.C.: Congressional Quarterly, 1977), p. 48-A.

28. Hoover Commission, *Task Force Report on Regulatory Commissions* [Appendix N], pp. 31–32, 46–49.

29. Hoover Commission, *Concluding Report* (May 1949), p. 72; C. Herman Pritchett, "The Regulatory Commissions Revisited," *American Political Science Review* 43 (1949): 978.

30. On the FTC, see Reorganization Plan No. 8 of 1950, 64 Stat. 1264 (1976); on the FPC, see Reorganization Plan No. 9 of 1950, 64 Stat. 1265; see also the provisions for its successor, the Federal Energy Regulatory Commission (FERC), 91 Stat. 582, sec. 401(b) (c), which authorizes the president to designate the chair and makes the chair responsible for executive and administrative operations. On the SEC, see Reorganization Plan No. 10 of 1950, 64 Stat. 1265. On the CAB, see Reorganization Plan No. 13 of 1950, 64 Stat. 1266, and Reorganization Plan No. 3 of 1961, 75 Stat. 837. On the FMC, see Reorganization Plan No.

7 of 1961, 75 Stat. 840. On the ICC, see Reorganization Plan No. 1 of 1969, 83 Stat. 859. On the FCC, see 48 Stat. 1066, sec. 4(a) (1934).

31. Commission on Money and Credit, *Money and Credit: Their Influence on Jobs, Prices, and Growth* (Englewood Cliffs, N.J.: Prentice-Hall, 1961), pp. 85–87.

32. 91 Stat. 1388, sec. 204 (1977).

33. "'Impartial' Regulators Stump for Nixon," *Washington Star-News*, Oct. 8, 1972, p. C5.

34. *Humphrey's Executor v. United States*, 295 U.S. 602, 612–13 (1935).

35. Ibid. at 617, 624.

36. Ibid. at 629.

37. Ibid. at 630. See J. D. Andrew, ed., *The Works of James Wilson*, 2 vols. (Chicago: Callaghan, 1896), 1:367–68; and Joseph Story, *Commentaries on the Constitution of the United States*, 4th ed., 2 vols. (Boston: Little, Brown, 1905), 1:525.

38. Cushman, *The Independent Regulatory Commissions*, pp. 447–48.

39. *Morgan v. Tennessee Valley Authority*, 28 F. Supp. 732 (E.D. Tenn. 1939); *Morgan v. Tennessee Valley Authority*, 115 F.2d 990 (6th Cir. 1940), *cert. denied*, 312 U.S. 701 (1941); *Wiener v. United States*, 357 U.S. 349 (1958); *Nader v. Bork*, 366 F. Supp. 104 (D.D.C. 1973); *Morrison v. Olson*, 487 U.S. 654 (1988).

40. *Humphrey's Executor v. United States* at 602, 632.

41. *Timm v. United States*, 223 Ct. Cl. 639 (1980).

42. 42 Stat. 20, sec. 2 (1921); 53 Stat. 565, sec. 201 (1939). See also H. Rept. 120, 76th Cong., 1st sess., 1939, p. 3.

43. OMB Circular No. A-10, Nov. 12, 1976, para. 3.

44. 86 Stat. 1229, sec. 27(k)(1) (1972); 7 U.S.C. 4a(h)(1) (1994).

45. In order of listing: for 1973, 87 Stat. 553, sec. 601(b)(1); for 1974, 87 Stat. 992, sec. 202(g)(2), 88 Stat. 1283, sec. 311(d)(1), 88 Stat. 1390–91, sec. 101(9)(A), and 88 Stat. 1906, sec. 5(a)(5)(A); for 1975, 88 Stat. 2170, sec. 304(b)(7); and for 1976, 90 Stat. 60, sec. 311.

46. 91 Stat. 583, sec. 401(j).

47. 92 Stat. 1125, sec. 1205(j).

48. Senate Committee on Government Operations, *Regulatory Agency Budgets* (Part 2) (hearings), 92d Cong., 2d sess., 1972, pp. 299, 301.

49. 88 Stat. 2011, sec. 175(a)(1). See H. Rept. 62, 96th Cong., 1st sess., 1979, p. 4.

50. 88 Stat. 288, sec. 3.

51. OMB Circular No. A-11, June 1995, sec. 11.1.

52. Assessments: 12 U.S.C. 243 (1994). GAO audits: 92 Stat. 391 (1978); 31 U.S.C. 714 (1994).

53. 7 U.S.C. 4a(h)(2) (1994). In signing the bill with this provision, Ford objected that the extension of the procedure "would make it difficult for me to develop and present to the Congress a coherent, coordinated legislative program." See *Public Papers of the Presidents, 1974*, p. 462.

54. 88 Stat. 1506, sec. 111 (1974).

55. 90 Stat. 60, sec. 311 (1976); 91 Stat. 583, sec. 401(j)(1977); 92 Stat. 1125, sec. 1205(k), 1209 (1978).

56. 28 U.S.C. 518 (1994). For exceptions to centralizing litigation in the Department of Justice, see Robert G. Dixon, Jr., "The Independent Commissions and Political Responsibility," *Administrative Law Review* 27 (1975): 1, 7–8 n.26. On the litigation issue, see also Senate Committee on Governmental Affairs,

Study on Federal Regulation, vol. 5, 95th Cong., 1st sess., Dec. 1977, pp. 54–67.

57. For the ICC, see 28 U.S.C. 2323 (1994). For other agencies, see A. Everette MacIntyre, "The Status of Regulatory Independence," *Federal Bar Journal* 29 (1969): 1, 6–9.

58. 87 Stat. 592, sec. 408(d) (1973); *Public Papers of the Presidents*, 1973, pp. 945–46.

59. See *Regulatory Commissions' Independence Act, S. 704: Compendium of Materials*, pp. 135–37.

60. Susan M. Olson, "Agency Litigating Authority as a Factor in Court Policy Making" (Paper delivered at the annual meeting of the American Political Science Association, Chicago, Sept. 1–4, 1983).

61. *Mail Order Ass'n v. U.S. Postal Service*, 986 F.2d 509 (D.C. Cir. 1993); *Mackie v. Clinton*, 827 F.Supp. 56 (D.D.C. 1993); *Mackie v. Bush*, 809 F.Supp. 144 (D.D.C. 1993); Neal Devins, "Tempest in an Envelope: Reflections on the Bush White House's Failed Takeover of the U.S. Postal Service," *UCLA Law Review* 41 (1994): 1035.

62. Neal Devins, "Political Will and the Unitary Executive: What Makes an Independent Agency Independent?" *Cardoza Law Review* 15 (1993): 273, 298–306.

63. MacIntyre, "The Status of Regulatory Independence," pp. 10–12.

64. 87 Stat. 576, 593–94 (1973); 119 *Congressional Record* 23883–87 (1973).

65. *Public Papers of the Presidents*, 1973, 946; General Accounting Office, *Status of GAO's Responsibilities under the Federal Reports Act: Independent Federal Regulatory Agencies*, OSP-76-14, May 28, 1976; 94 Stat. 2820 (1980); 44 U.S.C. 3507(c) (1994).

66. 94 Stat. 393–96 (1980).

67. *United States Senate v. FTC*, 463 U.S. 1216 (1983).

68. Jessica Korn, *The Power of Separation: American Constitutionalism and the Myth of the Legislative Veto* (Princeton, N.J.: Princeton University Press, 1996), pp. 48–68.

69. *Administrative Management in the Government of the United States*, p. 37; Hoover Commission, *Concluding Report*, pp. 9, 72; President's Advisory Council on Executive Reorganization, *A New Regulatory Framework: Report on Selected Independent Regulatory Agencies* (Washington, D.C.: Government Printing Office, Jan. 1971). This report was widely criticized for reaching conclusions and making generalizations in the absence of factual and analytical evidence. See Glen O. Robinson, "On Reorganizing the Independent Regulatory Agencies," *Virginia Law Review* 57 (1971): 947; and Roger G. Noll, *Reforming Regulation: An Evaluation of the Ash Council Proposal* (Washington, D.C.: Brookings Institution, 1971), pp. 12–13.

70. Emmette S. Redford, *The President and the Regulatory Commissions* (Unpublished report prepared for the President's Advisory Committee on Government Organization, 1960), p. 2. See also Redford's article, "The President and the Regulatory Commissions," *Texas Law Review* 44 (1965): 288.

71. David L. Shapiro, "The Choice of Rulemaking or Adjudication in the Development of Administrative Policy," *Harvard Law Review* 78 (1965): 921; *NLRB v. Bell Aerospace*, 416 U.S. 267, 294 (1974).

72. *Nat. Res. Def. Council v. U.S. Nuclear Reg. Com'n.*, 547 F.2d 633, 655 (D.C. Cir. 1976) (footnote omitted).

73. *Phillips Petroleum Co. v. Federal Power Com'n*, 475 F.2d 842, 844–45 (10th Cir. 1973), *cert. denied*, 414 U.S. 1146 (1974); *National Petroleum Refiners As-*

sociation v. FTC, 482 F.2d 672 (D.C. Cir. 1973), *cert. denied*, 415 U.S. 951 (1974).

74. Stephen F. Williams, "'Hybrid Rulemaking' under the Administrative Procedure Act: A Legal and Empirical Analysis," *University of Chicago Law Review* 42 (1975): 401.

75. 107 *Congressional Record* 3927–33 (1961). See Hugh M. Hall, Jr., "Responsibility of President and Congress for Regulatory Policy Development," *Law and Contemporary Problems* 26 (1961): 261.

76. *Public Papers of the Presidents*, 1961, pp. 267–76.

77. Ibid., 1963–1964, p. 18.

78. Ibid., 1975, Book 1:949–76; Robinson, "The Federal Communications Commission: An Essay on Regulatory Watchdogs," pp. 211–12.

79. 42 *Federal Register* 59741 (1977); 124 *Congressional Record* 8810–14 (1978); 43 *Federal Register* 12664, sec. 6(b)(5).

80. 43 *Federal Register* 12670 (1978). The exempted agencies include the CAB, CFTC, CPSC, FCC, FDIC, FEC, FERC, FHLBB, FMC, FRB, FTC, ICC, NLRB, NRC, SEC, the Federal Mine Safety and Health Review Commission, the Occupational Safety and Health Review Commission, and the Postal Rate Commission.

81. *Public Papers of the Presidents*, 1981, p. 104, sec. 1(d); see 44 U.S.C. 3502(10) (1982) for the exempted list of independent agencies.

82. Cutler and Johnson, "Regulation and the Political Process," pp. 1395, 1414–17.

83. Commission on Law and the Economy of the American Bar Association, *Federal Regulation: Roads to Reform*, Final Report 1979, With Recommendations, pp. 79–82, 88–91.

84. Ibid., pp. 82–84. See also Harold H. Bruff, "Presidential Power and Administrative Rulemaking," *Yale Law Journal* 88 (1979): 451. This article supports greater involvement by the president in the proceedings of regulatory agencies. This proposed delegation of power to the president is challenged by Douglas H. Rosenberg, "Delegation and Regulatory Reform: Letting the President Change the Rules," *Yale Law Journal* 89 (1980): 561.

85. *Melcher v. FOMC*, 644 F. Supp. 511 (D.D.C. 1986).

86. *Melcher v. FOMC*, 836 F.2d 561 (D.C. Cir. 1987), *cert. denied*, 486 U.S. 1042 (1988).

87. *Committee for Monetary Reform v. Board of Governors*, 766 F.2d 538 (D.C. Cir. 1985); *Riegle v. FOMC*, 656 F.2d 873 (D.C. Cir. 1981), *cert. denied*, 454 U.S. 1082 (1981); *Reuss v. Balles*, 584 F.2d 461 (D.C. Cir. 1978), *cert. denied*, 439 U.S. 997 (1978).

88. Edwin Meese III, "Towards Increased Government Accountability," *Federal Bar News and Journal* 32 (1985), 406, 408. Emphasis in original.

89. *Synar v. United States*, 626 F. Supp. 1374, 1398 (D.D.C. 1986) (three-judge court). The court consisted of Circuit Judge Antonin Scalia and District Judges Norma Johnson and Oliver Gasch. Any doubt about Scalia's authorship of this passage can be erased by reading his "Historical Anomalies in Administrative Law," in *Yearbook 1985* (Washington, D.C.: Supreme Court Historical Society), esp. pp. 106–10.

90. 272 U.S. 52, 135 (1926).

91. Ibid. at 135.

92. "Brief for the United States," *Bowsher v. Synar*, Supreme Court of the United States, October Term, 1985, p. 21.

93. Susan Sommer, "Independent Agencies as Article One Tribunals: Foundations of a Theory of Agency Independence," *Administrative Law Review* 39 (1987): 83.

94. *Landmark Briefs and Arguments of the Supreme Court of the United States: Constitutional Law*, ed. Philip B. Kurland and Gerhard Casper (Frederick, Md.: University Publications of America, 1987), 160:604.

95. Bernard Schwartz, "An Administrative Law 'Might Have Been'—Chief Justice Burger's *Bowsher* v. *Synar* Draft," *Administrative Law Review* 42 (1990): 221.

96. *Bowsher* v. *Synar*, 478 U.S. 714, 725 n.4 (1986).

97. *Commodity Futures Trading Com'n* v. *Schor*, 478 U.S. 833, 851 (1986).

98. "Complaint," *Ticor Title Ins. Co.* v. *FTC* (D.D.C. Sept. 26, 1985), p. 6.

99. *Ticor Title Ins. Co.* v. *FTC*, 814 F.2d 731 (D.C. Cir. 1987); *Ticor Title Ins. Co.* v. *FTC*, 625 F. Supp. 747 (D.D.C. 1986).

100. *SEC* v. *Blinder, Robinson & Co., Inc.*, 855 F.2d 677 (10th Cir. 1988), *cert. denied*, 489 U.S. 1033 (1989).

101. 487 U.S. 654 (1988).

102. *Mistretta* v. *United States*, 488 U.S. 361 (1989).

103. Friendly, *The Federal Administrative Agencies*, p. 154.

104. Commission on Law and the Economy of the American Bar Association, *Federal Regulation: Roads to Reform*, pp. 163–64.

Chapter 6. War Powers and Foreign Affairs

1. *United States* v. *Curtiss-Wright*, 299 U.S. 304, 315 (1936).

2. Ibid. at 319, 320.

3. Joel Francis Paschal, *Mr. Justice Sutherland: A Man against the State* (Princeton: Princeton University Press, 1951), p. 93. See also George Sutherland, *Constitutional Power and World Affairs* (New York: Columbia University Press, 1919) and S. Doc. No. 417, 61st Cong., 2d sess. (1910).

4. *Youngstown Co.* v. *Sawyer*, 343 U.S. 579, 636, n.2 (1952).

5. Ibid.

6. *American Intern. Group* v. *Islamic Republic of Iran*, 657 F.2d 430, 438 n.6 (D.C. Cir. 1981).

7. *United States* v. *Curtiss-Wright*, 299 U.S. at 319 (citing Annals of congress, 6th Cong. (1800): 613). 8. Annals of Congress, 6th Cong. (1800): 613. 9. United States v. Curtiss-Wright, 299 U.S. at 315.

10. Claude H. Van Tyne, "Sovereignty in the American Revolution: An Historical Study," *American Historical Review* 12 (1907): 529; David M. Levitan, "The Foreign Relations Power: An Analysis of Mr. Justice Sutherland's Theory," *Yale Law Journal* 55 (1946): 467; Charles A. Lofgren, "United States v. Curtiss-Wright Export Corporation: An Historical Assessment," *Yale Law Journal* 83 (1973): 1.

11. *United States* v. *California*, 332 U.S. 19, 31 (1947); *Texas* v. *White*, 74 U.S. 700, 725 (1869).

12. *Dames & Moore* v. *Regan*, 453 U.S. 654, 669 (1981). See also Rehnquist's comment at 678.

13. *Rostker* v. *Goldberg*, 453 U.S. 57, 66 (1981), quoting *Parker* v. *Levy*, 417 U.S. 733, 756 (1974).

14. For broad delegation arguments see *Ex parte Endo*, 323 U.S. 283, 298 n.21 (1944); *Zemel* v. *Rusk*, 381 U.S. 1, 17 (1965); *Goldwater* v. *Carter*, 444 U.S. 996, 1000 n.1 (1979). Inherent powers are discussed in *United States* v. *Pink*, 315 U.S. 203, 229 (1942); *Knauff* v. *Shaughnessy*, 338 U.S. 537, 542 (1950); *United States* v. *Mazurie*, 419 U.S. 544, 566–67 (1975).

15. Aaron Wildavsky, "The Two Presidencies," in *Perspectives on the Presidency,* ed. Aaron Wildavsky (Boston: Little, Brown, 1975), pp. 448–61.

16. Donald A. Peppers, "'The Two Presidencies': Eight Years Later," in *Perspectives on the Presidency,* pp. 462–71.

17. George C. Edwards III, "The Two Presidencies: A Reevaluation," *American Politics Quarterly* 14 (1986): 247.

18. Bayless Manning, "The Congress, the Executive and Intermestic Affairs: Three Proposals," *Foreign Affairs* 55 (1977): 306.

19. *United States v. Hoffman,* 334 F.Supp. 504, 506 (D.D.C. 1971). For a hybrid case, in which the activities of a domestic organization (the Jewish Defense League) affected foreign relations, leading the Justice Department to wiretap the league's office without a warrant, see *Zweibon v. Mitchell,* 516 F.2d 594 (D.C. Cir. 1975).

20. *Public Papers of the Presidents,* 1991 (II), p. 1629.

21. *Public Papers of the Presidents,* 1993 (II), p. 2.

22. *The Constitution of the United States of America: Analysis and Interpretation,* S. Doc. No. 103-6, 1996, p. 470.

23. Edward S. Corwin, *The President: Office and Powers 1787–1957* (New York: New York University Press, 1957), pp. 211–12.

24. *United States v. Curtiss-Wright,* 299 U.S. at 319.

25. John C. Fitzpatrick, ed., *Writings of Washington,* 39 vols. (Washington, D.C.: Government Printing Office, 1931–1944), 30:373.

26. Ibid., 378.

27. William Maclay, *Sketches of Debate in the First Senate of the United States, 1789–1791* (Harrisburg, Pa.: Lane S. Hart, 1880), pp. 122–26.

28. Thomas M. Franck and Edward Weisband, *Foreign Policy by Congress* (New York: Oxford University Press, 1979), p. 136.

29. George H. Haynes, *The Senate of the United States: Its History and Practice,* 2 vols. (Boston: Houghton Mifflin, 1938), 2:576–602; Louis Fisher, "Congressional Participation in the Treaty Process," *University of Pennsylvania Law Review* 137 (1989): 1511–22.

30. Francis O. Wilcox, *Congress, the Executive, and Foreign Policy* (New York: Harper & Row, 1971), p. 52.

31. Senate Judiciary Committee, *Executive Privilege: The Withholding of Information from the Executive* (hearings), 92d Cong., 1st sess., 1971, pp. 262–64.

32. I. M. Destler, "Executive-Congressional Conflict in Foreign Policy: Explaining It, Coping with It," in *Congress Reconsidered,* ed. Lawrence C. Dodd and Bruce Oppenheimer (Washington, D.C.: Congressional Quarterly Press, 1981), p. 310.

33. Wilson's constitutional analysis of the treaty process has been decisively refuted by Forrest R. Black, "The United States Senate and the Treaty Power," *Rocky Mountain Law Review* 4 (1931): 1; and by Richard E. Webb, "Treaty-Making and the President's Obligation to Seek the Advice and Consent of the Senate with Special Reference to the Vietnam Peace Negotiations," *Ohio State Law Journal* 31 (1970): 490.

34. Senate Finance Committee, *Extension of Fast Track Legislative Procedures* (hearings), 102d Cong., 1st sess. (1991): 9.

35. *Weekly Compilation of Presidential Documents* 27 (May 1, 1991): 537.

36. Annals of Congress, 4th Cong., 1st sess. (1796): 426–28.

37. Ibid., pp. 437, 466–74.

38. Ibid., pp. 771–82. This language has been adopted on subsequent occasions, such

as on Apr. 20, 1871; *Hinds' Precedents of the House of Representatives,* 5 vols. (Washington, D.C.: Government Printing Office, 1907), 2:1523. See also Ivan M. Stone, "The House of Representatives and the Treaty-Making Power," *Kentucky Law Journal* 17 (1929): 217.

39. Chalfant Robinson, "The Treaty-Making Power of the House of Representatives," *Yale Review* 12 (1903): 191.

40. *Hinds' Precedents,* 2:1524.

41. Louis Fisher, *President and Congress* (New York: Free Press, 1972), pp. 133–35.

42. James D. Richardson, ed., *A Compilation of Messages and Papers of the Presidents,* 20 vols. (New York: Bureau of National Literature, 1897–1925), 5:2176.

43. 9 Stat. 1 (1845).

44. 68 Stat. 92 (1954).

45. 90 Stat. 765, sec. 507 (1976); 90 Stat. 2498 (1976).

46. "Agreement on Friendship, Defense, and Cooperation between the United States and the Kingdom of Spain," Complementary Agreement Three, Article 2 (signed July 2, 1982).

47. *Digest of United States Practice in International Law,* 1978, at 734–65.

48. Louis Fisher, *Constitutional Conflicts between Congress and the President* (Lawrence: University Press of Kansas, 1997), pp. 243–44.

49. *Goldwater v. Carter,* 617 F.2d 697, 707, 714 (D.C. Cir. 1979).

50. *Goldwater v. Carter,* 444 U.S. 996, 998 (1979).

51. *Rainbow Nav., Inc. v. Department of Navy,* 699 F.Supp. 339 (D.D.C. 1988); *Rainbow Nav., Inc. v. Department of Navy,* 686 F.Supp. 354 (D.D.C. 1988).

52. Abram Chayes and Antonio Handler Chayes, "Testing and Development of 'Exotic' Systems under the ABM Treaty: The Great Reinterpretation Caper," *Harvard Law Review* 99 (1986): 1956; Abraham D. Sofaer, "The ABM Treaty and the Strategic Defense Initiative," *Harvard Law Review* 99 (1986): 1972.

53. Senate Committees on Foreign Relations and the Judiciary, *The ABM Treaty and the Constitution* (joint hearings), 100th Cong., 1st sess. (1987): 122–23.

54. Ibid., p. 143.

55. 101 Stat. 1057, sec. 226 (1987).

56. S. Exec. Rept. No. 100-15, 100th Cong., 2d sess. (1988): 442.

57. Ibid., p. 443.

58. 134 *Congressional Record* 12593, 12655 (1988).

59. Ibid. at 12655.

60. *Weekly Compilation of Presidential Documents* 24 (June 10, 1988): 780.

61. 1 Stat. 239 (1792).

62. *Altman & Co. v. United States,* 224 U.S. 583, 600–601 (1912). In *United States v. Pink,* 315 U.S. 203, 230 (1942), Justice Douglas regarded executive agreements as having a "similar dignity" with treaties. For an opinion by Acting Attorney General McGranery in 1946 upholding the legality of an executive agreement made pursuant to a joint resolution, see 40 Op. Att'y Gen. 469.

63. *United States v. Belmont,* 301 U.S. 324 (1937); *United States v. Pink,* 315 U.S. 203 (1941). For more recent decisions upholding the president's authority to enter into international executive agreements, see *Dames & Moore v. Regan,* 453 U.S. 654 (1981) and *Japan Whaling Assn. v. American Cetacean Soc.,* 478 U.S. 221 (1986).

64. *Foreign Affairs Manual* 11 (1974): 721.2(b)(3).

65. *United States v. Guy W. Capps, Inc.*, 204 F.2d 655, 660 (4th Cir. 1953), *aff'd on other grounds*, 348 U.S. 296 (1955).

66. *Seery v. United States*, 127 F.Supp. 601, 606 (Ct. Cl. 1955); and *Reid v. Covert*, 354 U.S. 1, 16 (1957).

67. 86 Stat. 619 (1972); 1 U.S.C. 112b (1988); 91 Stat. 224, sec. 5 (1977).

68. Franck and Weisband, *Foreign Policy by Congress*, pp. 152–54.

69. 22 CFR § 181 (1994); 141 *Congressional Record* S4050–53 (daily ed. Mar. 16, 1995).

70. John Locke, *Second Treatise of Government* (1690), §§ 146–47.

71. Ibid. at § 148.

72. William Blackstone, *Commentaries on the Laws of England*, 2 vols. (1803), 2:237–80.

73. Benjamin Fletcher Wright, ed., *The Federalist* (Cambridge, Mass.: Harvard University Press, 1961), p. 450. Emphasis in original.

74. Ibid. Emphasis in original.

75. Max Farrand, ed., *The Records of the Federal Convention of 1787*, 4 vols. (New Haven: Yale University Press, 1937), 2:318–19.

76. Jonathan Elliot, ed., *The Debates in the Several State Conventions, on the Adoption of the Federal Constitution*, 5 vols. (Washington, D.C., 1836–1845), 2:528.

77. Gaillard Hunt, ed., *The Writings of James Madison*, 9 vols. (New York: G. P. Putnam's, 1900–1910), 6:148. Emphasis in original.

78. Paul Leicester Ford, ed., *The Writings of Thomas Jefferson*, 10 vols. (New York: G. P. Putnam's, 1892–1899), 5:123.

79. Farrand, 1:139–40. Emphasis in original.

80. 8 *Annals of Congress* 1519 (1798).

81. *Bas v. Tingy*, 4 U.S. 37 (1800).

82. *Talbot v. Seeman*, 5 U.S. 1, 28 (1801); Barry M. Blechman and Stephen S. Kaplan, *Force without War* (Washington, D.C.: Brookings Institution, 1978).

83. *Congressional Glove*, 30th Cong., 1st sess. (1848): 95.

84. Roy Basler, ed., *The Collected Works of Abraham Lincoln*, 9 vols. (New Brunswick, N.J.: Rutgers University Press, 1953–1955), 1:451–52. Emphasis in original.

85. Richardson, *Messages and Papers of the Presidents*, 7:3225.

86. 12 Stat. 326 (1861).

87. *Ex parte Merryman*, 17 F. Cas. 144, 153 (C.C. Md. 1861) (No. 9, 487).

88. 12 Stat. 755 (1863).

89. Edward S. Corwin, "The President's Power," *New Republic*, Jan. 29, 1951, p. 16.

90. Michael J. Glennon, "The Constitution and Chapter VII of the United Nations Charter," *American Journal of International Law* 85 (1991): 75–77.

91. House Committee on Foreign Affairs, *Participation by the United States in the United Nations Organization* (hearings), 79th Cong., 1st sess. (1945): 23.

92. Ibid. (response to Congressman Roger) and 25–26 (response to Congressman Kee).

93. S. Rept. No. 717, 79th Cong., 1st sess. (1945): 5; 91 *Congressional Record* 12267 (1945).

94. 91 *Congressional Record* 11303 (1945). See also H. Rept. No. 1383, 79th Cong., 1st sess. (1945): 7.

95. 63 Stat. 735–36, § 5 (1949).

96. *Department of State Bulletin* 23 (July 10, 1950): 43 and 46.

97. Dean Acheson, *Present at the Creation* (New York: W. W. Norton, 1969), p. 408.

98. Ibid., p. 415.

99. Merle Miller, *Plain Speaking: An Oral Biography of Harry S Truman* (New York: Berkley Publishing Co., 1974), p. 297n.

100. For further details on the UN Charter and the Korean War, see Louis Fisher, *Presidential War* (Lawrence: University Press of Kansas, 1995), pp. 70–91, and Louis Fisher, "The Korean War: On What Legal Basis Did Truman Act?" *American Journal of International Law* 89 (1995): 21.

101. *Youngstown Co. v. Sawyer*, 103 F.Supp. 569 (D.D.C. 1952); *Youngstown Co. v. Sawyer*, 343 U.S. 579 (1952).

102. 69 Stat. 7 (1955); 71 Stat. 4 (1957).

103. Dwight D. Eisenhower, *Waging Peace, 1956–1961* (Garden City, N.Y.: Doubleday, 1965), p. 179.

104. *Public Papers of the Presidents, 1962*: 674, 679; 76 Stat. 697 (1962).

105. 78 Stat. 384 (1964).

106. Fisher, *Constitutional Conflicts between Congress and the President*, pp. 279–80.

107. 97 Stat. 805 (1983).

108. Senate Committee on Armed Services, *Crisis in the Persian Gulf Region: U.S. Policy Options and Implications* (hearings), 101st Cong., 2d sess. (1990), p. 701.

109. *Dellums v. Bush*, 752 F.Supp. 1141, 1145 (D.D.C. 1990).

110. *Public Papers of the Presidents, 1991* (I), p. 20.

111. 105 Stat. 3 (1991).

112. *Public Papers of the Presidents, 1991* (I), p. 40.

113. *Public Papers of the Presidents, 1993* (I), pp. 938, 940.

114. Michael Ratner and Jules Lobel, "Bombing Baghdad: Illegal Reprisal or Self-Defense?" *Legal Times*, July 5, 1993, p. 24.

115. Ruth Marcus and Daniel Williams, "Show of Strength Offers Benefits for Clinton," *Washington Post*, June 28, 1993, p. A1.

116. 107 Stat. 1475–77, sec. 8151 (1993).

117. *Public Papers of the Presidents, 1994* (II), p. 1419.

118. Ibid., p. 1559.

119. Ibid., p. 1551.

120. 108 Stat. 4358, sec. 1(b) (1994).

121. *Public Papers of the Presidents, 1993* (I), p. 594; *Public Papers of the Presidents, 1993* (II), pp. 1455, 1781.

122. *Public Papers of the Presidents, 1993* (II), pp. 1763–64, 1768, 1770.

123. *Public Papers of the Presidents, 1994* (I), p. 186.

124. *Weekly Compilation of Presidential Documents* 31 (Sept. 1, 1995): 1473, 1474; *Weekly Compilation of Presidential Documents* 31 (Sept. 12, 1995): 1553.

125. 141 *Congressional Record* H13228 (daily ed. Nov. 17, 1995).

126. Senate Committee on Foreign Relations, *Security and Development Assistance* (hearings), 99th Cong., 1st sess. (1985), pp. 908–10; House Committee on Appropriations, *Department of Defense Appropriations for 1986* (Part 2) (hearings), 99th Cong., 1st sess. (1985), p. 1092.

127. *Iran-Contra Affair*, H. Rept. No. 100-433 and S. Rept. No. 100-216 (Nov. 1987), p. 423.

128. Senate Select Committee on Intelligence, *Oversight Legislation* (hearings), 100th Cong., 2d sess. (1987), pp. 81–86.

129. *Public Papers of the Presidents, 1990* (II), pp. 1729–30.

130. 105 Stat. 441–45 (1991).

131. Iran-Contra Committees, *Iran-Contra Investigation* (joint hearings), 100th Cong., 1st sess. (Vol. 100-8, p. 158, and Vol. 100-7, Part II, p. 37).

132. Benjamin Fletcher Wright, ed., *The Federalist*, p. 450. Emphasis in original.

133. Hunt, ed., *The Writings of James Madison*, 6:148. Emphasis in original.

134. 99 Stat. 254, sec. 722(d) (1985).

135. *Public Papers of the Presidents*, 1989 (II), pp. 1567–69.

136. Ibid., p. 1546.

137. 103 Stat. 1251, sec. 582 (1989).

138. *Public Papers of the Presidents*, 1989 (II), p. 1573. For analyses of the Iran-Contra affair, see Lawrence E. Walsh, *Firewall: The Iran-Contra Conspiracy and Cover-up* (New York: W. W. Norton, 1997); Theodore Draper, *A Very Thin Line: The Iran-Contra Affairs* (New York: Hill and Wang, 1991); and Louis Fisher, "The Foundations of a Scandal," *Corruption and Reform* 3 (1988): 157–69.

139. *Department of State Bulletin*, No. 1871, 72 (May 5, 1975): 562.

140. House Committee on International Affairs, *Executive-Legislative Consultations on U.S. Arms Sales*, 97th Cong., 2d sess. (Committee Print, Dec. 1982).

141. Office of the White House Press Secretary, *Briefing by Attorney General Griffin B. Bell, Stuart E. Eizenstat, Assistant to the President for Domestic Affairs and Policy, and John Harmon, Office of Legal Counsel*, June 21, 1978, p. 4.

142. 100 Stat. 9 (1986).

143. *Commission on the Organization of the Government for the Conduct of Foreign Policy* (Washington, D.C.: Government Printing Office, June 1975), p. 195.

144. Thomas M. Franck and Edward Weisband, *Foreign Policy by Congress*, pp. 113–14, 183–84.

145. Douglas J. Bennett, Jr., "Congress in Foreign Policy: Who Needs It?" *Foreign Affairs* 57 (1978): 40, 49.

146. Patsy M. Mink, "Institutional Perspectives: Misunderstandings, Myths, and Misperceptions: How Congress and the State Department See Each Other," in *The Tethered Presidency*, ed. Thomas M. Franck (New York: New York University Press, 1981), p. 74.

147. "Bush Hears Debate on Japan Trade," *Washington Post*, May 23, 1989, p. C1.

Chapter 7. Budgetary Control

1. Louis Fisher, *Presidential Spending Power* (Princeton: Princeton University Press, 1975), pp. 12–13.

2. Ibid., pp. 17–18. For the efforts of other presidents and secretaries of the treasury, see other sections in this chapter.

3. Ibid., pp. 20–24.

4. *Harper's Weekly*, Aug. 12, 1882, p. 497.

5. Ibid., July 3, 1886, p. 421. For discussion of the Arthur and Cleveland vetoes, see Fisher, *Presidential Spending Power*, pp. 25–27.

6. 33 Stat. 1257, sec. 4 (1905).

7. 35 Stat. 1027, sec. 7 (1909); Taft's Executive Order is reprinted in Henry Jones Ford, *The Cost of Our National Government* (New York: Columbia University Press, 1910), pp. 115–16.

8. *The Need for a National Budget*, H. Doc. 854, 62d Cong., 2d sess., 1912, p. 138. Emphases in original.

9. 37 Stat. 415 (1912).

10. Frederick A. Cleveland, "The Federal Budget," *Proceedings of the Academy of Political Science* 3 (1912–1913): 167. Emphasis in original.

11. William Howard Taft, *Our Chief Magistrate and His Powers* (New York: Columbia University Press, 1916), pp. 64–65.

12. H. Rept. 362, 66th Cong., 1st sess., 1919, pp. 1–3.

13. H. Rept. 14, 67th Cong., 1st sess., 1921, pp. 4–5.

14. Ibid., pp. 6–7.

15. For Fitzgerald, see "Budget Systems, *Municipal Research* 62 (June 1915): 312, 322, 327, 340, and also William Franklin Willoughby, *The Problem of a National Budget* (New York: Appleton, 1918), pp. 146–49. For Houston, see David Houston, *Eight Years with Wilson's Cabinet* (Garden City, N.Y.: Doubleday, Page, 1926), 2:88. Wilson's other secretaries of the treasury took the same position. See *Annual Report of the Secretary of the Treasury*, 1918–1919, p. 121 (testimony of William McAdoo) and ibid., p. 117 (testimony of Carter Glass).

16. Charles Wallace Collins, "Constitutional Aspects of a National Budget System," *Yale Law Journal* 25 (1916): 376.

17. S. Rept. 524, 66th Cong., 2d sess., 1920, p. 4.

18. 42 Stat. 20 (1921).

19. Department of the Treasury, *Combined Statement of Receipts, Expenditures and Balances of the United States Government*, June 30, 1973, pp. 542–62.

20. *Weekly Compilation of Presidential Documents* 8 (Dec. 11, 1972): 1752.

21. Fisher, *Presidential Spending Power*, pp. 175–201.

22. *Washington Post*, Mar. 7, 1973, p. A4.

23. H. Rept. 147, 93d Cong., 1st sess., 1973, p. 39.

24. Paul E. Peterson, "The New Politics of Deficits," in *The New Direction in American Politics*, ed. John E. Chubb and Paul E. Peterson (Washington, D.C.: American Enterprise Institute, 1985), p. 375.

25. Senate Committee on the Budget, *Can Congress Control the Power of the Purse?* (hearings), 95th Cong., 2d sess., 1978, p. 13.

26. "Congress Must Get Serious," *Washington Post*, June 4, 1982, p. A19.

27. H. Rept. 1152, Pt. 1, 98th Cong., 2d sess., 1984, p. 43. See also my charts reprinted in "Issue Presentations before the Rules Committee Task Force on the Budget Process," prepared by the House Committee on Rules, 98th Cong., 2d sess., 1984, pp. 81, 83.

28. 122 *Congressional Record* 13761 (1976).

29. Ibid., 10519.

30. Trent Lott, "The Need to Improve the Budget Process: A Republican's View," in *Crisis in the Budget Process*, ed. Allen Schick (Washington, D.C.: American Enterprise Institute, 1985), p. 72.

31. Rudolph G. Penner, "An Appraisal of the Congressional Budget Process," in *Crisis in the Budget Process*, p. 69.

32. Allen Schick, "How the Budget Was Won and Lost," in *President and Congress: Assessing Reagan's First Year*, ed. Norman J. Ornstein (Washington, D.C.: American Enterprise Institute, 1982), p. 25.

33. David A. Stockman, *The Triumph of Politics* (New York: Harper & Row, 1986), p. 159.

34. Ibid., p. 91.

35. 127 *Congressional Record* 6292 (1981).

36. Jean Peters, "Reconciliation 1982: What Happened?" *PS* 14 (1981): 732; *Congressional Quarterly Weekly Report*, Aug. 15, 1981, p. 1466.

37. House Committee on Appropriations, *Views and Estimates on the Budget Proposed for Fiscal Year 1983*, 97th Cong., 2d sess. (Committee Print, 1982), p. 12.

38. 129 *Congressional Record* 25417 (1983).

39. 122 *Congressional Record* 17843 (1976).

40. *Weekly Compilation of Presidential Documents* 21 (Nov. 15, 1983): 1411.

41. 124 *Congressional Record* 12082 (1978).

42. *Bowsher v. Synar*, 478 U.S. 714 (1986).

43. Senate Committees on Governmental Affairs and the Budget, *Budget Reform Proposals* (joint hearings), 101st Cong., 1st sess., 1989, p. 3.

44. Raphael Thelwell, "Gramm-Rudman-Hollings Four Years Later: A Dangerous Illusion," *Public Administration Review* 50 (Mar./Apr. 1990): 197.

45. Senate Committees on Governmental Affairs and the Budget, *Budget Reform Proposals* (joint hearings), 101st Cong., 1st sess., 1989, p. 2.

46. House Committee on the Budget, *Budget Process Reform* (hearings), 101st Cong., 2d sess., 1990 , p. 1.

47. Helen Dewar, "Bush, Mitchell Take Aim at Slashing the Defense Budget," *Washington Post*, Jan. 17, 1991, p. B1.

48. Ibid.

49. *Weekly Compilation of Presidential Documents* 33 (May 16, 1997): 717.

50. 83 *Congressional Record* 355–56 (1938). This section on the item veto is based on a paper I presented at the Aug. 29–31, 1985, Annual Meeting of the American Political Science Association in New Orleans, and an article I co-authored with Neal Devins, "How Successfully Can the Item Veto Be Transferred to the President?" *Georgetown Law Journal* 75 (1986): 159.

51. 130 *Congressional Record* 10844–70 (1984).

52. 131 *Congressional Record* 20268–97 (1985).

53. *Public Papers of the Presidents*, 1986(I), p. 127.

54. Executive Office of the President, *Executive Policy Study #12*, 59 (Sept. 6, 1983).

55. *State v. Holder*, 76 Miss. 158, 181 (1898).

56. *Fergus v. Russel*, 270 Ill. 304, 348 (1915).

57. *State ex rel. Kleczka v. Conta*, 264 N.W.2d 539, 557 (Wis. 1978) (Hansen, J., concurring in part, dissenting in part).

58. *Cascade Telephone Co. v. State Tax Commission*, 176 Wash. 616 (1934); *Tacoma v. State Tax Commission*, 177 Wash. 604 (1934).

59. *Cascade Telephone Co. v. State Tax Commission*, 176 Wash. at 623 (Steinert, J., dissenting). See also *Washington Ass'n of Apt. Ass'ns v. Evans*, 88 Wash.2d 563 (1977).

60. *Commonwealth v. Dodson*, 176 Va. 281, 290 (1940).

61. Ibid. at 302.

62. *State ex rel. Kleczka v. Conta*, 264 N.W.2d at 557 (Hansen, J., concurring in part, dissenting in part). See also *Washington Federation of State Employees v. State*, 682 P.2d 869 (Wash. 1984).

63. *State ex rel. Wisc. Senate v. Thompson*, 424 N.W.2d 385 (Wis. 1988).

64. Wis. Const., art. V, § 10(1)(c).

65. *Anderson v. Lamm*, 579 P.2d 620, 624 (Colo. 1978).

66. La. Const., art. III. § 16.

67. Ala. Const., VI, § 45.

68. 109 Stat. 403 (1995); H. Rept. No. 293, 104th Cong., 1st sess., 1995, pp. 34–38.

69. *Public Papers of the Presidents*, 1988 (I), p. 86.

70. H. Rept. 498, 100th Cong., 1st sess., 1987, pp. 1099–1100. The "study of crawfish" shows up only by implication on page 1100 as "$200,000 for research in Louisiana."

71. 130 *Congressional Record* 10854 (1984).

72. House Committee on the Judiciary, *Item Veto* (hearings), 85th Cong., 1st sess., 1957, p. 94.

73. *Economic Report of the President*, Feb. 1985, p. 96.

74. Stephen Glazier, "Reagan Already Has Line-Item Veto," *Wall Street Journal*, Dec. 4, 1987, p. 14. See also David Rapp, "Does Reagan Already Have a Line-Item Veto?" *Congressional Quarterly Weekly Report*, May 14, 1988, p. 1284.

75. See the articles by Charles J. Cooper and Louis Fisher in *Pork Barrels and Principles: The Politics of the Presidential Veto* (National Legal Center for the Public Interest, 1988), pp. 17–45.

76. *Public Papers of the Presidents*, 1992 (I), p. 479.

77. *Byrd v. Raines*, 956 F.Supp. 25, 35 (D.D.C. 1997).

Epilogue

1. Congressman Jim Wright, *You and Your Congressman* (New York: Capricorn Books, 1976), pp. 60–63; statement by Senator Mike Mansfield in 105 *Congressional Record* 18873–74 (1959).

2. Willmoore Kendall, "The New Majorities," *Midwest Journal of Political Science* 4 (1960): 317.

3. *Weekly Compilation of Presidential Documents* 15 (May 11, 1979): 840; and ibid. (Aug. 7, 1979): 1410.

4. Stephen Hess, *Organizing the Presidency* (Washington, D.C.: Brookings Institution, 1976), pp. 9–10.

5. Joel D. Aberbach and Bert A. Rockman, "The Overlapping Worlds of American Federal Executives and Congressmen," *British Journal of Political Science* 7 (1977): 23, 33.

6. Francis O. Wilcox, *Congress, the Executive, and Foreign Policy* (New York: Harper & Row, 1971), p. 61.

7. "Reagan Has Power to Remold Bureaucracy," *Washington Post*, Nov. 19, 1980, p. A1.

8. "Reflections on a System Spinning Out of Control," *Washington Post*, Dec. 11, 1986, p. A21. Emphasis in original.

SELECTED BIBLIOGRAPHY

———◆———

I. General Studies

Books

Arnold, R. Douglas. *Congress and the Bureaucracy*. New Haven: Yale University Press, 1979.

Barber, Sotirios A. *The Constitution and the Delegation of Congressional Power*. Chicago: University of Chicago Press, 1975.

Berger, Raoul. *Executive Privilege: A Constitutional Myth*. Cambridge: Harvard University Press, 1974.

Binkley, Wilfred E. *President and Congress*. New York: Vintage Books, 1962.

Bowles, Nigel. *The White House and Capitol Hill*. Oxford, Clarendon Press, 1987.

Crovitz, L. Gordon, and Jeremy A. Rabkin, eds. *The Fettered Presidency: Legal Constraints on the Executive Branch*. Washington, D. C.: American Enterprise Institute, 1989.

Davidson, Roger H., ed. *Congress and the Presidency: Invitation to Struggle. The Annals* 499 (1988).

Dodd, Lawrence C., and Richard L. Schott. *Congress and the Administrative State*. New York: John Wiley and Sons, 1979.

Edwards, George C. III. *At the Margins: Presidential Leadership of Congress*. New Haven: Yale University Press, 1989.

———. *Presidential Influence in Congress*. San Francisco: W. H. Freeman, 1978.

Egger, Rowland, and Joseph P. Harris. *The President and Congress*. New York: Free Press, 1972.

Fisher, Louis. *President and Congress: Power and Policy*. New York: McGraw-Hill, 1963.

———. *Presidential Spending Power*. Princeton: Princeton University Press, 1975.

———. *Constitutional Conflicts between Congress and the President*. 4th ed. Lawrence: University Press of Kansas, 1977.

Foley, Michael, and John E. Owens. *Congress and the Presidency: Institutional Politics in a Separated System*. Manchester, England: Manchester University Press, 1996

Freeman, J. Leiper. *The Political Process: Executive Bureau–Legislative Committee Relations*. New York: Random House, 1965

Gibson, Martha Liebler. *Weapons of Influence: The Legislative Veto, American Foreign Policy, and the Irony of Reform*. Boulder: Westview Press, 1992.

Goldwin, Robert A., and Art Kaufman, eds. *Separation of Powers—Does It Still Work?* Washington, D.C.: American Enterprise Institute, 1986.

Hamilton, James. *The Power to Probe: A Study in Congressional Investigations*. New York: Random House, 1976.

Harriger, Katy J. *Independent Justice: The Federal Special Prosecutor in American Politics*. Lawrence: University Press of Kansas, 1992.

Heclo, Hugh, and Lester M. Salamon, eds. *The Illusion of Presidential Government*. Boulder: Westview Press, 1981.

Johannes, John R. *To Serve the People: Congress and Constituency Service*. Lincoln: University of Nebraska Press, 1984.

Jones, Charles O. *The Presidency in a Separated System*. Washington, D.C.: Brookings Institution, 1994.

———. *Separate But Equal Branches: Congress and the Presidency*. Chatham, N.J.: Chatham House Publishers, 1995.

King, Anthony, ed. *Both Ends of the Avenue: The Presidency, the Executive Branch, and Congress in the 1980s*. Washington, D.C.: American Enterprise Institute, 1983.

Korn, Jessica. *The Power of Separation: American Constitutionalism and the Myth of the Legislative Veto*. Princeton: Princeton University Press, 1996.

Kurland, Philip B. *Watergate and the Constitution*. Chicago: University of Chicago Press, 1978.

Merry, Henry J. *Five-Branch Government: The Full Measure of Constitutional Checks and Balances*. Urbana: University of Illinois Press, 1980.

Mezey, Michael L. *Congress, the President, and Public Policy*. Boulder: Westview Press, 1989.

Ornstein, Norman J., ed. *President and Congress: Assessing Reagan's First Year*. Washington, D.C.: American Enterprise Institute, 1982.

Peterson, Mark A. *Legislating Together: The White House and Capitol Hill from Eisenhower to Reagan*. Cambridge: Harvard University Press, 1990.

Pfiffner, James P. *The President, the Budget, and Congress: Impoundment and the 1974 Budget Act*. Boulder: Westview Press, 1979.

Polsby, Nelson W. *Congress and the Presidency*. 4th ed. Englewood Cliffs, N.J.: Prentice-Hall, 1986.

Pork Barrels and Principles: The Politics of the Presidential Veto. Washington, D.C.: National Legal Center for the Public Interest, 1988.

Pyle, Christopher H., and Richard A Pious. *The President, Congress, and the Constitution*. New York: Free Press, 1984.

Ripley, Randall B., and Grace A. Franklin. *Congress, the Bureaucracy, and Public Policy*. 5th ed. Homewood, Ill.: Dorsey Press, 1991

Salamon, Lester M., and Michael S. Lund, eds. *The Reagan Presidency and the Governing of America*. Washington, D.C.: Urban Institute, 1985.

Schick, Allen. *Congress and Money*. Washington, D.C.: Urban Institute, 1980.

Shuman, Howard E. *Politics and the Budget: The Struggle Between the President and the Congress*. 2d ed. Englewood Cliffs, N.J.: Prentice-Hall, 1988.

Spitzer, Robert J. *The Presidential Veto*. Albany: State University of New York Press, 1988.

———. *President and Congress*. Philadelphia: Temple University Press, 1993.

Sundquist, James L. *The Decline and Resurgence of Congress*. Washington, D.C.: Brookings Institution, 1981.

Thurber, James A., ed. *Divided Democracy: Cooperation and Conflict between the President and Congress*. Washington, D.C.: CQ Press, 1991.

————. *Rivals for Power: Presidential-Congressional Relations.* Washington, D.C.: CQ Press, 1996.

Tiefer, Charles. *The Semi-Sovereign Presidency: The Bush Administration's Strategy for Governing without Congress.* Boulder: Westview Press, 1994.

Watson, Richard A. *Presidential Vetoes and Public Policy.* Lawrence: University Press of Kansas, 1993.

Wayne, Stephen J. *The Legislative Presidency.* New York: Harper and Row, 1978.

Wilson, Bradford P., and Peter W. Schramm, eds. *Separation of Powers and Good Government.* Landham, Md.: Rowman and Littlefield, 1994.

Articles

Brooks, Jack. "Gramm-Rudman: Can Congress and the President Pass This Buck?" *Texas Law Review* 66 (1985): 131

Davis, Eric L. "Legislative Liaison in the Carter Administration." *Political Science Quarterly* 94 (1979): 287.

————. "The President and Congress." In *Politics and Oval Office,* ed. Arnold J. Meltsner. San Francisco: Institute for Contemporary Studies, 1981.

Dodd, Lawrence C. "Congress, the Constitution, and the Crisis of Legitimation." In *Congress Reconsidered,* 2d ed., Lawrence C. Dodd and Bruce I. Oppenheimer. Washington, D.C.: CQ Press, 1981.

Dry, Murray. "The Separation of Powers and Representative Government." *Political Science Review* 3 (1973): 43.

Fisher, Louis. "Separation of Powers Doctrine: Interpretation Outside the Courts." *Pepperdine Law Review* 18 (1990): 57.

————. "The Legislative Veto: Invalidated, It Survives." *Law and Contemporary Problems* 56 (1993): 273.

————. "Congress and the President in the Administrative Process: The Uneasy Alliance." In *The Illusion of Presidential Government,* ed. Hugh Heclo and Lester Salamon. Boulder: Westview Press, 1981, 21–43.

————. "Congress and the Removal Power." *Congress and the Presidency* 10 (Spring 1983): 63.

Harriger, Katy J. "Separation of Powers and the Politics of Independent Counsels." *Political Science Quarterly* 109 (1994): 261.

Heaphy, Maura E. "Executive Legislative Liaison." *Presidential Studies Quarterly* 5 (1975): 43.

Jones, Charles O. "Congress and the Presidency." In *The New Congress,* eds. Thomas E. Mann and Norman J. Ornstein. Washington, D.C.: American Enterprise Institute, 1981.

————. "Keeping Faith and Losing Congress: The Carter Experience in Washington." *Presidential Studies Quarterly* 14 (Summer 1984): 437.

Manley, John F. "Presidential Power and White House Lobbying." *Political Science Quarterly* 93 (1978): 255.

Mullen, William F. "Perceptions of Carter's Legislative Process and Failures: Views from the Hill and the Liaison Staff." *Presidential Studies Quarterly* 12 (1982): 522.

Parnell, Archie. "Congressional Interference in Agency Enforcement: The IRS Experience." *Yale Law Journal* 89 (1980): 1360.

Stathis, Stephen W. "Executive Cooperation: Presidential Recognition of the Investigative Authority of Congress and the Courts." *Journal of Law and Politics* 3 (1986): 183.

Strauss, Peter L. "The Place of Agencies in Government: Separation of Powers and the Fourth Branch." *Columbia Law Review* 84 (1984): 573.

Tiefer, Charles. "The Constitutionality of Independent Officers as Checks on the Abuses of Executive Power."*Boston University Law Review* 63 (1983): 59.

Zeidenstein, Harvey G. "The Reassertion of Congressional Power: New Curbs on the President." *Political Science Quarterly* 93 (1978): 393.

II. Foreign Affairs and War Power

Books

Abshire, David M. *Foreign Policy Matters: President vs. Congress.* Beverly Hills, Calif.: Sage Publications, 1979.

Adler, David Gray, and Larry N. George, eds. *The Constitution and the Conduct of American Foreign Policy.* Lawrence: University Press of Kansas, 1996.

Crabb, Cecil V., Jr., and Pat M. Holt. *Invitation to Struggle: Congress, the President and Foreign Policy.* 4th ed. Washington, D.C.: CQ Press, 1992.

Draper, Theodore. *A Very Thin Line: The Iran-Contra Affairs.* New York: Hill and Wang, 1991.

Ely, John Hart. *War and Responsibility: Constitutional Lessons of Vietnam and Its Aftermath.* Princeton: Princeton University Press, 1993.

Fisher, Louis. *Presidential War Power.* Lawrence: University Press of Kansas, 1995.

Franck, Thomas M., ed. *The Tethered Presidency: Congressional Restraints on Executive Power.* New York: New York University Press, 1981.

Franck, Thomas M., and Edward Weisband. *Foreign Policy by Congress.* New York: Oxford University Press, 1979.

Glennon, Michael J. *Constitutional Diplomacy.* Princeton: Princeton University Press, 1990.

Henkin, Louis. *Constitutionalism, Democracy, and Foreign Affairs.* New York: Columbia University Press, 1990.

Henkin, Louis, Michael J. Glennon, and William D. Rogers, eds. *Foreign Affairs and the U.S. Constitution.* Ardsley-on-Hudson, N.Y.: Transnational Publishers, 1990.

Keynes, Edward. *Undeclared War: Twilight Zone of Constitutional Power.* University Park: Pennsylvania State University Press, 1991.

Koh, Harold Hongju. *The National Security Constitution: Sharing Power after the Iran-Contra Affair.* New Haven: Yale University Press, 1990.

Mann, Thomas E., ed. *A Question of Balance: The President, the Congress, and Foreign Policy.* Washington, D.C.: Brookings Institution, 1990.

Muskie, Edmund S., Kenneth Rush, and Kenneth W. Thompson, eds. *The President, the Congress, and Foreign Policy.* Lanham, Md.: University Press of America, 1986.

Reveley, W. Taylor III. *War Powers of the President and Congress: Who Holds the Arrows and Olive Branch?* Charlottesville: University Press of Virginia, 1981.

Silverstein, Gordon. *Imbalance of Powers: Constitutional Interpretation and the Making of American Foreign Policy.* New York: Oxford University Press, 1997.

Spanier, John, and Joseph Nogee, eds. *Congress, the Presidency and American Foreign Policy.* New York: Pergamon Press, 1981.

Thomas, Ann Van Wynen, and A. J. Thomas, Jr. *The War-Making Powers of the President: Constitutional and International Law Aspects.* Dallas: SMU Press, 1982.

Turner, Robert F. *Repealing the War Powers Resolution: Restoring the Rule of Law in U.S. Foreign Policy*. New York: Brassey's, 1991.

Wormuth, Francis D., and Edwin B. Firmage. *To Chain the Dog of War: The War Power of Congress in History and Law*. Urbana: University of Illinois Press, 1989.

Articles

Adler, David Gray. "The Constitution and Presidential Warmaking: The Enduring Debate." *Political Science Quarterly* 103 (1988): 1.

Elkin, Steven L. "Contempt of Congress: The Iran-Contra Affair and the American Constitution." *Congress and the Presidency* 18 (1991): 1.

Fisher, Louis. "President Clinton as Commander in Chief." In *Rivals for Power: Presidential-Congressional Relations*, ed. James A. Thurber. Washington, D.C.: CQ Press, 1996.

———. "The Korean War: On What Legal Basis Did Truman Act?" *American Journal of International Law* 89 (1995): 21.

———. "Congressional Participation in the Treaty Process." *University of Pennsylvania Law Review* 137 (1989): 151.

———. "Foreign Policy Powers of the President and Congress." *The Annals* 499 (1988): 148.

Glennon, Michael J. "The Senate Role in Treaty Ratification." *American Journal of International Law* 77 (1983): 257.

Hilsman, Roger. "Congressional-Executive Relations and the Foreign Policy Consensus." *American Political Science Review* 52 (1978): 725.

Lofgren, Charles A. "War-Making Under the Constitution: The Original Understanding." *Yale Law Journal* 81 (1972): 672.

Manning, Bayless. "The Congress, the Executive and Intermestic Affairs: Three Proposals." *Foreign Affairs* 55 (1977): 306.

Rovine, Arthur W. "Separation of Powers and International Executive Agreements." *Indiana Law Journal* 52 (1977): 397.

Silverberg, Marshall. "The Separation of Powers and Control of the CIA's Covert Operations." *Texas Law Review* 68 (1990): 575.

INDEX OF CASES

INDEX

Felt, Mark, 11
Fenwick, Millicent, 88
Ferris, Charles, 157–58
Fiers, Alan D., 13
Fiske, Robert B., Jr., 140
Fitzgerald, John J., 59, 224
Flanigan, Peter, 72
Fogarty, Joseph R., 159
Ford, Gerald, 37, 120, 162, 169, 187, 200–201; and congressional interference, 68; and lobbying, 55–56, 63; and pardon power, 12; and pocket veto, 19
foreign affairs, 9–11, 94–95, 102–103, 177–82, 214–17
Foster, Henry W., 119
Foster, Vincent, 140
Fried, Charles, 172
Friedersdorf, Max, 55, 56
Friendly, Henry J., 175

Gallatin, Albert, 43–44, 185
Galloway, George B., 50
General Accounting Office. *See* Comptroller General
George, Clair, 13
George, Walter, 184
Gephardt, Richard, 27
Gerry, Elbridge, 193
Giaimo, Bob, 227–28
Giles, William B., 43
Gillett, Frederick, 59
Gilligan, John, 94–95
Goldwater, Barry, 10, 188
Gore, Al, 39
Gorsuch, Anne, 16
Gorton, Slade, 9
Gradison, Heather J., 157
Gramm, Phil, 234
Grant, Ulysses S., 219
Grassley, Charles, 57
Gray, C. Boyden, 38, 103, 248
Griffin, Patrick, 58
Griffin, Robert P., 159
Guinier, Lani, 119

Haig, Alexander M., Jr., 135
Hakim, Albert, 209
Haldeman, H. R., 54, 55

Hamilton, Alexander, 5, 28, 41–42, 70, 110, 112, 192–93, 211, 219
Hamilton, Lee, 46–47
Hansen, Kent F., 157
Harding, Warren, 156
Harlow, Bryce, 53, 54, 55
Harris, Joseph P., 73
Harrison, William Henry, 24
Hart, Philip A., 166
Hatfield, Mark, 247
Hathaway, William D., 158
Hayes, Rutherford B., 29
Helms, Jesse, 74
Hendrie, Joseph, 160
Herlong, A. Sydney, Jr., 156

Hilley, John, 58
Hills, Carla A., 185
Holmes, Oliver Wendell, Jr., 14
Hoover, Herbert, 91, 116–17
Hoover Commission, 148–51, 159, 167
Houston, David, 224
Howrey, Edward F., 131
Humphrey, Hubert H., 63
Humphrey, William, 160
Hunter, Robert P., 158
Huntington, Samuel P., 50
Hussein, bin Talal, 215
Hussein, Saddam, 202
Hutchinson, Ronald, 82

Ichord, Richard, 159
impeachment power, 7, 12, 138, 238
impoundment of funds, 83–85, 95–96, 128, 226, 228, 248
independent counsel, 136–42, 174
information, access to. *See* executive privilege
Inouye, Daniel K., 94–95
investigative power, 41, 73–75
Iran-Contra affair, 13, 57, 64, 103, 105, 139, 144, 206–10, 216
Iraq, war with, 58, 202–203
item veto, 85, 114–15, 242–50

Jackson, Andrew, 110–11, 112
Jackson, Jesse, 10–11
Jackson, Robert H., 5, 93, 179

Wilson, James, 5, 69, 161, 193
Wilson, Woodrow, 3, 4, 48–49, 68, 156, 184, 224
wiretaps. *See* electronic surveillance

Wirt, William, 129
Wright, Jim, 103, 235–36

Zuckerman, Jeffrey I., 157